THE BOOK OF THE
ENGLISH SPRINGER SPANIEL

by Anna Katherine Nicholas
with special sections by Evelyn Monte Van Horn,
Anne Pope, Elliot More, and Joseph P. Sayres, DVM

Dedicated to Triple Lina, who also loves and appreciates the English Springer Spaniel.

0-87666-744-2

Distributed in the UNITED STATES by T.F.H. Publications, Inc., 211 West Sylvania Avenue, Neptune City, NJ 07753; in CANADA by Rolf C. Hagen Ltd., 3225 Sartelon Street, Montreal 382 Quebec; in ENGLAND by T.F.H. (Great Britain) Ltd., 11 Ormside Way, Holmethorpe Industrial Estate, Redhill, Surrey RH1 2PX; in AUSTRALIA AND THE SOUTH PACIFIC by Pet Imports Pty. Ltd., Box 149 Brookvale 2100 N.S.W., Australia; in SOUTH AFRICA by Multipet (Pty.) Ltd., 30 Turners Avenue, Durban 4001. Published by T.F.H. Publications Inc. Ltd., The British Crown Colony of Hong Kong.

Title Page: A lovely headstudy of Ch. Judge's Pride Jennifer, Top Producing Springer Bitch in 1979, belonging to the Kay N Dee Kennels of Dr. Mary B. Gibbs, Spencerville, Maryland.

Contents

In Appreciation.. 6

About the Author.. 9

CHAPTER ONE
Origin and Early British History of the English Springer Spaniel.......11

CHAPTER TWO
English Springer Spaniels in Canada.................................17

CHAPTER THREE
Early English Springer Spaniels in the United States.................21

CHAPTER FOUR
Important Kennels of the Present Day................................49

CHAPTER FIVE
English Springer Spaniels at Westminster.............................145

CHAPTER SIX
Official Standard of the English Springer Spaniel...................165

CHAPTER SEVEN
Anne Pope Discusses the English Springer Spaniel..................175

CHAPTER EIGHT
The English Springer Spaniel Field Trial Association—Parent Club of the Breed............185

CHAPTER NINE
Evelyn Monte Van Horn Discusses English Springer Spaniel Field Trials...............191

CHAPTER TEN
Evelyn Monte Van Horn Explains the Working Certificates.............207

CHAPTER ELEVEN
Selection of Your English Springer Spaniel..........................225

CHAPTER TWELVE
Advance Preparation for Your Springer Puppy's Arrival.................233

CHAPTER THIRTEEN
Your Springer Spaniel Puppy Joins the Family.......................237

CHAPTER FOURTEEN
Elliot More Discusses Grooming the English Springer Spaniel.........243

CHAPTER FIFTEEN
Responsibilities of Springer Owners and Breeders....................249

CHAPTER SIXTEEN
Showing Your Springer Puppy.......................................253

CHAPTER SEVENTEEN
Pre-show Preparation for You and for Your Springer..................263

CHAPTER EIGHTEEN
Junior Showmanship with Springers.................................291

CHAPTER NINETEEN
You, Your Springer and Obedience...297

CHAPTER TWENTY
The English Springer Spaniel Brood Bitch...315

CHAPTER TWENTY-ONE
The English Springer Spaniel Stud Dog...323

CHAPTER TWENTY-TWO
Your English Springer Spaniel's Gestation, Whelping and Litter.........................331

CHAPTER TWENTY-THREE
Pedigrees—The Background of a Breeding Program..353

CHAPTER TWENTY-FOUR
The Veterinarian's Corner, by Joseph P. Sayres, DVM.......................................379

Glossary...399

Index..407

In Appreciation

There are many Springer fanciers who have helped most generously towards making this book a complete and beautifully illustrated presentation of English Springer Spaniels. Those who loaned photographs of dogs and those who sent historical information and background on breeding programs for kennel stories have contributed enormously, as these features do much to make a book of interest.

Anne Pope has spent time and effort helping us collect material and has written some extremely noteworthy and valuable chapters which are featured.

Evelyn Monte Van Horn, a very outstanding authority on Field Trials and Springers, took charge of that section with her usual skill.

Steve Dreiseszun collected information on our Great Obedience Springers and is largely responsible for the chapter on this subject.

The noted professional handler, Elliot More, who has conditioned, trained, groomed and shown very many successful winning Springers, has prepared an outstanding chapter on care of the coat and grooming of the breed. The chapter should prove invaluable to those owning a Springer, whether for show or other activities, as

it takes one from simplest essentials on through the most sophisticated show ring preparations.

Alice Berd did so much in helping me research the background of the breed, both here and abroad.

Our knowledgeable, widely respected veterinarian, Dr. Joseph P. Sayres, has written another of his fine chapters, "The Veterinarian's Corner," which we are proud to present. Dr. Sayres, in addition to being a fine veterinarian, grew up "in dogs," being the son of the renowned Terrier expert Edwin A. Sayres, Sr., and the brother of equally well-known professional handlers Ed Sayres, Jr., and Henry Sayres. He is an A.K.C. approved judge of Terriers and, like his Dad, an Irish Terrier breeder. He understands the problems of the breeder as well as of the one-dog owner.

Marcia Foy has assisted in numerous ways, helping to collect photos, checking copy for errors, as well as collecting material for several of our chapters.

To all of these folks, a heartfelt "thank you." We hope you will find this book worthy of every effort that went into it, and we are grateful and appreciative of your helpfulness and support.

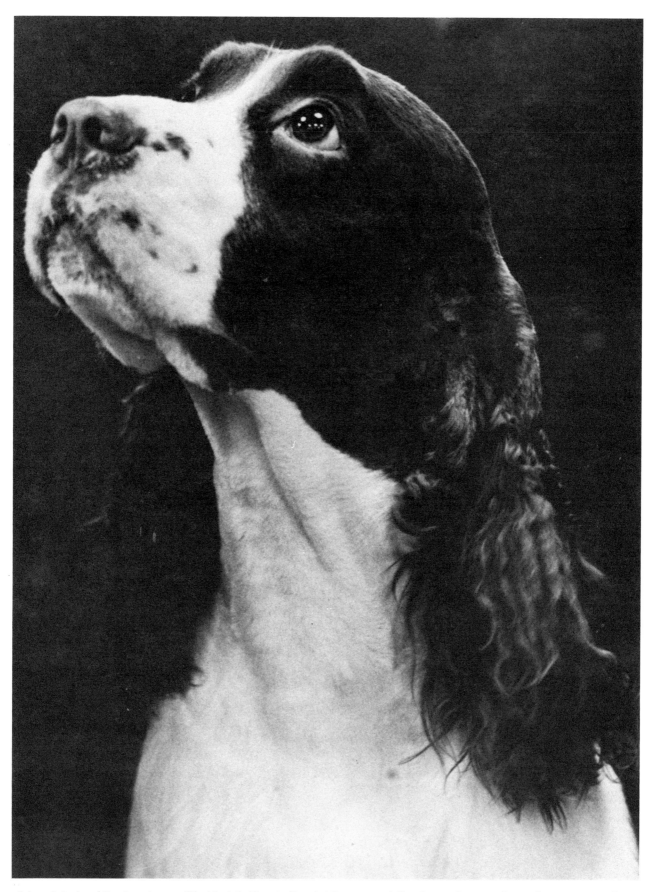

A headstudy of the handsome Ch. Lleda's Keeps Comin' On, a specialty show winner and consistent group placement winner, by Ch. Veron's Marco Polo ex Ch. Clancy's Erin of Packanack. Owned by Ray and Estelle Adell and Karen Adell Garetano.

Ch. Carey's Pride and Joy, U.D.T., W.D., and Ch. Carey's Prince Michael, U.D.T., W.D.X. (shown at 16 years of age). These are the first and second Ch., U.D.T., W.D. Springers in history. Grandfather and grandson, they belong to the Pride 'n' Joy Kennels of Julie Hogan and Donna Thompson in Manassas, Virginia.

About the Author

Since early childhood, Anna Katherine Nicholas has been involved with dogs. Her first pets were a Boston Terrier, an Airedale and a German Shepherd. Then, in 1925, came the first Pekingese—a gift from a friend who raised the breed. Now her home is shared with a Miniature Poodle and a dozen or so Beagles including her noted Best in Show dog and National Beagle Club Specialty winner, Champion Rockaplenty's Wild Oats, one of the breed's truly great sires who as a show dog was Top Beagle in the Nation in 1973. She also owns Champion Foyscroft True Blue Lou, Foyscroft Aces Are Wild, and, in co-ownership with Marcia Foy, who lives with her, Champion Foyscroft Triple Mitey Migit.

Miss Nicholas is best known throughout the Dog Fancy as a writer and as a judge. Her first magazine articles, published in *Dog News* magazine around 1930 were about Pekingese. This was followed by a widely acclaimed breed column "Peeking at the Pekingese" which appeared for at least two decades, originally in *Dogdom* and when that magazine ceased to exist, in *Popular Dogs*. During the 1940's she was Boxer columnist for *The American Kennel Gazette* and for *Boxer Briefs*. More recently many of her articles of general interest have appeared in *Popular Dogs*, and *The American Kennel Gazette—Pure Bred Dogs*. Currently she is a featured regular columnist in *Kennel Review*, *Dog World*, *Canine Chronicle* and *Dog Fancier* magazine, with occasional special features in *Dogs in Canada*. Her *Dog World* column, "Here, There and Everywhere," was the Dog Writers Association of America's winner of the "Best Series in a Dog Magazine" for 1979. She also has written for *The World of The Working Dog*.

It was during the late 1930's that Miss Nicholas' first book, *The Pekingese*, appeared, published by the Judy Publishing Company. This book completely sold out and is now a collector's item, as is her *The Skye Terrier Book*, which was published through the Skye Terrier Club of America during the early 1960's.

In 1970 Miss Nicholas won the Dog Writers Association of America Award for the Best Technical Book of the Year with her *Nicholas Guide to Dog Judging*, published by Howell Book House. In 1979, the revision of this book again won the Dog Writers Association of America's Best Technical Book Award, the first time ever that a *revision* has been so honored by this Association.

In the early 1970's, Miss Nicholas co-authored, with Joan Brearley, five breed books which were published by T.F.H. Publications, Inc. These were: *This is the Bichon Frise, The Wonderful World of Beagles and Beagling, The Book of the Pekingese, This is the Skye Terrier,* and *The Book of the Boxer. The Wonderful World of Beagles and Beagling* won a Dog Writers Association Honorable Mention Award the year it was published.

Successful Dog Show Exhibiting and *The Book of the Rottweiler*, Miss Nicholas' two latest books off the press, are being received with enthusiasm and acclaim. Both are T.F.H. Publications, as is the recently published classic, *The Book of the Poodle*, now eagerly awaited by fanciers of that breed.

Miss Nicholas, in addition to her four Dog Writers Association of America Awards, has on two occasions been awarded *Kennel Review* "Winkies" Awards as Dog Writer of the Year. Also, in 1977, she was winner of the Gaines "Fido" Award as Journalist of the Year in Dogs.

Her first appearance as a judge was at the First Company Governors Foot Guard in Hartford, Connecticut, in 1934, where she drew the largest Pekingese entry ever assembled at this show. At the present time she is approved to judge all Hounds, Terriers, Toys and Non-Sporting, Pointers, English and Gordon Setters, Vizslas, Weimaraners, Wire-haired Pointing Griffons, Boxers and Doberman Pinschers. In 1970 she became the third woman in history to judge Best in Show at the prestigious Westminster Kennel Club Dog Show, where she has officiated on some 16 other occasions over the years. She has judged in almost every one of the mainland United States, in four Canadian provinces, and her services are constantly sought in other countries. In addition to her many Westminster assignments, Miss Nicholas has officiated at such important events as Santa Barbara, Trenton, Chicago International, the Sportsmans in Canada, the Metropolitan in Canada and Specialty shows in several dozen breeds both here and in Canada.

Through the years, Miss Nicholas has held important offices in a great many all-breed and Specialty clubs. She still remains an honorary member of several of them.

Portrait of a Springer Spaniel of the late 1900's, from Anna Katherine Nicholas' collection of Maud Earl prints.

10

CHAPTER ONE

Origin and Early British History of the English Springer Spaniel

Lorna, Countess Howe, owned fine Springers as well as Labradors. This dog, Ch. Banchory Boy, is a splendid example.

It is generally agreed that English Springer Spaniels are the dogs behind all Spaniels, or as one writer has put it, "The Adams of the Spaniel family." From the earliest Springers, other Spaniels have been developed until now there are at least 10 varieties of Sporting Spaniel breeds. The new varieties are quite different from those of ancient times when all were referred to simply as "spaniels" or "spaniells," a designation covering all of the dogs of this type said to have originated in Spain.

The famous book *English Dogges,* so widely quoted by canine historians, was written more than 400 years ago. Its author, Dr. Johannes Caius, makes the following reference to the ancestors of modern Springers. We quote, "The common sort of people call them by one general word, namely spaniells, as tho these kind of dogges came originally and first of all out of Spaine. The most part of their skynnes are white, and if they be marked with any spottes, they are commonly red, and somewhat great therewithall, the heares not growing in such thickness but that the mixture of them may easely be perceaved. Othersome of them be reddishe and blackishe, but of that sorte there be but a very few."

Another famous writer, Dame Juliana Berners, the prioress of Hopewell Nunnery, in her *Boke of St. Albans* dated about 1487, mentions a "Spanyell" as one of the "divres manners of houndes" popular in the England of her day.

Reference to "Spanyells" has, in fact, been found at least as far back as 1392; and it is interesting to note that a Spaniel was one of the two dogs (the other a Mastiff) that came to America in 1620 aboard the Mayflower, although we have no way of ascertaining that it was a Springer.

As the different types of Spaniel gradually took shape, the Springer seemed to be dominant above the others. A medium-sized dog, well balanced, strong and sturdy, free of any exaggeration, he was fast and a good worker. This dog takes his name from "springing" the birds, originally for the nets, later for the guns. Robert Leighton in his *Dogs and All About Them,* copyright 1910, comments that this designation "was not, perhaps, a happy choice, as all Spaniels, properly speaking, are 'springers' in contradistinction to 'setters'." Also from Mr. Leighton's book we learn that the complete official name on the Kennel Club's register of the period was "English Springers other than Clumbers, Sussex and Field," which is certainly quite a mouthful! And for a time the old-fashioned liver-and-white or black Spaniels, longer in leg than the Sussex or Field Spaniels, were known officially as "Norfolk Spaniels," and as such the Spaniel Club had published a description (or early Standard) of them.

The name "Norfolk Spaniel" had evidently caused considerable controversy, there having been actually no territorial connection between these dogs and Norfolk; however, one of the Dukes of Norfolk had owned the breed with tremendous pride. Blaine, writing in *Rural Sports* said that the Duke's jealousy of his strain reached such proportions that he was loathe to part with one of his dogs and that when he did so, it was with the express condition that the dog would not be bred back into his direct line. It was the Sporting Spaniel Society that objected to calling the breed "Norfolk Spaniel," and that brought about the change back to Springer.

Ch. Worthing Suspense was a contender at Cruft's in 1934. Mrs. T. Ford-Lowe, owner.

We find, as we check back into history, that soon after the turn of the century the Caistor Kennels, owned by the Green family in Norwich, had dogs that were descended from the Norfolk Spaniels. They are described as having been mostly black, tan and white. One of them, Caistor Rex, born in 1908, was an important sire behind many generations of Springer Field Trial winners, including the three Dual Champions, Horsford Hetman, Flint of Avendale, and Thoughtful of Harting.

Of these Norfolk Spaniels Mr. Leighton mentions, "There is no doubt that this variety of Spaniel retains more resemblance to the old strains which belonged to our forefathers, before the long and low idea found favor in the eyes of exhibitors, and it was certainly well worth preserving. The only way nowadays by which uniformity of type can be obtained is by somebody having authority drawing up a standard and scale of points for breeders to go by, and the Sporting Spaniel Society are to be commended for having done this for the breed under notice, the fruit of their action being already apparent in the larger and more uniform classes to be seen at the shows."

One of the oldest descriptions we have seen of the dogs behind our modern English Springer Spaniels was originally published in 1616. It describes a "gentle, loving and courteous dog; a sturdy and clever hunter; with a round, thick head, a long and hairie ear, a broad breast, short, well knit joints, good round ribs, gaunt bellie, short broad backe, and a thick, bushie, long-haired taile."

Somewhere preceding the turn of the century, England's Sporting Spaniel Society drew up the following Standard for them:

Skull: Long and slightly arched on top, fairly broad, with a stop and well developed temples.

Jaws: Long and broad, not snipy, with plenty of thin lip.

Eyes: Medium size, not too full, bright and intelligent, of a rich brown.

Ears: Of fair length, low set and lobular in shape.

Neck: Long, strong and slightly arched.

Shoulders: Long and sloping.

Forelegs: Moderate length, straight, with flat, strong bone.

Body: Strong with well sprung ribs, good girth, chest deep and fairly broad.

Loin: Rather long, strong, and slightly arched.

Hindquarters and hindlegs: Very muscular, hocks well let down, stifles moderately bent, and not twisted either inwards or outwards.

Feet: Strong and compact.

Stern: Low carried, not above the level of the back, with a vibratory motion.

Coat: Thick and smooth or very slightly wavy. Must not be too long. Feathering on ears only moderate, scanty on the legs but right down to the heels.

Colour: Liver and white or black and white (with or without tan), fawn and white, yellow and white, also roans and self colours of all these tints. The pied colours are preferable.

Active, compact dog, upstanding but by no means stilty. Shoulder height about equal length from top of withers to root of tail.

It was in the 17th century that, very gradually, size differences started having impact on the persons using Spaniels for hunting, with the result that the larger ones soon were springing game while the smaller ones were used for hunting woodcock. The names Springer and Cocker, descriptive of the manner in which the dogs were used, quite naturally followed, until in 1892 the English Kennel Club registered them as separate breeds: the English Springer Spaniel and the English Cocker Spaniel. At this time, size alone was the distinguishing factor between the two breeds, which were actually born in the same litters, both before and after the Kennel Club separation of them. General type, hunting skills and coloring naturally were similar, since the two breeds shared their heritage.

The earliest Springer kennel to which we have found reference was Aqualate, whose liver-and-white Springers developed by the family of Sir Thomas Boughey date back as far as 1812 prior to the recognition of Springers as a breed. These dogs are said to have been the forerunners of the Denne and the Beechgrove lines which provided the principal background of early importations to America.

Beechgrove Kennels was established around 1890 by J. Winton Smith of England. This kennel is noted for having the world's first Springer champion, Beechgrove Will, whelped in 1898. He gained his title by winning the Challenge Certificate at the Crystal Palace Dog Show in London in 1902. He repeated the victory in 1903 and gained the necessary third C.C. to complete his English championship later in 1903 at Birmingham.

Denne Springers, the property of C.C. Eversfield, were located at Denne Park in Sussex. Probably the best known dog from here was Field Champion Velox Powder, grandsire of English Field Champion Denne Duke, winner of the first Championship Field Trial for Springers in England in 1914.

Other Springer breeders of the early 1900's, in addition to those already mentioned, include John and Godfrey Kent, J.P. Gardner, Colonel Williams and Mr. and Mrs. Lewis Wigan.

The Kents owned England's famed Chrishall Springers, where at least one of which, English Field Champion Silverstar of Chrishall, can be found in the pedigrees of early American importations.

Mr. Gardner's dogs were identified by the kennel prefix Hagley. His original stock had come from J.H. Mildon, another early breeder from Devon, England.

Colonel Williams operated the Gerwyn Kennels in Wales. Canadian Champion Don Juan of Gerwyn, that we have read was actually of Welsh Cocker breeding, was registered as a Springer and won fame in America following his purchase in Canada.

The suffix Cairnies was frequently seen in pedigrees during the early part of this century, as they were Springers of importance. These belonged to Mr. and Mrs. Lewis Wigan of Scotland, and this strain was well represented in the bloodlines of Springers coming to the United States and Canada in the early 1900's. The kennel was especially famed for such outstanding matrons as Witch of the Cairnies, Nell of the Cairnies, Bess of the Cairnies, Rip of the Cairnies and Susan of the Cairnies, all of which made their mark as important producers, particularly when bred to Rivington Sam and Prince of Avendale. The Wigans' famed producing bitch, Pinehawk, was by Spy O'Vara from Rip of the Cairnies. Their important sire, Jed of the Cairnies, was the grandsire of Staindrop Spitfire, a dog still to be found if one digs back to the beginning in the pedigrees of present day winners.

Then there were the Rivingtons, a Scottish kennel at Castle Douglas whence came the aforementioned Rivington Sam. Described as "one-fourth Field Spaniel, three-fourths Cocker," Sam was an illustrious progenitor of the modern Springer and at one time was

One of the Duke of Hamilton's noted Springers at a Scottish Field Trial Association meeting.

credited with being in the pedigree of more Bench and Field Springers than any other single early dog. C.A. Phillips was the owner.

Leam was another well known kennel, this one in England, owned by John Anderson. The best remembered dog from here was English Champion Andon of Leam, ancestor of numerous American winners, both on the bench and in the field.

Ranscombe was still another noted Springer kennel in England producing top quality dogs for both bench and field. Miss Dorothy Morland Hooper, owner, was a great enthusiast, having served as a judge of Field Trials and Championship dog shows and as author of a splendid book on Springers in England.

It is generally conceded that five of the most important British dogs behind present day Springers were: English Field Champion Velox Powder, born in 1903, bred by Sir Thomas Boughey, with a pedigree authenticated as far back as 1817; Dash of Hagley, born in 1905, bred by J.P. Hagley, from parents whose ancestry was uncertain; Horsford Honour, born in 1910, bred by William Humphrey, by Caister Rex from Horsford Heiress; Rivington Sam, previously described; and Cornwallis Cavalier,

born in 1914, by Shot ex Beanie, which we have read were "field dogs of Spaniel type."

William Humphrey's Horsford Kennels were in Shropshire, England and based on foundation stock headed by his home-bred Horsford Heiress and by Field Champion Bush. The latter was a gift from Sir Hugo Fitz Herbert, another successful early breeder of outstanding producers through the Tissington strain. Throughout the 1920's, literally hundreds of Horsford dogs came to the United States and Canada; among them was the first United States Champion of the breed, Dr. Gifford's Horsford Highness.

By the time the 1920's had arrived, England's Springer breeders were numerous and very busy. There were the Ellwyns, owned by J.C. Dagliesh in Scotland; the Carnfields, with whom George Taylor carried on for more than 40 years; and Aughrim, whose prefix belonged to J. Edgarton of Scotland. Aughrim was famous for a Springer bearing its prefix, Aughrim's Flashing, (bred by the Duke of Hamilton and Brandon) the first Springer to win a Field Trial Championship in the United States.

The Duke of Hamilton and Brandon's own kennel, Avendale, was one of Scotland's finest. Established in 1919, it was noted as being the home of English Dual Champion Flint of Avendale which was exported to the Avandale Kennels (note difference in spelling) in Canada and it was also the home of English Field Champion Rex of Avendale, grandsire of English and American Champion Rufton Recorder.

This also was the period in which H. Grierson of England established Solway Kennels from which came the American Best in Show winner Champion Love Bird of Solway. Additionally, English, American and Canadian Champion Advert of Solway had favorable impact on the breed and was the sire of Beauchief Outcross that produced the U.S.A. winners Champion Showman of Shottan and Speculation of Shottan and Greenfair.

There was Skegness in Northern England; Merlin, owned by G. Tomkinson; and Matford, well known under the ownership of E. Trimble in England. M.N. Lee had Stowmarket, Scadbury represented A. Higgs, and O'Vara, started in 1920, was doing well for C.S. Jones.

Inveresk Kennels became widely famed for A. McNab Chassels of Coatsbridge, Scotland. These Springers included English Champion Inveresk Coronation, Supreme Best in Show in

Rufton Repeater, owned by J.A. Wenger, was a lovely example of the English Springer Spaniel.

London in 1926; the splendid producer Champion Inveresk Countess; the successful Pacific Coast sire Champion Inveresk Chip; and Champion Inveresk Careful, dam of English and American Champion Inveresk Cocksure. A dog that was originally Dilkusha Punch, bred by Miss Pike, was purchased by Inveresk and renamed Inveresk Chancellor. After becoming an English Champion he was sold to a fancier in Canada, where American and Canadian titles were quickly added to his laurels.

Isaac Sharpe had lovely Springers which bore the Stylish kennel identification. Tedwyn and Troquehain were two other kennels producing dogs of quality.

One of the "turn of the century" Springer fanciers, William Arkwright, who had been the organizer of the first Field Trial ever held exclusively for Springers, had a niece who carried on his interest in the breed. Lady Lambe placed paramount importance on her Whaddon Chase dogs being excellent workers, although their appearance was not neglected and she demanded that these working attributes be combined with conformation as outlined in the Standard.

Also in the 1920's there were the Dalshangan Springers, owned by A.L. Trotter in Scotland, who exported progeny of Dalshangan Dandy Boy to the United States. Archie Butler in England had Faskally Kennels. Noted field dogs came from Scotland's Deveron Kennels, owned by J.W. Spencer, and also from Fintry where F.A. Rottenberg was the breeder.

Around 1920 Laverstoke was the Scottish kennel from which Lady Portal was sending out good Springers. American and Canadian Champion Laverstoke Powder Horn, English Champion Laverstoke Pepper and English Champion Laverstoke Pattern were exported to America. This kennel name was used in the United States starting in about 1924 by Henry B. Shaw of Burlington, Vermont, who had purchased numerous Laverstoke dogs for his foundation stock here, thus identifying his own breeding program with this same prefix. We understand that this was quite usual during that period.

Another Scottish fancier, David McDonald of Dundee, bred English Champion Little Brand and owned English and American Champion Nuthill Dignity. Langtoun, owned by W. Armstrong, was founded in the mid-1920's.

Many other people were actively breeding Springers in the British Isles of course, but we feel that the ones we have mentioned here will give a well-rounded view of what was taking place there in the breed as the 1930's approached.

The English Springer Spaniel in a portrait done by Ernest H. Hart.

E·H·HART

Am., Can. Ch. Shinnecock's Rapid Transit, by Ch. Winacko's Classic Replay, C.D., ex Ch. Loujon Femininity. Bred by Maureen Brady and Patty Alston; owned by Barry Davis and Tad Dunham, Charlotte, North Carolina. Finished his Canadian title, owner-handled, at seven months in three shows undefeated. Shortly thereafter was Best of Winners from the 6-9 month Puppy Class at the American Spaniel Club 1980, going on to complete his U.S.A. title at 13 months with three "majors."

CHAPTER TWO

English Springer Spaniels in Canada

Am., Can. Ch. Canarch Telltale Saga is an American T.D. and C.D.X., a Canadian C.D. and T.D. Also an ILLINI Search and Rescue Dog. Owned by Jim and Irene Eadie, Canarch Springers, Park Ridge, Illinois.

Most of the breeds whose history I have researched came to North America from their original birthplace, first by way of the United States, then later made their way to Canada. However, this was not so with the English Springer Spaniel, for it was the Canadian fancy that "discovered" the breed's talents and virtues, and it was there that the earliest great Springers on the North American continent were first imported.

It all started when a gentleman from Winnipeg, Mr. W.H. Gardner, made a trip from his home to England. During part of the trip he attended the great Crufts Dog Show in 1913. While there, Mr. Gardner had his attention taken by a handsome dark eyed black-and-white dog that was for sale, and when he returned to Canada this dog accompanied him.

The dog was Don Juan of Gerwyn, officially registered in England as an English Springer Spaniel (although we read that it was an accepted fact that there was Welsh Cocker blood behind him) by Duke of Gerwyn ex Flora and purchased from Colonel A.T. Williams of North Wales. Don Juan is said to have measured approximately 18½ inches at the withers and weighed about 45 pounds.

The following year Mr. Gardner boarded Don Juan with Eudore Chevrier, also of Winnipeg, who operated a boarding kennel there. We have found no explanation of the circumstances, but Mr. Chevrier (who had long been associated with hunting breeds and was highly appreciative of the quality and talents of his new boarder) started showing Don Juan in the Field Trials with very notable results, doing so under his own name as owner. Whether there had been a sale or a gift made or an agreement I have never seen stated, Don Juan became Mr. Chevrier's dog, and the rest is history. Certainly the dog could not have been in better hands so far as the future of his breed was concerned.

One thing led to another and Mr. Chevrier's enthusiasm for Springers grew quickly and steadily. Soon he had purchased two bitches that had been imported to Canada from the Beechgrove Kennels, both of which he bred to Don Juan. Two of these puppies went to Toronto, to Harry Johnston, and it was at this gentleman's home that Freeman Lloyd (that most eminent Sporting dog authority) became interested in the puppies and their breed. When he returned to his home in New York, Mr. Lloyd is said to have contacted Mr. Chevrier with the suggestion that his Springers be advertised in *Field and Stream* (the magazine with which Mr. Lloyd was associated) as it looked to him like a breed with a future here. How right he was! Mr. Chevrier did place the advertisement and soon was swamped with far greater numbers of inquiries than he could possibly produce the puppies to fill.

As the 1920's approached, a rush was getting under way from both American and Canadian fanciers to import Springers from the British Isles; thus, the breed was definitely on its way to popularity.

Mr. Chevrier's kennels were known as Avandale (not to be confused with the Avendale Kennels in Scotland, or the Avondale Kennels owned by Arthur Ellison also in Canada). Avandale was the oldest major Springer kennel in North America, having started in 1914, and it remained active until 1964.

Mr. Chevrier's influence on the Springer breed was tremendous. He imported many splendid Springers from Great Britain and thus played an important role in the development of correct Springer type and quality on this side of the Atlantic, both in Canada and in the States.

This photo, taken in 1965 at the National Amateur Championship, Indiantown Gap, Annville, Pennsylvania, shows Mrs. Herbert S. Routley, Peterborough, Ontario, with her Canadian Field Champion Trent Valley Bee. At age 75, and just returned from elk hunting in Canada, Mrs. Routley took Better Bee through all series and finished the trial.

His most prestigious dogs included Flint of Avendale (from the Scottish kennel of similar name), Springbok of Ware, Laverstoke Powder Horn and Little Messenger Boy which were included in his foundation stock. His American and Canadian Champion Marvel of Avandale won no less than 25 Bests in Show in Canada and the United States. A lovely liver-white-and-tan bitch, her show accomplishments were especially notable as those were not yet the years of "big record dogs" and the vigorous campaigning we know today.

The first Field Trials for Springers in Canada were initiated by Mr. Chevrier, who seemed to divide his interest pretty evenly between the field and the bench. It certainly must have been impressive to see his 12 dogs on the benches at Westminster, a show he attended (and where he wound up in the ribbons) with regularity. It would be difficult to say how many Springers Mr. Chevrier imported to his kennels during his years of operation. We have read that in 1923, described as "a typical year," he brought over about fifty.

Trent Valley was another outstanding Canadian Springer kennel of the early days, this one not quite so old as Avandale but founded around 1922.

Herbert S. Routley of Peterborough, Ontario was the owner and shared the hobby with his wife, also a great Springer enthusiast.

Foundation behind Trent Valley came by way of such Canadian importations as Inveresk Cocksure and Inveresk Chancellor, Mossend Dick, Loyal Lord, Limelight, Corselette's Son of a Gun, and other fine producers. So successful were the Routley dogs that they were known throughout the United States and Canada in both field and bench competition. One of the most famous was Champion Trent Valley Luckystrike that under Wallace Larsen's ownership gained wide acclaim. This kennel, second in size only to Avandale in its day, remained active well into the 1960's.

Belmoss is another famous name in Canadian Springer history, representing Hollis J. Placey of Sherbrooke, Quebec who started it in 1926. English, American and Canadian Champion Inveresk Chancellor and English, American and Canadian Champion Inveresk Cocksure (that figured so prominently in the establishment of other kennels as well as his own) were among those owned by this gentleman.

Smaller, but still prestigious, Springer kennels from the early days in Canada include Woodland, owned by Harry Crook, and started in the 1930's; and Lansdowne, owned by John Ritchey of Ottawa. Active through the 1920's and 1930's, Lansdowne's foundation bloodlines were provided by Solway, Inveresk and Pierpoint.

Founded principally on Beechgrove bloodlines, Maple Grove Springers was started in 1923 by H.D. Gilmour and provided the foundation bitch for Abilene Kennels in Kansas with Canadian Champion Yenda of Maple Grove.

Robert Fox had a kennel that was popular with breeders in the United States, and many of his dogs were imported there during the 1920's and the 1930's bearing his Eskdale prefix.

More recently, during the mid-1950's, Mrs. Anne Snelling founded Oaktree Springers based on Salilyn and Melilotus lines and many of her dogs are in a number of pedigrees as material is gathered for this book.

Some handsome young hopefuls from the Salilyn Kennels of Mrs. Julie Gasow, Troy, Michigan.

What a lot of memories this photo will arouse! Ch. Amos of Melilotus winning Best of Breed at Morris and Essex in 1946, Billy Lang handling, Paul Quay judging. Amos was by Dual Ch. Fast from Tranquillity of Well Sweep, foundation bitch at Melilotus, that was sired by Green Valley Hercules out of Orientia, half-brother and sister by Ch. Rufton Recorder.

CHAPTER THREE

Early English Springer Spaniels in the United States

Talented artist Jodie Lee Pearl of Kauneonga Lake, New York, has done this excellent drawing of a Springer for us. Her work appears in portrait form and on beautiful leather objects including wallets, key chains, purses, and many other items.

The American Spaniel Club was founded in 1880, and one of its earliest tasks was the sorting out by size of the different varieties of the breed. Cockers were already extremely popular in show ring competition at that period, with Springers far more rarely seen. The maximum size limit for Cockers was set at 28 pounds and dogs heavier than this were classified as Springers.

The first person we have found mentioned as having imported Springers from England to the United States was Robert D. Foote, of Morristown, New Jersey, who brought over two in 1907. No record seems to exist of any descendents from these dogs; therefore, they cannot be credited with any influence on the future development of the breed here.

The 1920's can well be described as the decade of the emergence of the Springer in the United States, and some well known kennels were founded by leading sportsmen of that period.

Freeman Lloyd wrote much in glowing praise of the breed in *Field and Stream* magazine and in his columns in the *American Kennel Club*. He felt the breed deserved an enthusiastic reception here from gun dog devotees, and his words were both prophetic and influential as Mr. Lloyd was well respected by his peers. The influx of Springers from Great Britain via Canada got under way with the importation on a large scale of great show Springers.

One of the earliest Springer breeders we find listed in the United States was Howard Stout Neilson, of Althea Farms in Darien, Connecticut. He raised and kept numerous breeds, Springers among them, around the year 1911.

Henry Ferguson established the Falcon Hill Kennels on Fisher's Island, New York in 1924, and his foundation stock included about half a dozen importations from Great Britain. Mr. Ferguson was a charter member of the English Springer Spaniel Field Trial Association and was its Honorary President until his death in 1959, at which time his kennel was disbanded. Mr. Ferguson made a tremendously important contribution to the breed as author of the excellent book, *English Springer Spaniels In America*.

Mr. and Mrs. Walton Ferguson, Jr. of Greenwich, Connecticut imported Morewood Horsford Heater in 1924 which marked the beginning of their Morewood Kennels. As successful breeders, they produced Morewood Rough, Morewood Pat and Morewood Rush which distinguished them in Fisher's Island Field Trials and in the conformation classes at the dog shows.

This is the famous Fishers Island, home of the Fishers Island Spaniel Field Trials, photographed many years ago. Photo courtesy of Evelyn Monte Van Horn, Southbury, Connecticut.

Clarion Kennels, another of the earlier ones, was established in 1924 by Charles Toy of Princeton, New Jersey, with Henry Cameron as manager. During 1930 four Springers were imported by Mr. Toy from Mr. Robert Cornthwaite, owner of Rufton Kennels in England, a kennel which has been described as both "famous" and "controversial." Mr. Toy's importations became Champion Clarion Rufton Dinah, Champion Clarion Rufton Tandy, Champion Clarion Rufton Ruler and Clarion Rufton Roger. The latter became the sire of such famed American-breds as Dual Champion Fast and Champion Clarion Trumpet, both of which became Westminster Best of Breed winners. Mr. Toy was Secretary of the English Springer Spaniel Field Trial Association (the breed's Parent Club) and the first Springer breed columnist for the *American Kennel Club Gazette*. It is interesting to note that Julie Gasow also selected

dogs from the Rufton bloodlines on which to base her Salilyn breeding program.

During the 1920's, an extremely prominent member of the dog fancy, Mrs. David Wagstaff, along with her husband, decided to add Springers to their famous Ledgelands Kennels (principally associated with Labrador Retrievers and Chow Chows) in Tuxedo Park, New York. Mrs. Wagstaff visited England for the specific purpose of selecting and purchasing Springers, and among those that came to Ledgelands were several of the Horsford dogs, including Canadian Champion Springbok of Ware. Interestingly, it was Ernest Wells, the capable trainer and kennel manager here, who was a member of the committee which drew up the Standard of the Breed in 1932.

Also in the East, New Jerseyites William Hutchinson and David Earle imported a number of field and show dogs from Horsford Kennels.

In Oshkosh, Wisconsin, Dr. A.C. Gifford was busy with his Winnebago Kennels which began operations around 1920, and remained active for about two decades. With no fewer than 17 champions to its credit, Winnebago was a respected force in the Springer world and one of the largest and best kennels of its day. Show and breeding stock were imported from Horsford and from the Beechgrove lines and included many descendents of Fleet of Avendale and Cornwallis Cavalier.

The first Springer to attain championship in the United States was the liver-and-white bitch, Horsford Highness, owned and imported by Dr. Gifford. Highness had a Westminster Best of Breed to her credit, among numerous other honors. Winnebago Kennels was also the home of English and American Champion Horsford Harbour, an outstanding worker and a highly successful stud dog, and of another respected and popular stud dog, Champion Inveresk Careful. An avid student of Springer bloodlines, Dr. Gifford was also a distinguished judge.

Omaha, Nebraska then later Denver, Colorado were the homes of Greenflint Kennels, another active Springer operation founded around 1920. Ben Gallagher owned these dogs, among them the importations Rag of Avendale, Drag of the Cairnies, and Woodelf of Ware. It is interesting to note that Mr. Gallagher also owned a chateau near France where Springers were raised. It was here that the U.S.A.-born bitch, Green Valley Jingle, was bred to the famous French dog, Ham de Sandricourt, a Field Trial Champion in France, Holland and Belgium but descended from principally leading English bloodlines. World War II began while the Gallaghers were visiting at home in the United States, and their chateau was taken over by German officers who permitted the caretaker to remain. When the Gallaghers returned to their chateau at the close of the war, they found the caretaker still in residence along with a son of Ham and Jingle. This Springer, Niblic of Gunflint, accompanied his owners to Colorado where he was treated for malnutrition and poor condition. Eventually a French born bitch that had been sent over to the United States prior to the occupation was bred to this dog, and the resulting litter included a bitch, Warren's Bobette of Kay Four, that proved a valuable producer at Mrs. Gladys Wood's Nor East Kennels.

From 1925 until 1950, Mrs. Betty Buchanan made history with her Breeze Springers in Edgewater, Colorado. Flint's Whimsey, a blue roan dog from Vivandiere of Avandale and sired by English Dual Champion Flint of Avandale, embarked on a show career as the result of Mrs. Buchanan's wanting to help a good friend assemble a big Springer entry for the show of which her friend was chairman. There Whimsey took the points which prompted Mrs. Buchanan to continue showing him to his title. During the late 1920's Breeze Kennels was raising an average of seven to eight litters annually.

Two fine bitches resulted from the mating of Dilkusha Darkie to English and American Champion Nuthill Dignity. These became Champion Woodelf of Breeze and Miss Dignity of Breeze. Woodelf was leased by Mrs. Buchanan to Mr. and Mrs. Fred Hunt of Green Valley Kennels for breeding to their magnificent imported dog, English and American Champion Rufton Recorder. This had taken quite a bit of persuasion on Mrs. Buchanan's part as Recorder was then along in years and not in the best of health—thus used only on a limited basis and to the Hunts' own bitches. But Mrs. Buchanan had a good case in her favor as Recorder's best English progeny had come from his breeding to Dignity daughters (which this would be duplicating) the merit of which was quite apparent to Fred Hunt too. This first litter by Recorder and Woodelf abundantly fulfilled all expectations with seven puppies, six of which became champions, plus the fabulous producing bitch, Orientia. Everyone agreed that it must be repeated. Unhappily, however, distemper struck this next litter and only two of the puppies grew up to become champions. The total from the two litters gave Woodelf eight champions, a record which remained unchallenged among Springer bitches over many years.

There was early Springer activity on the Pacific Coast too, where Mr. and Mrs. C.H. Jackson imported and bred excellent stock beginning around 1925 under the Blue Leader banner. For at least 10 years this kennel remained in the Winners Circle with such renowned dogs as Champion Love Bird Solway, Champion Boghurst Bushe, Champion Inveresk Clip, English and American Champion Adcombe Yakoob, Champion Inveresk Comfort and American and Canadian Champion Norman of Ramsey, the first Springer ever to win the Sporting Group at

Westminster. Norman, Yakoob and Love Bird all were Best in Show winners.

Fred and Mary Agnes Hunt bred Springers under the Green Valley prefix from 1929–1942 in the beautiful country near Devon, Pennsylvania. Their contribution to the breed was important, their dogs still being found behind many leading American-bred Springers. The Hunts were among the astute breeders who selected Rufton dogs for their breeding program and imported Rufton Ringleader, Rufton Reveller, Rufton Rosita, Rufton Recorder, and also the Field Trial bitches Breckonhill Baroness and Field Champion Sobenhall Donna. Some 22 champions, including a dual champion, helped make the Green Valley name so highly respected.

Another famous kennel that started around 1926 was Abilene, owned by Dr. R.B. Miller of Abilene, Kansas. Canadian Champion Yenda of Maple Grove was purchased in whelp to Champion Springbok of Ware from the Canadian kennel, Avandale, and they produced a litter that became well renowned. Champion Pat of Abilene gained titles for Tuscawilla Kennels; Champion Maggie of Abilene did likewise for Blue Leader Kennels; and Belle of Abilene gained Winners Bitch and favorable comment for L.B. Gould when shown in the stiff competition of Morris and Essex.

Airiebrooke Springers was registered with the American Kennel Club in 1925 by William C. Coleman of Eccleston, Maryland who divided his interest between dog shows and Field Trials. The previous year, 1924, saw the foundation of Allegheny Springers owned by Benjamin Newton at Salamanca, New York. Mr. Newton had Canadian dogs for his foundation stock from Inveresk Cocksure and Springbok of Ware lines. Later, during the 1930's, Rufton Rogerson and Rufton Rubicon joined the kennel from England, both becoming American champions.

Robert Morrow of Mendham, New Jersey founded Audley Farm in 1928 with three excellent bitches; these were Wisdom's Flush, Hardin's Wig Wag and Reynolda. The prominent stud dog here was Champion Field Marshall from the previously mentioned first breeding of Champion Woodelf of Breeze to English and American Champion Rufton Recorder.

Champion Langtoun Light and Champion Southwick Don, along with the Canadian Best in Show dog American and Canadian Champion Royal Flush of Avalon and the Canadian-bred Champion Belmoss Cocksure, helped to carry the Avalon Springer banner high for A.M. Nichter of Canal Fulton, Ohio who entered the Springer world in 1926.

During 1924 L.E. Barber of Grand Forks, North Dakota registered Beechgrove as his kennel name with the American Kennel Club. Thus the United States, England and Canada all had registered kennels bearing this same name. Mr. Barber used the prefix with which to register his puppies from his Beechgrove Valerie.

It was in 1925 when George Higgs of Rosemead, California set forth on a program for breeding Springers. The following year, importing Boghurst Rover from England, he adopted Boghurst as his kennel name. Rover was a Group winner and a popular stud dog.

Three owners, James Barnes, John Ferguson and Lester Knapp, were involved with the formation of Boisdale Kennels in Buffalo, New York during the late 1920's. It was they who sold Duchess of Boisdale to Robert Walgate—that great Springer enthusiast who passed away in 1980—and Duchess is behind many of the Walpride champions and other winners.

Emmett Randall of Jamestown, New York established Butternut Springers in 1924. A highly successful dog from there was Champion Butternut Lucky that had an exciting show career under the ownership of Bradford Warner of Fairfield, Connecticut.

Chadakoin, featuring Beechgrove and Horsford stock, was located in Forestville, New York, and owned by Dr. Edwin D. Putnam in the 1920's. On the Pacific Coast, Mr. and Mrs. R.G. Sternberg of Ventura, California had many winners of Blue Leader breeding under the name of Clipfort, starting about 1929. One year previously had seen the formation of Cornhusker Springers (based on England's Canfield bloodlines) by David M. Tourtelot of Marshalltown, Iowa.

It is interesting to note that Freeman Lloyd's wife, actress Margaret Drew, was a Springer enthusiast. Using Drew Farm as her kennel identification, she exhibited her dogs in the 1920's, at such events as the American Spaniel Club shows held in those days at the famous Waldorf Astoria Hotel.

Earlsmoor was the kennel name acquired by Dr. and Mrs. Samuel Milbank in 1925. The name had been registered to a butcher in Wales who, as he was about to retire, had allowed the Milbanks to register it with both the English and the American Kennel Clubs. The first of Dr. and Mrs. Milbank's Springers was a bitch, Field Champion Banchory Flame, from Lady Howe's kennel in England and then came English and American Field Champion Rivington Countryman, described as a good worker and an excellent sire. Among his long list of credits are second in the 1956 National Championship and Best Amateur-handled Dog.

Ernest de K. Leffingwell of Whittier, California between 1925 and 1935 operated under the Dilkusha prefix, having purchased several Springers from there. The famous Champion Woodelf of Breeze was out of Dilkusha Darkie.

In 1926 the Raymond Beales of Buffalo, New York founded Dormond Kennels on Bellmoss Cocksure, Bellmoss Jacqueline and the Best in Show winner Champion Marol Sir Hector.

In 1928 Elwood was established by Harold Baker of Huntington, New York. Also in the 1920's Colonel and Mrs. Guggenheim started their Firenze Kennels which became the home of noted Springers and Bedlington Terriers. Donald Fordyce was involved with both Bench and Field Springers, mainly of Horsford des-

cent, in Allentown, Pennsylvania.

The Foremost Kennels, established in California in 1926 and owned by Henry Schenker, bred Champion Foremost Stalker and Champion Foremost Esquire by Champion Nuthill Dignity.

Marobar Kennels was founded in 1928 on Long Island by Dr. and Mrs. Herman B. Baruch. The Baruchs imported Inveresk Cashier after Cashier had won Best of Breed at the Crystal Palace in London. Marobar Springers were successfully run in Field Trial competition and exhibited in the conformation classes at bench shows. Another event of 1928 was Pug breeder Dr. Aristine Pixley Munn's entry into the Springer world with her Jonmunn Kennels located in Long Branch, New Jersey.

Menhall Farm, 1927–1950, in Edgerton, Wisconsin was owned by Mr. and Mrs. James E. Menhall. Their Penelope of Menhall Farm was Winners Bitch at Morris and Essex in 1935, and their Champion Duke of Kent of Menhall was a Best in Show winner.

Edward Dana Knight entered the Springer world in 1926 with his Tuscawilla Kennels in Charleston, West Virginia. His first Springer, a pet named "Kim," won him completely to the breed. He then purchased Pat of Abilene, who later became a champion. Approximately eight of Mr. Knight's dogs have earned titles.

The late Dr. Samuel Milbank of Earlsmoor Kennels, with Rivington Countryman and Chuck Goodall, talking it out with Countryman.

Ch. Sir Lancelot of Salilyn, born in 1945, bred and owned by Mrs. Julie Gasow, Troy, Michigan.

Ch. Timpanogos Beauchief Cross, a well-known winner and son of two famous dogs, pictured at Harry Sangster's house in 1948. Bred and owned by R.E. Allen, Provo, Utah. By Ch. Rodrique of Sandblown Acre ex Ch. Timpanogos Melinda, she a daughter of Ch. Showman of Shotton, the Westminster Sporting Group winner of 1942. Our thanks to Dana Hopkins for use of this important photo.

This is the great Ch. Timpanogo's Radar winning Best in Show at Golden Gate Kennel Club in 1948. Breeder-owner, R.E. Allen, Timpanogo's Kennels; handler, George Sangster. Photo courtesy of Mrs. Sangster. Radar, who figures prominently in the background of numerous winning Springers, was by Ch. Showman of Shotton ex Ch. Timpanogo's Bette.

Ch. Roger's Justus of Barblythe (Ch. Roger of Hunter's Hill ex Barblythe's Jinjer) won Best in Show at Golden Gate Kennel Club in 1949 and many Sporting Groups in top California competition. Pictured winning the Group at Santa Ana Valley in April 1953, handled by his breeder, Lucille M. Parkening, under judge Helen Walsh. Owned by O.H. Parkening, Beverly Hills, California. This is one of the dogs behind Ch. Salilyn's Design.

Ch. Prince Charlie of Melilotus winning Best in Show at Oakland, California, in 1952. Handled by the late K.M. McDonald for Mrs. R. Gilman Smith, now Mrs. Frederick D. Brown.

Ch. Barblythe's Bankroll (Ch. Roger's Justus of Barblythe ex Ch. Hilen's Flicka's Duplicate) finishes his title at 18 months under judge William Pym at the 1953 Specialty of the Gateway Cities English Springer Spaniel Club, in conjunction with Glendale Kennel Club. Handled by Lucille M. Parkening for owner O.H. Parkening, Beverly Hills, California. A son of Ch. Frejax Mark Time, "Banky" won two Specialty Best of Breeds and other honors during his show career in the 1950s.

Ch. Barblythe Top Tune wins the Sporting Group at Beverly Riviera in 1954 under judge Eva Hill. Top Tune, by Ch. Timpanogos Radar ex Ch. Babblythe Jennifer, sired seven or more top champions and was a Group and Specialty Show winner. He was a grandson of Ch. Showman of Shotton and Ch. Roger of Hunter's Hill. Bred, owned, and shown by Lucille M. Parkening. Photo from Dana Hopkins' collection.

Ch. Field Knight II of Hampton (Merrimac of Hampton ex Knight's Varga Girl of Hampton) was purchased by Mrs. E.A. Klocke from the estate of Janet Henneberry. Pictured winning the Sporting Group under judge Charles Siever at Santa Barbara Kennel Club in 1955, handled by Harry Sangster. Photo courtesy of Dana Hopkins.

Best of Breed at the American Spaniel Club Specialty, New York City, 1955, is won by Champion King Peter of Salilyn for Mrs. Julie Gasow, Troy, Michigan.

Ch. Salilyn's Citation II, an International Champion and winner of many Bests in Show and Groups. Sire of Ch. Inchidony Prince Charming. Dick Cooper handling to Best in Show in 1960 for Mrs. Julie Gasow, owner.

Ch. Barblythe Topperson (by Ch. Barblythe Top Tune ex Skovalley Blithe Spirit) was bred, owned, and shown by Lucille M. Parkening, Beverly Hills, California. Here taking Best of Breed at the Gateway Cities English Springer Spaniel Association Specialty in 1957. Our thanks to Dana Hopkins for loaning us this picture.

Above: A day to be remembered! The Eastern English Springer Spaniel Club Futurity of June 24, 1961. The future champion Kaintuck Winston, owned by Stewart Johnson and handled by Laddie Carswell to Best in Futurity is on the right. Mr. Johnson is standing in the background behind his dog. On the left, future champion Another Star of Pequa, owned by Mr. and Mrs. A.W. Matson and handled by their daughter, Patty Matson Alston, takes Best of Opposite Sex. Mr. Matson is standing behind his bitch. The judge is Atha Whitaker of Athadele Springers.

Right: Anne Pope's famous Best in Show winning Ch. Charlyle Fair Warning with Laddie Carswell at Old Dominion in 1966.

29

Left: Ch. Flaming Ember of Berclee is pictured winning at the Suffolk County Kennel Club in September 1964, with Dorothy Callahan handling.

Below: Ch. Syringa Claudette, black-and-white bitch by Ch. Kaintuck Marc Antony ex Ch. Syringa Sue, pictured taking Best of Opposite Sex under Herb Roling at the Eastern English Springer Spaniel Club Specialty in 1961. Dorothy Callahan is handling, and Atha Whitaker is smiling on the left. Claudette was owned by Mr. and Mrs. Whitaker of Ambler, Pennsylvania.

Above: A picture filled with Springer history! Bob Walgate is judging the Eastern Springer Spaniel Club Specialty in 1966. On the left, George Alston is winning Best in Sweepstakes with Ch. Beryltown Virginian of Pequa. On the right, Ch. Beryltown Lucky Victoria is taking Best of Opposite Sex with Dorothy Callahan, handling.

Right: Ch. Tara's Sovereign, born August 27, 1967, bred and owned by Lillian and Robert Gough, Syosset, New York. By Ch. Fortune's King William ex Ch. Fortune's Judy Belle.

31

Left: The great winning Springer, Ch. Charlyle Fair Warning, handled by Laddie Carswell for Anne Pope, at the Trenton Kennel Club, adding to his many wins.

Below: Ch. Salilyn's Aristocrat is handled here to Best in Show by Dick Cooper for Mrs. Julie Gasow. Mrs. Amanda West, left, presents the trophy as Mrs. Erica Huggina Thomson makes the award.

PROGRESSIVE DOG
CLUB OF WAYNE, INC.
OCT. 9, 1966
BEST
IN SHOW
JUDGE:
MRS. E. D. HUGGINS
E H FRANK PHOTO

Ch. Salilyn's Sophistication, Aristocrat daughter and MacDuff great grand-daughter, was **Top Springer** Bitch in 1970 and No. 8 among all Springers. She is the dam of ten champions, of which three are **Best in** Show winners. Her son, Ch. Salilyn's Continental, has been a current top winner and Quaker Oats recipient in 1978. Mrs. Julie Gasow, owner.

33

Ch. Filicia's Crescendo, by Ch. Filicia's Anlon Patriot ex Ch. Filicia's Aliden Bisket, bred by Anne Pope, co-owned by the Robert Goughs and Anne Pope, recently sold to Maureen Brady.

Opposite: Ch. Filicia's Monarch, June 17, 1970, by Ch. Filicia's Matinee Idol ex Ch. Kaintuck Pixie, C.D.; bred by Anne Pope; owned by the Robert Goughs, Syosset, New York. Dorothy Callahan, handler.

Lleda's Lady Meg wins Best of Opposite Sex to Best in Sweepstakes under noted breeder-judge Anne Pope at the Eastern English Springer Spaniel Club in 1973. Lleda Springers are owned by the Adells at Huntington, New York.

Opposite: Ch. Danaho's Firebird (Ch. Filicia's Anlon Patriot ex Ch. Danaho's Ballet Russe), is handled by her breeder-owner Dana Hopkins to Best of Breed under Madge Ziessow at Antelope Valley Kennel Club.

B.O.B.

photo by Ashbey

38

Ch. Filicia's Wescot Justin, born April 1972, by Ch. Salilyn's Aristocrat ex Ch. Kaintuck Pixie, C.D., is pictured winning Best in Show at Greenwich Kennel Club under Mrs. Francis V. Crane. Handled by Robert S. Forsyth for co-owners Mr. and Mrs. Robert Gough and Anne Pope.

Opposite: Ch. Pembroke Inheritance, by Ch. Salilyn's Aristocrat ex Ch. Pembroke Yankee Heritage, belongs to Mrs. Walter Berd, Tolland, Connecticut.

Ch. Salilyn's Hallmark adds to his impressive list of Bests in Show under Dick Cooper's handling for owner, Julie Gasow.

Ch. Lou Jon's Femininity, at the American Spaniel Club in 1977, is handled to Winners Bitch by Patty Alston, and to Best of Winners and Best of Opposite Sex by Jane Alston (pictured).

A well-known winning Springer, Ch. Lleda's Spartacus of Sunnykay takes a Group placement at the Kenilworth Kennel Club in 1977. Owned by Barbara Weingarten and Karen Adell Garetano.

Lleda's Welcome Vintage (by Ch. Welcome Great Day ex Ch. Clancy's Erin of Packanack) is shown winning Best in Sweepstakes at the Eastern Springer Spaniel Club in 1975 under Mrs. Anne Snelling. Bred by Estelle Adell and Karen Adell Garetano; owned by Kathleen Kelly and Mary Jo Hosteny.

Ch. Salilyn's Private Stock, bred by Salilyn Kennels and co-owned by the Robert Goughs and Julie Gasow, handled by George Alston, is by Ch. Filicia's Bequest (a Ch. Salilyn Classic son) ex Ch. Salilyn's Sonnet (a Ch. Salilyn Aristocrat daughter). Stock's record at press time was 21 Bests in Show, 100 Group Firsts, and 10 Independent Specialties including the National.

Ch. Salilyn's Tempo is the current Top Winning English Springer Spaniel in the United States (as of June 1981). Handled by Houston Clark for owners Sonnie and Alan Novick, Rustic Woods Kennels, Plantation Acres, Florida.

Am., Can. Ch. Shinnecock's Rapid Transit, by Ch. Winacko's Classic Replay, C.D., ex Ch. Lou Jon's Femininity, became a Canadian champion undefeated at 7 months, completed U.S.A. title at 13 months. Winners Dog, Best of Winners, and Best Puppy at American Spaniel Club 1980, this splendid Springer is from Shinnecock Kennels, Maureen Brady and Patty Alston, Flanders, New York.

Wayfarer's Bridget relaxes on the lawn. Debra Valvo, owner, Sure-Wyn Springers.

Opposite: Chuzzlewit's Rule of Thumb and Chuzzlewit's Pentimento were photographed during an informal moment. Francie Nelson owns these two beauties from Fanfare Kennels, Minneapolis, Minnesota.

Champion Kevriett's Kay N Dee Damnation, pictured at 13 months of age, is owned by Bruce and Jeane Harkins, Ellicott City, Maryland. Photographed by Bruce Harkins.

48

CHAPTER FOUR

Important Kennels of the Present Day

A "look of eagles" is characteristic of field trial bred Springers. F.C. Brackenbriar Snapshot, Jr., looks disdainfully at the rest of the world. Third in 1973 and second in the 1974 National Championship, he is owned by Brackenbriar Kennels.

The growing appreciation of English Springer Spaniels can be credited to the reputable breeders who are devoted to raising good, healthy puppies from worthy stock to insure the future of the breed. We also owe a debt of gratitude to the majority of owners who have just one or two dogs and, presenting the breed at its best, contribute in their own way to its popularity.

Brackenbriar

Brackenbriar Kennels was registered in 1929 by Mr. and Mrs. George E. Watson, Jr. of Greenwich, Connecticut. Springers of Horsford breeding were owned, bred-from and run in Field Trials from this establishment. Following Mr. Watson's death, the Brackenbriar prefix was re-registered by Mr. Watson's daughters, Elisabeth Watson and Mrs. James C. Kineon (also of Greenwich, Connecticut), who made their father's dream come true where his Springers were concerned.

The combination of Earlsmoor Brackenbriar, a son of F.C. Rivington Countryman and Brackenbriar Blaze, daughter of F.C. Ludlovian Scamp, produced 1967 National Field Cham-

pion Brackenbriar Snapshot. Also in this litter were Field Champion Brackenbriar Bonfire, Amateur Field Champion Brackenbriar Boulder and Top Brood Bitch Brackenbriar Bequest. Snapshot sired one son, 1969 National Field Champion and National Amateur Field Champion Dansmirth's Gunshot, that in turn sired National Field Champion, National Amateur Field Champion and Canadian National Field Champion Joysam's Solo Sam. Another son of Snapshot, Field Champion Brackenbriar Snapshot, Jr. was third in the 1973 Nationals and second in the Nationals the following year. He too has sired champion sons and daughters and has grandchildren currently placing in Field Trials. Another Brackenbriar bloodline stemming from Earlsmoor Brackenbriar's son, Brackenbriar Bonus, produced Field Champion Brackenbriar Boomerang that was Top Point Springer (Field) in 1971 and Boomerang's sister, Hogan's Hawk, that was the dam of 1972 National Field Champion Dot of Charel. Tradition has continued with Mrs. Kineon's daughter Forsyth running her Springer, Prairie Rose, in Field Trials, making Brackenbriar a three generation hobby for this family.

Forsyth Kineon and Brackenbriar Bosun try a "look-alike" pose for the camera in this informal shot from Brackenbriar Kennels.

Camden

A successful strain of Field Trial Springers which resides at the Craig Kennels in Lebanon, Ohio founded by Lew Craig back in 1958 has been established under the Camden identification. David S. Ingalls, then editor of the *Post-Times-Star* newspaper, was financially associated with this kennel, and his son David, Jr. has some outstanding Camden field dogs there now. A dog, Sam O'Vara, was the basis of the stock and was of Field Trial Champion Rivington Landmark and double National Champion of England Scramble O'Vara lineage. Field Trial Champion Pam's Smarty of Camden II and Pam's Thumzup of Camden are among the distinguished winners produced by this kennel.

This young field Springer, Pam's Thumzup of Camden, placed in a Puppy Stake at 7 months and was doing well in Open All Age Stakes at the time of this writing. Owned by the Camden Springers in Ohio.

Field Trial Ch. Pam's Smarty of Camden, II, was the high-scoring bitch in field trials a few years back. Her record includes 3 firsts, 1 second, 2 thirds and 1 fourth. Owned by David Ingalls, Jr., Cleveland, Ohio.

Am., Can. Ch. Telltale Valleybrook Secret, liver-and-white bitch, is also an American and Canadian C.D., T.D., and C.D.X. This daughter of Ch. Telltale Prime Minister ex Canadian Ch. Valleybrook U.E. Loyalist belongs to the Canamar Springers of James and Irene Eadie at Park Ridge, Illinois.

Canamer

Canamer Springers is owned by James and Irene Eadie of Park Ridge, Illinois and was founded with the purchase of their first Springer, Telltale Valleybrook Secret, that went on to become an American and Canadian Champion, C.D., T.D. and C.D.X. The kennel prefix was selected due to Secret having been bred in CANada with an AMERican sire, from which the name Canamer was coined.

Secret was whelped on August 17, 1973, and bred by Howard Northey, of St. Thomas, Ontario. She was simultaneously trained in tracking, breed ring and obedience, many times going from the breed ring to the obedience ring at the same show. She won her American Tracking Dog title in May 1974 at only eight months of age, following this in November of the same year with a Canadian T.D. During 1975 she completed her Companion Dog degrees in both Canada and the United States, plus her Canadian Championship. Next was her American Championship in February 1976, during which year she also became an American C.D.X. Then in 1979, following time out for puppies, she gained her Canadian C.D.X., bringing her total number of titles to six. Very nice going, indeed!

In addition to her own accomplishments, Secret is proving herself to be a Top Producer. As this is written, a son and two daughters have gained their titles in the show ring, and one of them has added a T.D. as well. They are the dog, Champion Canamar Commodore, owned by Dr. Milton Prickett; the bitch, Champion Canamer Chantilly, owned by Karen Prickett and Jim Eadie; and the bitch, Champion Canamer Blue Ribbon, T.D., owned by Jim and Irene Eadie. Commodore and Chantilly, who are littermates, won the National Sweepstakes in Philadelphia in 1978 under Juanita Howard, going Best Puppy and Best of Opposite Sex respectively. They went back to back at many shows on the way up the ladder and finished their championships on the same day at Ann Arbor on April 27, 1981, under judge Richard N. Thomas. Blue Ribbon finished her championship under Mrs. Patterson at Clearwater and earned her tracking title in March 1981.

Then there is Canamer High Life, Canadian T.D., owned by Irene Eadie and Delores Streng, that was Best Puppy in Futurity at the Great Lakes English Springer Spaniel Breeders Association in 1979, plus Best Puppy in Sweepstakes and Reserve Winners Bitch at the Michigan Specialty the same year. Temporarily retired for breeding in 1980, she is back in the ring as this is written and has her "major" points.

Canamer Telltale High Life, Am., Can. T.D., by Ch. Coventry's Allegro ex Am., Can. Ch. Telltale Valleybrook Secret, Am. T.D. and C.D.X., Can. C.D. and T.D.X., was whelped in July 1978, and is owned by Jim and Irene Eadie and Delores Streng.

American and Canadian Champion Canarch Telltale Saga, American and Canadian T.D., C.D. and C.D.X., is another of the Eadies' Springers holding a distinguished record. This liver-and-white male was whelped March 19, 1973, bred by Delores Streng and John Hilt, by Champion Salilyn's Aristocrat ex Canarch Siren. During 1976 he earned six titles, American and Canadian T.D., American and Canadian C.D. and American and Canadian Championships. Then in 1978 came American C.D.X., and the Eadies are hoping that he will have earned his U.D. and T.D.X. by the end of 1981. It is noteworthy that his Canadian C.D. and Championship were both earned over the same four-show weekend where he placed Group Two and Group Four as "frosting on the cake."

Saga has never been used at stud. Interestingly, he is a member of the *Illini Search and Rescue Group*, proving that a Springer can succeed in this capacity too. His owner, Jim Eadie, who is an American Kennel Club judge of tracking, trained and handles him for this important work. It is the Eadies' special interest in tracking that has led to all the T.D. titles on their own dogs and the offspring of these Springers.

Canarch

Canarch Springers, Reg. belongs to Mr. and Mrs. Charles F. Hendee of Barrington, Illinois. Their foundation bitch in 1959 was to have been Rock Fair's Eliza, a daughter of Champion Cartref Cosmic ex Champion Deuces Wild of Donniedhu. Her show career was interrupted at nine points to make way for a breeding to Champion Syringa Disc Jockey; however, the resulting pregnancy ended in her death just prior to the delivery of nine puppies which were also dead . . . truly a sad disappointment.

A new start was made with the purchase of Melilotus Hufty Tufty, by the imported Champion Rostherne Hunter ex Melilotus Princess Dona, the latter a daughter of Champion Melilotus Prince Charlie. Hufty Tufty was bred to Champion Syringa Disc Jockey, producing, among others, the black-and-white Canarch Sunnyside that became a champion and earned a C.D. and became the fine "resident producer" for Canarch with nine American Champions to her credit—three of which also became Canadian Champions—plus a tenth that was a Canadian Champion only. Sunnyside's daughter, Champion Canarch Inchidony Brook, sired by Cham-

Finishing their championships at the same show, these two lovely Springers also started out together by being Best Puppy and Best of Opposite Sex at the National Springer Specialty in Philadelphia. They are Ch. Canamer Chantilly, now owned by Karen Prickett and Jim Eadie, and Ch. Canamer Commodore, owned by Dr. Milton Prickett. Bred by Jim and Irene Eadie and D. Streng, they are by Ch. Loujon Counter Point ex Am., Can. Ch. Telltale Valleybrook Secret, Am. T.D., C.D.X., and Can. C.D., T.D.X.

Am., Can. Ch. Canarch Yankee Patriot, C.D., is owned by Mr. and Mrs. Charles F. Hendee.

pion Inchidony Prince Charming, became an outstanding producer herself with numerous champions to her credit including the magnificent Champion Chinoe's Adamant James, winner of two consecutive Westminster Bests in Show and a record-breaking number of all-breed shows in one year.

It was during those early years that the Hendees produced two American Best in Show dogs, these being Champion Canarch Juniper Five and American and Canadian Champion Canarch Inchidony Sparkler. American and Canadian Champion Canarch Gold Eagle became a Best in Show winner in Canada. Champion Canarch Yankee Patriot drew attention as a big winner, but the Best in Show spotlight seemed always to elude him.

It became apparent to Mr. and Mrs. Hendee that three things were necessary for record-setting: the right dog, the right handler, and being in the right spot at the right time. Chasing the top win spot became less interesting to them, and trying new combinations in their breeding program was more absorbing. Champions still dotted the list of dogs produced, but some of the best were not campaigned even so far as to championship status. Among the latter were Canarch Triple Crown, Canarch Yankee Tea Party, Canarch Reverie, Canarch Contemplation, Canarch Storm Center and Canarch Roman Fiddler. Many of these dogs, however, eventually gained wide recognition as fine producers

Staying primarily within the strong Prince Charming line, with an outcross of American, Canadian and Mexican Champion Muller's Blazing Kane, such dogs as the Group winning Champion Canarch Exchequer, Champion Canarch Meltaway Pippin, Champion Canarch Show Bird, C.D., W.D. and Champion Canarch Carillon, T.D. were produced. From Carillon came Champion Canarch Cardinal's Lancer, a fine, upstanding, free-moving dog that is passing these qualities to his offspring.

The attempt to combine the fine Spaniel qualities of the two brothers, American and Canadian Champion Canarch Inchidony Sparkler and American and Canadian Champion Canarch Yankee Patriot, C.D., was at the same time rewarding and frustrating. A Sparkler daughter, Incandescent, bred to Yankee Patriot, produced most successfully. The progeny included Canarch Yankee Tea Party, a foundation bitch of the Winacko line in Michigan, Canarch Minute Man, a foundation stud at Valleybrook in Ontario, and Canarch Town Crier, a foundation stud at Wingdale in Pennsylvania, all of which were littermates.

The Sunnyside daughter (by Champion Salilyn's Aristocrat), group winning American and Canadian Champion Canarch High Society, was bred to a Prince Charming line-bred dog, Champion Canarch Three Alarm. In this litter were three bitches that became famed producers: Canarch Reverie, foundation bitch at Willowside, Canarch Contemplation that put Chuzzlewit/Fanfare into production; and Canarch Meditation who was used successfully in the home kennel.

Left to right are Ch. Canarch Spring Peeper, C.D., foundation bitch Melilotus Hufty Tufty, and Ch. Canarch Sunnyside, C.D. These are three highly important members of the Hendees' Canarch Kennel. Photo made in 1965.

Some other results were less rewarding, and for a while the Hendees had the feeling that Canarch was marking time; but it was only over a brief period, as the new challenges of new breedings are continuing to produce dogs in which to take pride. Some of those coming along as this is written include Canarch Expertise, Canarch Soft Music, Canarch Warning Bell and Canarch Anchor Man, among others.

With a breeder's true dedication, the Hendees keep foremost in mind the desire to produce a *Spanielly* Springer, an animal that is functional with few exaggerations and limiting faults. Their foremost aim is good temperament with every attempt being made to socialize a well-bred animal early enough to produce the well known, gentle, intelligent Canarch Springer.

The Best in Show winner, Am., Can. Ch. Canarch Inchidony Sparkler, from the Canarch Kennels, Reg., of Mr. and Mrs. Charles F. Hendee at Barrington, Illinois.

Carey's

Carey's Springer Spaniels, in Fairfax, Virginia, has been widely renowned and respected in the Fancy since the early 1950's when Mary and Andy Carey (Mr. and Mrs. Andrew M.) started in the breed with a bitch puppy of Frejax breeding, soon afterwards purchasing another bitch from the Melilotus strain. These were bred into Walpride and Kaintuck bloodlines with resulting success in the form of some truly lovely litters. The puppies were sold mostly to military people, due to the large number of military establishments in the area.

It had never occurred to the Careys to enter any of their Springers in a dog show until one day when a professional handler stopped by to

The black-and-white Springer bitch, Ch. Canarch Soft Music, whelped in January 1978, winning a "major" from judge Georgia Buttram, Waukesha, Wisconsin, 1980. Owned by Canarch Kennels, Mr. and Mrs. Charles F. Hendee.

say that he had long admired the quality of Carey Springers and that he would like to handle some of them in show competition. The suggestion seemed interesting, so Mr. and Mrs. Carey sent one out with him. The first time in the ring she came away with Winners Bitch. Need we say more? Of course the Careys, as has been the case with so many of us, were promptly bitten by the dog show bug.

Ch. Carey's Flaming Glory is shown taking Best of Opposite Sex at the National Specialty in August 1967. Owned by Mr. and Mrs. Andrew M. Carey of Fairfax, Virginia. Mr. Carey is handling.

Mr. Carey, long prior to that time, had been doing field work, tracking and obedience with the dogs. Now here was an added interest and source of pleasure. By 1970 the Careys had produced 18 home-bred conformation champions and achieved National fame for the excellence of their dogs.

By the time of this writing, Andy and Mary Carey have raised 29 litters of Springers and one litter of Irish Setters. Because so many of their Springers have gone to military families who move about a great deal, dogs from this kennel are known and admired all around the world for their outstanding beauty and personality, making splendid goodwill ambassadors for the Springer breed.

Mr. and Mrs. Andrew M. Carey's noted winner, Ch. Carey's Brown Derby, in June 1965.

It was about 1971 when Andrew Carey was granted a license to judge English Springer Spaniels, English Cocker Spaniels and Irish Setters, after which time this became his principal interest where show dogs are concerned. Thus there has been a slowdown in the Carey breeding program along with a curtailment of showing, which they now do only occasionally. Obedience, tracking and field work, however, continue.

Carey's Springers have distinguished themselves notably in obedience competition as well as in conformation over the years. At the time of this writing, 12 have earned their Companion Dog titles (C.D.), four have Companion Dog Excellent (C.D.X.), and two have Working Dog Excellent (W.D.X.), this latter degree being that of the Parent Club for Springers.

Ch. Carey's Brown Betty, C.D., completing her championship at Virginia Kennel Club, April 1959. Owned by Mr. and Mrs. Andrew M. Carey.

The Careys have given generously of their time and effort to club activities. Mr. Carey was first President of the Potomac Valley English Springer Spaniel Club, which was organized in 1956, and was also its first Show Chairman. He was Show Chairman for the Parent Club Specialties in Northern Virginia in 1961 and again in 1971 and has held a position on the National Board of Directors over many years. Both he and Mrs. Carey are honorary lifetime members of the Potomac Valley English Springer Spaniel Club and of the Potomac Irish Setter club. Additionally Mr. Carey has been twice President of the Capital Dog Training Club in Washington, D.C., each time for two-year terms, and is an honorary member of the Mattaponi Kennel Club in Northern Virginia and the Dulles Gateway Obedience Club. Both he and Mrs. Carey are honorary members of the Old Dominion Kennel Club of Northern Virginia, for which Mr. Carey was the American Kennel Club delegate for 12 years, 1968-1980. One other club in which these dedicated fanciers actively participate is the Eastern English Springer

Spaniel Association, to which they have belonged for more than 25 years, and of which they are now honorary members. Mrs. Carey was Chairman for this association's 1968 Specialty in Ridgefield, Connecticut, an event which drew a record entry at that time.

Champion Carey's Brown Betty, C.D. was the Careys' first champion in breed competition, and they were very proud of her. Mrs. Carey describes her as "a natural liver-and-white beauty requiring no posing or handling in the ring." Gordon Barton showed and finished her with either Best of Breed or Best of Opposite Sex in entries averaging around 30 Springers each time she entered the ring. She was born in 1958, lived to be 12 years of age and produced two handsome litters of puppies. Several of them became champions and, by an English Field Champion, several became good Field Springers. Betty was by Carey's Royal Bill (Champion Chrisbrick Starflight-Carey's Trants Sheila) from Laurestra's Royal Beauty (Champion Frejax Royal Command-Frejax Virginia Miss).

Carey's Brown Bomber, U.D.T., W.D.X., in June 1964 at seven years age. Mr. and Mrs. Andrew M. Carey, owners.

Ch. Carey's Flaming Glory taking Winners Bitch, Best of Winners, and Best of Opposite Sex for a 5-point "major" at the Keystone Specialty, May 1966. Mr. and Mrs. Andrew M. Carey, owners.

Carey's Brown Bomber, U.D.T., W.D.X. (1957-1972) was the Careys' first all-obedience champion, having earned six obedience titles and Water Trial degrees by the age of six years. He was twice the Highest Scoring Dog in Trial and a talented retriever that spent many days bringing in ducks from the rough waters of the Chesapeake Bay during competitive Water Trials.

Bomber was also a talented tracking dog, and he was called upon several times to help find lost dogs (and on one occasion a lost small child). He invariably found his prey. As for personality and temperament, he was the ideal of what one likes to find in a Springer. Bomber performed often with several other obedience-trained dogs that visited childrens' and veterans' hospitals and also homes for the old and for retarded citizens. The dogs gave much pleasure and Bomber was always the center of attention.

Sired by Champion Chrisbrick Starflight (Champion Sunhi's Christmas Star-Salilyn's Adoration) ex Carey's Trants Sheila (Chestnut Blaze-Zimm's Lady), he brought 15 years of pleasure to his owners and is still missed very much by them.

American and Canadian Champion Carey's Lucky Knight, C.D. (1961–1974) was by Champion Legend's Baron Blennerhasset (Champion Sandolyn's Davy Crocket-Champion Melilotus Winter Starlight) from Champion Shamrock's Black Pepper, C.D. (International Champion Walpride Flaming Rocket-Champion Upland Merrie Sunshine). This gorgeous black-and-white dog was not shown in the breed until three years of age, when he was entered in three shows in North Carolina during September 1964. He was Best of Breed from the classes all three days and placed each time in the Sporting Group, winning second, third and fourth respectively. From these wins he went to shows in Ohio and Pennsylvania with Tom Glassford, gaining his title in less than two months, winning one Group First and four other placements along the way. He was Best of Breed at the Potomac Valley Specialty in April 1965 over 150 entries which included the top Springers of the day. Then he went to Canada, gained his title there, and was rated second highest ranking dog in Canada for that year. Also in 1965 he was the number four Sporting Dog in the United States.

Lucky Knight had considerable impact as a sire and in the ring. Two daughters of his in particular became very famous; one was Champion Carey's Flaming Glory and the other was Champion Carey's Dusty Rose.

Ch. Carey's Lucky Knight, C.D., taking Best of Breed at the Potomac Valley English Springer Spaniel Specialty, April 1965. Mr. and Mrs. Andrew Carey, owners. Tom Glassford, handler. George Pugh, judge.

Ch. Oakeire Minit Man of Carey finishing his title.

Lucky Knight's daughter, Champion Carey's Flaming Glory, was from Richlin's Debutante (Champion Walpride Bright Flame-Champion Beryltown Rocket of Rovenn). Born in 1965, she completed her championship in May 1966 at the Keystone English Springer Spaniel Specialty with five points from the Bred-by-Exhibitor Class under Ray Beale. She also took Best of Winners and Best of Opposite Sex over a goodly entry. Additionally she was Best of Opposite Sex in the Potomac Valley Sweepstakes in April 1966 judged by Bernice Roe, and then she went to the National Specialty in August 1967 where she was Best of Opposite Sex in a quality-laden turnout. Glory produced one litter of eight, five of which completed their titles; two of them won Specialty events.

Lucky Knight's other best known daughter, Champion Carey's Dusty Rose, was rated Bitch of the Year for 1971 by the *Springer Review*, having produced seven champions out of a litter of 10, the other three of which won obedience titles. Rose herself finished her title in three straight weekends with six "majors" for a total of 18 points.

Champion Carey's Prince Michael, U.D.T., W.D.X. (1958–1974) was sired by Champion Kaintuck Marc Anthony (Champion Kaintuck Prince Hamlet-Kaintuck Roxane) from Bonnie Minx of Lakeland, C.D. (Jou's Durmont Ned-Glenwood's Augusta). He was thought to be the most titled Springer in the United States, having been shown successfully in obedience, tracking and field and water trials, in all of which he had gained many titles before he was ever entered in conformation. At four years of age he made his bench show debut and finished quickly with a four point "major." Michael was a great tracking dog who won several tracking trials, and he was called upon more than a few times to help find lost dogs and other lost animals. He was bred to an English Field Champion and produced a number of fine field dogs, as well as several conformation champions.

Champion Carey's Brown Derby (1962–1973) was a liver-and-white son of Champion Melilotus Destiny (Champion Melilotus Royal Oak-Champion Melilotus Barbary Ann) from Champion Carey's Brown Jewel, C.D (Champion Kaintuck Marc Anthony-Bonnie Minx of Lakeland, C.D.). At the age of 13 months he finished his championship in 17 days from the Bred-by-Exhibitor Class with several Bests of Breed and Group placements along the way. Shown for a short time as a "special," he won the Group at Susque-Nango in 1963, as well as several other Group placements. He sired numerous fine litters which included some outstanding champions.

Included among the Brown Derby progeny, Champion Oakeire Minit Man of Carey was sold as a puppy to an Irish Setter breeder in Georgia. The Careys considered him to be the pick of the litter from Champion Carey's Flaming Glory, so they were hardly prepared for the purchaser to have kept the dog for two years— evidently in the kennel—and then telephone to say that he was "no good" and that he wanted to get rid of him. The Careys asked that Minit Man be shipped home immediately. Two weeks later they met him at the airport and were shocked to see him stripped of all featherings with his ears practically shaven to the skin. The Careys' original opinion of his show potential obviously had been correct, however, as five months later he was entered in the Bred-by-Exhibitor Class at the Winchester, Virginia dog show. Here he went

Ch. Carey's Jet Rocket in August 1964, taking Best of Winners at Annapolis. Mr. and Mrs. Andrew M. Carey owners.

Winners Dog, Best of Winners, then Best of Breed over five top professionally-handled "specials" under Ted Eldredge, a very knowledgeable Sporting Dog authority.

Minit Man completed his title a few months later under a breeder-judge from England at Maryland Kennel Club over a very large entry with several consistent "specials" competing. He went Best of Breed there, too.

As a sire, Minit Man produced at least a dozen splendid litters, and many of his offspring became champions in obedience and tracking as well as in conformation.

Another very lovely Springer owned by the Careys was the black-and-white Champion Carey's Jet Rocket (1961–1974). Shown for the first time at age three years, he went through within a few months from the Bred-by-Exhibitor Class, winning first in the Sporting Group at Penn Ridge in 1964, and also winning five other Group placements during that and the following year.

Jet Rocket then spent the next five years in Hawaii with some military friends of the Careys who had wanted him from the time he was a puppy. There he became the foundation sire of a

new Springer breeder, and the Careys understand that he had offspring all over Hawaii being enjoyed and being shown in the ring. The family was eventually transferred back to the United States, and they shipped the dog back to the Careys, with whom he remained for the balance of his life, about six years. He was by Champion Legend's Blannerhasset ex Champion Shamrock's Black Pepper, C.D.

As of 1981, the Careys had two entries at the Eastern Specialty. These were Carey's Pride of Virginia, T.D. by Champion Carey's Pride and Joy, U.D.T. ex Carey's Lady Tiffany, T.D., born in May 1979 and Carey's Rainbow of Love, by Cricket's Venetian Count ex Carey's Lady Tiffany, born in October 1980.

Chinoe

It was a fateful day in 1964 when a chubby black-and-white Springer bitch puppy left Canarch Kennels to journey to Lexington, Kentucky. She went to fill the gap left by the death of a beloved pet Springer in a pet home; but when Ann Roberts took "Brook" she also took the pressure of her sister, Mary Lee Hendee (owner of Canarch) and her brother, professional handler Clint Harris, to show this puppy when the time came.

Chinoe Kennels, Reg., came about as the result. It was not long until the bug bit, and within a short time the then grown-up Springer puppy became Champion Canarch Inchidony Brook. When Brook's first litter, by Champion Salilyn's Inchidony Banquo, was whelped on lease to Canarch Kennels, a liver-and-white male was kept at Chinoe as Canarch Juniper Five. This was the start of an active time, as Juniper became a Multi Best in Show winner.

Within the next few years, Brook was bred to various fine studs; Champion Salilyn's Aristocrat twice, a repeat to Champion Salilyn's Inchidony Banquo and twice to Champion Willowbank's Make It Snappy. There were many fine show dogs produced under the Chinoe prefix, such as Delightful Jezebel, Libation, Ace High, Eminent Judge and others.

Everyone the least bit familiar with modern show Springers is aware of Champion Chinoe's Adamant James, by Champion Salilyn's Aristocrat ex Champion Canarch Inchidony Brook. In the ring his flawless showmanship won countless fanciers to the breed as his easy personality, shown in closer contact, convinced those people that Springers are indeed a superior breed. Born at Chinoe Kennels in 1968, "D.J.," who had been nicknamed "Diamond Jim" as a wee pup, became the friend and companion of Dr. Milton Prickett, a Kentucky veterinarian who later practiced in Michigan. D.J. will always be remembered for his 1971 and 1972 Best in Show wins at the Westminster Kennel Club at Madison Square Garden where he literally brought down the house on both occasions. There are only a few dogs among all breeds that have been double Best in Show winners at Westminster, thus it truly is a most note-worthy achievement. Additionally, during this same period D.J. set a record by winning 48 Bests in Show within one year, a record which only very recently has been broken.

The last fine dog to gain the limelight from this kennel was Champion Chinoe's Applause, another Best in Show liver-and-white dog, this one by Champion Salilyn's Aristocrat ex Champion Chinoe's L.E. Roban.

The closing of the Chinoe Kennel doors after nearly 15 years of breeding was a sad day. Many fine Springers had been produced here, and many good friends made for the breed. Our thanks to Ann Roberts and her husband Lloyd for this page in Springer history.

The multi-Best in Show winner, Ch. Canarch Juniper Five, owned by Ann Roberts, handled by Clint Harris, is here gaining the top award from Virgil Johnson in 1969 at the Huntington Kennel Club, Huntington, West Virginia.

Ch. Chinoe's Applause, liver-and-white dog by Ch. Salilyn's Aristocrat ex Ch. Chinoe's L.E. Roban, is the last Best in Show dog from Ann Roberts' famed Chinoe Kennels at Lexington, Kentucky. Winning Best in Show here at a recent St. Louis Dog Breeders Kennel Club event, handled by Mrs. Roberts' brother, Clint Harris.

Danaho

The purchase of "Lucy Lou," a charming liver-white-and-tan bitch puppy registered by Dana Hopkins as a ten-year-old child in 1952, was the start of his involvement with Springers that led to the founding and success of the now very famous Danaho Springers in Los Angeles, California. Lucy was sired by Barblythe Judge, the littermate to those widely admired champions, Barblythe Top Tune, Sparkle Plenty and Fire Belle. A visit to the Beverly Riviera show at the Miramar Hotel put the finishing touches on Dana Hopkins' enthusiasm for showing, as he watched an "invader" from the East, Champion Prince Charlie of Melilotus, go on to Best in Show. Lucy was in due course bred to Champion Barblythe Bankroll and produced a nice litter.

School and the army interrupted dog activities for this young fancier but in 1970, with these concerns now in the past, Dana Hopkins had the good fortune to purchase Champion Kaintuck Tolstoy from Anne Pope. "Toy" was the son of the famed Champion Charlyle Fair Warning (which Mr. Hopkins had seen when attending East Coast shows) ex Champion Kaintuck Fortune Huntress, an excellent bitch owned by Stuart Johnson whose Kaintuck dogs were Dana's favorites. Tolstoy, in addition to being a most handsome Springer, had the happy faculty of a truly *Great* stud, being able to produce excellent progeny in every litter, regardless of the bloodlines, regardless of faults the bitch might possess. He sired more than 11 champions, although he was not extensively used at stud.

Spennymoor's Noblesse Oblige (Ch. Spenny-moor's Doc's Boy ex Billet Doux of Spennymoor), owned and bred by Mrs. John G. Fletcher of Sacramento, California, and leased to Dana Hopkins. Photo courtesy of Mr. Hopkins.

Mr. Hopkins leased a bitch to breed to Tolstoy from Ruth Fletcher, whose dedication to Springers and diligent, intelligent linebreeding from her foundation bitch, Frejax Sweet Memory, produced outstanding stock. The bitch chosen by Mr. Hopkins was exquisite in head, bone, feet and outline and was of unique, unrepeatable pedigree—entirely Frejax, Barblythe, and Toprock. She was a grand-daughter of Champion Toprock's Glory's Repeat and of Champion Frejax Royalist Am-bassador. Her name was Spennymoor's Noblesse Oblige, and she produced for Mr. Hopkins those high-flying littermates, Champion Danaho's Moonfleet and his sister Champion Danaho's Ballet Russe, Mr. Hopkins' first two champions.

These two young home-breds hit the show ring with considerable impact. In 1974 at the Sacramento Specialty they took, owner-handled, Best in Sweeps and Best of Opposite Sex under judge Barbara Jane Gates. At the Santa Barbara Kennel Club they were Best of Breed and Best of Opposite Sex from the classes under George Sangster, where Ballet Russe finished at 18 months of age with four "majors" in only nine shows. Moonfleet also finished handily with four "majors," but it was Ballet Russe who had the truly startling show career and has consistently produced the goods.

Ballet Russe was the 1975 Parent Club Bitch of the Year, shown by her owner at only the large California events. She won several Special-ty Best Opposites and was also winner of Bests of Breed and Group placements. She then had the honor of being leased for her first litter by Julie Gasow, and together with Champion Salilyn's Encore she produced those fine pro-ducers, Salilyn's Curtain Call for Mrs. Gasow, Danaho's Salilyn Blackamoor for Mr. Hopkins and Salilyn's Doll Babe for Mrs. Ferguson. For her second litter Ballet Russe was bred to Cham-pion Filicia's Anlon Patriot, producing those ex-cellent bitches, Champion Danaho's Firebird and Champion Danaho's Lalique of Stanton. And from her third litter, by Champion Foyscroft's Signed Edition, she produced Mr. Hopkins' Champion Danaho's Hedy Tondelayo that started her "specials" career by going Best of Breed at the Santa Clara Valley English Springer Spaniel Association Specialty in an en-try of 135, which she has followed up with several Best of Breed victories, owner-handled, in stiffest California competition.

Ch. Danaho's Ballet Russe (Ch. Kaïntuck Tolstoy ex Spennymoor's Noblesse Oblige) is the dam of champions and was the Parent Club's Bitch of the Year for 1975. Owned, bred, and handled by Dana Hopkins, Los Angeles, California.

Mr. Hopkins feels that Springer breeders "should place more concentration on correct, sturdy type and good nature, and place less emphasis on newly discovered fads of the day, which are reduced to irrelevance if the dog is either unreliable temperamentally or incorrect in looks."

Above left: Ch. Danaho's Hedy Tondelayo (by Ch. Foyscroft Signed Edition ex Ch. Danaho's Ballet Russe) is handled by her breeder-owner Dana Hopkins to Best of Breed at South Bay Kennel Club in 1981 under judge Raphael Schulte. **Above right:** Ch. Danaho's Moonfleet (Ch. Kaintuck's Tolstoy ex Spennymoor's Noblesse Oblige) finishes his championship with his fourth "major" under judge Winifred Heckman at San Antonio in 1976, handled by Ray McGinnis, Jr.

Santa Barbara Kennel Club, 1974. Littermates taking it all are (left) Best of Breed to future Ch. Danaho's Moonfleet and Best of Opposite Sex to Ch. Danaho's Ballet Russe, the latter completing her title on the day.

National Field Trial Champion and National Amateur Field Trial Champion Dansmirth's Gunshot (bred, owned, and trained by Daniel K. Langhans) won five Open wins, back-to-back National and National Amateur in 1969, and was awarded Best Dog Handled by an Amateur. Additionally, he has sired ten champions.

Dansmirth's

Dansmirth's Kennels, owned by Marie and Daniel K. Langhans of Harvard, Illinois are breeders of some highly successful Field Trial winners.

Some years back when they were looking for a Field-bred Spaniel, the Langhans found very little breeding of them being done in this country. Finally they located and purchased one from John Harding named Athena L of Davellis Shot. "Tina" did not make it as a Field Trial dog, but she lived with Mr. and Mrs. Langhans as a fine hunting dog and pet until she was 17 years old.

As soon as Dan Langhans discovered that Tina would not do for Field Trials, he searched further and this time came up with Vivacious Victoria from a litter out of Ludlovian Socks. Victoria placed in Puppy Stakes and had a win in the Amateur and a second, when her owners lost her at three-and-one-half years in a training mishap. Fortunately they had bred this lovely bitch to E.F.T.C. Gwibernant Abereithy Skip, and had kept a bitch, Amateur Field Trial Champion Dansmirth's Cricket, that placed in Open Stakes, in two National Amateur Championships and in one National Championship.

Cricket was bred twice: first to National Field Trial Champion Brackenbriar Snapshot, which produced National Field Trial Champion and National Amateur Field Trial Champion Dansmirth's Gunshot and Field Trial Champion and Amateur Field Trial Champion Orm's Emissary; and for her second litter to Field Trial Champion Pepe of Shrewsbury, which produced Field Trial Champion and Amateur Field Trial Champion Vivacious Penny.

Dansmirth's Gunshot, or "Gunner," was and still is a dream come true for Mr. and Mrs. Langhans. He was (as was Cricket) bred, owned, trained and handled by Dan. He took five Open wins, back-to-back National and National Amateur in 1969 and was awarded the "Best Dog Handled by An Amateur," as Cricket had been. During Gunner's three years at stud he produced 10 champions, among them National Field Trial Champion, National Amateur Field Trial Champion and Canadian Field Trial Champion Joysan's Solo Sam.

After training and competing in trials since 1961, Dan Langhans decided to turn professional in 1974. Since then he has trained and handled Field Trial Champion Slattery of Saighton, Top Dog in 1977; Field Trial Champion Dewfield Flicker of Brickcourse, Top Dog in 1978; and Field Trial Champion Chrishall Rover, Top Dog in 1980.

In 1978 Marie and Dan Langhans purchased an 80 acre farm and built a new kennel where they have 20 acres planted in brome for a licensed training area. They do some breeding, with some dogs still in the Cricket–Gunner line which now are being bred to the Saighton and Chishall lines.

Donahan

Donahan Springers "officially" began when Don and Carol Callahan of Prineville, Oregon purchased Lilley's Holiday Cheer from Joe and Daisy Lilley of the Holiday Kennels. A liver-and-white daughter of Champion Geiger's Chief Geronimo, C.D. ex Champion Lilley's Pheasant Quest, C.D., Cheer was born in 1966 and went back in her pedigree to Rexford, Melilotus and Salilyn bloodlines. Owner-handled, she quickly gained her championship and Companion Dog Excellent title. Two months after finishing, again owner-handled, she took Best of Opposite Sex at the 1969 National Specialty Show under judge Ray Beale.

Prior to purchasing Cheer, the Callahans had owned a dog that was actually their first Springer that they had bought as a hunting dog and family pet in 1960, a grandson of Field Trial Champion Whittlemoor George. An obedience class which they attended led to an interest in obedience trials, then eventually to exhibiting in conformation competition.

Cheer became the dam of five champions and the grand-dam of two Best in Show and Specialty winners, namely American and Canadian Champion Perri's Timothy Von Zuda, C.D. (by Bipa's Western Yankee of Sujax, C.D.X., T.D., a Champion Canarch Yankee Patriot son ex a Champion Magill's Patrick, C.D. daughter); and American and Canadian Champion Donahan's Mark Twain (by Champion Telltale Author ex the same Champion Magill's Patrick, C.D. daughter). Timothy was born in October 1972; Mark, June 4, 1977.

Timothy won Best of Breed at the Sacramento English Springer Spaniel Specialty in 1975 and at the Puget Sound Specialty in 1977, in addition to his two all-breed Bests in Show.

Mark, bred and owned by the Callahans, at mid-1981 won three all-breed Bests in Show, Best of Breed at the Puget Sound Specialty in 1981 and at the American Spaniel Club in 1981, plus 11 Group Firsts. He was among the Top 10 Springers of 1980 and is well on the way to repeating the honor in 1981. He is the sire of two champions, with others on the way.

Am., Can. Ch. Donahan's Mark Twain is handled here by Jim Hall to Best in Show under Howard Tyler. Mark is owned by Donahan Kennels, Don and Carol Callahan, Prineville, Oregon.

To date the Callahans have bred 10 champions. In addition to Mark these include: Champion Donahan's Quinn of Crestridge, C.D.X.; Champion Donahan's Kiss Me Kate, C.D.; American and Canadian Champion Donahan's Sandpiper, C.D.X.; American and Canadian Champion Donahan's Gingersnap, C.D.; Champion Donahan's Bartholomew; Canadian Champion Tabaka's Tradition of Donahan, C.D.; American and Canadian Champion Donahan's Agatha Christie; Champion Donahan's Pen 'n' Ink and American and Canadian Champion Donahan's Reflection, C.D.

Dungarvan

Dungarvan Kennels was famous for its Cocker Spaniels in both show ring and Field Trial competition during the decades from the 1920's to the 1950's, when Mrs. Francis P. Garvan of Roslyn, New York, maintained a fine establishment under this prefix. Field Springers were added when Mrs. Garvan's son Peter, and his wife Wilhelmina, became interested in owning and working that breed in trial competition.

Mrs. Wilhelmina Garvan and Dungarvan Trampoline, a daughter of Tramp, at a summer water trial held by the Bushy Hill Club in Connecticut, 1980.

In 1961 the Peter Garvans took over the kennel and although Cockers were still bred as gun dogs, Cocker Trials had died out; therefore, all attention was focused on the Springers.

Widowed in 1976, Mrs. Peter Garvan continued her interest in the trials and in running her own dogs from her home in Warwick, New York. One of her most noted trial dogs, and a highly successful stud, was Amateur Field Champion Denalisunflo Coffey. He is in the background of numerous present winners. A later acquisition from England was Field Champion Wivenwood Tramp, a strong-running darkly marked dog whose progeny can be found in the catalogues of the majority of Field Trials— generally in the Winner's Circle.

At the present time Mrs. Garvan is campaigning My Own Dino, a young dog that has attracted attention in the Eastern trials. He qualified for the 1980 National Open where he was handled by his trainer, Ray Cacchio. Mrs. Garvan is a dedicated Field Trial devotee, taking enormous pleasure in her Springers. This is a field pedigree quite typical of many, especially in the East, showing how prominent the English imports were. The Saighton prefix, for example, belonging to Talbot Radcliffe of Isle of Anglesey, Wales is to be found identifying many dogs currently owned in the United States and running in trials.

Fanfare

Fanfare Springers came about in the summer of 1969 through Francie Nelson, who asked for and received as an engagement gift from her fiance, an English Springer Spaniel puppy (remarking "some prefer rings"). The engagement was broken that fall, but the puppy remained with Francie and grew up to become, despite her obscure newspaper-ad-origins, a top scoring obedience dog and a beloved pet. Here began the understanding of, and love for, the breed that led Francie deeper and deeper into an emerging program of her own.

The arrival during May 1971 of ten-month-old Chinoe's Eminent Judge led to Francie's first efforts at conformation competition and a championship for Judge before his second birthday. Judge also holds his C.D.X. degree. Utility has been abandoned due to Judge's preference for

Ch. Chinoe's Eminent Judge, C.D.X., a black-and-white male born in 1970, owned by Frances Nelson, Minneapolis, Minnesota.

Liz Hanson, co-owner with Francie Nelson, handling Ch. Chuzzlewit's Polonaise to Winners Bitch, St. Croix Valley Kennel Club, 1980.

clowning in the ring; at the age of eleven years, he can still run a Utility pattern competently but only at the training club!

Francie worked to combine Midwest and East Coast bloodlines for a time, hoping to create the soundness and style that she so loved in Judge; but in 1973 she approached Mary Lee and Charles Hendee (of Canarch Springers) for assistance with a bitch puppy, and she has continued with the Canarch program pre-eminent in her own breeding ever since.

Until 1979, Francie Nelson's Springers were registered under the Chuzzlewit prefix, indicating her love for literature and acknowledging the breed's British tradition. The obscure literary reference was a delight to some and a confusion to many, so in 1978 the prefix was changed to Fanfare. Francie's initials, "FAN," inspired the change.

Balance, style, and soundness produce the functional Spaniels that Francie, through her dependence on the guidance of the Canarch program, is striving to produce in her own kennel.

There may be a litter every two years or so. Francie is currently Director of Development for the Children's Theatre Company and School of Minneapolis, one of the largest non-profit professional theatre companies; and her developing career in the field of non-profit management and administration dictates conservation in the sport of dogs. She is assisted in her efforts by her parents, Frances and Russ Nelson, who each have a Springer of their own. Judge travels from Francie's home to the senior Nelsons' home for "dog sitting" on those days when Francie's business schedule keeps her from taking him along to her office, where he usually sleeps under her desk!

Fanfare Chuzzlewit Springers have been successful in the breed ring, in obedience, and in the field. The program is known for producing stable, eminently livable housedog temperament. Francie credits Judge for creating a national awareness, through his travels around the country, of the kind of special friendship a Springer has to offer his people.

Her foundation bitch is Canarch Contemplation who has proven herself a potent producer. Retired now to a life of leisure with her best friend Judge, she is taking great delight in watching her first crop of grandchildren from several different litters distinguish themselves in the ring. Contemplation's duties have been assumed by a lovely new puppy, her granddaughter in fact, Canarch Madeira, who, as we write, is busy in the show ring.

Francie has been, for several years, a member of the English Springer Spaniel Field Trial Association and serves on its Heritable Defects Control Committee. She currently writes the breed's column for *Pure-Bred Dogs American Kennel Gazette*. She takes particular pride in her role as incorporator of the Voyageur English Springer Spaniel Association of Minnesota, the state's largest breed and obedience club which, although not yet sanctioned, draws larger match entries than licensed Specialty Shows in surrounding states. Additionally, the VESSA organization had for two consecutive years held the nation's largest Working Dog Certification test.

Champion Canarch Contemplation is the dam of six champions sired by Champion Winacko's Editor's Choice, one by Champion Coventree's Allegro and one that is pointed, and another with a Tracking Dog title by Champion Canarch Cardinal's Lancer. Pentimento Rousing Fanfare had Reserves from the Puppy Class during 1980; and along with the newly acquired Canarch Madeira, he will be working on completing his title as we go to press.

Ch. Chuzzlewit's Editorial, by Ch. Winacko's Editor's Choice, C.D., ex Canarch Contemplation, black-and-white male, born November 1976. Francie Nelson, owner, Fanfare Kennels, Minneapolis, Minnesota.

A beautiful headstudy of the Springer bitch, Ch. Filicia's Fidelis of Sulo, owned by the Fidelis Kennels of Nancy S. Cowley at Woodstock, Connecticut.

Fidelis

Fidelis Springers, now located at Woodstock, Connecticut, are owned by Mrs. Nancy S. Cowley who until 1971 "had never considered attending a dog show." In North Carolina during that year she acquired her first Springer, Heather, and at about the same time met a couple who showed their German Shepherd and persuaded Mrs. Cowley to start coming along with them. Her interest was aroused by their tales of dog show weekends but it was not until 1974 in El Paso, Texas that she found herself becoming actively caught up in our exciting sport.

Her husband had been transferred to El Paso and Mrs. Cowley joined the English Springer Spaniel Association there. Although she still did not start to show her Springer, she did attend meetings and conformation classes and took lessons in Springer grooming. Then a second Springer joined the household, and Mrs. Cowley began her personal association with the shows as an exhibitor.

Traveling the Texas show circuits with Estrellita de Abril, Mrs. Cowley got off to a good novice start winning Classes and Reserves. In spite of this mild success, Mrs. Cowley soon realized that "April" was not a top flight show dog; but, she *was* a marvelous teacher. To this day Mrs. Cowley refers to April as her "training aid" because from her she learned so much about showmanship of the breed.

After returning to North Carolina, Filicia's Fidelis of Sulo was purchased, and Mrs. Cowley was really on her way. This handsome bitch finished at 15 months, after being owner-handled from her first four-point "major" through to 10 points. Illness however, prevented Mrs. Cowley from showing her so she was turned over to a handler for the remaining points rather than having her show career interrupted. Mrs. Cowley will never forget the excitement of taking her bitch into its first "major" Open Class—and winning!

This bitch, known as "Liz," was bred to Champion Foyscroft Signed Edition in 1978, producing for her first litter five pups from

Ch. Foyscroft Signed Edition, at 11 months old, with his then-owner Marcia Foy. By Ch. Salilyn's Signature ex Ch. Kaintuck Pixie, bred by Anne Pope, "Grumpy" is now a famous winner and Top Producer living in California.

Fidelis Halls of Montezuma winning his first "major" in July 1980, handled by Elliot More for owner, Nancy S. Cowley, Woodstock, Connecticut.

Filicia

Filicia Springers owner Anne Pope used to show horses, but a serious accident necessitated the termination of that hobby. Upon recovery from the accident, Anne had taken her young Springer, Melilotus May Flower, to the veterinarian for a routine check-up. Admiring the bitch, the veterinarian asked if Anne intended showing her. Actually she had not planned on doing so, but being without a hobby at the moment, the idea intrigued her; the result was that Anne and "Phoebe," as May Flower was called, went to a show. Anne had entered Phoebe in all of the Bitch Classes which surely must have branded her a complete novice in the eyes of the judge, Mr. I. Irving Eldredge, who kept going over the same bitch all those times at the same show. Anne was pleased, however, when she won Reserve Winners.

Those were the days of benched dog shows, and when Anne took Phoebe to find her place, it was right next to the famous Champion Wake-

which one male was kept. He is Fidelis' Halls of Montezuma that should have gained his title by now, having had 13 points as this was written.

For her second litter, Champion Telltale Author was the sire selected for Liz's breeding in 1980. This was a litter of six, which promptly started out in their show careers.

In answer to my question regarding the Fidelis prefix Mrs. Cowley explains, "My kennel name, Fidelis, resulted from my husband's 30-year association with the Marine Corps, where the motto 'Semper Fidelis' (meaning "always faithful") seemed especially appropriate for the consistently faithful nature for which we so dearly love our Springers." Fidelis Halls of Montezuma was so named as a salute to Mr. Cowley's long association with the Marine Corps as his retirement drew near.

Following that retirement, the Cowleys moved to Connecticut, to new friends and to new challenges. Since relocating, occasionally she has been "specialing" her bitch Liz with Elliot and Linda More. It was really exciting when at four years old and after two litters Liz had her last "fling" in the show ring by taking Best of Breed and a Group third. Now Liz is retired in favor of the younger generation of her family from whom a bit of worthwhile winning is anticipated.

Anne Pope and her brother with their Springer, a son of Frejax Royal Salute, at their very first dog show.

field's Black Knight whose owner, Mrs. Borie, was sitting with her dog. The two women started talking and Mrs. Borie introduced Anne to her handler, Laddie Carswell. A seed was planted when she told Anne that "the real fun is in breeding dogs," suggesting that she do so with Phoebe.

Winning Reserve Winners at one show and talking with Mrs. Borie at another were two important events that led to the beginning of the Filicia bloodline. Laddie Carswell became a good friend and teacher plus handler of Anne's dogs for many years, including her famous Best in Show winner, Champion Charlyle Fair Warning.

In the beginning, Laddie suggested that Phoebe be bred to Champion Kaintuck Christmas Carol. So she was, and when Anne visited Stuart Johnson's kennel for the breeding, she was tremendously impressed with the Springers there. Her years of working with horses had given her a strong appreciation of the "sound, honest quality" she noted in the Kaintuck dogs.

This is Ch. Filicia's Uncle Tom, born in 1963 from the first Filicia litter, son of Ch. Kaintuck Christmas Carol ex Ch. Melilotus May Flower.

An informal pose of Ch. Charlyle Fair Warning with Laddie Carswell. One of the many outstanding Springers from Anne Pope's Filicia Kennels.

Melilotus May Flower produced six puppies in May in Anne's one-room New York City apartment (which Anne shared with a roommate and another adult dog)—right when final exams were rapidly approaching! Anne says, but I do not believe actually *means*, "to this day I hate puppies as a result." From this litter she kept one male, that was her favorite pet, plus a successful show dog that completed his title in just six ring appearances. This was Champion Filicia's Uncle Tom, that won at the Keystone Specialty his first time in the ring. The year was 1962, one year after Tom had been born.

Following Tom, Anne acquired several other dogs that were all very nice, but none were exactly what she wanted which was a Springer as sound and honest as Mr. Johnson's but, at the same time, pretty. Laddie Carswell knew that she was looking for a top dog and sent her out a few times to see some that he thought she might like to consider. One of those was a dog named "Sam" that Charles Clement had in Wisconsin. Anne had ". . . never seen a Springer that pretty. No freckles, lots of coat, beautiful shape, lovely attitude." He cost a lot more than she had planned on spending, so she decided to breed to him rather than buy him. Soon thereafter someone showed Anne a dog with which they expected to "clean up." Anne thought Charlie Clement's dog was far superior to this person's dog, and on a dare she called Mr. Clement and said that she would buy Sam.

Laddie Carswell wasn't even sure he could win with Sam as he was so different, the first of the "new" type, sired by Champion Inchidony Prince Charming out of Charlyle's Nanette. The rest stands in Springer history, as Champion Charlyle Fair Warning (Sam) did indeed win, taking 15 Specialty Bests of Breed, over 60 Sporting Groups and a goodly number of all-breed Bests in Show. Twice he was the Number One Springer in the country, the Number One Springer sire (despite very limited breeding) and the Number Three Sporting Dog, all breeds. Fair Warning lived his entire lifetime with Laddie Carswell, even after Laddie's retirement. Meanwhile, Anne moved to Boston and rarely saw Sam who was quite happy and content with his friends the Carswells.

Filicia's bloodlines started with the combining of Champion Charlyle Fair Warning (the pretty one) with Mr. Johnson's dogs (the honest, sound ones). Mr. Johnson and Anne co-owned several Springers, all of them representing that cross in their breeding. Among them were Champion Kaintuck Tolstoy and Champion Kaintuck Pixie. Following Mr. Johnson's death, Anne sold Tolstoy to Dana Hopkins and kept Pixie.

Ch. Charlyle Fair Warning takes Best in Show at the Long Island Kennel Club in 1967. Anne Pope, owner, Filicia Kennels, Acton, Massachusetts.

Pixie had been raised from the time she was six months old by Anne who handled her exclusively once she had finished (being defeated only once) with two Specialty wins. Anne's attending school in Boston limited the number of dog shows she could attend, but despite this "handicap," Pixie became the Number two Springer bitch in the United States in only 14 shows —obviously big ones—never defeated. Interestingly, prior to Pixie, Anne owned a bitch, Nora of Canorwoll, which could not be shown as she had no teeth. Anne comments, "Laddie did show her once, but I had forgotten to mention her having no teeth." In spite of this, Nora did herself proud as she became the Number One Brood Bitch.

Pixie had five litters sired by five different dogs, and was Number One Brood Bitch on the strength of having produced 16 champions that accounted for over 40 Specialty wins (either Best in Sweepstakes, point winners or Best of Breed). Anne "... never advertised or sought show homes. Had I done so, God alone knows what kind of producing record she might have attained."

Of Pixie's offspring, Anne kept Champion Filicia's Coronation that finished in four shows including Winners Bitch at Keystone and

Anne Pope with Ch. Charlyle Fair Warning and Ch. Kaintuck Pixie, two winning Springers that contributed tremendously to the Filicia breeding program.

Anne Pope, breeder-owner-handler, with Ch. Filicia's Coronation, taking Best in Sweepstakes at the National Specialty in 1971.

Michigan and Best in Sweepstakes at the National before her first birthday. Coronation also was a "specials" winning bitch, with at least one Group to her credit. She produced five champions in her two litters.

From Pixie's second litter, Champion Foyscroft Signed Edition became well known as a producer; among his progeny is the Number One Springer Bitch in California now. From Pixie's third litter came Champion Filicia's Westcot Justin. An all-breed and Specialty Best in Show winner, "Sherman," as he is known, became sterile and could not be used for breeding. A sad loss to the breed from this standpoint, Sherman is his owner's very special pet and famous for his work with disturbed people who are among Anne's patients.

The next of Pixie's litters produced Champion Filicia's Etching, also an all-breed and Specialty Best in Show dog, whose brief 11-month career was ended abruptly by a serious illness shortly after he had won the breed and Group Second at Westminster a few years ago. Champion Filicia's Anlon Patriot, by Etching, turned out to be a Top Sire among all breeds.

Filicia bloodlines are based on repeating the cross of Kaintuck and Fair Warning, a cross

Anne continues to make successfully today. Her current dog is Champion Filicia's Crescendo who just started his "specials" career in mid-1981 and is already doing well. He is co-owned with Maureen Brady and handled by Patty Alston.

Then there is Filicia's Dividend, a young, extremely promising dog that is starting out well as a sire with some beautiful litters and soon will make his debut in the ring. Both of these dogs carry the cross of "pretty" and "sound" for several generations.

When Anne first started showing dogs, she had two extremely unpleasant experiences of selling a "show" puppy to so-called "future exhibitors," and finding out later that the dogs died due to neglect or carelessness. So now, although occasionally she will sell show dogs, it is only by recommendation from someone or to people whom she personally knows well; therefore, she does not advertise. She attributes her longevity in dogs to the fact that she has not turned the dogs into a second full-time job. She took a few years off, after breeding for around 10 years, then bred a couple of litters, then took another rest. Now she is more enthusiastic than ever in actively raising and showing Springers and pleased with the present generation of bitches with which she is working. These are Champion's Filicia's Bequest (Champion

Ch. Filicia's Etching winning the Keystone Specialty. Etching had two Bests of Breed from the classes, in 11 months of "specialing," took 21 Groups, and is a Best in Show winner.

Ch. Filicia's Bequest, by Ch. Salilyn's Classic ex Ch. Kaintuck Pixie, C.D., shown here with owner-handler Anne Pope, has already produced several championship litters.

Ch. Filicia's Crescendo, starting out on what should become a brilliant show career, is owned by Anne Pope and Maureen Brady, the latter handling here.

Salilyn's Classic ex Champion Kaintuck Pixie, C.D.), Champion Filicia's Custom Maid (Tara's Aquarious ex Champion Filicia's Liberty Belle of Sulo) and Liberty Belle herself, a Specialty winner including the National, by Champion Filicia's Anlon Patriot ex Champion Filicia's Black Magic of Sulo. The outline of the next three generations at Filicia has already been planned, using the Shinnecock Springers in conjunction with Anne Pope's own line.

Recently the breeding pattern at Filicia has been to cross Champion Kaintuck Pixie (Champion Charlyle's Fair Warning ex Kaintuck Sprite) and Champion Kaintuck Tolstoy (Champion Charlyle's Fair Warning ex Champion Kaintuck Fortune Huntress) with Mrs. Julie Gasow's Salilyn Springers. Pixie produced Champion Filicia's Coronation, sired by Champion Filicia's Matinee Idol. She in turn, bred to Champion Salilyn's Aristocrat, produced the Specialty winning bitch, Champion Filicia's Enchanted Evening, that was bred only once and produced Champion Filicia's Aliden Biskit by Champion Filicia's Bequest. Biskit was one of four puppies in Enchanted Evening's only litter that finished easily and in turn was bred to Champion Filicia's Anlon Patriot. This latter dog, known as "Ben," made an outstanding

show record at prestigious Specialty and all-breed events and also has been an extremely successful sire, becoming one of the Top Producers for all breeds in 1980. He is by champion Filicia's Etching (Champion Salilyn's Classic son) ex Champion Filicia's Wescot Joy of Anlon (Champion Salilyn's Aristocrat ex Champion Kaintuck Pixie), an example of the successful blending between Salilyn and Filicia.

The bloodline of Champion Kaintuck Tolstoy (Champion Charlyle's Fair Warning ex Champion Kaintuck Fortune Huntress) is kept active through Champion Danaho's Ballet Russe (Tolstoy ex Spennymore's Noblesse Oblige). "Raindrop" in her own right has been outstanding, having been the Top Springer Bitch in the country a few years back. She is owned by Dana Hopkins. Bred to Champion Filicia's Anlon Patriot, she produced two champions, one of which, Champion Danaho's Lalique of Stanton, is owned by Anne Pope. "Rita," bred to Champion Salilyn's Private Stock (Champion Filicia's Bequest ex Champion Salilyn's Sonnette) has produced the previously mentioned exciting young male, Filicia's Dividend. Tara's Aquarious is a son of Kaintuck Tolstoy also, on his dam's side going to Kaintuck through the successful Fortune bloodlines.

Dogs bred or owned by Anne Pope have accounted for more than 50 top awards at Specialty events. She adds, "I honestly cannot remember an exact count on how many champions I have bred or owned other than my special pets 'Tom' and 'Sherman.' I keep my dogs with me no more than three or four years, during which time they are shown, conditioned, then bred once or twice. Then I select and place them in good and loving pet homes. This enables me to continue a breeding pattern, and the dog benefits by remaining a household member with his own home and family." Anne rarely keeps more than three adult dogs with her as all live in the house as pets. She feels that this type of life is important for a Springer's temperament and mental stability, and she has found that some dogs that are constantly kept in a kennel environment cannot tolerate the uncertainties of home life.

The Filicia breeding program is kept extremely limited for two reasons. Anne does not really enjoy puppies, and her work schedule is such that she does not have sufficient time to devote to them. When there is a litter, she makes a definite effort to arrange her schedule so that she can be home to give time to them and to help develop their personalities. Feeling as she does that temperament takes precedence over all else in Springers, she takes very seriously the idea that puppies grow up well socialized and accustomed to people and activity.

Anne likes to start her puppies out at the point shows when they are at least six months old rather than at the match shows where most breeders do their ground work. In her opinion, too much stress is placed upon a puppy that is younger than show age; thus the process of being shown becomes something to be learned rather than enjoyed and she feels that often a Springer pup can be turned off as an outgoing show campaigner by too early and too severe a start. So when the six-month birthday arrives, off they go with Anne, who handles them herself while they become accustomed to the world of competition. Sometimes, she says, by the time the puppy is show-trained, it is also a finished champion. This is fun for their owner too who likes to show some of the dogs personally but feels that once they enter "specials" competition there is too much work involved for her to manage. At this point she feels that the dogs are more competitively presented by a professional.

Ch. Filicia's Liberty Belle of Sulo, by Ch. Filicia's Anlon Patriot ex Ch. Filicia's Black Magik of Sulo. Taking Best of Winners at Springfield in 1978, handled by owner Anne Pope.

Ch. Filicia's Aliden Biskit, by Ch. Filicia's Anlon Patriot ex Ch. Filicia's Enchanted Evening, at the 1976 Eastern Futurity. Owned by Susan Dash and Anne Pope.

Fortune's

Mr. and Mrs. James O. Fortuna established their Fortune's Kennels back in the 1960's while living on Long Island.

Their foundation bitch was Champion Syringa Sue, representing Rufton and Audley bloodlines on her sire's side of the family, while her dam was strong in Frejax, Melilotus and Salilyn. Syringa Sue was every breeder's dream, a most excellent producing dam whose puppies were consistent in type and quality. She herself produced seven champions.

Sue's granddaughter, Champion Fortune's Dorsue Diana of Day, won her title from the Puppy Classes. She too produced seven champions, among them a daughter, Champion Fortune's Regina, that was runner-up bitch for the year 1970 and Best of Opposite Sex at Westminster in 1972. These bitches were all black-and-white and very much alike.

The Fortunas now live in Ponte Vedra Beach, Florida. Although they no longer are breeding Springers, they still maintain a great love of the breed and an interest in its welfare.

Ch. Wakefield's Black Knight and Ch. Fortune's Dorsue Diana of Day taking the top awards at the 1964 Specialty of the Potomac Valley English Springer Spaniel Club. Laddie Carswell is handling Black Knight as Dorothy Callahan presents Diana.

Ch. Fortune's Regina taking Best of Winners at Westminster around 1970. Dorothy Callahan handling for owners, Mr. and Mrs. James O. Fortuna of Ponte Vedra Beach, Florida.

Could you stand it NOT to have a Springer puppy? These handsome babies belong to Henriette Schmidt's Hillcrest Kennels at Brookfield, Wisconsin.

Hillcrest

Hillcrest Springers, belonging to Miss Henriette A. Schmidt and located in Brookfield, Wisconsin, is not a large kennel. Only a small group of Springers live there where they are valued both as pets and as show dogs. Miss Schmidt does not produce as great a number of generations as some breeders do within a given period of time because the longevity and good health of her dogs is of prime importance to her.

The Hillcrest name was originated by Henry and Tekla Phillips who began with Springers in the 1930's. Henriette learned a great deal from this couple whose integrity and genuine concern for each individual animal she admired. Often she saw the Phillips place pointed dogs in pet homes because they cared more that the dogs

should have a fine home than a title. Under their direction Miss Schmidt saw that mental and physical soundness are essential prerequisites in a breeding program; thus, she strove to maintain the breed's function as an easily trained hunting companion. From the Phillips she also learned the importance of selective breeding.

Believing in the principle—it is better to sell one that should have been kept than to keep one that should have been sold—she was not "allowed" to keep for herself any of the puppies she had bred until the third litter from her foundation bitch, Champion Ginger Snap of Hillcrest, that incidentally was to become a Parent Club Dam of the Year in 1964. It was these pups, born in 1961 which were the major basis for future success.

Ch. Hillcrest Happy Go Lucky, C.D., as a puppy. Hillcrest Springers are owned by Henriette Schmidt.

Obviously Gingerbread Boy's litter sisters produced fewer puppies, but each produced a daughter that was amateur-handled to the Best of Opposite Sex win at a National Specialty. Champion Amanda Hunter of Hillcrest produced Champion Hillcrest Happy Go Lucky, C.D., W.D., a Best of Opposite Sex winner at the 1971 National Specialty. Champion Gingerbread Gal of Hillcrest, C.D. produced Champion Cookie Crisp of Hillcrest who won Best of Opposite Sex at the 1970 National Specialty, and also Champion Hillcrest's Pretty Penny who took Winners Bitch and Best of Winners at the 1967 National Specialty.

Hillcrest Springers are dogs that must be physically sound, free of health problems, easily adaptable to varying activities and environments and just plain pleasant to live with. Additionally, they are easy to train for field and obedience work due to their strong natural instincts and their great desire to please.

Ch. Hillcrest Most Happy Fella, W.D., C.D.X. one of the versatile Springers owned by Henriette Schmidt.

Sired by Champion Rostherne Hunter, W.D., an English dog that had been imported by Mrs. Beatrice Smith (Melilotus), this litter was filled with quality. For herself Miss Schmidt kept the future Champion Gingerbread Boy of Hillcrest, C.D. that, although never heavily campaigned, produced 23 champions. Each of these progeny distinguished itself in some way above the usual with extra "majors," Group placements, wins at the National Specialty, Obedience degrees, Working Dog certificates and successes with an amateur handler. Champion Sugarbush Hillcrest Stinger, C.D. was Best of Opposite Sex in the 1968 National Futurity; Champion Happy Hank of Hillcrest was Best of Opposite Sex in the 1971 National Sweepstakes and Winners Dog there; and Champion Nam Tan Forget Me Not, C.D. was Winners Bitch at the 1972 National Specialty. It is interesting to note that all of the above wins were made with amateur handlers.

Ch. Gingerbread Boy of Hillcrest, C.D., is the sire of 23 champions. This winner of three Sporting Groups is owned by Henriette Schmidt.

So well has Miss Schmidt succeeded in attaining these goals that she can point with pride to the versatility of her stock. For example, Champion Hillcrest Happy Go Lucky, C.D., W.D. mentioned above and her sons, Champion Hillcrest Most Happy Fella, C.D.X., W.D. and Champion Hillcrest Exuberance, C.D., W.D., have distinguished themselves in obedience, field work and the show ring—as has Champion Michael Konig of Hillcrest, U.D., W.D., a Gingerbread Boy—Cookie Crisp son.

These handsome Springers, left to right, are Ch. Crooked Pine's Frederick, Ch. Cookie Crisp of Hillcrest, and Hillcrest Abbie of Stanton. All are from Hillcrest Springers, Henriette A. Schmidt, Brookfield, Wisconsin.

Homestead

Homestead Springers owner Louise Bilby of Oneida, New York, purchased her first English Springer Spaniel in 1968. Within a year she had joined the Onandaga Kennel Association and soon after that became interested in showing dogs.

Before too long she was breeding Springers. Her first litters were sired by Bob Walgate's dogs, and later she bred a bitch to Champion Horizon's Pathfinder. The latter produced a

Am., Can. Ch. Homestead's Rippling Rhythym (by Am., Can. Ch. Bordalyn's By The Way, C.D.X., W.D.X., from Ch. Homestead's Summersong) is a homebred belonging to Mrs. Louise Bilby, Oneida, New York. Here he is taking Best of Winners for a 5-point "major" under judge Robert Wills at the Potomac Valley English Springer Spaniel Specialty in April 1979.

black-and-white bitch which Mrs. Bilby bred to Champion Salilyn's Aristocrat. It was from this litter that she finished her first champion, namely, the handsome black-and-white bitch Champion Homestead's Summersong, who, nearing seven years of age as this was written, appeared as sound and lovely as when she was two years old.

Summersong was bred to American and Canadian Champion Bordalyn's By The Way, C.D.X., W.D.X. A son from these two, Champion Homestead's Rippling Rhythym, was shown in Canada by Parker Harris, who also put eight points on this dog in the States. "Bailey," as he is called, was with Parker the night he (Parker) was so tragically killed in an auto accident in March 1979. The dog, however, was unhurt and three weeks later was Best of Winners for a five point "major" at Potomac Valley Springer Specialty under Robert Wills. He finished in May 1979 in Lancaster, Pennsylvania. "Bailey" is the sire of several young Springers now in competition that are nearing completion of their titles.

A litter sister, Homestead's August Melody, has nine points and will return to the show ring soon, having taken a break to produce a litter sired by Bordalyn's By Request, the Best of Winners dog at the American Spaniel Club, January 1981. From this litter Mrs. Bilby has kept two puppies that she plans on showing.

Although shown on a limited basis, the Homestead dogs do a nice amount of winning. Mrs. Bilby is proud of the fact that her champions are *homebred* and that her kennel is known for producing Springers sound in mind, body and temperament, and of correct size.

Horizon

Horizon Kennels came about as the result of Lois Bates' having purchased a black-and-white six-month-old male Springer puppy back in 1967. So completely did this youngster capture the family's heart that a year later a liver-and-white half sister joined him at their Canastota, New York home.

The Bates' daughter Betty (then 12) started showing the Springers in Junior Showmanship, winning four Open Classes the very first summer. At 13, she trained and handled the male to his C.D., and the next year she did the same with the bitch, winning the *Dog World* award as well. These two Springers were known as Champion Ring A Ding's Jet Pilot, C.D. and Ring A Ding's I Love A Parade, C.D. Jet Pilot was owner-handled half of the way to his championship and then finished by Phil Fairfield. The

Ch. Horizon's Pathfinder at 2½ years wins Best of Breed at the Eastern English Springer Spaniel Club Specialty in June 1973. Maxwell Riddle judging, Betty Bates Davis handling. Owned by Mrs. Lois K. Bates.

Ch. Horizon's Parade has just taken Best of Opposite Sex at the Eastern English Springer Spaniel Club Futurity. Lois K. Bates, owner-handler.

Mrs. Bates has raised only six litters to date but certainly with striking success. One of her bitches became the dam of the Virgin Islands' first American Springer champion. Two other bitches bred at Horizon have earned their C.D. titles in three straight trials; one of these is in Virginia and the other in Michigan. Another puppy from Mrs. Bates' latest litter is in Virginia also, and at eight months he is the star of his obedience class and has taken Puppy Sporting Group awards at the matches.

Mrs. Bates has been a member of the Eastern English Springer Spaniel Club for 14 years, during nine of which she has served as a member of its Board of Governors.

The Bates family is another example of how the fun and success of raising, training and showing this wonderful breed can be a worthwhile family project for all its members.

Ch. Horizon's Vibrance taking Winners Bitch at Suffolk County, 1973, for a "major", then going on to Best of Opposite Sex. Handled by Betty Bates Davis; owned by Lois Bates.

other champions finished by Horizon have all been completely owner-handled by members of the Bates family.

Parade retired with 15 points, including a four point "major." For the second Horizon litter, Mrs. Bates bred Parade to Jet Pilot with excellent results, as it included the future Champion Horizon's Pathfinder. This black-and-white dog earned his title with four "majors" (one a four-pointer), took Reserve Dog at the Eastern English Springer Spaniel Club en route to the title and then returned to the Eastern as a "special" the following year and won Best of Breed, handled by Betty Bates. At this same show, his daughter won a strong Puppy Class and later finished with three "majors." She is Champion Horizon's Vibrance. A Parade granddaughter, Champion Horizon's Parade, finished and was Best of Opposite Sex in Eastern's 1974 Futurity.

Betty Bates continued to succeed in Junior Showmanship. She competed five times and the last three times was a finalist in these classes at Westminster.

Ch. Venetian Jove's Jester, Top Winning black-and-white Springer in 1977 and 1978, handled here by Tom Glassford for Andrea Glassford, Jester Springers, Ashtabula, Ohio.

Jester

Andrea Glassford's first show dog was a Springer, Champion Venetian Jove's Jester, and it is for him that the Jester Springers, at Ashtabula, Ohio were named.

Mrs. Glassford considers herself extremely lucky in acquiring this dog. Before making a purchase she had talked with many breeders and felt that Marjorie Rollins, from whom Jester was purchased, was one of the most helpful of any breeders with whom she has ever dealt. (This assistance, incidentally, is very important to a novice, as Mrs. Glassford was then, especially when the breeder is willing to "tell it like it is" and then follow through with aid in training, grooming and the like.)

Champion Venetian Jove's Jester was a Best in Show dog and the Top Winning black-and-white Springer in 1977 and 1978. He is the sire of Champion Jester's Jinjer Snap that was a stud fee puppy. She did her sire proud with some important wins including several Specialty Shows, and she was among the Top Ten Bitches in 1978 and 1979.

Being so pleased with her original purchase, Mrs. Glassford returned to Marge Rollins for a bitch and purchased Champion Venetian Jester's Jypsi. This one was finished in six shows as an open bitch and then started her duties in the whelping box. She is the dam of the current highly successful dog, Champion Jester's Jack In The Box, that at the time of writing was Number Seven Sporting Dog, *Kennel Review* System, and Number Two Springer in the United States. Handled by Mrs. Glassford's husband, noted professional handler Tom Glassford, "Boxer," as Jack In The Box is known to his friends, became a noted Best in Show dog and Specialty winner. He is also coming into his own as a sire. Among his progeny is Champion Jester's Southwind Twister, another stud fee puppy that finished recently from the Puppy Classes, as did his sire before him. Twister will be the dog to replace Boxer in the "specials" ring upon the latter's retirement.

Ch. Jester's Jack In The Box at 11 months old, owned at that time by Andrea Glassford, shown with handler Tom Glassford.

Andrea Glassford with her Ch. Venetian Jester's Jypsi, by Ch. Goodwill Copyright Reserved ex Ch. Venetian Cricket's Shannon, C.D.

Other successful Springers bred or owned by Mrs. Glassford include Champion Jester's Advocate for Agape, Champion Tara's Just A Jester and Champion Jester's Justification. The lines that have been most successful for her have come through the Venetian dogs, and she especially likes the combination of Canarch and Salilyn that this kennel offers. Also she has successfully used Willowbank, Loujon, Winacko and others when she feels that they have something she needs for her own line.

It is interesting to note that in addition to being an American Champion, Jack In The Box also has his title in Canada, Columbia, Uruguay, Puerto Rico and a South American International. Very nice going, indeed!

Ch. Jester's Jinjer Snap relaxes in front of the fireplace. Andrea Glassford, owner.

Kalyn

Kalyn Springers started in the late 1960's as a small "husband and wife project" by Kathryn and Lynn Freese of Burdett, New York. The black-and-white foundation bitch, Pokohaven's Howling Success, represented Hillcrest breeding and was shown by Henrietta Schmidt to some pleasing wins. Next came what the Freeses refer to as their "main guy," Champion Kalyn's Command Performance, C.D., W.D.X. (the Parent Club's Working Dog Excellent Certificate), obtained through Nancy Pokorney. Currently this dog's quality and contribution to the breed are being seen through his

Kalyn's High Society took Winners Bitch and Best of Winners under William L. Kendrick at the Bytown Springer Spaniel Specialty in 1979. Owned by Kathy Freese, Burdett, New York.

grandchildren, but along the way he produced Kalyn's Peppermint Patti, Kalyn's High Society, Kalyn's Star Performance and now his newest hopeful, Fordacre's Act III of Kalyn. The last three are outcrosses to the Tamridge line and quite successfully owner-handled to all their points.

Right from the beginning Mr. and Mrs. Freese have been firm in their belief that the Springer is capable of doing many things and with great joy. Give them a chance and they will try to do their best whether it be hunting, obedience, tracking or whatever; but uppermost in mind has been the thought that the breed would achieve no success if lacking soundness of mind and body.

Kalyn has now expanded to include Welsh Springers and Field Spaniels, and both owners are aiming towards eventually becoming judges.

Ch. Beryltown Lively Chatter, C.D.X., by Ch. Inchidony's Prince Charming ex Ch. Beryltown Lively Rocket, C.D. Amy was the first Kay N Dee Springer champion to take Best of Opposite Sex at Potomac Valley English Springer Spaniel Club (which she did in 1968-69). Owned by Deborah Kirk, bred by Beryl D. Hines.

Kalyn's Star Performer, Winners Dog, Bytown Springer Spaniel Specialty, 1979. Owned by Kalyn Kennels, Kathryn and Lynn Freese. The judge is William L. Kendrick.

Kay N Dee

Kay N Dee Springers was founded in 1966 as a small breeding kennel by Dr. Mary S. Gibbs and her daughter, Deborah Kirk, of Spencerville, Maryland, where quality rather than quantity has been the keynote through the years. Show litters have been produced on an average of one every 16 months here since 1974 with some excellent and beautiful Springers as a result.

It was Champion Beryltown Lively Chatter, C.D.X., also known as "Amy," with which Kay N Dee started out in 1966. This beautiful bitch was obedience-trained exclusively by her then nine-year-old owner, Debbie Kirk, so well that she had smooth sailing on the road to her C.D.X. In the show ring too Amy distinguished herself by completing her championship in Philadelphia in 1968 under Mrs. Julie Gasow with a five point "major." Then she was Best of Opposite Sex at the Pioneer Valley English Springer Spaniel Club Specialty in 1969. Amy rounded out her career and proved her versatility by appearing in the 1969, 1970 and 1971 Westminster Junior Showmanship Finals.

In 1972 Kay N Dee's first litter from their Champion Judge's Pride Jennifer, C.D., was produced. This bitch is now the dam of 11 champions and in 1979 was the English Springer Spaniel Dam of the Year.

Among Jennifer's progeny is the outstanding winner, Champion Kay N Dee Geoffrey, that has remained in the Top Ten English Springer Spaniels for the past three consecutive years, 1979, 1980 and 1981. Bred by Deborah Kirk and owned by Dr. Mary B. Gibbs, Geoffrey is by Champion Salilyn's Classic.

Dr. Mary B. Gibbs, the breeder, handling Ch. Jennifer and Ch. Chatter to win Best Brace under Julie Gasow, judge.

Ch. Kay N Dee's Maginna's Gibson Girl, C.D., by Ch. Veron's Marco Polo ex Ch. Loujon Maginna's Victoria, taking Winners Bitch at the English Springer Spaniel Field Trial Association under Melbourne Downing; handled by Kathy Kirk for Dr. Mary B. Gibbs, Spencerville, Maryland.

Ch. Kay N Dee Geoffrey, multi-Group winner that finished in 1979 and became No. 10 Springer for that year, then in 1980 was No. 6 top winner in the breed. Handled by Kathy Kirk for Dr. Mary B. Gibbs, Kay N Dee Springers.

Champion Kay N Dee Maginnes Gibson Girl, C.D., was Winners Bitch at the 1980 English Springer Spaniel Field Trial Association Specialty and was the 1980 Pioneer Valley English Springer Spaniel Club Sweepstakes winner. She and Champion Geoffrey are perpetuating well the Kay N Dee line.

Highlights from Kay N Dee's records include 13 bench show Champions to their credit, one International Champion, six Obedience titles and a South American Group winner.

Ch. Judge's Pride Jennifer, C.D., was the foundation bitch for Kay N Dee Springers. Pictured taking Best of Opposite Sex at the Pioneer Valley English Springer Spaniel Club Specialty in 1974.

Kevriett Acres

Bordalyn's Kevriett Charisma, W.D.X., is pictured here retrieving a pheasant while earning her Working Dog Excellent. She is the foundation bitch at Kevriett Acres, major pointed, and (in the words of her owners, Bruce and Jeane Harkins, Ellicott City, Maryland) "she trained us on birds." Photo by Bruce Harkins.

Kevriett Acres is a three-acre home in Ellicott City, Maryland, where Bruce and Jeane Harkins live with their small but extremely select family of Springers.

The Harkins show their Springers in conformation, work with them in obedience and encourage all hunting instincts of their dogs. Their goal is to raise Springers with titles in conformation, obedience, field and tracking.

The foundation bitch at Kevriett Acres is Bordalyn's Kevriett Charisma, W.D.X., a daughter of American and Canadian Champion Bordalyn's By The Way (Champion Salilyn's Classic ex Champion Bordalyn's Begin Again) from Champion Bordalyn's Silhouette (Cham-

Ch. Kevriett's Kay N Dee Damnation winning a 5-point major at the Potomac Valley English Springer Spaniel Specialty to complete his title. Mrs. Michele Billings, judge. Owners, Bruce and Jeane Harkins, Ellicott City, Maryland. Photo by Mr. Harkins.

Going through field training on quail, at six months old, is "Dameon," who grew up to become Ch. Kevriett's Kay N Dee Damnation. Bruce and Jeane Harkins, owners. Photo by Mr. Harkins.

pion Salilyn's Paramount ex Champion Welcome Joie De Vivre). "Crissy," as she is called, is producing well with several from her first litter pointed in the show ring, competing in obedience and actually working in the field.

Enjoying the "do it yourself" method, the Harkins' next purchase was an eight-week-old male puppy for them to raise, train and personally handle in the ring. When he was one year of age they started him on his show career and he finished his title in good order with a five point "major" at the Potomac Valley English Springer Spaniel Club Specialty. This is Champion Kevriett's Kay N Dee Damnation, the Harkins' first champion, a son of Champion Salilyn's Encore (Champion Salilyn's Colonel's Overlord—Champion Salilyn's Something Special) out of Champion Judge's Pride Jennifer, C.D (Champion Salilyn's Aristocrat—Champion Judge's Pride Missy).

The future looks bright for the Kevriett Acres Springers, owing to the quality of the stock on which the kennel is based and the enthusiasm and dedication of the owners.

Lleda

Lleda Springers, located in the heart of Long Island, New York, is a family project that has been exciting and successful for all concerned. It is shared by Ray and Estelle Adell and their two daughters, Karen Adell Garetano and Teri Adell.

During January of 1963 the Adells bought the first of their show Springers, a four-month-old liver-and-white puppy from the Pequa Kennels of Al and Elsie Matson. This young dog completed his title in March of the following year, after which owner-handled as a "special" and with limited showing, he made a Sporting Group First along with several additional Group placements.

Ch. Daphne of Recess, by Ch. Blairshinnock John D'Groats ex Ascot's Jeannie With, is the foundation bitch behind the Lleda Springers.

Then in 1964 the Adells purchased a fourteen-month-old liver-and-white bitch, Daphne of Recess, bred by Reed Hankwitz, a popular and well-known breeder and judge. Daphne made her championship in 1966 and then proceeded to become the foundation bitch at Lleda with some excellent progeny. Her litter sired by Champion Mister Tamridge of Stage Run contained Champion Randhaven Lleda Sue owned by Edna Randelph, Champion Lleda's Something Special owned by the Adells and Champion Viking Eric of Lleda owned by Marshal and Thea Berbit. Her litter by Champion Point Spa's Gay Star gave the Adells Champion Lleda Spring Hill April Fools, and her litter sired by Champion Scotch Mist of Pequa included Clancy's Copper Penny of Lleda, owned by Mary Clancy and shown by Karen Adell. After acquiring some

A double family portrait, the Springers being littermates and their handlers the sisters Karen and Teri Adell of Huntington, New York. Ch. Penny's Clown Prince of Lleda is taking Winners Dog at the Eastern English Springer Spaniel Club Specialty in 1972 as Ch. Clancy's Erin of Packanack takes Winners Bitch, Best of Winners, and Best of Opposite Sex.

points towards her championship, Copper Penny was bred to Champion Beryltown Virginian of Pequa owned by Patty Alston. Penny had this one litter which produced Champion Penny's Clown Prince of Lleda and the Top Producer bitch, Champion Clancy's Erin of Packanack. They were born on September 10, 1969. Unfortunately it became necessary for Penny to be spayed, due to illness; therefore she was never again bred.

Her daughter Erin, however, had seven champions and was awarded a Top Producer Certificate by the Eastern English Springer Spaniel Club in June 1972. Three of these champions were sired by Champion Welcome Great Day, owned by Mary J. Hosteny. These were Champion Lleda's Syncopation, owned by D. Rockefeller and Karen Adell; Champion Welcome Lleda's Delegate, owned by Mary J. Hosteny; and Champion Lleda's Aegena of Rube co-owned by the Adells, that was Winners Bitch at the Eastern Specialty for a five point "major" in 1976 and is dam of two champions.

Four of Erin's champions are by Champion Verons Marco Polo. They are Champion Lleda's Spartacus of Sunnykay and Champion Lleda's Athena of Sunnykay owned by Barbara Weingarten Champion Lleda's Keeps Comin' On owned by Estelle Adell and Karen Adell Garetano and Champion Lleda's Majestic Prince owned by Dave Schwartz. Spartacus died at an early age, but two of his progeny have finished so far from Champion Salilyn's Combo of Trulu. They are Champion Sunnykay's Sir Winston Cromwell and Champion Sunnykay's September Song. Athena has produced one champion, Lleda's Ariana, by Champion Duncan's Fife. Champion Lleda's Keeps Comin' On is a Specialty Best of Breed winner with many Group placements.

Another Erin daughter, Lleda's Replica of Erin, sired by Champion Ronlaine's Ebony Emperor, had two daughters in competition during 1981. These were Lleda's Angelique and Lleda's Legacy to Croft Harbor, both sired by Champion Filicia's Bequest.

Back in 1966, the Adells also acquired a lovely eight-week-old black-and-white male puppy from Mrs. Dorothy Fortuna of Fortune Kennels. Interestingly, he was from the very first litter ever sired by Champion Salilyn's Aristocrat. His dam was a beautiful bitch of Kaintuck breeding, Champion Fortune's Dorsue Diana of Day. This dog became Champion Fortune's Trouble Ted of Lleda, and he sired four well known winners. These were Champion Croft Harbor's Triumph owned by M. and T. Berbit, Champion Lleda's Blaze of Coral Cables owned by J. Muchtin, Champion Pequa's Checkmate owned by L. Beyrer and Champion Torbin Pequa Mischief Maker owned by L. Beyrer.

To date about 18 champions have been raised at Lleda. Based on the knowledge and enthusiasm of the Adells, it would seem a fair prediction that many, many more will follow.

All four of the Adells have been active in the English Springer Spaniel Club of Long Island, of which they are founder members. It was they who saw the need for such an organization in

This handsome headstudy is of Ch. Lleda's Legacy to Croft Harbor, owned by Lisa Berbit, Huntington, New York.

their area back around 1970. They sent letters to many people for an opinion on the subject and were largely responsible for the turnout of 60 Springer enthusiasts at the first meeting. It was at this first meeting that the Springer Spaniel Club of Long Island was formed. The Club holds a Specialty each year in conjunction with the Ladies Kennel Association, and in 1981 hosted the National Specialty of the Parent Club.

An informal study of Ch. Lleda's Spartacus of Sunnykay, owned by Barbara Weingarten and Karen Adell Garetano.

Lleda's Lady Meg is the Springer pictured in this very interesting "all angles" series of studies. Owned by the Adells, Lleda Kennels, Huntington, New York.

Maginna

Maginna Kennels was founded in 1976 by Helen M. Maginnes of Exeter, New Hampshire. The foundation brood bitch was Champion Loujon Maginna's Victoria, born in March 1976, a granddaughter of Champion Chinoe's Adamant James. Victoria made her championship in short order with two Bests of Breed and one Best of Opposite Sex over "specials" en route to the title and then settled down to some good work in the maternity box. She whelped two litters, the first of which was sired by Champion Cricket's Rhody Mac (Champion Salilyn's Aristocrat ex American and Canadian Champion Venetian Cricket's Cinnamon), whelped in 1978. The second was by American and Canadian Champion Veron's Marco Polo (Salilyn's Morning Breeze II ex Salilyn's Dolly Veron). Sadly, Victoria died in February 1980.

Then came Champion Maginna's Royal Heiress by Champion Cricket's Rhody Mac from Champion Loujon Maginna's Victoria that had been Mrs. Maginnes' first home-bred Champion and that stepped into her dam's position as the current brood bitch. In the show ring, she had finished her title at 13 months with three "majors," had been Reserve Winners Bitch at the Keystone Specialty and had gone Best of Breed and Best of Opposite Sex from the classes over "specials." The stud selected for her first litter was Champion Shinnecock's Overdrive (Champion Salilyn's Exclusive ex Champion Loujon's Femininity). Eight show quality puppies were the result, and by the time they were a year old, two were pointed with "majors," two had been reserve in good entries and all had match show experience. Her second litter, this one by the Best in Show winning Champion Telltale Author (Champion Salilyn's Aristocrat ex Telltale Victoria) was due to arrive as this was written.

Maginna's Sir Sandringham (Marco Polo—Victoria) is the young stud dog at Maginna and is proving himself well both as a sire and in the show ring.

Ch. Maginna's Royal Heiress is leading five of her eight show quality puppies (sired by Ch. Shinnecock's Overdrive). Owned by Maginna's Springers, Helen H. Maginnes, Exeter, New Hampshire.

Ch. Maidenhead's Remembrance finishing his title. The previous day he had been Reserve Winners Dog from the Bred-by Exhibitor class at the Eastern English Springer Spaniel Specialty. Handled by Laddie Carswell for Judy and Bud DiDonato, Lawrenceville, New Jersey.

Maidenhead

Maidenhead Springers came about as a result of the purchase in 1971 of Maidenhead's Bineski Koda by Judy and Bud DiDonato who live in Lawrenceville, New Jersey. At that time the DiDonatos had not even thought of becoming seriously involved with breeding and exhibiting, but after one Specialty match, that of the English Springer Spaniel Field Trial Association, they were "hooked." The noted professional handler Laddie Carswell was introduced to the DiDonatos, and by the time Koda was 15 months old he had completed his title, gaining the final points at Sussex Hills in a supported Springer entry.

The DiDonatos then selected a pointed brood bitch to join their family, Wakefield's Cinderella, that was linebred from Kaintuck but too small and light-boned to consider finishing. Koda's conformation suited Cinderella's perfectly, so twice they were bred to each other and produced some good pups; but unfortunately the DiDonatos were not successful in placing them, as they would have preferred, in show homes. Some of the owners did take a couple of them to match shows, and some even had points, but regretfully, none of the owners was sufficiently interested to stick with it and finish the dogs.

The next decision was that Cinderella's breeding might fit well with some of the Salilyn lines, so she was bred to Champion Salilyn's Bravo, litter brother to Champion Salilyn's Classic. It was from this litter that the DiDonatos gained their first home-bred champion, Maidenhead's Rememberance, and two others were pointed, Nigel of Maidenhead and Bravo's Brynne of Maidenhead, both of which belonged to other owners.

Champion Maidenhead's Rememberance became a Specialty Sweepstakes winner and twice was Reserve Winners Dog from the Bred-by Exhibitor Class at Specialty events.

About this time Bud DiDonato met Jim Hyslop, who was just getting into Springers, and they decided to jointly purchase a brood bitch from more contemporary lines. After a careful search it was decided that Maitre's Dawn of Maidenhead would be the one. "Chelsea," as she was called, was all they had ever dreamed of in a bitch. A Specialty winner from the Puppy Class and Reserve Winners Bitch at two other Specialties, her real contribution, however, began in the whelping box. Bred to Champion Bordalyn's Behold, she produced 11 puppies in her first litter, seven of which were sold to show homes. The DiDonatos kept a male from this litter for themselves. This one quickly made his presence felt in the show ring, becoming Champion Bryden's Marque on Maidenhead. At his first Specialty, following an exciting match show career, this puppy took Reserve Winners Dog

Ch. Maitre's Dawn of Maidenhead winning the Rocky Mountain English Springer Spaniel Club Specialty from the puppy class. Maidenhead Springers belong to Bud and Judy DiDonato.

Nigel of Maidenhead winning under Ralph Del Deo at the English Springer Spaniel Field Trial Association Specialty Show, July 8, 1977. Handled by owner Bud DiDonato, Nigel is a litter brother to Ch. Maidenhead Remembrance, by Ch. Salilyn's Bravo ex Wakefield Cinderella.

from the 9–12 month class and won Best of Breed several times over "specials" en route to gaining his title. He is now a Group winner.

As this was written, four champions had finished from this litter, which included Marque, and the DiDonatos anticipate the total rising to seven as three others seem destined to finish soon. This is a noteworthy accomplishment for a bitch in any breed. Chelsea's talents as a producer have been well honored, as she won the Brood Bitch Class at the Eastern English Springer Spaniel Specialty under Derek Rayne in an entry of eight and Best Brood Bitch at two smaller Specialties. Then at the 1980 National Specialty, in an entry of 12, it was again Champion Maitre's Dawn of Maidenhead (Chelsea) that earned the Best Brood Bitch award.

In between the breeding and exhibiting, Bud DiDonato has also found the time to become interested in the Keystone English Springer Spaniel Club, becoming its President in June 1981. He is Vice President of the Trenton Kennel Club and is a Director of the New Jersey Dog Federation. In November 1980 he was approved to judge Springer Spaniels on a provisional basis by the American Kennel Club.

Melilotus

Although no longer active as a Springer breeder, Mrs. Frederick D. Brown (the former Mrs. R. Gilman Smith) now of St. Croix, Virgin Islands, who so successfully operated Melilotus Springers in Barrington, Illinois and later in Bethel, Connecticut, has lost not one jot of her enthusiasm for and interest in her long-time favorite breed. She makes frequent visits here for important dog shows, such as Westminster, the National Specialty and others, and it must be a source of pride and satisfaction for her to observe the quality and success of the descendants of her famed Melilotus "pillars of the breed." Surely this strain has had tremendous impact on the quality not only of their own but also of future generations of English Springer Spaniels.

The Melilotus kennel prefix was registered in 1944. Tranquillity of Well Sweep was the foundation bitch, a daughter of Champion Green Valley Hercules ex Orientia, both by the noted Rufton Recorder. The name Melilotus was taken from *Melilotus alba*, a variety of clover that grew in the fields surrounding the original kennel in Barrington. The kennel's greatest activity and fame were reached between 1948 and 1959 after a move to Bethel, Connecticut where about 35 Springers were constantly in residence.

From the beginning, Mrs. Brown was interested in the "dual purpose" ideal. All Melilotus puppies had a chance to run in the

Ch. Tranquility of Melilotus with six of her progeny sired by Ch. Frejax Royal Salute. From the left: Tranquility, Ch. Her Ladyship of Melilotus, Ch. Melilotus Royal Oak, Ch. Prince Charlie of Melilotus, all from litter number one.

field where it was easy to see which ones were natural hunters and which were less concerned with the sport, and all had a chance to swim and retrieve from water. A good many had some field training. The magnificent dog, Champion Amos of Melilotus (by Dual Champion Fast), sired dozens of field workers. The same bitches came back to him year after year for his services because his pups were in demand as hunters. The Smiths (Mrs. Brown and her former husband) themselves never got into Field Trial competition, although a son of Champion Melilotus Royal Oaks became a Dual Champion in Canada (field and bench). This dog, Canadian Dual Champion Dan Dee of Melilotus, was trained and campaigned by his owner, a young man with no previous experience and no money to hire a trainer. He watched the trials, talked to people who took an interest in helping him and did a great job of piloting his own dog to two titles. Most people had said it couldn't be done! In appearance, Mrs. Brown describes Dan Dee as "... not the most elegant and beautiful Springer, but he was sound, put together well and good enough to win a show championship in either Canada or the United States." Mrs. Brown comments, "I tell you all this because people are too ready to give up the dual purpose ideal!" Dan Dee was three-quarters Melilotus and one-quarter field breeding.

Then from the repeat breeding a year later, litter number two, came the three completing the row: Ch. Melilotus Highland Cream, Melilotus Duff Gordon (a beautiful puppy that died before she was old enough to campaign), and Ch. Melilotus Peter Dawson. Photo courtesy of Mrs. R. Gilman Smith, owner of the Melilotus Springers, taken at Berks County Dog Show in 1950. Mrs. Smith is now Mrs. Frederick D. Brown of St. Croix, Virgin Islands.

Of the more than 40 champions carrying the Melilotus identification, one is a Dual Champion and six are Best in Show winners. Included among the latter are such Springers as Champion Tranquillity of Melilotus that produced four Best in Show winners herself; Champion Prince Charlie of Melilotus, Tranquillity's son by Champion Frejax Royal Salute, with seven Bests in Show within one year during his campaigning days; Champion Melilotus Royal Oak, same breeding as Prince Charlie, with more than half a dozen Bests in Show; and Champion Melilotus Lucky Star, again the same breeding as the above.

A noted Best in Show winner, Ch. Prince Charlie of Melilotus, litter brother to Ch. Melilotus Royal Oak, was one of the many outstanding Springers from Mrs. R. Gilman Smith's famed kennel at Bethel, Connecticut.

Ch. Amos of Melilotus, the first champion at this famed kennel, was sired by Dual Ch. Fast ex Tranquillity of Well Sweep. Bred and owned by Mrs. R. Gilman Smith, now Mrs. Frederick D. Brown.

Ocoee

Ocoee Springers, owned by Kathleen Reiss Lorentzen of Saginaw, Michigan is famous as the home of the great winning and producing dog, American and Canadian Champion Winacko's Classic Replay, C.D. This magnificent Springer, handled to most of his ring successes by his owner (although Houston Clark showed him to one of his Bests in Show and a few Group victories while Mrs. Lorentzen was temporarily sidelined having a baby), has amassed the impressive record of three all-breed Bests in Show, three Specialty Bests of Breed (two of them during 1980 from the Veterans Class) and 16 Group Firsts.

Ch. Cricket Hill Cover Girl is by Ch. Winacko's Classic Replay, C.D., ex Cricket Hill Columnist. This black-and-white bitch earned three "majors" and Best of Winners six of the seven times she was Winners Bitch. Handled by Ken Murray and bred by Judy Steve, who co-owns her with Kathleen Lorentzen.

His successes put him on the Top Ten Springer lists under all the various Systems for 1974, 1975 and 1976. He has distinguished himself as a sire in a highly creditable manner with 18 champions to his credit as this was written.

Am., Can. Ch. Willowbank's Second Look, liver and white, by Ch. Winacko's Classic Replay, C.D., ex Willowbank Armar's Mirage. Bred by John Merriman and Mary Roberts; owned by K.R. Lorentzen, Saginaw, Michigan. Finished in Canada while still a puppy with 3 Bests of Breed and 2 Group placements, her American title came in just 15 days' time as she earned her first points on January 5 and finished on January 20, 1980. She continued on to wind up 1980 as the Number 2 bitch in breed competition. Handled throughout her show career by Ken and Virginia Murray.

Among the latter, Champion Bushlo's Ephor, T.D. is a Best in Show winner. Five from one litter ex Champion Salilyn's Cosmopolitan, have finished, including: Champion Salilyn's Atlantis that is another multiple Group winner; a daughter owned by Mrs. Lorentzen, American and Canadian Champion Willowbank's Second Look, who completed her championship in 15 days and then went on to become the Number Two Springer Bitch in the Nation in 1980, based on breed points; a daughter, Shinnecock's Simply Smashing, who was recently Best in Sweepstakes at both the Potomac Valley English

Springer Spaniel Club and the Long Island English Springer Spaniel Club; and another daughter, Orion's Essence of Lee Vee, who was just Winners Bitch at the West Texas English Springer Spaniel Club.

Classic Replay is a son of Champion Salilyn's Classic from Canarch Yankee Tea Party, C.D. He was whelped September 18, 1972, bred by David L. Morman and he is the sire of two U.D.T. daughters, Champion Bushlo's Arion, U.D.T. and Kaleros Amy, U.D.T. It's no wonder that Kathleen Lorentzen is really proud of these two bitches!

Ch. Bordalyn's Behold, pictured here winning one of his Sporting Group Firsts, is the sire of eleven champions and seven Sweepstakes winners which include Group Winners and Top Producers, was born in April 1974 by Ch. Salilyn's Classic ex Ch. Bordalyn's Begin Again, C.D. Bred by Bonita Bosley, owned by Susan Ritter, handled by Mary Ann and George Alston.

Patrician

Patrician Springers came about when Debbie and Ron Ritter made their first purchase of the breed back in 1973. Now they maintain a small number of dogs at their kennel in Chesapeake, Virginia where quality rather than quantity remains the keynote.

The breeding foundation here is based on Bordalyn, Salilyn, Bushlo and Shinnecock strains, and the results of the Patrician program are now competing in both show and obedience rings.

Among the noted Springers owned by the Ritters are Champion Bordalyn's Silhouette by Champion Salilyn's Paramount ex Champion Welcome Joie de Vivre. Born in 1972 and bred by Bonita J. Bosley, Silhouette's show career included such outstanding successes as Winners Bitch at the Potomac Valley English Springer Spaniel Specialty in 1974, Winners Bitch and Best of Opposite Sex at the Keystone Specialty

the same year and Best of Opposite Sex at the 1974 Eastern Specialty. In 1975 she was Best of Opposite Sex at Westminster and in 1977, after time out for maternal duties, she was Best of Opposite Sex at the Potomac Valley Specialty. Silhouette was a 1979 *Kennel Review* Top Producer. She is the dam of Champion Bordalyn's Blockade, T.D.; Champion Bordalyn's Burlesque, C.D., Champion Bordalyn's Beezlebub; Champion Bordalyn's Devil's Advocate, plus several others with "major" points. Three of her get are Sweepstakes winners.

Then there is Champion Bordalyn's Behold who was bred by Bonita Bosley and whelped April 24, 1974 by Champion Salilyn's Classic ex Champion Bordalyn's Begin Again. His accomplishments include Best in Sweepstakes at the National Specialty in 1975, Best of Breed at the American Spaniel Club in 1978, Best of Breed at the Potomac Specialty that same year and, still in 1978, Best of Opposite Sex at the National in July. A multiple Group winner, Behold was the Nation's Number Four Springer in 1979. He was the sire of 11 champions and seven Sweepstakes winners as this book was written. His progeny include Group winners and Top Producers and he is the grandsire of two Best in Show winners.

Patrician is also the home of Champion Carey's On Pride's magic, C.D., T.D., by Champion Carey's Pride and Joy, U.D.T., W.D., ex Champion Carey's April Shower. Champion Bordalyn's Blockade, T.D., by American and Canadian Champion Bordalyn's By The Way, C.D.X., W.D.X., ex Champion Bordalyn's Silhouette; Champion Bushlo's Calling Card by American and Canadian Champion Bordalyn's By The Way, C.D.X., W.D.X., ex Champion Highcliffe's Kandy Kisses, C.D.; and Champion Bordalyn's Burlesque, C.D., from Silhouette by All The Way, are others which have brought success to Patrician Springers.

The Ritters are working to maintain both mental and physical soundness along with a blending of various bloodlines which evidently is proving highly successful. Due to family considerations (a Naval Officer husband and three young children), all of the Patrician dogs are handled by Mary Ann and George Alston, as much as Debbie Ritter would enjoy doing some of it herself. The oldest child, Courtney, is currently showing in the Open Junior Showmanship Class.

Pembroke

Pembroke Springers, which has been so successful over the years, belongs to Mrs. Walter Berd and is now located in Tolland, Connecticut. This kennel probably showed its first glimmer of light back in 1937 when Alice Berd's father took pity on his youngest daughter who was grieving for their Gordon Setter that had recently died. Alice's father took her to look for a replacement for the Gordon (unbeknownst to her mother) but found the price was very high for this breed during those depression years. They had seen and liked a Springer, however, and luckily had found Robert Morrow of Audley Farms with a nice litter at a price they could afford. Alice's mother was surprised when presented with a new puppy to housebreak, but she too loved dogs and quickly took the young pup to her heart—where he remained for the next 14 years.

Mrs. Berd describes this first Springer as having been a good one for his day, but the only people who wanted to show him were his breeder and herself (her parents were not at all interested), and so the dog was never shown. The thought of dog shows and Springer Spaniels had been firmly implanted in the future Mrs. Berd's mind, however.

Mrs. Berd was married in 1949 and she and her husband settled in Birmingham, Michigan after her husband's company had transferred him to Detroit. Alice had left her old Springer with her parents but she found out that their new home town seemed to be filled with Springers although this was a fairly rare breed at the time. Only a few miles away were both Salilyn and Frejax kennels, so literally they were in a "hot bed" of this lady's favorite breed. In a short time the Berds had a puppy—Walter Berd's first dog. This puppy was entered in the classes at the 1950 Detroit Kennel Club Show, and though Mr. and Mrs. Berd were both complete novices and did nothing, the dog show bug had bitten again! Mrs. Berd recalls that the winner of the Puppy Class in which she had competed went on to Best of Winners, something she did not quite understand at that time. She does remember that puppy well, however, as he was to become Champion King Peter of Salilyn. The Best of Breed and finally Best in Show winner that day was Champion Frejax Royal Salute. This was another dazzling introduction to the dog show world for this young fancier.

Ch. Valderae's Pembroke Sea Mist, C.D., was Best in the Futurity and Winners Bitch at the National Specialty in 1968. Owned by Mrs. Walter Berd, Tolland, Connecticut.

A star of the future! Pembroke Just William, at 15 months of age, taking Best of Opposite Sex in Sweepstakes at Long Island in 1981. Elliott More handled for Mrs. Walter Berd, Pembroke Springers.

Soon Mrs. Berd realized that her own dog, though well-bred, was not of the quality to compete in the show ring, so she trained him for obedience and had fun being part of the Fancy in that way.

The Berds' home was soon filled with three small children, and the few hours a week Alice spent with the dog were a good respite from diapers, toilet training and nursery school car pools.

In 1958 the Berds purchased a nice bitch, Grande Pointe's First Lady. This bitch, sired by Salilyn's Sensation out of a King Peter daughter, was bred to a King Peter son, Salilyn's Santa Claus, and the Berds produced three champions at last. One was a Group winner and another their home-bred foundation bitch, Phyliss Duchess of Pembroke. The kennel name Pembroke came from the street where the Berds' first home in Michigan was located, ". . . a rather poor choice as I think back," comments Mrs. Berd, "but as dogs with the Pembroke prefix were becoming known and doing their share of winning, we decided not to change."

Ch. Pembroke Inchidony Scot, C.D. (Ch. Inchidony Prince Charming ex Ch. Phyliss Duchess of Pembroke, C.D.), taking the Sporting Group under Denis Grivas at Monroe Kennel Club, June 1971, handled by Bob Schmitz. One of the most outstanding winners from Mrs. Walter Berd's Pembroke Kennels, Scot's show record included 9 or more all-breed Bests in Show, at least 37 Group Firsts, and a Specialty Best of Breed.

Ch. Pembroke Satin Doll at the English Springer Spaniel Club of Michigan Specialty, March 1977, taking Winners Bitch for a 5-point "major" handled by Karen Prickett under judge John Marvin for owner Mrs. Walter Berd, Pembroke Springers.

Pembroke Springers has always been a small operation with only one or rarely two litters a year. Some very excellent quality Springers have been produced from these breedings, and the Pembroke stud dogs have had some lovely bitches to breed. All of the Berds' Springers live together as house dogs, and the present five, as this is written, are described by their owner as being "a most amiable crew."

Since 1978 the Berds have lived on 12 beautiful acres in Connecticut with a bona fide hobby kennel license, legal at last, after years of being "over limit" in suburban Birmingham. Although Walter Berd loves the dogs and is proud of their wins, it is Alice who is the active participant in the show world. The dog game has been good to her, giving her an absorbing and satisfying hobby, many good times and friends from all over the country with similar interests. She comments, "I hope that my long years as a part of this fascinating hobby have given me perspective, understanding and appreciation of a good animal in any breed."

Phylwayne

Phylwayne Springers, owned by Wayne and Phyllis Magill of Kent, Washington, has made history with some very famous members of this breed.

American and Canadian Champion Magill's Patrick, C.D., W.D.X., by American and Canadian Champion Geiger's Chief Geronimo ex Cindy's Delight was bred by the Magills, who say of him, "he was a much loved family pet and sometimes a hunting companion for Wayne." Pat was also a dream come true for anyone breeding or owning show dogs. He won five all-breed Bests in Show, the Sporting Group at Westminster in 1969 and seven Specialty Bests of Breed, including the National Specialty in 1972 where he was also the winner of the Stud Dog Class. His total record included 105 Bests of Breed, 51 Group firsts and 42 additional Group placements.

The proof of the pudding is that Pat's greatness continued through his offspring. He has sired many champions, including Group winners, obedience title holders, working certificate holders, hunting dogs and great pets. Among

Multiple Best in Show winner, Am., Can. Ch. Magill's Patrick, C.D., W.D.X., bred and owned by Wayne and Phyllis Magill, Kent, Washington.

The Multiple Sporting Group winner, Am., Can. Ch. Phylwayne's Bred Gun Fighter, C.D., W.D.X. Bred by Wayne and Phyllis Magill, owned by Rodney C. Luchsinger.

them is American and Canadian Champion Phylwayne's Bred Gun Fighter, C.D., W.D.X., who is an amateur-handled multiple Sporting Group winner and sire of the 1981 National Specialty Best of Opposite Sex winner.

Pat's other noted grandchildren are two Best in Show winners, Champion Perrie's Timothy Von Zuda and Champion Donahan's Mark Twain, both Specialty Best of Breed winners. Another grandson, Champion Tamrod's Legend of Bali, has many Group wins to his credit and a granddaughter, Champion Fenway's Tricia, was Best of Opposite Sex at the 1981 National Specialty.

According to the Phillips System, Pat was in the Top Ten Springers for the years 1967, 1968, 1969 and 1972. He was Number two in 1968 and 1969, Number six in 1967 and 1970 and Number eight in 1972.

Champion Phylwayne's Genie, Pat's younger sister, was also bred by the Magills and sired by American and Canadian Champion Geiger's Chief Geronimo ex Cindy's Delight. She was completely owner-handled and finished her championship in only four months with three "majors" and was awarded Best of Winners on

four occasions. Genie has 11 Best of Opposite Sex wins, including two at Specialties, to her credit. She is a grandmother to American and Canadian Champion Phylwayne's Bred Gun Fighter, C.D., W.D.X.

The latter dog, "Gunner," was also bred by the Magills, by Patrick ex Phylwayne's Samantha, W.D.X. As a puppy he was sold to the Rodney Luchsingers who own the Tamrod Springers and who are the breeders of the multiple Sporting Group winner, Champion Tamrod's Legend of Bali. Gunner was always amateur-handled by Wayne Magill and won the P.S. .S.S.A. "Gun Dog of the Year" Award for three years.

Pride 'n' Joy

The Pride 'n' Joy Springers belong to Julie Hogan and Donna Thompson and are located in Manassas, Virginia. The Springers are all house pets and currently there are ten of them, including some impressive title holders.

The foundation dog here, for which the kennel was named, is Champion Carey's Pride 'n' Joy, U.D.T., W.D., who was purchased in 1969 by Donna and Bernie Thompson from Andy and Mary Carey. The Careys had owned a very active kennel with dogs well-known for all around accomplishments in conformation, obedience and field; this became the aim at Pride 'n' Joy too.

For over five years Pride was the only living Champion Utility Dog, Tracking Dog, Working Dog Springer—and he is only the second in the breed thus distinguished—the first having been his grandsire, Champion Carey's Prince Michael, U.D.T., W.D.X. Pride's children have, as this was written, earned a total of three bench championships, 11 C.D. titles, three C.D.X., 12 T.D. titles and one W.D.X.

Among the other Springers owned by Julie Hogan and Donna Thompson are Champion Carey on Pride's April Luv, C.D.X., T.D., by Champion Carey's Pride 'n' Joy ex Carey's April Shower that earned her Tracking title at six months of age. Then there is Tak-A-Chance of Windyridge, C.D.X., T.D., by Champion Canarch's Yankee Patriot ex Champion Carey's Christmas Star, and Carey's Navy Admiral, C.D., T.D., by Champion King Andrew of Carey ex Champion Carey's Sweet Sue. Of identical breeding to Luv are Carey On Pride's Joy, C.D., T.D.; Carey Hi Pride's Banner, C.D.,

T.D.; and Carey Hi Pride's April Juniper, C.D. (the latter two now owned by Pride 'n' Joy). Champion Carey On Pride's Magic, C.D., T.D., is owned by Debbie Ritter, and Jasper of Carey's Pride, C.D. is owned by J. and C. Snyder. Pride 'n' Joy's Duplicate, C.D., T.D., W.D.X., by Champion Filicia's Etching ex Carey On Pride's Joy gained a Tracking degree at seven months. Pride 'n' Joy's Flaming Pennant, C.D.X., T.D.X., W.D.X., by Champion El Taro's Scotch Flag ex Carey On Pride's Joy was the first T.D.X. Springer in the United States; both he and his son passed the requirements on March 8, 1981. Pride 'n' Joy's Holiday Punch, C.D., T.D., same breeding as Pennant, and Pride 'n' Joy's Rhyme 'n' Reason, C.D.X., T.D., by Champion Carey's Pride 'n' Joy ex Pride 'n' Joy's Duplicate are others keeping this kennel in the limelight, as is Fanfare's Bright Salute, T.D., by Champion Canarch's Cardinal Dancer ex Canarch's Contemplation.

The magnificent Ch. Carey On Pride's April Luv, C.D.X., T.D. This lovely Springer died prematurely at 4½ years of age of cardiomyopathy, a very sad loss to his owners, Julia Hogan and Donna Thompson of Pride 'n' Joy Kennels.

Champion Chuzzlewit's Courier, a black-and-white tri-color, lately has been added to the Springers at Pride 'n' Joy, as has Shinnecock's One For The Money, barely a year old, purchased from Maureen Brady and Patti Alston.

The owners of Pride 'n' Joy would like to have all Champion U.D.T. Springers. They love putting championships on the dogs but are not interested in specialing them. Field and obedience work are equally enjoyed. As Julie Hogan states, "We want to stay right in the middle if we can, producing lovely all-'round Springers."

Ch. Carey On Pride's April Luv, C.D.X., T.D., owned by Pride 'n' Joy Springers, Manassas, Virginia.

Salilyn

Salilyn Springers is among the world's most famous and respected kennels in any breed of dog. Founded during the 1930's by Mrs. Julie Gasow of Troy, Michigan, the name has become synonymous with quality and true greatness.

Salilyn, named for Mrs. Gasow's two daughters, was based on the Rufton bloodlines to which Mrs. Gasow has strongly linebred through her dogs from the beginning. Starting back in 1936 with the purchase of a bitch, Champion Hibank Hopeful, this has been the strain she preferred; however, despite Hopeful having been sired by a Rufton dog, success was not immediate, and Mrs. Gasow notes that due to her inexperience and lack of knowledge at that point with the breed, several fruitless years followed until she had collected sufficient Rufton breeding on which to base a program as she planned. It was an "un-show-worthy bitch" that, bred to a Rufton dog, produced Julie Gasow's first Best in Show winner, Champion Sir Lancelot of Salilyn, in 1945. This dog took many Groups and three Bests in Show before his son started to beat him. The latter was the great and famous Champion Frejax Royal Salute.

Royal Salute came from Lancelot's first breeding and was an outstanding dog of his day. A daughter from the litter, Salutation of Salilyn, was kept by Mrs. Gasow and was eventually mated to a strongly inbred Rufton dog. The combination justified Mrs. Gasow's faith in this breeding plan, so she repeated it on three additional occasions. Each litter gave her one Best in Show dog, plus many champions. The two of the Best in Show dogs that she kept were Champion King Peter of Salilyn and Champion King William of Salilyn. Both proved themselves as highly successful producers and as noted winners. In 1953 Champion King Peter of Salilyn became the first recipient at Salilyn of the Quaker Oats Award, which has come so frequently and consistently over subsequent years to this kennel. He is the sire of 36 champions, in-

Ch. King Peter of Salilyn taking a Best in Show in 1953.

Ch. King William of Salilyn, a winner of the 1950s from Mrs. Julie Gasow's Salilyn Kennels, Troy, Michigan.

cluding Champion Salilyn's Cinderella that became the granddam of Champion Salilyn's Aristocrat that in turn was the Top Sire in the breed over quite a lengthy period of time. Champion King William of Salilyn made a splendid record on his own, surpassed in those days only by that of his brother, King Peter. He won five Bests in Show, numerous Groups and produced several champion sons and daughters including the handsome Champion Salilyn's MacDuff.

MacDuff was the 1957 Quaker Oaks Award winner with thirty-one Group firsts and was then sold to William L. and Elaine P. Randall for whom he again won the Quaker Oats Award in 1958. His record by 1959, making him the Top Show winning Springer up until that time, stood at 39 Bests in Show and 81 Group firsts. He thus surpassed the show record of American and Canadian Champion Frejax Royal Salute, then had to bow to his uncle, Champion Salilyn's Aristocrat. He was Best in Show at the National Specialty in 1959 and had the second highest number of Best in Show wins for any dog of any breed in the country. He was honored by taking the Parent Club Award for Springer of the Year three times in 1958, 1959 and 1960.

Ch. Salilyn's Aristocrat on August 13, 1967, winning a Best in Show from judge Alva Rosenberg for breeder-owner Mrs. Julie Gasow.

Ch. Salilyn MacDuff, by Ch. King William of Salilyn ex Shercliff's Lady Debbie, an Aristocrat daughter. Best in Show at the Progressive Dog Club of Wayne County in 1959 for Mrs. Julie Gasow.

The liver-and-white Champion Salilyn's Aristocrat, in 1967 before his third birthday, won a total of 45 Bests in Show and 71 Group firsts to establish a record for all breeds—it being a Phillips System rating of a total of 34,553 points. His record stood until 1971 when it was surpassed by his son, Champion Chinoe's Adamant James.

Aristocrat finished his championship at nine months of age from the Puppy Class. During his career in the ring, he won 61 Bests in Show, 108 Sporting Groups and 5 Specialties, including Best in Show at the American Spaniel Club in 1967 under Percy Roberts. That same year he won the Quaker Oats Award and Parent Club Springer of the year award. Sired by Champion Inchidony Prince Charming from Champion Salilyn's Lily of the Valley, he was voted in 1971 "The Greatest Winning Show Dog in History" in the *Kennel Review Awards*, thus becoming the only living dog to be put in the *Kennel Review Hall of Fame*. Aristocrat was 12 years a Top Producer; this amazing record of 183 Champions out of 92 dams is an all-time record for all breeds.

Ch. Salilyn's Classic (by Ch. Salilyn's Encore ex an Aristocrat daughter) winning Best in Show at the International Kennel Club in 1974. Mrs. Julie Gasow, owner; Dick Cooper, handler; Mrs. James Edward Clark, judge.

Champion Salilyn's Classic was whelped in 1971, won the National Specialty three times and won the Quaker Oats Award in 1975. He was Top Springer in the United States in 1974 and 1975, and his championship progeny include at least 75 that have gained the title, among them six Best in Show winners. As a Show dog himself, he collected 39 Bests in Show, 111 Groups and eight Specialties, including three National Specialties, two English Springer Spaniel Club of Michigan Specialties, two Great Lakes English Springer Spaniel Breeders Association Specialties and Best of Breed at the American Spaniel Club Specialty.

Champion Salilyn's Hallmark, with more than 12 champion get, is a second generation Top Producer, being a son of Champion Salilyn's Classic. In 1976 he won the Quaker Oats Award for Top Sporting Dog.

The most recent Quaker Oats Award winner here has been Champion Prelude's Echo for two years in a row, 1979 and 1980, co-owned by Julie Gasow and Jacqueline Tousley. The Quaker Oats Award, incidently, goes annually to the dog or bitch in each of the Variety Groups that has won first in that Variety Group most times throughout the dog show year.

Mrs. Gasow notes that there have been many other top winning champions along the way, but in this resume she has discussed only those that have played an important role in becoming the backbone of her bloodlines. In this regard there are two dogs to which she gives particular credit; they are Champion Salilyn's Sensation (out of a Sir Lancelot sister) and Sensation's son, Champion Salilyn's Citation, because it is through them that she developed a positive program still in use today.

It was in the early 1950's that Julie Gasow realized the existence of two distinct types of Springer within her own breeding program, practically all of them resulting from different combinations of the same dogs. She liked both types as "... there was not a great difference between the two," to quote her, and one of them she called the "Sensation line" or the "short-legged family." This was a compact, cobby dog measuring perfectly into standard with heavy bone, excellent feet, stylish top-line and outstanding showmanship, but appearing perhaps on the small side when compared with Salilyn's "King Peter line" or the "long-legged family." The latter also fits well into standard, but they have more elegance both in conformation and bearing, slightly less bone, flash and showmanship, plus better heads and more neck. Again quoting Mrs. Gasow, "I found it possible to hold both types and that crossing the two so called 'families' with an occasional outcross worked successfully." She considers the best Salilyn show dogs and producers to have come from this combination and they still continue to do so.

Best in Show at Livonia Kennel Club in 1976 was won by Ch. Salilyn's Hallmark for Mrs. Julie Gasow.

Ch. Prelude's Echo won the Quaker Oats Award two years in a row (1979 and 1980). Co-owned by Julie Gasow and Jacqueline Tousley, handled by Dick Cooper. Sire, Ch. Salilyn's Colonel's Overlord; dam, Ch. Salilyn's Debutante II.

In introducing new blood, Mrs. Gasow prefers to buy a bitch, then breed it to her own stud dogs, making sure that the bitch was linebred for the characteristics needed to overcome faults in her dogs.

The most outstanding of the Salilyn Springers have been, in chronological order, Champion King Peter of Salilyn, Champion Salilyn's Mac-Duff, Champion Salilyn's Aristocrat, Champion Salilyn's Classic and Champion Salilyn's Hallmark. King Peter, as mentioned, won the Quaker Oats Award in 1953; MacDuff in 1957 and 1958; Aristocrat in 1967; Classic in 1974 and 1975; Hallmark in 1976; Salilyn's Continental in 1978; and Champion Prelude's Echo, co-owned by Julie Gasow and Jacqueline Tousley, in 1979 and 1980. This latter dog was by Champion Salilyn's Colonel's Overlord ex Champion Salilyn's Debutante.

While on the subject of awards, in addition to all these Quaker Oats honors, Salilyn has seven times won the *Kennel Review* "Winkie" for Best Sporting Dog of the Year and three times the "Winkie" for Best Dog of the Year all breeds with Champion Salilyn Aristocrat—plus this dog's entry into the *Kennel Review Hall of Fame* as previously mentioned.

Of the current top winners at Salilyn, Mrs. Gasow points with pride to Champion Salilyn's Private Stock, sired by Champion Filicia's Bequest (a Classic son) out of Champion Salilyn's Sonnet (an Aristocrat daughter), the latter bred by Salilyn and co-owned by Julie Gasow and the Robert Goughs.

Looking towards the future, Champion Salilyn's Design has just finished his title with five "majors." He is a black-and-white son of Champion Salilyn's Classic from Champion Salilyn's Applause.

As the pages of this book are studied, readers will become increasingly aware of the impact Salilyn breeding has had on the modern Springer in this country. Few and far between are the kennels which do not somewhere trace back to it and to the dogs that are not in some way descended from it. Mrs. Gasow has personally won many awards as a successful breeder, which she modestly refrains from mentioning. They certainly have been well deserved.

Profile of a superb Springer! Ch. Salilyn's Aristocrat at ten years old. Mrs. Julie Gasow, owner.

Sandyhill

Sandyhill Springers was established in 1971 and named for the old section of Ottawa, Canada, from where their owner, Carmen Berci, originally came. Now located in Detroit, Michigan, Sandyhill is making itself well known in the Springer world at present with the handsome American and Canadian Champion Sandyhill's Major Domino, which is being successfully campaigned by Dennis Kniola here and by his owner in Canada.

Am., Can. Ch. Sandyhill's Major Domino, black and white, was born on January 6, 1978, sired by Ch. Salilyn's Classic ex Ch. Salilyn's Soubrette. Carmen Berci and Salilyn Kennels co-own this handsome dog that was bred by Mrs. Anne Snelling. Handled in Canada by owner and in the United States by Dennis J. Kniola.

Carmen Berci joined the English Springer Spaniel Club of Michigan in 1971 at the same time he purchased a Springer dog from the Hendees' noted Canarch Kennels and a bitch from the Pembroke line. The latter was bred to American and Canadian Champion Pembroke Inchidony Scot and produced Carmen's first Canadian Champion, Sandyhill's Power Play.

Sandyhill has done considerably well in Canada, finishing six Springers there, three from the Puppy Classes along with three Best Puppy in Show awards.

Major Domino, "Amos" to his friends, is the first U.S.A. Sandyhill champion and is of Salilyn breeding by Classic from Champion Salilyn's Soubrette.

Shalimar

The establishment of the Shalimar Kennels came as nothing of a surprise to owner Sharon Mabrey of Odessa, Delaware, as she has been interested in animals all her life and active in the show arena since the age of ten. The local 4-H program developed most of her interest and allowed the interest to blossom into many areas of success in the field of animals.

Sharon's first love was horses and no sooner had she become an owner of one when she was in the show ring with it. Most of her participation was at local shows and at 4-H events. Her horse project branched into her using horses in demonstration contests, parades and 4-H horse-judging. Three years later her parents bought her a registered quarter horse, and she was off to the show circuit; this horse did continue to be used in the 4-H program, however. After the second quarter horse came along, more emphasis was placed on national shows and on earning points to qualify for both team competition and Delaware Quarter Horse Association Queen. Sharon later began a breeding program which resulted in the raising and breaking of two foals. There were situations that arose which required her to do a lot of research on the subject of breeding, and later, with regard to therapy and nutrition.

Sharon's hobby turned into a profession as she entered a pre-veterinary curriculum at the University of Delaware in hopes of someday finding a job in animal research. After college Sharon married, and the horses that were to have established Dufford Club Farms were sold.

As might have been expected with one so devoted to animals and to competition with them, Sharon found that her cravings for the show ring were still very strong. No sooner were the horses gone when she found herself at the Wilmington Kennel Club, a local dog show. Sharon's first dog had been a Springer, given to her by her Dad on her 16th birthday, to be used as a hunting dog. Actually, it was a disappointment at the time, as Cockers were the breed she really loved and wanted to own. She recalls being crestfallen, but as she grew to love the Springer and see her work, she was soon converted. (Today she would not own any breed in preference to an English Springer Spaniel.)

Naturally, the first place Sharon headed for at that Wilmington show was the Springer section.

There she met Dr. Mary Gibbs of Kay n Dee fame, who was most helpful and cordial to this new fancier. Next came a match show sponsored by a New Jersey Springer Club (no longer in existence) where she met Bonnie Bosley and saw a lovely group of Springers. After that, she found herself going home to her own Springer with a new perspective.

Suddenly, this pet Springer came under a different type of scrutiny. A whole new objective was planned for her, as her owner became excited over turning her into a show dog. Thus, the earlier dreams of Dufford Club Farms turned into Shalimar Kennels. This was in the spring of 1977 when the "kennel" consisted of two dogs, both of good solid field-breeding. The younger bitch, daughter of her first Springer, was sired by a son of Champion Gieger's Chief Geronimo and seemed like a good choice on which to base a breeding program. She, Bertalion Flirtation, was bred to Champion Wheeler Ridge One Man Band. The first litter was ill fated, as only one of seven puppies survived beyond several days. This one puppy, Shalimar's New Morning, was raised by hand and struggled to live; she grew up to be a nice bitch suitable for showing and she became a constant companion and good teammate for Sharon's initiation into the world of Springers. They started out, quite correctly, in the match shows, graduating to the point shows. Sharon was always observant of how the handlers proceeded, asked many breeders questions and at the end of her first year, joined one of George Alston's handling classes.

"Toby," as New Morning is called, gained a point or two in competition, but her true value has been in the whelping box, as she produced three beautiful litters with the first just beginning to show accomplishment in the ring and the third only several weeks old as this was written. The most exciting of these to date was Champion Shalimar's Springtime and his sister, Shalimar's Norwegian Wood, already pointed. Springtime belongs to William Rich and his daughter, Anne, and has really done well, handled by George Alston. He has gained his points at Westminster, the Eastern Specialty and the National Specialty.

Mrs. Mabrey's plans for the future are now being made, and she looks forward to producing many more splendid champions at Shalimar.

Ch. Pequa Choir Boy, the first homebred Pequa champion owned by Mr. and Mrs. A.W. Matson. By Ch. Melilotus Star of Pequa ex Ch. Maquam's Psalm Singer.

Shinnecock

The Shinnecock English Springer Spaniels in Flanders, New York is owned by Patricia Matson Alston and Maureen Brady, and is the result of a former successful kennel, two generations of interest in Springers and many years of devotion to the breed. Back in 1949, Mr. and Mrs. A.W. Matson of Long Island founded Pequa Kennels, with the purchase of a dog they named Pequa Don, as a hobby project for their family.

Don was a son of Champion Maquam's Psalm Singer ex Flored Gypsy. He won enough to keep the family interested, starting off with a countless series of Reserves, handled by Jackie Matson Forbes. He was finished by Laddie Carswell, thus becoming one of this talented professional handler's first Springer champions. Don's principal claim to fame (and surely not a bad one) was Winners Dog at the American Spaniel Club Specialty, plus the fact that he was a member of the family until the day he died.

Best in the Eastern English Springer Spaniel Club
Futurity, 1957, is Ch. Pequa September Song at nine
months old. Owned by Pequa Kennels, handled by
Patty Alston.

Four generations of fine Springers, photographed
at the Eastern Specialty in 1955. On the left is Atha
Whitaker with his great Champion Runor's
Deacon; the other three are with Jackie Matson
Forbes, Patty Alston, and Billy Matson.

Don's many Reserves had made the Matsons
aware that, even back in the early 1950's, his
dark face with no blaze was a handicap. So in
their second Springer they looked for a "pretty"
one, which they found in a beautiful six-month-
old puppy by Champion Runor's Deacon ex
Champion Melilotus Highland Cream.
"Clover," as she was called, was destined to
become Champion Melilotus Star of Pequa.
Handled by Laddie Carswell, she finished with a
Best of Opposite Sex to Champion Melilotus
Royal Oak at the American Spaniel Club and
proceeded along to garner multiple Group placements at a time when Springer bitches had not
yet heard of equal rights. In the whelping box,
Clover became the foundation bitch of the Matsons' Pequa Kennel. At least one direct descen-
dant of hers, Champion Torlin's Spellbinder,
finished as recently as 1980. Clover produced
the Matsons' first home-bred champion, the
well-known Champion Pequa Choir Boy, sired
by Champion Maquam's Psalm Singer. This
was the Matsons' initial attempt at combining
extreme soundness with style. Choir Boy was
the Springer on the end of the lead when he and
Patty Alston (nee Matson) won Junior
Showmanship at Westminster in 1957. Another
titled offspring from this breeding was Champion Pequa September Song, winner of the 1957
Eastern Futurity from the six to nine Puppy
Bitch Class. The influence of Champion
Runor's Deacon, owned and handled by Atha
Whitaker, is very apparent in the four-
generation photo taken at the Eastern that year.

At the time Patty Matson and George Alston were married, Patty owned only one Springer, Champion Elkgrove Black Watch of Pequa, which was acquired on her first trip to Michigan as a gift from Alice and Hap Herwig. This dog became the first Pequa Group winner, and as Patty says, "It took us 10 years, and even then we didn't breed him but only owned him." In an attempt to combine the soundness and type of the Eastern dogs with the style and elegance of the mid-Western ones, the Matsons then bred Champion Melilotus Star of Pequa to Champion Elkgrove Black Watch of Pequa. The result was highly successful, producing Champion Another Star of Pequa that took "majors" at four Specialties as she gained her title, did a fair share of Best of Opposite Sex placing in Sweepstakes along the way, and then took Best of Opposite Sex to the great Champion Wakefield's Black Knight at the Potomac Specialty in 1962.

Needless to say, even though now married and retired to motherhood herself, Patty could not stay out of the ring. It became obvious, too, that a third generation Springer fan was also emerging, as it grew increasingly difficult to keep young daughter Jane out of the ring even before she was old enough to show a dog.

Mr. Matson (Patty's father) died about this time, and Mrs. Matson seldom got to the shows due to the severity of her arthritis. She did, however, keep her hand in with the Springers by agreeing to finance and co-own Patty's new purchase, an eight-week-old liver-and-white male from Beryl Hines that was by Anne Pope's famous Best in Show winner, Champion Charlyle Fair Warning ex Champion Beryltown Lively Rocket, another Eastern—mid-West type of cross. This puppy, the future Champion Beryltown Virginian of Pequa, brought renewed interest to the entire family when he won the Eastern Futurity in 1966, under Bob Walgate, and captured his first points a year later, with Julie Gasow judging. At this point, Patty, with three children to look after, really was finding it difficult to campaign a dog.

An impending divorce from her husband George brought about a total change of location plus many added responsibilities for Patty. Even so, she and her mother were eager to have their fine young dog go through to his title, and so Patty decided to try her hand with him. Everyone came along to the shows—Mrs. Matson (on crutches), the youngsters—while Patty did the driving and handled the dog. It paid off and was

Ch. Elkgrove Black Watch of Pequa, owned by Patricia Matson Alston, bred by Alice Herwig, handled by George Alston. Shown winning Pequa Kennels' first Group 1 award in 1962 under judge Maxwell Riddle at Williamsport, Pennsylvania. This dog was the sire of Ch. Another Star of Pequa.

worth the effort when, at Newtown 1969, Patty piloted Champion Beryltown Virginian of Pequa to first in the Sporting Group. Unfortunately, they lost "Josh," as he was known, shortly after this win. Mrs. Matson, too, passed away not long after that.

Patty and her children relocated to New Hampshire where she set out to establish herself as a professional handler. She concentrated mainly on Springers, commenting, ". . . but it seemed I was hired mostly for problem dogs . . ." and soon she was doing well with a number of them, these having been far from the "problem" category. Patty affectionately refers to Pete Skinner's "Oxford" and to a dog called "Deuce", owned by Ardella and Noel Pease, that was one of her favorites. Patty describes Deuce as "one of the finest examples of Spaniel movement and temperament that I've seen." Their first time in the ring led to a "major" and

Best of Breed over "specials," and this dog added another "first" to Patty's own list of successes, as it was with him that she won the Keystone Specialty in 1975. Although he never took a Group first, he had the distinction of placing in the Sporting Group every time he won Best of Breed. More formally, Deuce was Champion Arel's Deuce, a dog with a host of admiring friends.

This was a very exceptional Springer in Patty's opinion. She also compliments Ardella Pease's efficiency as an obedience trainer as even Patty helped him to win a leg on his C.D.; Jane Alston took him to the final leg, and also got the Highest Scoring Junior Handler with him at the New York National in 1975. Patty says of this dog, "he seemed to mellow and soften up any harsh spots with age," as proven by his win of the Veterans Class at the Eastern Specialty in 1979.

Ch. Beryltown Virginian of Pequa going Best of Winners at the Eastern English Springer Spaniel Specialty under Julia Gasow in 1967. George Alston is handling for owner Patty Alston. By Ch. Charlyle's Fair Warning ex Ch. Beryltown Lively Rocket.

Ch. Arel's Deuce, owned by Ardella and Noel Pease, winning one of his numerous Bests of Breed. Handled by Patty Alston.

At the time Deuce was being shown, one of his greatest admirers was a young lady named Maureen Brady. She had a few Springers of her own and asked Patty's opinion of them . . . and there you have the start of Shinnecock Kennels! Patty and Maureen formed a fast friendship; as they discussed Springers (Maureen preferred the "pretty" ones while Patty was all out for the "sound" ones), the picture of a combination dog formed in their minds. Both of them could see him: Maureen's picture was beautifully stylish, but boy, could he move; Patty's picture was a flawless mover and stylish besides. The decision was reached to co-purchase a bitch they hoped would produce this wonder dog. Patty says, "We will always thank Karen Prickett for offering us pick of a promising litter by Champion Lou Jon's Executor ex Varis Cinderella Star." The litter was bred and owned by David Slagle, but Karen Prickett was acting as a sales agent for the pups. The one that the girls settled on was not the flashiest, but could surely cover ground, even at eight weeks. They also fell in love with a half brother, marked with a full stocking, which came home, too, to become the "pride and joy" of Shinnecock.

It became immediatly obvious at her very first show that the bitch, Lou Jon's Femininity, was the kind we get once in a lifetime. Even having had no show training, she instinctively played up to the judge and ringside like a Best in Show winner. Her first five-point "major" was the Long Island Specialty in 1976 from the Puppy Class under Fred Hunt, after going Best of Opposite Sex in Sweeps and Reserve Winners Bitch at the Potomac Specialty as a "warm up." Shown sparingly over that summer, she went to the American Spaniel Club under Anne Clark and came home with Best of Winners and Best of Opposite Sex over "specials," repeating these wins to finish at Westminster. Within six weeks, the owners found her to be the Number one Springer Bitch in the country. Specialed for exactly nine months, her record included 13 Bests of Breed, one Sporting Group first and multiple Group placements—certainly putting Shinnecock off to a fine start.

Ch. Lou-Gin's Femininity winning the Sporting Group at Sand and Sea. Owned by Maureen Brady and Patty Alston, Shinnecock Springers, Flanders, New York.

Ch. Shinnecock Overdrive, winner of the Eastern Futurity in 1978, here is taking Best of Winners at Trenton that same year for Shinnecock Kennels.

Here is "Soc" gaining his first points at Trenton in May 1978 for Shinnecock Kennels. He completed his title in August of that same year.

After great deliberation, it was decided to breed Femininity to an unknown stud, Champion Salilyn's Exclusive. While awaiting this litter, the girls started off with "Soc," the male puppy they had brought back with them too. He won a "major" at his first show and finished with a Best of Breed over Best in Show "specials" in August 1978.

Meanwhile, the anticipated litter arrived and of five puppies, four became champions and the fifth one pointed. Included among them were Champion Shinnecock's Overdrive, winner of the Eastern Futurity 1979; a National Best in Sweeps, Champion Shinnecock's Tumbleweed, and Champion Shinnecock's Understudy that was Winners Bitch at the Long Island Specialty in 1979.

Femininity's second litter was sired by Champion Winacko's Classic Replay, C.D., producing the 1980 Eastern Best in Futurity, Welcome Aboard Shinnecock. Unfortunately, this lovely dog succumbed to pneumonia in January 1981 when only 18 months old, a sad loss to his owner, Mary Jo Hosteny. This litter also included American and Canadian Champion Shinnecock's Rapid Transit that completed his Cana-

dian title undefeated at seven months, and finished his championship here at 13 months, where he included among his victories Best of Winners and Best Puppy at the American Spaniel Club 1980.

Ch. Shinnecock Tumbleweed, on the way to Best in the National Sweepstakes at Colorado, handled by Maureen Brady, who is co-owner with Patty Alston.

The third Femininity litter was a repeat breeding to Classic Replay, again highly successful, as the puppies included Shinnecock's Simply Smashing which the girls describe as "possibly our winningest yet." At 12 months old, she had topped the Sweeps at both the Potomac Valley Specialty and the Long Island Specialty, and her sister, Shinnecock's Rave Notice, has garnered both "majors," with George Alston handling.

Patty Alston comments, "As the time for Femininity's 1981 breeding approached, we tried to re-evaluate what 'Amy' had produced previously and how we would change them. We decided we could use a tad more bone and a few deeper angles. The dog we chose was Champion Filicia's Crescendo, so we took a trip to Connecticut for breeding purposes, fell madly in love and acquired still another dog. It seems that Miss Anne Pope (owner of Filicia) had the same idea we did, and we feel confident that the Crescendo—Femininity offspring should provide the final step in the merger of soundness with style, elegance with strength and type with temperament."

Shinnecock's Simply Smashing, from the second litter by Ch. Winacko's Classic Replay, C.D., ex Ch. Lou-Jon's Femininity, is co-owned by Christine Miller and Maureen Brady, bred by Shinnecock Kennels. Topped the Sweepstakes at both the Potomac Valley Specialty and the Long Island Specialty, the latter pictured.

This handsome dog is Welcome Aboard Shinnecock, Best in the Eastern Futurity 1980, owned by Mary Jo Hosteny, from the second litter by Champion Winacko's Classic Replay, C.D., ex Ch. Lou Jon's Femininity. Unfortunately died in January 1981 at only 18 months old. Bred by Patty Alston and Maureen Brady.

Certainly Maureen Brady and Patty Alston can pause with satisfaction as they contemplate what already has been accomplished at Shinnecock in just five short years, based on, as they put it, "two dogs in the backyard." Their list of credits includes the Number one Springer Show Bitch in the country for 1977, the Top Producer of 1980 and the recent winning by Champion Shinnecock Tumbleweed of two Bests in Show. This kennel certainly has had an exciting course to follow and one which will surely lead to many future successes.

Silverbow

The foundation for Silver Bow Springers was acquired by Cecil and Nancy Kemp of Las Vegas, Nevada, with the purchase of their first show-quality puppy from Mrs. Gasow of Salilyn. This bitch became Champion Salilyn's Touch of Mink, and although bred only three times, she gave the Kemps some especially beautiful puppies. One daughter was the future American and Mexican Champion Silverbow's December Dawn sired by Champion Salilyn's Aristocrat that started her show career at six months of age by taking Reserve Winners Bitch at the National Specialty in 1973. She was also presented the Gateway Cities English Springer Spaniel Association Best of Opposite Sex Award in 1974 and 1975.

December Dawn's first litter of five was sired by Champion Salilyn's Classic and produced three pups that went on to their titles. These were Champion Salilyn's Lyra, a multiple Group winning bitch; Champion Silverbow's Royal Heritage that gained several Bests of Breed and a Group placement, and Champion Silverbow's Misty Dawn that acquired most of her points from the Puppy Classes, including a Best of Breed, and that produced Champion Silverbow's Poetry in Motion by a sire of Kaintuck bloodlines. December Dawn added three more champions from her two other litters, bringing her total to six.

The Kemp's other Springers include Champion Silverbow's Touch of Class, a Champion Salilyn's Classic son, that finished with three five-point majors and is a multiple Best of Breed winner with several Group placements. He has sired two champions with several more pointed. Another Aristocrat daughter, Champion First Impression of Silverbows, has produced 12 champions and was the Parent Club's Top Producing Dam for 1976.

This is Am., Mex. Ch. Silverbow's December Dawn, by Ch. Salilyn's Aristocrat ex Ch. Salilyn's Touch of Mink, bred and owned by Cecil and Nancy Kemp, Silver Bow Springers, Las Vegas, Nevada.

Although their kennel is a small one and the Kemps have maintained a limited breeding program over the years, they certainly can point with pride to the accomplishments they have attained. Always, temperament has been foremost in their minds, sharing equally with type. Their dogs excel in sweet and loving dispositions, most have kept their natural hunting instincts and they also do well in obedience.

This young Springer is Sure-Wyn's Black Magic, by Ch. Wheeler Ridge One Man Band ex Ring-A-Ding's My Sin, C.D., just starting out in the obedience ring and conformation classes. Owned by Debby Valvo, Sure-Wyn Springers, Middletown, Connecticut.

Sure-Wyn

Although Sure-Wyn Kennels is very young, Debra Valvo and her family had owned Springers for about six years prior to the decision to seriously breed and campaign them. As Debby says, "My husband and I started with a Springer as a Christmas gift and just got hooked, pure and simple."

Their eldest Springer, Wayfarer's Bridget, is still Mr. Valvo's favorite companion and hunting dog. She is a daughter of Ascot's Wayfarer from Wayfarer's Mocha.

Other Springers currently belonging to the Valvos include Champion Ring-A-Ding's Ascot Royal Guard's lovely daughter, Ring-A-Ding's My Sin, C.D., that was bred by Mary V. Costello and is from Ring-A-Ding's Roulette. Mrs. Valvo has already put an obedience title on Sin and is now working towards her conformation championship.

Headstudy of Debby Valvo's Sure-Wyn's Black Magic.

Wayfarer's Bridget, by Ascot's Wayfarer ex Wayfarer's Mocha, is "head lady" at the Valvos' Sure Wyn Kennels.

Sure-Wyn's Night Watch, bred and co-owned by Mrs. Valvo, has only just begun working towards his bench championship; and there is another young dog in which she takes particular pride, Sure-Wyn's Black Magic, now working in obedience and soon to enter the breed ring. He is by Champion Wheeler Ridge One Man Band ex Ring-A-Ding's My Sin, C.D.

The Valvos are well pleased with the several litters born to date at Sure-Wyn and look forward to an exciting future with the breed.

Triagain

Triagain Springers in Cockeysville, Maryland, are owned by Mrs. Susanne B. Howard who has been breeding for approximately 10 years. This is a small kennel, producing about one litter annually. The foundation bitches, both black-tan-and-white tri-colors, were purchased as puppies and come from different bloodlines. Champion Ledger Hill Royal Scotch Mist, W.D., represents the Walpride-Beryltown strains, while Champion Excaliber's Royal Maiden is from the Salilyn-Wakefield-Stage Run strains.

The goal here is to produce soundness that is both physical and mental, and concentration is on the tri-colors, all of the breeding stock being either tri-colored itself or tri-factored.

Ch. Ledger Hill Royal Scotch Mist, W.D., the first of the tri-color Champions owned by Mrs. J.E. Howard, Jr., completed title at the Eastern Dog Club in 1973 under the late Louis Murr. George Alston is handling.

Ch. Triagain One More Time, from the Triagain Kennels of Mrs. J.E. Howard, Jr., of Cockeysville, Maryland, pictured gaining final points at the Kennel Club of Philadelphia, 1980, handled by George Alston.

Triagain Springers are seen not only in the show and obedience rings but also in the field as hunting companions. They have bred and/or owned six champions, four of which are tri's. There are also five Triagain-bred obedience-titled Springers.

Champion Ledger Hill Royal Scotch Mist, W.D., was Best of Breed from the classes for her first championship points. She attained the Parent Club's Working Dog title with only two weeks of field training and was a super hunting companion. She and the other foundation bitch, Champion Excaliber's Royal Maiden, certainly put this kennel off to an excellent start both in the ring and in their breeding program.

George Alston handles the Triagain Springers.

Waiterock

Waiterock Kennels, belonging to Mrs. Juanita Waite Howard of Lafayette, California, has the distinction of being one of the longest established and still active kennels of any breed in the United States, having had its beginning all the way back in 1935. Recently Mrs. Howard finished her 70th champion, and while all of these

have not been Springers (she has lately become extremely interested in English Cockers, six of which have completed titles for her), by far the majority have been of her original breed.

The original Waiterock Springers represented some excellent individuals of Elysian, Breeze, Boghurst, Tahquitz and Timpanogos lineage. Upon acquisition of her first member of the breed, Mrs. Howard attended a Field Trial (which she loved) and in 1936 she attended her first dog show held on the grounds of the old Del Monte Hotel. Her first entry in a dog show was at Santa Cruz and the silver trophy won by the Waiterock Springer shown that day did much to spark her interest in breeding for show conformation as well as for hunting. She says, "It was with a great deal of pride on my part that in 1964 a Waiterock Springer went Best in Show at Del Monte (the Club which held the first show I ever attended) even though it took me 28 years."

Ch. Waiterock Strongbow, the first of all the Waiterock champions owned by Juanita Waite Howard, Waiterock Ranch, Lafayette, California. Owner-handled, he took Best of Breed at the first National Show for Springers held in the West on July 21, 1946, at Vallejo, California, judged by Ed Knight. Strongbow also placed Group 2 at that show. He gained his title with three 5-point "majors" with a 2 point in the middle.

Am., Can. Ch. Waiterock Elmer Brown winning Best in Show at the Del Monte Kennel Club in 1964. Judge, Kyle M. McDonald; handler, R. McGinnis; presenter, Henry Tiedemann, club president. At this same show an Elmer Brown son and daughter took Winners Dog, Winners Bitch, Best of Winners, and Best of Opposite Sex—making it a real "grand slam" for breeder-owner Juanita Howard.

Champion Waiterock Strongbow was the first to gain this title for Mrs. Howard. He is by Elf's Sportsman of Breeze ex Timpanogo's Peg and made his title in four shows, three of which were five-point "majors," with a two-point win just prior to the final "major" which was at the first National Specialty held in the West, under Ed Knight. Strongbow took Best of Winners and Best of Breed. This was in July 1946.

Strongbow sired Champion Waiterock Firebow and Champion Waiterock Whistle that in turn sired the very famous and outstanding Champion Waiterock Elmer Brown. Champion Waiterock Firebow had the distinction of winning Working Dog Certificate Number one awarded to a Springer in the United States. Among his noted progeny were Champion Waiterock Fire Flare, Champion Waiterock Bow Key, Champion Waiterock Crossbow and Champion Waiterock Dogwood.

American and Canadian Champion Waiterock Elmer Brown earned himself a place of great honor in the Springer world when he won the Top Springer in the United States award, *Phillips System*, in 1962, 1963 and 1964. He also won the Parent Club Award as Top Springer Sire of the Year in 1964 and 1966 and the Parent Club Award as Top Springer of the Year in 1964. Additionally, he was Top Western Sporting Dog (western states) in 1962 and 1964, an award granted by *Kennel Review*, and he was the International Sporting Group Winner (first) at the World Championship Shows held in Nassau (the Bahamas) in 1966.

Eight all-breed Bests in Show and 16 Specialty shows (two of the latter from the Veterans Class at 12 years old) were won during his career, which also included 187 times Best of Breed and 44 times first in the Sporting Group. One of the latter victories, at Golden Gate in 1967, was scored from the Veterans Class when he was three months short of 12 years old . . . truly an amazing achievement!

More than 40 champions were sired by this grand dog including eight in one litter from Champion South Riding Wild Rose, bred by John Breslin, and eight in another litter from Champion Jayne's Cindy Girl (born in 1967), bred by Jane Lowy.

Born April 8, 1956, Elmer Brown lived to be 14 years of age. He was bred and owned by Mrs. Howard. His is an especially interesting story as he was sold at eight weeks of age then returned to Mrs. Howard at 4½ years because he "lorded it over all the other Springers" where he had gone to live. He was five years old before ever being used at stud and was not used for outside stud work ever, except by two breeders who outcrossed their champion bitches to him. Each of these, mentioned in the preceding paragraph, got eight champions by him. Elmer Brown made his title in three five-point shows. Among his admirers and those who gave him important wins were such respected authorities as Alva Rosenberg, Max Riddle, Charles Sievers, Louis Murr, Joe Quirk and many others.

Among the outstanding litters bred by Juanita Howard and sired by Elmer Brown were those from Champion Waiterock Oak Branch, which included Champion Waiterock Annie Laurie; Champion Waiterock Oak Leaf II, which included Champion Waiterock Elm Leaf and Champion Waiterock Emblem; Waiterock Dala, which included Champion Waiterock Elmo's Fire and Champion Waiterock Nobo Diana's Belle; and Waiterock Ceres, which included Champion Waiterock High Trill and Champion Waiterock Skykomish.

Another distinguished litter raised at Mrs. Howard's kennel was one which included five champions by Champion Melilotus Royal Oak ex Champion Tahquitz Solita, from which Waiterock Oak Twig, Waiterock Oak Bur, Waiterock Oak Leaf II, Waiterock Royal Wings and Waiterock Timber Oak were whelped on September 8, 1954. All gained their titles.

It is noted that over the years, Mrs. Howard has made judicious outcrosses in her breeding program, selecting such fine Springers as Champion Melilotus Royal Oak, Champion Prince Charlie of Melilotus, Champion Melilotus Larch, Champion Frejax Royal Salute and

Six famous Springer champions at home. Left to right, Ch. Waiterock Bowkey (sired by Ch. Waiterock Firebow), Ch. Waiterock Recruit (by Ch. Frejax Royal Salute), Ch. Waiterock Firebow (by Ch. Waiterock Strongbow), Ch. Waiterock Charlita (by Ch. Prince Charlie of Melilotus), Ch. Tahquitz Solita (by Ch. Prince Charlie of Melilotus), and Ch. Waiterock Whistle (by Ch. Waiterock Strongbow). At one period there were 15 living champions at Waiterock Ranch. Except for Solita (bred by Dr. Byron Mock), these were all bred by Juanita Waite Howard.

Champion Salilyn's Aristocrat upon occasion for her best home-bred bitches.

Some of the more current bench show winners belonging to Mrs. Howard are Champion Waiterock Trident, Champion Waiterock Danela, Champion Waiterock Triangle, Champion Waiterock Bodkin, Champion Waiterock Talion, Champion Waiterock Triumpher, Champion Waiterock Triple Sec, Champion Waiterock Arrow, Champion Waiterock Jada, Champion Waiterock Annabelle Lee and Champion Waiterock Tarra.

Through the years, Juanita Howard's two most exciting dog show days were the ones on which her kennel achieved "grand slams," i.e., the days on which Elmer Brown took Best of Breed, the Sporting Group and Best in Show while his get accounted for Winners Dog, Winners Bitch, Best of Winners and Best of Opposite Sex to their sire. This happened at both a Del Monte event and at San Fernando and were occasions to make *any* breeder's heart beat faster.

From the very beginning, Waiterock has been a "dual purpose" kennel. Mrs. Howard's first visit to a Field Trial even slightly preceded her first visit to a dog show, and its effect on her had much to do with her devotion to Springers over the past many years. The trial she attended in 1935 was the second such event to take place in California (she was told), the first having been in the Sacramento area the year before. This second trial was held on the banks of the Salinas River near Monterey.

The eagerness of the Springers to hunt, their willingness to be trained and their friendly, enthusiastic owners attracted Mrs. Howard immediatly and brought her to membership in the Northern California Field Trial Club, which she understands was the oldest such club in the West and which had Clarence Pfaffenberger as its first president.

When the Northern California Field Trial Club held its first Field Trial on the Rolph Ranch south of San Francisco in December 1937, Mrs. Howard was there to help and to learn. The owners of Waiterock Springers, however, had left their partially trained dogs at home while they, as novices, saw how it was done. There were some absentees, probably for the same reason, but the result was that one more entry was needed to make the six required for championship points in the Open All-Age Stake.

The Field Trial was delayed until Mrs. Howard could make a fast trip of 35 miles back to her home in Santa Cruz and return with a carsick Springer named Waiterock Hunter, a post entry to run in his first Field Trial. He placed third in Open with judges Dr. A.C. Gifford from Oshkosh, Wisconsin and Mr. Ralph White of Berkeley who placed King Lion first, making that dog the West Coast's first Dual Champion. O.W. Koeppen's Dawn of Day was second and then came the one-year-old Waiterock Hunter whose third place trophy, clutched proudly in his owner's arm, started her off "to that wonderful land of 'we'll do it next time,' plus years of hard work and fun."

From then on, Juanita Howard attempted to field train two pups out of every litter to prove her breeding program and she tried to have entries for each Field Trial (most of them were "post entries" after fast, mad rides from some distance). Most of her time during the following 14 years was spent training for field although she

Ch. Waiterock Bodkin, daughter of Am., Can. Ch. Waiterock Elmer Brown. Trained for hunting while being shown in the conformation classes and finished her championship with a "major" at the Specialty Show sponsored by the Sacramento English Springer Spaniel Club. Breeder-owner is Juanita Waite Howard.

Such a gorgeous Springer head-study! Ch. Waiterock Oak Leaf II, from a five-champion litter by Ch. Melilotus Royal Oak (National Specialty winner) ex Ch. Tahquitz Solita (Top Springer Bitch in the U.S. in 1951).

claims, "I never became proficient at the fine art of steadiness and control of my dogs for Field Trials. They were known as meat dogs but were always in there pitching." A number of trophies and placements in Field Trials kept Mrs. Howard trying in her limited time. The Pacific Cocker Spaniel Club, the English Springer Spaniel Club of Northern California and the Stockton Club, each with a Field Trial, kept up the activity.

Over the years, 21 Waiterock dogs distinguished themselves with Field Trial successes for Juanita Howard. All were owner-trained and all started in their owner's field training classes on her ranch as an extra way for her to more fully enjoy Springers.

Mrs. Howard's aims as a breeder have been to breed gun dogs true to the Standard; to breed, in the order named, for temperament, natural hunting instincts, health and soundness, mental stability (the natural willingness to please is so characteristic of the English Springer Spaniel) and conformation according to the Standard; to make selections for future breeding after five months of age; and to start the puppies' training

at four weeks of age, to train them by the positive method—praise for doing the right thing, ignoring them when they do it wrong. She does not breed for color, markings, lack of ticking, etc., nor for any of the other prevalent "fads."

Mrs. Howard likes to keep puppies until their second teeth are in, in order to frequently evaluate their growth and qualities. "Pets" are sold with "no breeding" agreements and the papers are withheld. Such agreements clearly state: "All breeding rights remain with the breeder." Puppies are gently trained prior to

Ch. Waiterock Arrow wins the Veteran's Class at the 1980 Specialty Show of the English Springer Spaniel Association of Central California. Juanita Howard, breeder-owner.

their adoption into a new family, then their further training is left in the hands of the new owner. To help accomplish her aims, Mrs. Howard has, in the past, provided field training classes once a week to people having Waiterock puppies, along with a class in home obedience and one in show training, which is about all that the most conscientious of breeders possibly can do to ascertain a good start and happy future for their puppies in new homes.

Willowbank

Willowbank Springers was started back in 1964 by Mr. and Mrs. Alexander B. Merriman of Blairstown, New Jersey with the acquisition of a lovely liver bitch, Tamridge Molly Malone, from Barbara Parker's Tamridge Kennels. Molly was a daughter of Champion Mister Tamridge of Stage Run ex Tamridge Silver Slipper, and she was retired from the ring with 10 points when it was realized that the puppies she was producing were outclassing their dam in show quality. Mrs. Merriman comments that in later years she has felt badly that they did not turn Molly over to a handler to get those "majors" along the way.

The Merrimans are very proud that all of their champions are home-bred, as indeed one in that fortunate position should be, for what could possibly be more satisfying to a dedicated breeder? Their first one to finish was Champion Willowbank's Make It Snappy, C.D., that sired 10 champions himself and was the first born puppy in the Merrimans' very first litter. He was obviously special from the beginning. The Merrimans never campaign their dogs, as they prefer to have them at home to be enjoyed. "Snapper" was shown about 12 times as a "special," and managed to win a Group and six or seven Bests of Breed during the process. A litter sister, Champion Willowbank's Easy On The Eye, also finished but was found to be dysplastic, thus was given away as a companion and spayed. Quoting Mrs. Merriman, "It was a heartbreaking lesson, and we vowed then and

Ch. Willowbank's Make It Snappy, C.D., owned by the Willowbank Springers, Mr. and Mrs. Alexander B. Merriman, Blairstown, New Jersey.

Ch. Willowbank's Hocus Pocus at eight years old, by Ch. Willowbank's Make It Snappy, C.D., ex Tamridge Cordial, a champion that finished with four "majors", owner-handled by Alex Merriman.

there to never, never, never compromise soundness with winning and glamour. We like to think our determination to maintain total honesty about our dogs' faults and virtues has made us friends. We were taking X-rays of hips long before the Orthopedic Foundation for Animals came on the scene, and because of recent developments with severe hereditary eye defects in our breed, we check all puppies' eyes prior to sale."

The Merrimans are keenly interested in maintaining the native intelligence and "birdiness" in their dogs and have successfully done so. Many puppies sold by them have been superb hunters. Obedience figures prominently in the challenges that have faced some of the Willowbank puppies in their new homes as they have been sold, and the Merrimans are gratified to hear of their successes. But most of all they take pleasure in producing liveable, lovable dogs that are good friends. Success in the show ring takes a back seat to this, in the opinion of these breeders.

In the beginning, the Merrimans extensively linebred with Tamridge, Stage Run, Cricket Hill and other long time eastern bloodlines.

Eventually, the judicious decision was reached that some careful outcrossing was needed, and with a few heartbreaks, but generally good success, several of their bitches have been bred to several of the Winacko studs sired by Champion Salilyn's Classic ex Canarch Yankee Teaparty, C.D. The titles have been completed on a number of the progeny from these breedings.

Mrs. Merriman notes that compared to some kennels that breed many litters a year and campaign their dogs vigorously, Willowbank seems like a small operation. It is especially commendable that a breeder who has raised just 30 litters (as this was written), thus averaging about two annually since the kennel began, has been so highly successful in producing correct type and dogs of quality. All of their dogs, except one, have had points put on them, handled by either Mr. or Mrs. Merriman, and several have been entirely owner-handled by them. They point with pride to Champion Willowbank's Hocus Pocus by Champion Willowbank's Make It Snappy, C.D. ex

Ch. Willowbank's Trendsetter, liver and white, taking Best of Winners at Bennington in 1978 under Mrs. Doris Wear. Owned by Willowbank Kennels, Mr. and Mrs. Alexander B. Merriman.

Ch. Willowbank's Now Hear This, by Ch. Tamridge Homestretch ex Ch. Willowbank's Simply Smashing, belongs to the Willowbank Springers, Mr. and Mrs. Alexander B. Merriman.

Tamridge Cordial that finished with four "majors," handled by Alex Merriman; to Champion Willowbank's Simply Smashing, her little sister, that finished in 10 shows, including Puppy and Bred-by Exhibitor Classes, handled by Mrs. Merriman; to Champion Willowbank's Now Hear This by Champion Tamridge Homestretch ex Champion Willowbank's Simply Smashing that was Best of Winners at a Potomac Specialty en route to the title; to Champion Willowbank's Warlock by Champion Tamridge Homestretch ex Champion Willowbank's Hocus Pocus that was also Best of Winners at a Potomac Specialty, handled by Mr. Merriman; and to Champion Willowbank's Yours Truly by Champion Willowbank's Now Hear This ex Tamridge Cordial that received her first major at nine months at her first show, handled by Mrs. Merriman, and that went on to Reserve Winners Bitch at the National Specialty. Taking time out for a litter, Yours Truly then returned to finish with a four-point "major" at the American Spaniel Club.

Ch. Willowbank's Pleasure Is Mine, C.D., one of the outstanding Springers owned by Mr. and Mrs. Alexander B. Merriman.

In addition, there is Champion Willowbank's Pleasure Is Mine, C.D., by Champion Willowbank's Warlock ex Willowbank's With Pleasure, handled by her owner, Sharon Zysk, that was the 1976 runner-up for Bitch of the Year Award from the Parent Club; and American and Canadian Champion Willowbank's Second Look by American and Canadian Champion Winacko's Classic Replay, C.D., ex Willowbank's Armar's Mirage was the 1980 runner-up for Bitch of the Year handled by her sire's owner, Kathy Lorentzen.

Champion Willowbank's Trendsetter by American and Canadian Champion Winacko's Editor's Choice, C.D., ex Champion Willowbank's Yours Truly finished at just over a year with some really super Specialty class wins, finishing with a "major" at the Meadowlands.

And of course, never to be forgotten by those who love him, "the grand old man" of Willowbank, Champion Willowbank's Make It Snappy, C.D., although no longer with the Merrimans, still continues to greet them through his many progeny with a familiar lift of the eyebrow or tilted head.

Windfall

Although a comparatively new kennel at the time that this was written, the Springer Spaniels at Windfall are based on the finest of backgrounds and would seem destined for a very bright and exciting future.

It was about 1973 when Mrs. Connie Mitchon of Springfield, Illinois, purchased her first Springer, Lady Dustin, C.D. Through love and appreciation of "Dusty," a steadily increasing interest in Springers developed, along with participation in dog shows in both obedience and conformation competition. Dusty completed her C.D. title at seven-and-one-half-years old.

Late in the 1970's, Mrs. Mitchon acquired her "dream foundation bitch" with which to embark on a breeding program of her own. This was Champion Telltale Windfall, a liver-and-white bitch purchased from Mrs. Delores Streng. Sired by Champion Filicia's Bequest ex Champion Telltale Rambling Heart, she was a granddaughter of Champion Salilyn's Classic on her sire's side and Champion Salilyn's Aristocrat through her dam.

Telltale Windfall distinguished herself in the show ring as her championship points included a "major" at the Fall 1980 Chicago International. She has taken up maternal duties with her first litter, eight males, sired by Champion Coventry's Allegro. Several of these youngsters look especially promising as they mature, so Mrs. Mitchon has high hopes for them along with enthusiastic plans for the future.

The kennel name, Windfall, was selected in honor of Champion Telltale Windfall, as she was to be the backbone of the breeding program.

Ch. Telltale Windfall en route to her title. Owned by Mrs. Connie Mitchon, Springfield, Illinois.

Right: Ch. Salilyn's Lily of the Valley, by Salilyn's Royal Consort ex Salilyn's Glenda, was whelped in April 1962 and became the dam of Ch. Salilyn's Aristocrat. Mrs. Julie Gasow, breeder-owner.

Opposite page, top: The fabulous liver-and-white Springer dog, Ch. Salilyn's Classic, here is winning one of his 39 Bests in Show, at Lafayette Kennel Club in September 1967. Dick Cooper is handling for Mrs. Julie Gasow of Troy Michigan.

Opposite page, bottom: Ch. Fortune's Judy Belle, born May 10, 1965, by Ch. Kaintuck's Vicar of Wakefield ex Ch. Fortune's Dorsue Diana of Day, bred by Dorothy Fortuna, owned by Mr. and Mrs. Robert Gough, Syosset, New York.

Below: A photo filled with greatness! Ch. Charlyle's Fair Warning, on the right, taking Best of Breed for Anne Pope, Laddie Carswell handling. Ch. Anastasia of Berclee, left, taking Best of Opposite Sex for Bernice Roe, Dorothy Callahan handling. Mrs. Julie Gasow is the judge at the Eastern English Springer Spaniel Club Specialty in 1967.

Top springer in the United States 1962, 1963, and 1964; Top Western Sporting Dog in 1962 and 1964. Am., Can. Ch. Waiterock Elmer Brown (whelped in 1956, by Ch. Waiterock Whistle ex Tahquitz Merry Mischief) is pictured at ten years of age with his owner, Mrs. Juanita Howard, Lafayette, California.

Ch. Canorwoll's Reflection, by Ch. Filicia's Anlon Patriot, Winners Bitch at Potomac Specialty and Michigan Specialty, Best of Opposite Sex at Westminster and American Spaniel Club, is another fine example of the quality produced by Anne Pope's Filicia bloodlines.

Ch. Jester's Jinjer Snap was among the Top Ten Springer bitches in both 1978 and 1979. Photographed at the Keystone Springer Specialty in 1978 by Per Axel Lindbloom, Jinjer Snap here is owner-handled by Andrea Glassford. Andrew Carey is the judge pictured.

Opposite: Ch. Homestead's Summersong, by Ch. Salilyn's Aristocrat ex Homestead's Silk and Satin, a homebred from the Homestead Kennels, Mrs. Louise Bilby, Oneida, New York. Handled by Patty Alston, handler; Don Booxbaum, judge.

BEST OF
OPPOSITE SEX

ONONDAGA
KENNEL ASSOC., INC.

KLEIN APRIL 30, 1977

131

Sunnykay's Shawn of Klaibar, shown here taking Winners Bitch at Queensboro in 1981, is owned by Michael and Barbara Hertz and Sharon Weingarten. Mrs. Arlene Thompson, judge.

Opposite: Canarch Madeira, by Ch. Canarch Robber Baron ex Chuzzlewit's Lead Story, on the way to his title for Francie Nelson, Fanfare Springers. Mrs. Anne Rogers Clark, judge.

9-12 PUPPY BITCH

WISC. ENG. SPRINGER

SPANIEL ASSOC.

MAY 3, 1981

MORRISSETTE PHOTO

KETTLE MORAINE
KENNEL CLUB
BEST IN SHOW

A RITTER PHOTO

The great Ch. Salilyn's Hallmark is pictured with his good friend and handler Dick Cooper. Mrs. Julie Gasow owns this magnificent and famous dog.

Anne Pope's Ch. Filicia's Aliden Bisket, another lovely Springer from the highly successful Filicia Kennels.

Dana Hopkins is the owner of this magnificent Springer, Ch. Danaho's Hedy Tondelayo, by Ch. Foyscroft Signed Edition ex Ch. Danaho's Ballet Russe. This is the second generation result of crossing Ch. Kaintuck Pixie and Ch. Kaintuck Tolstoy.

Ch. Filicia's Custom Maid, by Tara' Acquarius ex Ch. Filicia's Liberty Belle, from Anne Pope's Filicia Kennels. Donald Booxbaum, judge.

This is Ch. Kalyn's Command Performance, top dog at the Kalyn Springers owned by Kathryn and Lynn Freese, Burdett, New York.

Ch. Lleda's Ariana, a Specialty Show winner bred by Karen Adell Garetano, is by Ch. Duncan's Fife ex Ch. Lleda's Athena of Sunnykay; owned by Estelle Adell, Huntington, New York.

Opposite: Danaho's Salilyn Blackamoor, at five years of age in January 1981, by Ch. Salilyn's Encore ex Ch. Daniho's Ballet Russe, bred and owned by noted California Springer fancier Dana Hopkins.

BEST OF
BREED
SCHOOLEY'S MOUNTAIN
KENNEL CLUB
SEPTEMBER 1979
ASHBEY

140

A beautiful class of "specials" in the ring! George Alston, left, showing Ch. Filicia's Etching.

Opposite: Ch. Rube's Alicia of Lleda takes Best of Breed from the classes to finish her championship over four Best in Show "specials" under Michele Billings, at Schooley's Mountain Kennel Club in 1979. Owned by Estelle Adell, Alicia is by Ch. Somerset Sagas Sirius ex Ch. Lleda's Aegina of Rube.

BEST OF
BREED OR VARIETY

CAPE COD
KENNEL CLUB

1981

GILBERT PHOTO

142

Ch. Bryden's Marque on Maidenhead, a handsome Group winning Springer dog, is owned by Maidenhead Springers, Bud and Judy DiDonato of Lawrenceville, New Jersey. By Ch. Bordalyn's Behold ex Ch. Maitre's Dawn of Maidenhead.

Opposite: Ch. Filicia's Fidelis of Sulo is winning her first Best of Breed and going on to Group Third at Cape Cod Kennel Club, February 1981. Owned by Nancy S. Cowley, Woodstock, Connecticut, and handled by Linda More under judge Edith Hellerman. By Ch. Filicia's Anlon Patriot ex Ch. Filicia's Black Magic of Sulo.

Anne Pope with her beloved Ch. Kaintuck Pixie, C.D., receives the "Parade of Veterans" award at the English Springer Spaniel Field Trial Association, July 1978, from Langdon Skarda, judge of the Specialty.

144

CHAPTER FIVE

English Springer Spaniels at Westminster

Julie Gasow, Ch. King Peter of Salilyn, and New York City Mayor Robert Wagner, photographed at the Waldorf Astoria (where "no dogs are allowed") in 1954. His Honor has just presented the key to the city to King Peter, who was second in the Group at Westminster that year, then went on to win it in 1955.

The history of any breed of dog in the United States would be incomplete without some mention of what has taken place at Westminster, America's most famed and prestigious dog show for more than 100 years. Accordingly, I have checked what has happened in Springers there and I have come up with the following information to share.

Springers first appeared on the Westminster entry lists in 1921 where the lone breed entry, Beechgrove Duke, won the Miscellaneous Class over several other assorted canines. *Note*: The breed did not yet have its own classification. A Canadian dog, Duke belonged to Robert Smith of Port Hope, Ontario. There were four or five Springers entered the following year, but we have no record of how they fared; beyond that none took the first prize.

By 1923 the Springer entry had grown to 12. Five of these were from Eudore Chevrier's rapidly expanding kennel in Canada and included his great importation, Springbok of Ware; the others were Laverstoke Powder Horn, Laverstoke Powder Puff, L'lle Merle and Chastleton Belinda. The latter four, one would imagine, were brought to Westminster by their owner mainly to provide background for the mighty Springbok, which we have heard was quite a

dog. We can picture their owner's amazement when one of his Springers did turn out to be the winner—but it was Chastleton Belinda, a bitch that never completed her title! We understand that another of these Springers which created particular attention at the show was L'lle Merle, a daughter of the famed English Field Champion Rivington Sam.

In 1924, Springers had their own separate classification at Westminster and the famous English breeder, William Humphrey, was on hand to judge them. There were no "specials" classes as we know them today, at that time, and the champions competed against the non-champions on the same basis as in England. The Best of Breed was Dr. A.C. Gifford's Champion Horsford Highness, a liver-and-white daughter of English Dual Champion Horsford Hetman, imported for his Winnebago Kennels. As previously mentioned, Highness became the first member of her breed to gain a U.S.A. championship, which she completed in 1923. The Winners Dog was Donual, belonging to Emmett Randall of Jamestown, New York, that went on to gain his championship in 1926. The Reserve Winner was another destined for later titular honors, Winnebago Watchful II, again owned by Dr. Gifford.

By 1925, there was truly excellent and exciting competition in the breed here, with an entry of 66. Avandale led the entry list with 12. There were nine from Clarion Kennels (Charles Toy, owner) and four from Roycroft (G.W.G. Ferris, owner, of Franklinville, New York whose dogs principally were from Horsford strain and black-and-white in color). Other exhibitors included Mrs. Walton Ferguson, Herbert Routley and actress Margaret Drew (Mrs. Freeman Lloyd). The competition for Best of Breed must have really been something to see, as five famed champions were entered only to be defeated by a newcomer to Westminster, English Champion Boghurst Rover, the Winners Dog which took Best of Winners and Best of Breed under the judgeship of Walter Stoddard. Rover, owned by Mr. Chevrier, went on to still further glory gaining his title in both the United States and Canada. Eventually he was purchased by George Higgs from California, who named his kennel Boghurst in Rover's honor, an honor which he surely earned not only for his ring successes but as a splendid hunter and the sire of numerous winners.

Returning to Westminster 1925, the "specials" Rover had defeated there were Laverstoke Powder Horn, Horsford Harbour, Jambok of Ware, Loyal Lord and Inveresk Careful of Winnebago, all noted winners. Mrs. Ferguson gained the points in bitches with her Admaston Belle. The reserves were Langtoun Leader in dogs, owned by David P. Earle; and Marvel of Avandale, a future multiple Best in Show winner in bitches setting a record for her sex.

The entry dropped back to 40 in 1926. Champion Punch of Ruan was Best of Breed, owned by Walter S. LeFavour of New Bedford, Massachusetts, and described as a heavily ticked black-and-white excelling in neck and shoulders. He was a son of English and American Champion Horsford Harbour Punch. Shortly after Westminster he won Best in Show at his hometown event, the New Bedford Kennel Club. Canadian Champion Inveresk Cadet took the Winners Dog award back to Canada for P.S. Payne, while Winners Bitch was Mr. Routley's Trent Valley Cutie that went on to gain American and Canadian championships. Horsford Howitzer and Coleland Blackie were the respective reserves.

Mr. Chevrier had somewhat of a "clean sweep" when he came to Westminster in 1927.

English Champion L'lle Messenger Boy took Winners Dog and Best of Breed for him, and his Marvel of Avandale took Winners Bitch. The reserves were Winnebago Kennels' English Champion Southwick Don in dogs, that became a champion shortly thereafter in the United States, and Belmoss Countess in bitches, belonging to Canadian breeder Hollis Placey. Countess gained her title in 1929 and produced Westminster's 1935 Best of Breed winner. Messenger Boy lost no time in adding Canadian and American championships to his English title when shown in both countries.

Mrs. Walton Ferguson's imported dog, Champion Horsford Highlander, won Best of Breed from the classes at Westminster 1928. The judge was C.F. Neilson, who selected another import from Horsford as reserve, Champion Horsford Historical. It is interesting to note that although there were 14 bitches entered, the award for Winners Bitch was withheld, with no reason recorded.

In 1929 the decade closed with more than 30 Springers at Westminster for the opinion of Donald Fordyce, judge. Best of Breed was the noted Best in Show winner, Champion Marvel of Avandale, Mr. Chevrier's famous bitch. Willinez Bob was Winners Dog, with Clarion Gale Winners bitch from the Puppy Class. Edward Dana Knight took reserve in dogs with his Langtoun Lubricant, as did Mrs. Ferguson in bitches with Merlin Mytrust that went on to a nice career as a "special."

The thirties opened with a bang, as Springer entries increased to 53 at Westminster with the entries truly having come from far and wide. Walter Stoddard judged, selecting English Champion Nuthill Dignity for Best of Breed. Ernest Leffingwell of California owned this magnificent Springer by English Champion Andon of Leam ex English Champion Banchory Tranquil. A new award just added this year was Best of Opposite Sex, this going to Champion Lilac Wonder, another from Mr. Leffingwell's kennel. The trip East was no doubt a very worthwhile one for this gentleman.

It was Vale of Burnside who took the Garden Best of Breed in 1931 for W.C. Burns of Canada. This lovely bitch was entered in both Limit (a class since dropped) and Open, which she won en route to Winners Bitch and the eventual top award. Mr. Vale's kennel was located in Sidney, British Columbia and was active from the early to mid-1930's. Clarion Rufton Ruler was Winners Dog, one of the four Springers Charles Toy had imported from Robert Cornthwaite in England.

The Honorable Townsend Scudder, whose opinion was so highly respected in the Sporting Dog world, judged 41 entries at the 1932 Westminster Show. Mrs. C.K. Jackson of Santa Barbara, California turned out full force with her Blue Leader dogs, and when it was all over she had taken Best of Breed and a Group four with her American and Canadian Champion Norman of Hamsey, Winners Dog with Carlos Cavalier and Winners Bitch and Best of Winners with Inveresk Comfort. So far as I can see, Norman's Group placement was the first ever for a Springer at Westminster, and he really put the frosting on the cake when he returned in 1933 to win first in the Sporting Group—a real breakthrough for Springers at this prestigious show.

On the latter occasion, the Springer judge was the well known breeder Mrs. E.A. Sturdee, who lost no time in making Norman of Hansey the Best of Breed again. This time, in '33, there were 56 entries. Norman was handled superbly by Ben Brown and made many fanciers "Springer conscious" by his beautiful performance in the Group ring, which I personally recall watching. English Champion Advert of Solway was Winners Dog, while Winners Bitch was taken by Maggie of Abilene, bred by Dr. Miller but owned by Blue Leader. Chauncey Stillman had Kenridge Gunner entered, taking Reserve Dog with him.

Donald Fordyce did a return engagement judging Westminster Springers in 1934. Mr. and Mrs. Fred Hunt had an excellent win with their bitch, Linwhinney Crowle, a Rufton Recorder daughter, taking the purple in her sex. Kenridge Gunner was Winners Dog, a grandson of Dual Champion Tedwyn's Trex, then went on to Best of Winners and Best of Breed over a galaxy of champions in for "specials."

Westminster 1935 was noteworthy for its judge, William L. McClandish, who was Chairman of the Kennel Club in England and who had judged here at the 1930 Fisher's Island Field Trials. He drew an entry of 60 and intrigued the onlookers by demanding that the dogs be shown in the British fashion on the end of a loose lead. Edward Dana Knight's dog, White Knight, by Champion Pat of Abilene ex Champion Belmoss Countess, a home-bred from his Tuscawilla

Kennels, went from Winners Dog to Best of Breed, scoring (as was happening so frequently in Springers from the classes at Westminster) over a strong group of champions which competed for "specials." Winners Bitch was Bill Bailey's Hope. The reserves were Duke of Kent of Menhall Farm, owned by James Menhall of Wisconsin; and Worthen Suspense of Millstream, an import belonging to Mrs. Erwin R. Hilts of Greenwich, Connecticut.

Ed Knight switched from exhibitor to judge at the 1936 Westminster show and drew 62 dogs. Dual Champion Fast, winner of a keenly contested Field Trial Class, staged a hard fought contest for the Best of Breed award with the Canadian-bred bitch, Champion Quantock Beauty owned by Fred Hadley of Ohio. Fast finally came away the winner for Mrs. W.A.M. Morin, with Beauty taking Best of Opposite Sex. Winners Dog was the American-bred Bozo's Bar Mate owned by Rowcliffe Kennels (a future Dual Champion). Bud Lewis from California took Reserve Dog with his Clipfort Press Agent, a future Best in Show winner. There were no bitch awards from the classes noted.

By 1937 the Westminster Springer entry had climbed to 70 for Canadian judge William Pym. George Thorsby of St. Charles, Michigan took Winners Dog, Best of Winners, and Best of Breed over a strong lot of "specials" with his Thorsdale Fidelis. Mr. Thorsby was a respected breeder with a number of home-bred champions to his credit. Winners Bitch was Worthen

Ch. King Peter of Salilyn at 10 months old winning a Sporting Group for Mrs. Julie Gasow, Troy, Michigan.

147

Suspense of Millstream, dam of the puppy (by Dual Champion Fast) that had gone Reserve Dog. Reserve Bitch was Mrs. Gould's Berlu Beauty from Detroit.

There were 71 Springers in 1938, judged by David Wagstaff. Some very prestigious names were among the exhibitors, such as Mrs. Janet Henneberry who took the breed with her handsome black-and-white dog, American and Canadian Champion Dunoon Donald Dhu; Mr. and Mrs. Joseph C. Quirk who had Winners Dog with their imported Rufton Roberto of Greenfair; Henry Ferguson, who took Winners Bitch and Best of Winners with Faith of Falcon Hill; Clarion Kennels with Clarion Torch; and Reginald Lewis with Green Valley Holly, the respective reserves.

Mrs. A.R. Moffit judged Westminster Springers in 1939, taking Colonel of Audley, bred by Robert Morrow and owned by T. Norman Morrow, to Best of Breed from the classes. Donna Jean of Wampee was Winners Bitch for Mr. and Mrs. Lathrop Hopkins, with Reserve Dog, Well Sweep Kennels' Punchford Pete, and Reserve Bitch, Mr. Lewis's Green Valley Holly.

The 1940's started out for Westminster Springers with Ed Knight again on the woolsack, and the appearance of a destined-to-become-immortal in the Springer world: English, Canadian and American Champion Showman of Shotton owned by Mr. and Mrs. Paul Quay of Chagrin Valley, Ohio and handled by Billy Lang. Bowing only to Champion My Own Brucie, the American Cocker that went on to Best in Show, Shotton wound up second in a thrilling Sporting Group. Later he became a very famous Best in Show winner during a spectacular career. Fred Jackson's Frejax Woodelf Recordson was Winners Dog and Best of Winners while Mrs. C. Willmott's Cliffmar Countess won in bitches. Reserves went to Green Valley The Feudist and Greenfair Sue.

At Westminster 1941, with Atha Whitaker judging, it was Frejax Fire Flash from the classes who went Best of Breed while a kennelmate, Frejax's Showman's luck (a Showman of Shotton daughter) was Winners Bitch. Mr. and Mrs. Joseph C. Quirk had both of the reserves that day with Stingo of Shotton of Greenfair in dogs and Greenfair's April in bitches.

One of the truly great moments in Springer history is pictured here as Ch. Wakefield's Black Knight becomes the first of his breed ever to gain Best in Show at the Westminster Kennel Club event. Laddie Carswell handled this important and famous dog for Mrs. W.J.S. Borie.

Ch. King Peter of Salilyn, Best of Breed en route to Group First, handled by Dick Cooper for Mrs. Julie Gasow. Westminster 1955.

A brilliant Springer year at "the Garden" to remember was 1942 when a beautiful-moving, mostly white bitch with liver ticking won the nod from two such esteemed authorities as Joseph C. Quirk, who was judging the breed, and Dr. Samuel Milbank officiating in the Sporting Group, to become Best Sporting Dog at Westminster that year. She was Champion Timpanogo's Melinda, owned by R.E. Allen and handled by Harry Sangster, sired by English, American and Canadian Champion Showman of Shotton ex Champion Timpanogo's Belle; and the Winners Dog was Mr. Allen's Timpanogo's Squanto, bred from the same parents as Melinda. Timpanogo was a kennel located in Provo, Utah with a highly respected breeding record for dual purpose dogs. One of them Champion Timpanogo's Adonis, who with his brother Champion Timpanogo's Radar, won well here and was exported to Sweden, where he is credited with having been a fine influence as a stud dog. Back at the Westminster ring, a Showman of Shotton son, Champion Hellzapoppin, was Best of Opposite Sex for co-owners Fred Hadley and Ed Knight, while the Winners Bitch was Scamp's Hollywood Belle owned by G.C. Staber

of California. Reserves were Mrs. C.S. Hutchinson's Frejax Gay Cavalier in dogs and T. Mertes' Leading Lady of Caulier's in bitches.

It was a somewhat small entry that turned out for W.A. Price at Westminster 1943. A very notable dog, Champion Eldgyth Apollo, "star" of Ralph Rubinger's Greenhaven Kennels in Rye, New York, accounted for the Best of Breed there. Mr. and Mrs. Quirk had Best of Opposite Sex with Champion Greenfair's April, along with Best of Winners with another of their bitches, Greenfair's Easter Day.

In 1944, it was another dog bearing the Eldgyth prefix that gained Best of Breed at Westminster, Champion Eldgyth Adonis, belonging to W.E. Belleville. Champion Greenfair's April repeated her previous year's Best of Opposite Sex for Phyllis and Joe Quirk. Winners Dog was Silver Creek El Gee Marvo belonging to Leo Groombridge of Ontario. Winners Bitch was Kencia's Lorna owned by E.K. Lopeman. Two Springers that became notable dogs later on were the reserves at this show, Mrs. William McKelvy's Rumak's King Cole and Mrs. R. Gilman Smith's Tranquillity of Melilotus, that matured into Best in Show winners.

149

Another Westminster Best of Breed for Mrs. Gasow's Ch. Salilyn's King Peter, again Dick Cooper handling.

Champion Co-Pilot of Sandblown Acres, owned by W.E. Belleville, was Best Springer at Westminster 1945 under judge Fred Hunt. Sandblown Acres was established in the late 1930's by Mr. Belleville, who was the plant geneticist for Campbell Tomato Farms in the Riverton, New Jersey area during this period. Tranquillity of Melilotus was Winners Bitch, Best of Winners and Best of Opposite Sex this time for Mrs. Gilman Smith. Winners Dog was Wishihadadagal, owned by Fred Hadley and Ed Knight. Robert Walgate's black-and-white Walpride Sandeman was reserve in dogs and Robert Morrow's Audley Farm Windem was Reserve Bitch.

Ray Beale had an entry of 56 assembled for his judgment at Westminster 1946, where his principal winner was Champion Sir Robert of Happy Hunting over a large class of "specials" for Mr. and Mrs. Kenneth Kirtland. Champion Tranquillity of Melilotus was Best of Opposite Sex, Walpride Sandeman was Winners Dog and Victory Girl of Caulier took the bitch points and

Best of Winners. In Reserves, the dog was one of particular interest, since this was the first occasion that Mrs. Julie Gasow's name appeared in "the Garden" award columns, this time with her future "great," Sir Lancelot of Salilyn. Reserve Bitch was another Caulier entry, Charm of Caulier.

Champion Rumak's King Cole gained Westminster's 1947 Best of Breed award for Mrs. William McKelvy, under judge Mildred Imrie. Mrs. McKelvy was a breeder from the Pittsburgh area whose Rumak Springers made some fine records from the early 1940's until their owner's death in 1961. King Cole was a handsome contender at leading dog shows and was a liver-and-white product of Mr. Caulier's breeding. He was a consistent victor in Sporting Group and Best in Show competition as was his lovely son, Champion Sir Thomas of Rumak, the latter having three Eastern Specialties to his credit along with five Bests in Show at all-breed events. Mrs. Imrie selected the Quirks' Champion Greenfair Easter Day for Best of Opposite

Sex, and Mrs. Janet Henneberry garnered the points in both dogs and bitches with the littermates Donniedhu's G.I. Joe and Donniedhu's G.I. Jane to take home to her Illinois kennel. Mrs. Henneberry was a talented and respected breeder, probably best known for her American and Canadian Champion Dunoon Donald Dhu, a dog of Canadian breeding in whose honor his kennel was named.

In 1948, Champion Frejax Royal Salute led 45 entries under Clyde Heck's judging, then thrilled the Springer fans by taking first in a quality Sporting Group. Winners Dog was Mrs. McKelvy's Champion Sir Thomas of Rumak, while Winners Bitch was Mrs. W.W. Elder's Maquam's Gay Lady. The Elders maintained a large and busy kennel in Gladstone, New Jersey where a goodly number of lovely Springers were produced. Mrs. McKelvy also took Best of Opposite Sex with her Champion Pall Mall of Rumak.

Closing out another decade, 1949 saw Champion Frejax Royal Salute repeat the previous year's victory in the breed but this time as second in the Group. Winners Dog was Gordon Paton's Skyline Fast, Winners Bitch and Best of Opposite Sex was taken by W.E. MacKinney's Gypsy Maid and Reserves were Robert Walberg's Warpride Sir Accolon in dogs and Mrs. Smith's Melilotus Woodelf in bitches.

Twelve champions for "specials" were among the 42 Springers greeting Paul Quay when he officiated at the 1950 Westminster, from which he chose Champion Runor's Agent, owned by his breeder, Norman Morrow. Agent was a son of English, American and Canadian Champion Showman of Shotton ex Champion Audley Farms Judy, the Morrows' foundation bitch and the dam of 12 champions. This kennel was located in Avon, Connecticut and in addition to Agent the Morrows' owned numerous other winners in both bench shows and licensed trials, including some 20 champions. Winners Dog went to the future Best in Show dog, Lymburner's Covington Nim-Beau, that became a Canadian Best in Show dog. Winners Bitch, Best of Winners and Best of Opposite Sex were taken by Mrs. Henneberry's Donniedhu's Gypsy. This was the show debut of Mrs. Gilman Smith's two youngsters, Prince Charlie of Melilotus and Melilotus Royal Oak as a brace, and they won the Brace Class with little effort.

Mrs. Julie Gasow won her first Westminster Best of Breed in 1951, Fred Jackson judging, with Champion King Peter of Salilyn who later went on to second in the Group. Mrs. Smith's Prince Charlie of Melilotus was Best of Winners and Mrs. Henneberry's Charlyle's Royal Heiress was Winners Bitch. And Champion Donniedhu Gypsy, returning as a "special," repeated the previous year's Best of Opposite Sex.

Champion Melilotus Royal Oak took the Best of Breed from Clyde Heck at Westminster 1952 for Mrs. Gilman Smith. Best of Opposite Sex went to Mrs. Elder's Champion Maquam's Singing Star. Best of Winners went to the dog, Timpanogo's Ramon belonging to R.E. Allen, while the purple in bitches went to Dr. Andrew Klembara's Frejax Progress.

In 1953, Mrs. Joseph Quirk was on the Westminster Springer assignment of 31 entries. Best of Breed was Champion Wilmar's Whirlaway owned by Mrs. J.P. Barthold; Best of Opposite Sex was Mrs. R. Gilman Smith's Champion Melilotus Barbary Ann; Winners Dog, Seymour Roberts' Pen Bet Lee's Bonnivery; and Winners Bitch, Wilbur Amand's Amand's Black Magic.

On this historic occasion, Ch. Melilotus Royal Oak is winning his first Best in Show (at Longshore-Southport Kennel Club, June 1952). Tom Gately is handling for Mrs. R. Gilman Smith, now Mrs. Frederick D. Brown. This magnificent dog, a son of Ch. Frejax Royal Salute and Ch. Tranquility of Melilotus, also was the first Springer to win Best in Show at the American Spaniel Club Specialty.

152

The Veteran's Class at the Eastern English Springer Spaniel Specialty, June 25, 1960. Left to right: Norm Morrow with Ch. Runor's Agent, age 14; Gilman Smith with Ch. Melilotus Royal Oak, age 11; Ruth Williams with Ch. Prince Charlie of Melilotus, age 11; Bea Smith with Ch. Melilotus Barbary Ann, age 10; Herbert Schwerdle with Ch. Melilotus Lucky Star, age 10; Art Beaman with Ch. Melilotus Emily Gray, age 9; Elsie Matson with Ch. Melilotus Star of Pequa, age 7; and Laddie Carswell with Ch. Barrowdale Lady B, age 7. This fascinating photo was loaned to us by Mrs. Frederick D. Brown.

Entries seemed to slide downwards for Springers at Westminster during this period with only 27 for the 1954 event. Mrs. Julie Gasow's Champion King Peter of Salilyn returned to again take Best of Breed, repeating his 1951 success, this time under judge Ray Beale. Mrs. Elder's Maquam's Forty Niner was Winners Dog and Best of Winners. Winners Bitch and Best of Opposite Sex went to Mr. and Mrs. Albert Matson's Melilotus Star of Pequa, a young bitch representing a kennel which has flourished as a "family project" through the Matsons and their youngsters. Incidentally, Mr. and Mrs. Matson are the parents of Patty Matson Alston, a highly successful Springer breeder of the present day.

Champion King Peter of Salilyn won his third Westminster Best of Breed and an exciting first in the Sporting Group in 1955 under Paul Quay. Gordon Paton had Winners Dog with Bobbru's Barnstormer. Dr. Klembara had Winners Bitch with Frejax Progress. Best of Opposite Sex was Mrs. Richard Hopper's Champion Sunhi's Spray O'Hara.

Champion Royal Duke of Rexford scored for Best of Breed at Westminster 1956 under Clyde Heck in an entry of 35. Owned by Mr. and Mrs. Vincent Paul, this widely admired dog was on

Ch. Royal Duke of Rexford (Ch. Barblythe Top Tune ex Ch. Princess Victoria of Rexford), a stunning homebred owned by Mr. and Mrs. Vincent J. Paul, Brentwood, California. Duke was a Best in Show winner, won Best of Breed at Westminster in 1956, and here is winning Best of Breed at the English Springer Spaniel Club of Southern California Specialty in 1957, handled by Ben Brown. Photo courtesy of Dana Hopkins.

from Los Angeles. Best of Opposite Sex was Samuel Helfand's Champion Frejax Royal Maggie. Winners Dog, en route to his title, was the great youngster, Salilyn's Macduff owned by Mrs. Julie Gasow. Winners Bitch, from Canada, was Covington Spring Song owned by Mrs. Lilah Lymburner.

Returning in 1957 as a "special" to Westminster in an entry of 24, Champion Salilyn's Macduff took the breed from Atha Whitaker. James Forbes had Best of Opposite Sex in Champion Borrowdale's Lady B. Winners Dog and Best of Winners was Leonard Greenwald's Ascot's Ajax while Winners Bitch was Mrs. Placide Smyth's Bobbru's Blazing Star. Leonard Greenwald, by the way, is the owner of Ascot Springers and is still an active judge of the breed today. Based on Runor foundation stock, this gentleman bred at least 15 bench champions at his well known kennel in Connecticut.

Dr. Andrew Klembara stepped into the role of judge at the 1958 Westminster, where Miss Mary McCune took Best of Breed with Champion Covington Free Lance Reporter and where Best of Opposite Sex was the Winners Bitch, Alice Herweg's Elk Grove's Top Flight. Best of Winners went to Fred Jackson with Frejax Royalist Flash.

In 1959 it was Champion Kaintuck Christmas Carol taking the Westminster Best of Breed ribbon for Stuart Johnson under Dr. Joseph E. Redden. Leonard Greenwald had Winners Dog and Best of Winners in Ascot's Horatio At, while Peter Maher's Cartref Merri-O took Winners Bitch and Best of Opposite Sex.

Clyde Heck, judging his fifth Westminster Springer assignment in 1960, drew 40 entries this time, among which the winner was Champion Salilyn's Macduff for his owners (at that time) Mr. and Mrs. William Randall from Chicago. Leonard Greenwald had Winners Bitch and Best of Opposite Sex with Ascot's Maid of Honor and Winners Dog and Best of Winners was Mrs. R. Gilman Smith's imported Rostherne Hunter.

In 1961 Champion Blairshinnoch John O' Groats was Westminster's Best Springer under judge Dr. Elder; James Forbes was the owner of this dog. Leonard Greenwald's Champion Ascot Scarlet O was Best of Opposite Sex. Winners Dog went to Bernardine Tucker's Legand's Baron Blennerhasset. Winners Bitch was Mary McCune's Montour Tadg.

A picture filled with dog show history! The three Junior Handlers are Patty Matson Alston with the Springer, who took first prize. Bob Harris is with the Boxer, and Bethny Hall Mason with the English Setter. John P. Murphy, is the judge at the rear right, and in the center rear is Clint Callahan. All these very famous people in the fancy are shown at the Westminster Kennel Club, February 1957.

In 1962 it happened. The event eagerly awaited by Springer lovers throughout the United States was that first occasion on which a member of the breed scored the breakthrough to take Best in Show at this mightiest of dog shows. It was Champion Wakefield's Black Knight that did it, owned by Mrs. W.J.S. Borie and handled by Laddie Carswell. To make it all the more exciting, Black Knight was a home-bred by Champion Kaintuck Christmas Carol from the Bories' foundation bitch, a daughter of Champion Melilotus Royal Oak. Clark Thompson had been the breed judge, Fred Hunt had done the Group and Virgil Johnson did Best in Show, certainly a trio of Sporting Dog experts who made the victory especially satisfying. Best of Opposite Sex Springer was Mary Carey's Champion Shamrock's Black Pepper. The points went to Hubert Schwerdtle with Spring Hill's North Star in dogs (also Best of Winners) and Seymour

Roberts' Quonset Laurie in bitches.

A son of Black Knight, Champion Wakefield's Sir Galahad, was Best of Breed at Westminster 1963 under Mrs. R. Gilman Smith for Mrs. Borie; Wakefield's Bobby of Rabbit Run took Winners Dog for Mrs. Lloyd Reeves; The First Lady of Rodleigh was Winners Bitch and Best of Opposite Sex for Mrs. Roger Batchelder; and the Reserves were Carol Suder's Wodehouse of Richmond in dogs and Leonard Greenwald's Ascot's Miranda in bitches.

Vivian Diffendaffer's Champion Debonair Dandy was selected by Reed Hankwitz as Best of Breed at the 1965 Westminster show in an entry of 31. Arthur Westlund's Salilyn's Celestial Lady was Winners Bitch and Best of Opposite Sex while Lawrence Commiso's Marquis Richmond was Winners Dog. Reserves were Helen Romig's Sable Knight of Romig in dogs and M.A. and E.C. Gies' Andronicus Hecate in bitches.

Left: Ch. Randhaven's Lleda Sue, by Ch. Mister Tamridge of Stage Run ex Ch. Daphne of Recess, bred by owner Karen Adell, was Best of Opposite Sex at the Eastern English Springer Spaniel Futurity in 1968 and Winners Bitch that same year at the Chicago International.

Opposite page, top: Keystone English Springer Spaniel Club Specialty, Trenton 1968. Ch. Kaintuck Tolstoy, left, at 10 months, is going Best in Show and Ch. Wakefield Deborah is Best of Opposite Sex. Photo courtesy of Anne Pope. Tolstoy is owned by Anne Pope and Stuart H. Johnson; Deborah is owned by Martha Borie.

Opposite page, bottom: Ch. Tracy's Ebony Prince, black and white, by Ch. Charlyle's Fair Warning ex Starfoot Seneca Filly, owned and bred by Barbara Buesing, Parsippany, New Jersey, taking Winners Dog under Ted Gunderson.

Below: A dynasty of outstanding producing Springer bitches. Left to right, Ch. Syringa Sue; her daughter, Ch. Fortune's Lucky Penny; Penny's daughter, Ch. Dorsue Diana of Day; and Diana's daughter, Ch. Sea Witch. Syringa Sue was owned by Dorothy and Jim Fortuna, of Fortune's Springers, who also owned the granddaughter, Ch. Dorsue Diana of Day. Lucky Penny belonged to Jeanne C. Dayton of Day's Springers. Sea Witch was owned by Helen Shambaugh. Diana, bred to Ch. Kaintuck Vicar of Wakefield, really hit the jackpot when she earned Brood Bitch of the Year as the dam of the litter which included Ch. Sea Witch (dam of Ch. Dot's It of Mar-Len, a Group and Best of Breed winner that was runner up bitch of the year), Ch. Fortune's Charlie (sire of numerous champions), Ch. Kaintuck's Fortune's Huntress, and Ch. Fortune's Judy Belle. Our thanks to Dorothy Callahan for providing this historic photograph so it could be reproduced here.

157

Champion Salilyn's Aristocrat, then only little more than a puppy, scored a rousing Best of Breed in 34 entries at Westminster 1966 for Julie Gasow under Lee Murray. Best of Opposite Sex was the bitch, Champion Ascot's Etching, for Bernice Roe and Leah L. Douglas. Welcome Thunderlord Littee was Winners Dog and Best of Winners for Herbert and Maxine Wilkes, while Mary Costello took Winners Bitch with Ring A Ding's Lady Gwenivere. Mrs. Romig's Knight of Romig and W.B. Franklin's Richline Starlite were the Reserves.

It was Aristocrat again in 1967 under the Australian judge Leonard de Groen, and he went on to add the Sporting Group to his Westminster successes, the latter judged by Gordon Parham. Champion Ascot's Almond was Best of Opposite Sex and the point winners were Lonna Fargo's Readyset of Far Rae and Louise Harris' Honors Baby Polka Dot.

Aristocrat's third consecutive Best of Breed win at Westminster 1968 enabled him go on to second in the Sporting Group. Fred Hunt was again the judge, and he found his Best of Opposite Sex in Stuart Johnson's Champion Kaintuck Pixie later owned by Anne Pope. Leonard Greenwald, keeping up his consistent West-

At the Westminster Kennel Club, February 1969 is winner of first in the Sporting Group, Am., Can. Ch. Magill's Patrick, C.D., W.D.X., bred and owned by Wayne and Phyllis Magill of Kent, Washington.

minster successes, took Winners Dog with Ascot's Insurgent. Mrs. Borie's Wakefield Deborah was Winners Bitch. Reserves went to Raymond Sullivan with Ramar's First Try in dogs and Bernice Roe with Anastasia of Berclee in bitches.

The year 1969 was a double-barreled Westminster as this was the first time the show had taken place at the present Madison Square Garden, and a raging blizzard caused a very large portion of the entry to be absent. In the case of Springers, nine of the 23 failed to appear. Virgil Johnson judged with the following results: Champion Magill's Patrick, all the way from the state of Washington, was Best of Breed for owner Wayne Magill, then added frosting to the cake when he took the Sporting Group under Fred Hunt. Patrick was a son of Champion Geiger's Chief Geronimo ex Cindy's Delight. Lillian and Robert Gough had Winners Dog with Tara's Sovereign. Harold Hall had Winners Bitch with Starfoot Seneca's Gypsy. Best of Opposite Sex went to Bernice Roe's Champion Anastasia of Berclee that had been Reserve Winners Bitch the previous year.

The decade of the 1970's opened with Mrs. R. Gilman Smith on the Westminster woolsack, finding her Best of Breed in a liver-and-white dog, Champion Richmond's Hustler, by Champion Pommie's Black Ramrod out of Champion Richmond's Donna Dee, a home-bred owned by

Ch. Kaintuck Pixie taking Best of Opposite Sex at Westminster 1968. Anne Pope, owner-handler.

Mrs. James S. Wilschke of Illinois. Winners Dog was Elizabeth Clark's Salilyn's Tennessee Squire; Winners Bitch, Georgia Hobbs' Carey's Christmas Star. Mary Ellen Bates had the Best of Opposite Sex to Best of Breed in her Champion Charlyle's Fair Warning's daughter, Dot's It of Mar Len.

The year it happened was 1971; the one in which for the second time, and the first time in eight years, a Springer went Best in Show at Westminster. On this occasion it was a three year old from Lexington, Kentucky, Champion Chinoe's Adamant James, owned by Dr. Milton E. Prickett, bred by Ann H. Roberts, and handled by Mrs. Robert's brother, Clint Harris. Excitement was high in the Springer Fancy that night and even higher and more jubilant the *following* year when "D.J." returned to the Westminster Best in Show ring and again came away the victor, making him one of only several dogs ever to have repeated a Westminster Best in Show.

The Springer judge for 1971 was Joe Tacker, the Group was done by Virgil D. Johnson and Best in Show by O.C. Harriman. Other Springers entered for "specials" there were:

Ch. Dot's It of Mar-Len winning the Sporting Group at the Plainfield Kennel Club in 1970. By Ch. Charlyle's Fair Warning ex Ch. Sea Witch, this lovely bitch was the dam of Ch. Mar-Len's Mr. It of Romig and Ch. Short Acres Ariel.

To become a champion, Salilyn's Aristocrat took Winners Dog from the Puppy Class, then Best of Breed over seven champions including his sire, entered in "specials," to Group First, all at only nine months of age. This event was prophetic of the many exciting ring successes which in the future would continue coming to him. Breeder-owner is Mrs. Julie Gasow, Troy, Michigan.

PROGRESSIVE DOG
OF WAYNE COUNTY, INC.
APRIL 30, 1966
FIRST IN
SPORTING GROUP
JUDGE: MR.
LEE E. MURRAY

Champion Kaintuck's Heir Apparent, co-owned by D. Lawrence Carswell and Mrs. W.J.S. Borie, by Champion Kaintuck Tolstoy ex Champion Ring A Ding's Lady Gwenivere; C.D. Champion Silvershoe Spring Hill Mark by Champion Inchidony Prince Charming ex Champion Spring Hill's Ring A Rosy, owned by Elizabeth B. Schwerdtle; Champion Salilyn's Paramount, by champion Canarch Inchidony Sparkler ex Salilyn's Constellation, owned by Gary E. Engle handled by Dorothy Callahan; Champion Oaktree's Lancashire Poacher, by Oaktree's Drunken Piper ex Salilyn's Kissin Cousin, owned by Mrs. Anne E. Snelling, handled by William Trainor; Champion Starfoot Seneca Gypsy, C.D., by Champion Filicia's Uncle Tom ex Wakefield's Gin Fizz, C.D., owned by Harold L. Hall; Champion Salilyn's Tennessee Squire, by Champion Salilyn's Colonel's Overlord ex Champion Salilyn's Something Special, owned by Elizabeth D. Clark and handled by Bobby B. Barlow; Champion Salilyn's Sophistication, by Champion Salilyn's Aristocrat ex Champion Salilyn's Radiance, owned by Mrs. F.H. Gasow; Champion Anastasia of Berclee, by Champion Charlyle's Fair Warning ex Champion Flaming Ember of Berclee, owned by Bernice C. Roe and handled by Albert Kirby; Champion Ascot's Insurgent, by Champion Ascot's Emperor Jones ex Ascot's Vanilla, owned by George Danis, M.D. and handled by Jeanne Millet; Champion Salilyn's

Ch. Anastasia of Berclee, owned by Bernice C. Roe, is pictured taking Winners Bitch at the Eastern English Springer Specialty in June 1965, Dorothy Callahan handling. Mrs. R. Gilman Smith is the judge.

Colonel's Overlord, by Champion Salilyn's Aristocrat ex Champion Salilyn's Radiance, owned by Forrest Andrews and Julie Gasow and handled by Dick Cooper; and Champion Willowbank's Make It Snappy, by Champion Stage Run Native Son ex Tamridge Molly Malone, owned by Julia T. Merryman.

For his 1972 Westminster Best in Show, "D.J." gained the approval in the breed of Mrs. Julie Gasow, in the Sporting Group of Lee Murray and in Best in Show of William Brainard. On this occasion the Springer entry numbered just over 40. Several of the previous year's "specials" returned, among them Champion Oaktree's Lancashire Poacher, Champion Salilyn's Tennessee Squire, Champion Salilyn's Paramount, Champion Kaintuck's Heir Apparent and Champion Starfoot Seneca Gypsy, C.D.

The following entries also were added: Champion Marjon's Sweet Cassia by Champion Salilyn's Aristocrat ex Champion Marjon's Spice N Rice, owned by Peggy and Vern Johnson, handled by Corky Vroom; Champion Filicia's Coronation by Champion Filicia's Matinee Idol ex Champion Kaintuck's Pixie, owned by Anne Pope; Champion Canarch Fielder's Choice by Champion Salilyn's Aristocrat ex Canarch Paddock, C.D., owned by Dennis Calahan and Donald R. Snyder; Mt. Ascutney's Duchess of Snow by Champion Tamridge Homestretch ex Champion Ascot's Almond, owned by Douglas Heavisides, handled by Dorothy Briggs; Colonel's Shinfane Warlock by Champion Salilyn's Aristocrat ex Champion Salilyn's Radiance, owned by Patricia L. Grant; Filicia's Monarch by Champion Filicia's

Matinee Idol ex Champion Kaintuck's Pixie, owned by Lillian Gough; Verone's Marco Polo by Salilyn's Morning Breeze II ex Salilyn's Dolly Vernon, W. Westlake, owner, Ronald Pemberton, handler; Champion Dell's Freckled Fair by Champion Charlyle's Fair Warning ex Champion Dolly of Wakefield, Albert Della Porta, owner, Paul Edwards, handler; Champion Fortune's Regina by Champion Beryltown Virginian of Pequa ex Champion Fortune's Dorsu Diana of Day, owned by Dorothy and James Fortuna, handled by Dorothy Callahan; Champion Pequa's My Goodness Gracious by Champion Beryltown Virginian of Pequa ex Champion Another Star of Pequa, owned by Linda and Raymond Beyrer; Champion Pembroke Inchidony Scot, C.D. by Champion Inchidony Prince Charming ex Champion Phyliss Duchess of Pembroke, C.D., owned by Alice Berd and Donald Robb; Champion Salilyn's Encore by Champion Salilyn's Colonel Overlord ex Champion Salilyn's Something Special, owned by Robert Pryor and Variell Atkins; Champion Beryltown Lively Chatter, C.D.X. by Cham-

pion Inchidony Prince Charming ex Champion Beryltown Lively Rocket, C.D., owned by Debbie Kirk; Champion Salilyn's Zorro by Champion Salilyn's Paramount ex Champion Salilyn's Sophistication, owned by Ted M. Akin, handled by Dick Cooper; and Champion Ramegate's Scotch Mist by Champion Inchidony Prince Charming ex Delledo Merry Mark, owned by Mr. and Mrs. Richard Mau, handled by Jack Funk.

Mrs. James Warwick judged the Westminster Springers in 1973, drawing 49 of them, nearly half of which were "specials." Many of these had competed here previously, but additionally there were: Eli and Frances Franco's Champion El Ray's Reina of Whitney by Champion Salilyn's Aristocrat ex Champion Anglodale's Mocha Amulet, handled by Walt Shellenbarger; Constance C. and James H. Schuman's Champion Canarch Robber Baron by Champion Salilyn's Aristocrat ex Champion Canarch Sunnyside, C.D.; Barbara Gamache's Champion Venetian Count Ducat, C.D. by Champion Inchidony Prince Charming ex Champion

Ch. Rostherne Hunter, owned by Mrs. Frederick D. Brown, was imported from England by Melilotus Kennels. He is pictured here, handled by Ruth Williams, winning the Eastern English Springer Spaniel Specialty in 1962.

Ch. Kaintuck Pixie, pictured here at the age of 16 years, looks at us with a smile. Owned by Anne Pope, Filicia Springers.

161

Nobility's Venetian Dawn, U.D.; Earl Taisey's Champion El Taro's Scotch Flag by Champion Salilyn's Signature ex Champion Beryltown Gingersnap of Taro, C.D., handled by George Alston; Edward and Lillian Stapp's Champion Loresta's Storm King by Champion Salilyn's Aristocrat ex Champion Loresta's Lady Cynthia, Ray McGinnis, handler; Gary and Mary Engle's Champion Kirklyn's Firewater by Champion Salilyn's Aristocrat ex Champion Nobility's Patent Pending; Lawrence Koval's and Mary Jane Engle's Highcliffe's Tamalove by Champion Salilyn's Paramount ex Wakefield's Burgundy Sass; Connie J. Reikhoff's Champion Loujon Potter's Wheel by Champion Salilyn's Captain's Table ex Loujon Spinning Jenny; H. William Hoffman's Champion Chatham's Duke of Huntington by Champion Charlyle's Captain Brown ex Chatham's Pixie of Wakefield, Dorothy Callahan, handler; and Billy D. Evans' and Marshall Comerer, Jr.'s Champion Devan's Fitzpatrick by Champion Beaujeau Renown ex Champion Salilyn's Nancy II. Among the other "specials" that year, Susan Marx and Arlene M. Thompson (Mrs. Sid Marx and Mrs. Clark Thompson) had Champion Wingdale's Snow Prince by Champion Canarch Inchidony Sparkler ex Spring Hill's Glamour. Juanita Howard's Champion Waiterock Bodkin was entered, and we note that Mark Threlfall and Susan Matson had Champion Pequa Checkmate by Champion Fortune's Terrible Ted of Lleda ex Hoosier Star of Pequa. Julie Gasow had Aristocrat and Classic, and with Barbara Gates, Salilyn's Vanguard.

What a lot of Springer history this photo covers, taken at the English Springer Spaniel Field Trial Association National Specialty in 1973. On the left, Ch. Salilyn's Aristocrat, bred and owned by Mrs. Julie Gasow, received the award as Best Stud Dog in a class of eight with his son, Ch. Chinoe's Adamant James (twice Best in Show at Westminster, among many other honors), bred by Ann Roberts, owned by Dr. Milton Prickett, handled by Clint Harris, and another son, Ch. Salilyn's Colonel's Overlord, bred by Forrest Andrews, owned by Forrest Andrews and Julie Gasow, handled by Ruth Cooper. Photo by Francie Franco.

For Mrs. Virginia Hampton in 1974, there were 49 Springers. This event included the "specials" class in which the following were entered: Champion Inchidony Perpetual Motion, Bryan K. Martin, owner; Champion Tri Trump's Noble Bidder, Vivian Diffendaffer, owner; Champion Arel's Deuce, owned by Noel and Ardella Pease; Champion Kaintuck's Heir Apparent, Mrs. Borie and Laddie Carswell, co-owners; Champion Salilyn's April Flower, Lyman S. and Shirley Walker, owners; Champion Avenir Ezeliel of Bair, owned by Ann Bamford; Lee Vee's Jayson of Clarandon, Vivian Diffendaffer, owner; Champion Salilyn's Encore, co-owned by Edna Randolph and Donald Snyder; Champion Salilyn's Vanguard, and Champion Salilyn's Classic, co-owned by Julie Gasow and Barbara Jane Gates; Filicia's Westcot Justin, Anne Pope and Lillian Gough, co-owners; Champion Salilyn's Bravo, Matthew and Marian Bonnefond, owners; Champion El Taro's Scotch Flag, owned by Earl Taisey; Champion El Ray's Reina of Whitney, Eli and Frances Franco, owners; Champion Victoria's Copper Penny, Sherwood and Sandra Brown, owners; Champion Loresta's Storm King, Edward and Lillian Stapp, owners; Champion Highcliffe's Tamalove, Mary Engle and L. Koval, co-owners; Champion Salilyn's Paramount, owned by Gary Engle; Champion Starfoot Shawnee Prince, C.D., Harold L. Hall, owner; Champion Pequa's My Goodness Gracious, owned by Linda and Ray Beyrer; Champion Sogo Lord Randy of Huntington, owned by H. William Hoffman; Champion Wendankei's Ole Toledo Too, Daru J. and Clifton Smith, owners; and Champion Telltale Crown Darby, Thomas Hale and Jon Bailey, co-owners.

As of February 1981, the following English Springer Spaniels had won the Sporting Group at Westminster since 1942 when the William Rauch III Memorial Trophy came into the competition. The first Springer (and Sporting dog) to win this trophy was in that year, and the dog was Champion Timpanogos Melinda owned by R.E. Allen. In 1948 it was again a Springer, this time Champion Frejax Royal Salute owned by Fred Jackson. In 1955 Mrs. Julie Gasow gained the honor with Champion King Peter of Salilyn. In 1963, en route to Best in Show, it was Champion Wakefield's Black Knight for Mrs. W.J.S. Borie. In 1967 Mrs. Julie Gasow had the winner

A three-time Best of Breed winner at Westminster, Ch. King Peter of Salilyn is shown winning here on the first of these occasions, handled by Dick Cooper.

in Champion Salilyn's Aristocrat, and in 1969 Champion Magill's Patrick, C.D. did it for Wayne D. Magill. In 1971 and 1972, Champion Chinoe's Adamant James, went both times to his double Best in Show victories, and in 1976 it was Champion Loujon's Executor for JoAnn Larsen.

Shalimar's Springtime, by Ch. Bryden's Marque on Maidenhead ex Shalimar's New Warning, is pictured winning points at the Eastern English Springer Spaniel Club 1981 Specialty, handled by George Alston for owner William W. Rich of Wilmington, Delaware. "Shannon" was purchased from breeder Sharon Mabrey of Shalimar Kennels in January 1980. In addition to the pictured win (from which he went on to Best of Winners that day), he took Winners Dog at Westminster the same year.

Ch. Salilyn's Private Stock is pictured in September 1982 becoming the only Springer to go Best in Show at West-chester Kennel Club. George G. Alston is shown handling for owners Robert Gough and Julia Gasow. Bred by Salilyn Kennels (Julia Gasow), Stock compiled a record (through 1982) that included 21 All-Breed Bests in Show, 10 Specialty Bests of Breed, and 100 Group Firsts. At the time of writing this book, he was tied for Top Sire, All Breeds, 1982; he also had to his credit four Group-winning children in 1982.

CHAPTER SIX

Official Standard of the English Springer Spaniel

Ch. El Taro's Scotch Flag, a Number One Springer and Top Ten Sporting Dog, one of the many fine representatives of the breed owned by Earl Taisey, pictured here with handler George Alston, taking Best in Show under Ray Beale at the Ingham County Kennel Club event, May 1973.

A breed standard is the description of the perfect, or ideal, dog. It is used as a guideline for objectively measuring the appearance (and temperament, to a certain extent) of a given specimen of the breed. The degree of excellence of a particular dog is based on how well that dog meets the requirements described in the standard for its breed—how well the dog approaches the ideal.

The following standard for the English Springer Spaniel is that which was approved in 1978 by the American Kennel Club, the governing body for purebred dogs in the United States.

General Appearance and Type: The English Springer Spaniel is a medium-size sporting dog with a neat, compact body, and a docked tail. His coat is moderately long and glossy with feathering on his legs, ears, chest and brisket. His pendulous ears, soft gentle expression, sturdy build and friendly wagging tail proclaim him unmistakably a member of the ancient family of spaniels. He is above all a well proportioned dog, free from exaggeration, nicely balanced in every part. His carriage is proud and upstanding, body deep, legs strong and muscular with enough length to carry him with ease. His short level back, well developed thighs, good shoulders and excellent feet suggest power, endurance, agility. Taken as a whole, he looks the part of a dog that can go and keep going under difficult hunting conditions, and moreover he enjoys what he is doing. At his best, he is endowed with style, symmetry, balance, enthusiasm and is every inch a sporting dog of distinct spaniel character, combining beauty and utility. **To be penalized:** Those lacking true English Springer type in conformation, expression or behavior.

Temperament: The typical Springer is friendly, eager to please, quick to learn, willing to obey. In the show ring, he should exhibit poise, attentiveness, tractability, and should permit himself to be examined by the judge without resentment or cringing. **To be penalized:** Excessive timidity, with due allowance for puppies and novice exhibits. But no dog to receive a ribbon if he behaves in vicious manner toward handler or judge. Aggressiveness toward other dogs in the ring not to be construed as viciousness.

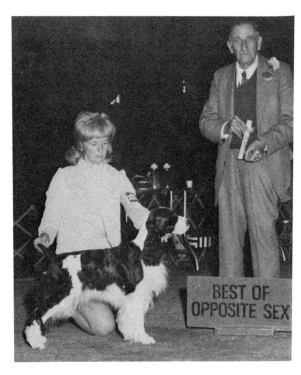

Ch. Pembroke Yankee Heritage with owner Janie Graham. By Ch. Canarch Yankee Patriot, C.D. ex Ch. Salilyn's Elegance of Pembroke. Alva Rosenberg is judging.

Size and Proportion: The Springer is built to cover rough ground with agility and reasonable speed. He should be kept to medium size—neither too small nor too large and heavy to do the work for which he is intended. The ideal shoulder height for dogs is 20 inches; for bitches, 19 inches. Length of topline (the distance from the top of the shoulders to the root of the tail) should be approximately equal to the dog's shoulder height—never longer than his height—and not appreciably less. The dog too long in body, especially when long in loin, tires easily and lacks the compact outline characteristic of the breed. Equally undesirable is the dog too short in body for the length of his legs, a condition that destroys his balance and restricts the gait.

Weight: Is dependent on the dog's other dimensions: a 20 inch dog, well proportioned, in good condition should weigh about 49-55 pounds. The resulting appearance is a well-knit, sturdy dog with good but not too heavy bone, in no way coarse or ponderous. **To be penalized:** Over-heavy specimens, cloddy in build. Leggy individuals, too tall for their length and substance. Oversize or undersize specimens (those more than one inch over or under the breed ideal).

Color: May be black or liver with white markings or predominantly white with black or liver markings; tricolor, black-and-white or liver-and-white with tan markings (usually found on eyebrows, cheeks, insides of ears, and under tail); blue or liver roan. Any white portions of coat may be flecked with ticking. All preceding combinations of colors and markings to be equally acceptable. **To be penalized:** Off colors such as lemon, red or orange not to place.

Coat: On ears, chest, legs and belly the Springer is nicely furnished with a fringe of feathering of moderate length and heaviness. On head, front of forelegs and below hocks on front of hindlegs, the hair is short and fine. The body coat is flat or wavy, of medium length and sufficiently dense to be waterproof, weatherproof and thornproof. The texture fine, and the hair should have the clean, glossy, live appearance indicative of good health. It is legitimite to trim about head, feet, ears; to remove dead hair; to thin and shorten excess feathering, particularly from the hocks to the feet and elsewhere as required, to give a smart, clean appearance. **To be penalized**: Rough, curly coat. Overtrimming especially of the body coat. Any chopped, barbered or artificial effect. Excessive feathering that destroys the clean outline desirable in a sporting dog.

Lleda's Angelique, Best of Opposite Sex at the Eastern English Springer Spaniel Club Futurity in 1978, is by Ch. Filicia's Bequest ex Lleda's Replica of Erin, was bred by Karen Adell Garetano and Estelle Adell, and is owned by Mrs. Garetano, Huntington Station, New York.

Ch. Kay N Dee's Chatter, C.D., by Ch. Salilyn Classic ex Ch. Judge's Pride Jennifer, C.D., finished her championship with Best of Breed from the classes at Maryland Kennel Club in 1978 under English judge M.J. Boothroyd in an entry of 27. Owned by Dr. Mary B. Gibbs, Spencerville, Maryland.

Head: The head is impressive without being heavy. Its beauty lies in a combination of strength and refinement. It is important that the size and proportion be in balance with the rest of the dog. Viewed in profile the head should appear approximately the same length as the neck and should blend with the body in substance. The skull (upper head) to be of medium length, fairly broad, flat on top, slightly rounded at the sides and back. The occiput bone inconspicuous, rounded rather than peaked or angular. The foreface (head in front of the eyes) approximately the same length as the skull, and in harmony as to width and general character. Looking down on the head, the muzzle to appear to be about one half the width of the skull. As the skull rises from the foreface, it makes a brow or "stop," divided by a groove or fluting between the eyes. This groove continues upward and gradually disappears as it reaches the middle of the forehead. The amount of "stop" can best be described as moderate. It must not be a pronounced feature; rather it is a subtle rise where the muzzle blends into the upper head, further emphasized by the groove and by the position and shape of the eyebrows which should be well-developed. The stop, eyebrow and the chiseling of the bony structure around the eye sockets contribute to the Springer's beautiful and characteristic expression. Viewed in profile, the topline of the skull and the muzzle lie in two approximately parallel planes. The nasal bone should be straight, with no inclination downward towards the tip of the nose which gives a downfaced look so undesirable in this breed. Neither should the nasal bone be concave resulting in a "dish-faced" profile; nor convex giving the dog a Roman nose. The jaws to be of sufficient length to allow the dog to carry game easily; fairly square, lean, strong and even (neither undershot nor overshot). The upper lip to come down full and rather square to cover the line of the lower jaw, but lips not to be pendulous or exaggerated. The nostrils well opened and broad, liver colored or black depending on the color of the coat. Flesh colored ("Dudley noses") or spotted ("butterfly noses") are undesirable. The cheeks to be flat (not rounded, full or thick) with nice chiseling under the eyes. **To be penalized:** Oval, pointed or heavy skull. Cheeks prominently rounded, thick and protruding. Too much or too little stop. Over-heavy muzzle. Muzzle too short, too thick or too narrow. Pendulous slobbery lips. Under- or over-shot jaws—a very serious fault to be heavily penalized.

Ch. Pembroke Romance taking Best of Winners at Lowell Kennel Club, 1981. Elliot More handles for Mrs. Walter Berd, Pembroke Springers, Tolland, Connecticut.

Teeth: The teeth should be strong, clean, not too small; and when the mouth is closed the teeth should meet in a close scissors bite (the lower incisors touching the inside of the upper incisors). **To be penalized:** Any deviation from above description. Irregularities due to faulty jaw formation to be severely penalized.

Eyes: More than any other feature, the eyes contribute to the Springer's appeal. Color, placement, size influence expression and attractiveness. The eyes to be of medium size, neither small, round, full and prominent, nor bold and hard in expression. Set rather well apart and fairly deep in their sockets. The color of the iris to harmonize with the color of the coat, preferably a good dark hazel in the liver dogs and black or deep brown in the black-and-white specimens. The expression to be alert, kindly, trusting. The lids tight with little or no haw showing. **To be penalized:** Eyes yellow or brassy in color or noticeably lighter than the coat. Sharp expression indicating unfriendly or suspicious nature. Loose, droopy lids. Prominent haw (the third eyelid or membrane in the inside corner of the eye).

Nora of Canorwoll in March 1967. She is a daughter of Ch. Wakefield Black Knight ex a daughter of Ch. Salilyn's King Peter. Owned by Anne Pope, Filicia Springers.

This well-known representative of Mr. Johnson's kennels is Ch. Kaintuck Tolstoy, by Ch. Charlyle Fair Warning ex Ch. Kaintuck Fortune Huntress. Owned by Anne Pope and Stuart A. Johnson.

Ears: The correct ear-set is on a level with the line of the eye, on the side of the skull and not too far back. The flaps to be long and fairly wide, hanging close to the cheeks, with no tendency to stand up or out. The leather thin, approximately long enough to reach the tip of the nose. **To be penalized:** Short, round ears. Ears set too high or too low or too far back on the head.

Neck: The neck to be moderately long, muscular, slightly arched at the crest, gradually blending into sloping shoulders. Not noticeably upright, or coming into the body at an abrupt angle. **To be penalized:** Short neck, often the sequence to steep shoulders. Concave neck, sometimes called "ewe neck" or "upside-down neck" (the opposite of arched). Excessive throatiness.

Body: The body to be well coupled, strong, compact; the chest deep but not so wide or round as to interfere with the action of the front legs; the brisket sufficiently developed to reach to the level of the elbows. The ribs fairly long, springing gradually to the middle of the body then tapering as they approach the end of the

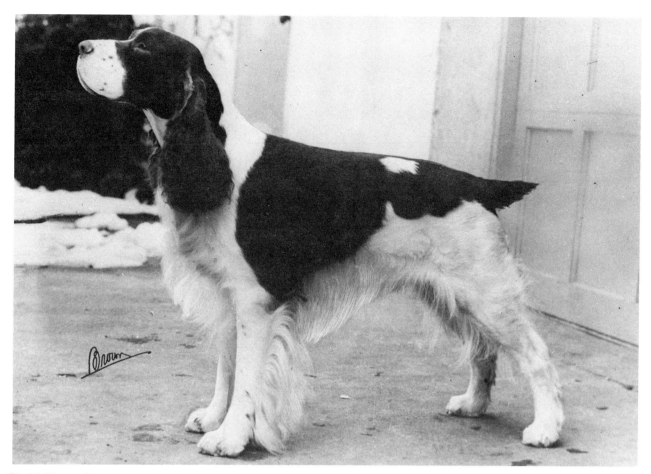

Ch. Melilotus Heritage, a Springer of superb style and temperament, is by Ch. Melilotus Royal Oak ex Oak's half sister, Ch. Melilotus Barbary Ann, she by Roger of Hunter's Hill. Owned by Mrs. R. Gilman Smith, now Mrs. Frederick D. Brown of St. Croix, Virgin Islands.

ribbed section. The back (section between the withers and loin) to be straight and strong, with no tendency to dip or roach. The loins to be strong, short; a slight arch over loins and hip bones. Hips nicely rounded, blending smoothly into hind legs. The resulting topline slopes very gently from withers to tail—the line from withers to back descending without a sharp drop; the back practically level; arch over hips somewhat lower than the withers; croup sloping gently to base of tail; tail carried to follow the natural line of the body. The bottom line, starting on a level with the elbows, to continue backward with almost no up-curve until reaching the end of the ribbed section, then a more noticeable up-curve to the flank, but not enough to make the dog appear small waisted or "tucked up." **To be penalized:** Body too shallow, indicating lack of brisket. Ribs too flat, sometimes due to immaturity. Ribs too round (barrel-shaped), hampering the gait. Swayback (dip in back), indicating weakness or lack of muscular development, particularly to be seen when dog is in ac-

tion and viewed from the side. Roach back (too much arch over loin and extending forward into middle section). Croup falling away too sharply; or croup too high—unsightly faults detrimental to outline and good movement. Topline sloping sharply, indicating steep withers (straight shoulder placement) and a too low tail-set.

Tail: The Springer's tail is an index to both his temperament and his conformation. Merry tail action is characteristic. The proper set is somewhat low, following the natural line of the croup. The carriage should be nearly horizontal, slightly elevated when dog is excited. Carried straight up is untypical of the breed. The tail should not be docked too short and should be well fringed with wavy feather. It is legitimate to shape and shorten the feathering but enough should be left to blend with the dog's other furnishings. **To be penalized:** Tail habitually upright. Tail set too high or too low. Clamped down tail (indicating timidity or undependable temperament, even less to be desired than the tail carried too gaily).

Ch. Geiger's Tiger Chief, C.D., W.D.X., jointly owned by Tillie and Robert C. Geiger, contributed to his breed as a show winner, obedience dog, and sire.

Forequarters: Efficient movement in front calls for proper shoulders, the blades sloping back to form an angle with the upper arm approximately 90 degrees, which permits the dog to swing his forelegs forward in an easy manner. Shoulders (fairly close together at the tips) to lie flat and mold smoothly into the contour of the body. The forelegs to be straight with the same degree of size to the foot. The bone strong, slightly flattened, not too heavy or round. The knee straight, almost flat; the pasterns short, strong; elbows close to the body with free action from the shoulders. **To be penalized:** Shoulders set at a steep angle limiting the stride. Loaded shoulders (the blades standing out from the body by overdevelopment of the muscles). Loose elbows, crooked legs. Bone too light or too coarse and heavy. Weak pasterns that let down the feet at a pronounced angle.

Hindquarters: The Springer should be shown in hard muscular condition, well developed in hips and thighs and the whole rear assembly should suggest strength and driving power. The hip joints to be set rather wide apart and the hips nicely rounded. The thighs broad and muscular; the stifle joint strong and moderately bent. The hock joint somewhat rounded, not small and sharp in contour, and moderately angulated. Leg from hock joint to foot pad, short and strong with good bone structure. When viewed from the rear, the hocks to be parallel, whether the dog is standing or in motion. **To be penalized:** Too little or too much angulation. Narrow, undeveloped thighs. Hocks too short or too long (a proportion of one-third the distance from hip joint to foot is ideal). Flabby muscles. Weakness of joints.

Feet: The feet to be round, or slightly oval, compact, well arched, medium-size with thick pads, well feathered between the toes. Excess hair to be removed to show the natural shape and size of the foot. **To be penalized:** Thin, open or splayed feet (flat with spreading toes). Hare foot (long, rather narrow, foot).

Movement: In judging the Springer, there should be emphasis on proper movement, which is the final test of a dog's conformation and soundness. Prerequisite to good movement is balance of the front and rear assemblies. The two must match in angulation and muscular development if the gait is to be smooth and effortless. Good shoulders laid back at an angle that permits a long stride are just as essential as the excellent rear quarters that provide the driving power. When viewed from the front, the dog's legs should appear to swing forward in a free and easy manner, with no tendency for the feet to cross over or interfere with each other. Viewed from the rear, the hocks should drive well under the body following on a line with the forelegs, neither too widely nor too closely spaced. As speed increases there is a natural tendency for the legs to converge toward the center line of gravity or single line of travel. Seen from the side, the Springer should exhibit a good, long forward stride, without high-stepping or wasted motion. **To be penalized:** Short choppy stride, mincing steps with up and down movement, hopping. Moving with forefeet wide, giving roll or swing to body. Weaving or crossing of fore or hind feet. Cowhocks—hocks turning in toward each other.

In judging the English Springer Spaniel, the overall picture is a primary consideration. It is urged that the judge look for type, which includes general appearance, outline and temperament and also for soundness, especially as seen when the dog is in motion. Inasmuch as the dog with a smooth, easy gait must be reasonably sound and well balanced, he is to be highly regarded in the show ring; however, not to the extent of forgiving him for not looking like an English Springer Spaniel. A quite untypical dog, leggy, foreign in head and expression, may move well. But he should not be placed over a good all-'round specimen that has a minor fault in movement. It should be remembered that the English Springer Spaniel is first and foremost a sporting dog of the spaniel family and he must look and behave and move in character.

Approved June 13, 1978 by the
American Kennel Club

Winning the nod of approval from Mrs. Winifred Heckman, Ch. Salilyn's Hallmark takes Best in Show again with Dick Cooper handling for owner, Mrs. Julie Gasow of Troy, Michigan.

Ch. Waiterock Barcarolle, current winning champion at Waiterock Ranch, by Ch. Waiterock Arrow (grandson of Elmer Brown) ex Waiterock Mistletoe Twig, winning at San Luis Obispo under Ed Dixon. Bred and owned by Juanita Waite Howard, Lafayette, California.

Ch. Pembroke's Dr. Milton (Ch. Pembroke Inchidony Scot, C.D., ex Ch. Pembroke Inheritance), handled here by Karen Prickett for Alice Berd, taking Winners Dog under Harrison Fagan at the Michigan Specialty in March 1976.

Disqualifications

A dog that is blind, deaf, castrated, spayed or whose appearance has been changed by artificial means beyond those specified in the Standard of its breed may not be shown under the rules of the American Kennel Club; nor may a dog that is a monorchid (with one testicle normally located in the scrotum) or cryptorchid (with neither testicle normally located in the scrotum). All such dogs are to be disqualified from competition, except for a spayed bitch which may be shown as a brood bitch in the Brood Bitch Class only, and a castrated dog which may be entered in the Stud Dog Class only.

Removal of dewclaws, docking of tail or cropping of ears in a breed where these acts are customary and in accordance with the Standard will not be considered as artificial changes of appearance.

A dog that is lame at a show cannot receive an award at that show and must be excused from competition for that day. A dog that appears to have any foreign substance in its coat, whether for cleaning purposes or otherwise, MAY NOT BE JUDGED AND MUST BE EXCUSED FROM THE RING WITH THE REASON NOTED IN THE JUDGE'S BOOK.

Do not show a lame dog in hopes that perhaps the judge may not notice or the dog may not happen to limp while being gaited for examination. Do not show a monorchid or a cryptorchid dog either, or a dog with any of the other disqualifications with the thought that it may succeed in slipping past the judge's eye. It is very unlikely that the latter will happen, and even if it does, you will almost certainly get caught next time. This can be extremely embarrassing. A reputation for honesty and fair play is vital and should be guarded zealously if one is to succeed in the Fancy.

If your dog is disqualified at a show for any reason whatsoever you then may appeal (and will want to do so if you feel that the judge was mistaken) to the American Kennel Club for the dog's reinstatement. An appointment will be arranged for official examination of the dog, followed by a decision rendered on whether the dog can again become eligible for competition. Should this happen to you, go immediately to the A.K.C. Field Representative at the show where the disqualification took place, explain what has happened and ask for instructions regarding application for reinstatement.

A handsome class of Springers being judged at Windham County. Photo courtesy of Debby Valvo.

With an admiring gallery in the background, Anne Pope wins another Best of Breed with her gorgeous liver dog, Ch. Filicia's Westcot Justin.

"To the victor. . .". Ch. Charlyle Fair Warning winning the Eastern Springer Spaniel Specialty, 1967. Anne Pope, owner.

CHAPTER SEVEN

Anne Pope Discusses the English Springer Spaniel

Anne Pope with Ch. Charlyle Fair Warning.

Author's Note

In earlier chapters of this book, we discussed characteristics of the English Springer Spaniel as this word is generally accepted by the layman. To the enthusiast of purebred dogs, however, the expressions "characteristics" and "breed character" take on a considerably wider meaning. In dog-show language, breed character is synonymous with "type," which means the physical appearance of the dog in addition to its traits of personality, talents and disposition.

When a breeder, a fancier or a judge of purebred dogs speaks of character, chances are he is referring to "type," in which case the reference is to the composite features making that breed of dog distinctive, i.e., setting it apart from all other breeds and making it easily recognizable. To be strong in breed character, or of good type, a dog must adhere not only in personality but also in conformation as well to what is considered ideal for his breed. The "ideal" is described in the Standard of Perfection which outlines the ideal animal breeders strive to produce and judges try to single out in our show rings. Such a Standard of Perfection is the breeder's guide and the judge's tool. It is the result of long and dedicated work on the part of the Parent Specialty Club based upon in-depth study of the breed's history, earlier Standards and the goals for which the breed was developed. In the case of Springers, I can think of no better person to discuss physical characteristics or type in Springers than Anne Pope, who has owned so many top dogs, bred such excellent ones and judges them so capably.

A.K.N.

Anne Pope Discusses Characteristics of the English Springer Spaniel

The English Springer Spaniel is a compact, medium-sized dog, free of exaggeration, with a notable exception—that being the long, pendulous ears. Because the Springer is free of exaggeration, it is a breed free of congenital health problems. Some breeds that have anatomical extremes do have health problems in the area which has been exaggerated. For example, Pekingese have problems with their large, globular eyes called for in their standard; Dachshunds have back problems which arise from their long body length. Since everything about a Springer is in balance and proportion, this is one of the breeds that escapes those difficulties brought about by man's attempts to exaggerate.

The Springer's most notable characteristic is his disposition, his ingratiating attitude towards the entire world. He loves people. He loves life, and this jolly appreciation of everything, coupled with uncanny human-like intelligence makes him a fascinating fellow, a wonderful companion not only for adults but particularly for children. With patient understanding he will endure eye-poking, ear-pulling—all manner of abuse—and in fact rather seem to enjoy it. He is not entirely a one-man dog in the ordinary sense of the word.

Anne Pope's Ch. Filicia's Aliden Biskit shown here at eight years old, is now owned by Susan Dash and Anne Pope.

His great affection embraces the entire family fortunate to be owned by him! On the other hand, he is a remarkably good watchdog as his loyalty gives him a fiercely protective spirit for his own family's safety. Strangers, particularly roughly dressed ones or those arriving after sunset, are not warmly greeted. Springers do not bite but their warning is fearsome.

An English Springer is such a cheerful fellow, always interested, curious and ready to start on any expedition. The Springer thinks he is a person, that he should do everything you do, go everywhere you go. You need only to get out your coat and hat to stir up a riot. Springers know cars are for pursuing adventure; therefore, they love to ride in them. They will raise utter bedlam when they see you gather whatever indicates to them that a car ride is imminent, and with a display of disappointment worthy of an "Oscar" award, they make it difficult for you to go off and leave them behind. Their ears seem to grow longer with their hanging head; their eyes become full of heartbreak, almost tears! They seem to lose several inches in height and their usually happy tail disappears in dejection. Once in the car, however, they are quite tractable as they sit quietly and look with great interest at the passing scenes. Truly this is a breed for people who intend to share companionship with their dog.

Springers make excellent hunting dogs. Their high intelligence makes them adaptable to all game birds—pheasant and quail (land birds) as well as duck (water birds). Their natural love for hunting and their wish to please you make them an exceptionally easy dog to train. The Springer's strong build and hard coat allow him to hunt the most treacherous of terrain in inclement weather without any dampening of his eagerness since he is physically equipped to tolerate weather extremes. He is a natural swimmer and, given a chance, he will be swimming even before he is ready to leave his litter-mates. The Springer is tireless hunting on land or in water.

The Springer's disposition is truly remarkable. I have discussed his spirit and gaiety; however, the most endearing characteristic of all in this breed is his sensitivity to his family. It is this sensitivity that gives the perfect balance to his character. The Springer has great dignity, a serenity of spirit. He knows his place and keeps it, never making a nuisance of himself. Generally he finds a place in the house which becomes his own where he will go for a nap when nothing interesting is happening. Springers have a terrific sense of humor and will do something to get you laughing whenever the opportunity arises. These dogs are sensitive to your moods and will stay with you quietly when you are sad or play

"Caught in the act!" Ch. Filicia's Uncle Tom looks guilty as he gets a final lick from the breakfast table. Anne Pope, owner.

Ch. Filicia's Coronation, owner-handled by Anne Pope to Best of Breed at Springfield in 1975.

At first glance, the Springer should impress one as being square, powerful, but at the same time graceful. When observed moving from the side, the dog should cover the ground with ease, his body moving as a unit: topline level, with a strong, even, powerful yet fluid gait.

The head of the English Springer Spaniel is what sets the breed apart from any other, it being the Springer's most distinctive feature. There are other medium-sized, square dogs but only *one* with the head of a Springer! A good Springer head is truly beautiful. It combines gentleness with sculptured elegance. The expression which, correctly, conveys a calm, sweet and intelligent dog, is all-important in the breed.

Anne Pope Discusses
Judging the English Springer Spaniel

First and foremost in evaluating the dogs before you, remember that a good Springer essentially must be well balanced. His gait, when viewed from the side, must be powerful and even, enabling the dog to cover the ground without effort as he travels. The overall picture must be pleasing, one of graceful strength.

The dog's attitude should be cooperative and happy. His head must be distinctively "spaniel," a gentle expression in a well-defined, balanced structure.

with you when you are happy. They are quiet dogs in the house, rarely barking unless they sense danger. As house dogs, they are neither destructive nor hyperactive. Also, they are a clean breed; this makes them easy to housebreak.

In summation, their size, good health and remarkable disposition make English Springer Spaniels one of the most popular and sought after breeds for family pets.

Anne Pope Discusses
Physical Characteristics or "Type"
of the English Springer Spaniel

The Springer's medium size is important to the character of the breed since it is a critical factor with regard to their hunting abilities as well as their desirability as a pet. The female is about 19 inches, weighing approximately 40–45 pounds; the male is about 20 inches, weighing 50–55 pounds.

The breed is aesthetically pleasing with its overall balance of appearance. A Springer's weight should be carried equally on the framework of the dog, the forequarters and hindquarters assuming equal responsibility in supporting and moving the body. No single section of a Springer's body should appear overdone or conspicuous. The rib cage should be somewhat rounded and deep between the forelegs with plenty of space for good lung power.

Ch. Canorwoll's Reflection (Patriot ex Hecate) owner-handled by Anne Pope at Cape Cod, 1980.

Since no dog is perfect, the art of judging becomes one of understanding which components are essential for the ideal of the breed to be realized. For example, if a Springer is to look and move as it should in accordance with the ideal, it must have the heavy, muscular thigh; thus, in making comparisons one should bear this fact in mind. A "flashy"-looking dog, although beautiful in some respects, never should take precedence, if it lacks the correct thigh, over one that is less elegant and beautiful but correct in this important feature. It is a matter of putting things in their proper perspective. Without a proper thigh, a Springer cannot be balanced or truly square nor can it move along correctly. Since balance and the box-like appearance coupled with correct action are essential to the breed, the lack of sufficient thigh constitutes a serious fault. A capable Springer judge knows how to weigh one problem against another, thus determining which of the dogs in front of him comes closest to breed type. Each component of the dog is important but it is the *overall* animal that must be considered.

Ch. Filicia's Etching, born June 1973 (breeder Anne Pope), by Ch. Salilyn's Classic ex Ch. Kaintuck Pixie, C.D. A Best in Show winner, Group 2 at Westminster, with many Bests of Breed including 2 Specialties. Handled by George Alston for the Robert Goughs, Syosset, New York.

Mrs. Winfred Heckman selects Ch. Charlyle Fair Warning as Best in Show at Newton Kennel Club. Laddie Carswell, handler; Anne Pope, owner.

As a judge, I resent over-handling on the part of an exhibitor and dislike the custom some handlers follow of repeatedly and busily pointing out by actions the animal's good points instead of setting the dog up and letting the judge go over it without all this excess motion from the exhibitor. I personally find this aggressive type of handler offensive. I know this breed. I know what I am looking for, and the pushy handler is insulting to my intelligence and knowledge. Moreover, this kind of handler is often so determined that you see his dog's head, for example, that you can hardly get a look at the entire dog or the overall picture it presents. I will not tolerate this in my ring and feel that judges should bear in mind that THEY are in command of the ring while officiating and that distasteful actions on the part of any exhibitor should not be condoned. Arrogant handlers do little to enhance a dog's chances of winning. On the other hand, a courteous, knowledgeable, expert handler can be all important in successful exhibiting.

Never underestimate the importance of condition and presentation when showing a Springer, as these are decidedly counted as the judge evaluates.

Basically there are two types of show Springers. Both are acceptable and both necessary to produce splendid representatives of the breed.

Ch. Kay N Dee Rudolph, by Ch. Kay N Dee Geoffrey ex Ch. Judge's Pride Jennifer, C.D., taking Best of Winners at the Long Island Springer Club supported Specialty under Anne Pope. "Rudy" finished in 12 shows in 1979, then was sold to Brazil where he became a champion and a multi-Group winner. Dr. Mary B. Gibbs, Kay N Dee Kennels, Spencerville, Maryland.

The first type is what I refer to as "stocky." This type of dog tends to be lower on leg, cobbier and generally heavier than the other type, or the "racy" ones. These latter are higher on leg, usually with less bone, and create a finer appearance. Both types should make square overall pictures. Both must be well-balanced. When breeding Springers, the breeder should always try to cross between the two types, thus keeping the offspring a "happy medium."

Too many judges and breeders place undue importance on markings. Litters are graded by the proximity to the ideally marked dog rather than the animal under the markings. Certainly markings do create an illusion and some markings are definitely detrimental to the overall appearance of the dog. A white slash through the loin, for example, usually makes the dog look long in back, while a white rump tends to make the dog look high in the rear. Markings which will adversely affect the dog are unfortunate; however, a competent judge should be able to differentiate between structure and optical illusion. All Springers should not need the solid blanket with white running gear and a shawl collar to successfully compete in the show ring. A good judge evaluates the dog—not the illusion the dog creates due to modern markings.

Perhaps the most common mistake made by judges and exhibitors alike is that of being deceived by excessive speed and flash as the animal moves in the ring. It certainly is true that a dog that shows with enthusiasm and flair will be more eye-catching and spectacular than one that trots lackadaisically around the ring. Since dog-show enthusiasts want to win with their dogs, speed and showmanship are becoming more and more important; in fact, I believe, to a fault. It is impossible to tell if the dog that races around the ring is moving correctly with proper balance and co-ordination. Moreover, this is not a natural gait for any animal to move at on its own. Ideally judges should fault these "racing machines." Our goal should be to evaluate the animal that moves happily and freely, demonstrating drive and reach in an unfrenzied manner. A flash of flying fur is not impressive—at least not to a knowledgeable judge.

Ch. Filicia's Hershey Kiss finished in three weeks of showing. Pictured here when seven months old at the Pioneer Valley English Springer Spaniel Specialty, 1979, owner-handled by Anne Pope.

Anne Pope Discusses
One Major Problem of the Springer Breed

Ideally, the Springer disposition should be, and generally is, as previously described. Certainly the majority of Springers make delightful companions; however, there is a serious temperament problem in some Springers which we feel we should not totally ignore in the presentation of this book to the public.

When considering a Springer as a pet, or when looking for an ideal mate for your dog or bitch, the knowledgeable consumer will remember to consider temperament carefully, for a problem does exist and should be avoided.

To explain what qualifies me to write this chapter, I have had Springers all my life. My family has always had two or more as house pets since before I was born. For more than 20 years, I have raised and shown them. For six years, following college, I studied chemical and physical aspects of behavior. As a result of that time and effort, I have a Ph. D., along with considerable knowledge of physical and/or chemical properties of behavior—specifically the physiology of violence. It was necessary that I learn how to investigate a problem; how to divide a problem into its smallest sub-groups and not to complicate the investigation by merging together two problems. Common sense tells us that answers cannot possibly be found without knowing the question.

There has been overwhelming evidence suggesting that Springers do have behavioral problems. With increasing frequency, one hears of Springers biting people or being put to sleep because they are unsatisfactory pets.

To understand these behavioral problems, we must divide the components of behavior into their most basic elements. In this case: first, disease; second, temperament; and third, environment.

Champion Filicia's Uncle Tom with his owner, Anne Pope.

Anne Pope handling Ch. Filicia's Crescendo, by Ch. Filicia's Anlon Patriot ex Ch. Filicia's Biskit, in August 1979.

Before going any further, let me emphasize that this problem is by no means present in *all* Springers. Most Springers are exactly what they should be, excellent family pets. A few of them are not. This section is about those few.

As I have mentioned, there are three primary variables influencing behavior. Starting with disease processes, I'm sure that everyone owning a dog is aware of lead poisoning. The addition of a chemical agent (lead) to an animal's blood causes behavioral symptons which are 1) hyperactivity, 2) excitability and 3) overreaction. The cause of these behaviors is due to a chemical reaction and in no way reflects the animal's normal temperament. When the chemical is removed, the behavior returns to normal. This demonstrates that primary symptoms of some diseases are behavioral.

A rare condition in people is one called Temporal Lobe Epilepsy (TLE). Uncontrollable rage attacks are its primary symptom. People with this disease can be like people everywhere, some charming, others unpleasant, with a whole range of personalities in between. Upon occasion (usually unpredictable) people with TLE have rage attacks during which time the victim has no control over his actions or any memory of the attack once the seizure ends. Through sophisticated tests, scientists have learned that during the rage attack, a part of the person's brain is showing the electrical activity associated with a seizure. So, what we are really seeing in these rage attacks amounts to an epileptic seizure. These seizures are different from the "normal" epileptic seizure which causes *grand mal* convulsions or *petit mal* blackout or temporary blackout, in that the result is violence. Just as the "normal" epileptic cannot control his seizures, the victim of TLE is unable to control his.

There is a striking resemblance between the "Rage" syndrome in Springers and TLE in people. These dogs—who are or are not otherwise friendly—seem temporarily dazed, then lash out viciously and aggressively. They neither respond to nor seem aware of verbal commands. They do not bite once and then back away. They attack and continue to attack until physically stopped or until they regain control. Following the attack, the dog seems confused, as though not quite sure what has happened.

Ch. Filicia's Royal Velvet, by Ch. Salilyn's Classic ex Ch. Kaintuck Pixie, is handled by Elliot More for Anne Pope of Filicia Springers.

Anne Pope handling her Filicia's Rainmaker of McDerry at 12½ months to Best of Winners at Wachusett Kennel Club in 1980.

Anne Pope with Ch. McDerry's Cameo.

TLE in people does not occur before puberty, usually after 16 years age. In Springers the "Rage" onset is generally around one to two years of age. I cannot state as a certainty that "Rage" Springers have TLE, only that the similarity is striking between the two.

Dogs with "Rage" do not necessarily have a temperament problem. They have a disease, the symptoms of which are behavorial. One cannot teach a dog not to have a disease, so if your dog has TLE, training will be useless. Let us not forget that people with TLE spend their lives in institutions, since they are uncontrollable, dangerous and unpredictable. The only solution with a dog under these circumstances is that it be humanely put down, sparing misery all around.

Ch. Filicia's Moonwind, by Ch. Forestwoods' Prime Minister ex Ch. Danaho's Lalique of Stanton. Owned by Anne Pope, Filicia Kennels. Linda More is handling.

The third component of behavorial problems is the environment in which the dog is raised. Nowadays Springers, especially show dogs are more physically active than they were say a dozen years ago and are encouraged to exhibit more animation, enthusiasm and speed than was formerly the case. Such behavior can perhaps get out of hand, producing what could be called "psyched-up" dogs as opposed to the calm, easy-to-live-with Springer we all love.

Do not purchase a Springer that appears to have any tendency towards timidity, over-exuberance or nervousness. If possible, see the parents before you buy. Do not breed to a dog in which you note any temperament instability, or to a bloodline in which you have noted any behavioral peculiarities. Timid or hyperactive dogs should not be used for breeding or taken on as pets.

We repeat that the majority of Springers are the same dependable, lovely canine personalities Springer folks have always known. But we do not feel it fair to release a book on the breed completely ignoring this problem, even though it is decidedly in the minority. Forewarned is forearmed. We want both the breed and its owners to have the protection that understanding the presence of a problem can create.

Ch. Kaintuck Pixie at 14 years old, the dam of 16 champions. Anne Pope, owner, Filicia Kennels, Acton, Massachusetts.

Ch. Kaintuck Pixie, C.D., with two of her well-known progeny, Ch. Filicia's Etching and Ch. Filicia's Capulet Fashion. Anne Pope, owner.

Ch. Salilyn's Aristocrat at three years of age when he retired. In 1971 he became the "greatest winning show dog in history," and was the first living dog to earn a place in the *Kennel Review Hall of Fame*. Sired by Ch. Inchidony Prince Charming (by Ch. Salilyn's Citation) ex Ch. Salilyn's Lily of the Valley. Mrs. Julie Gasow, owner.

The English Springer Spaniel Field Trial Association— Parent Club of the Breed

Fishers Island, 1938. An informal shot of judges Dr. Sam Milbank and Robert McLean, two gentlemen who contributed greatly to the progress of English Springer Spaniels in the United States. Both sincere and loyal fanciers, they were active participants who gave much thought and effort to anything for the good of Springers, and were highly successful, widely admired in all phases of the Fancy.

It was in 1926 that the English Springer Spaniel Field Trial Association was admitted to membership in the American Kennel Club and officially named Parent Club for the breed. Prior to that time, Springers had been under the wing of the American Spaniel Club, and it was becoming obvious that a Parent Club devoted solely to Springers was needed. As interest in the breed grew, small groups started to form clubs of their own. The transfer from the American Spaniel Club to the English Springer Spaniel Field Trial Association was amicable to all concerned, and as present day "Springerites" are well aware, the American Spaniel Club still includes classification for Springers at its Specialty shows.

Samuel Allen was President for the first two years of the new Parent Club. The founder members were Henry Ferguson, W.J. Hutchinson, David Wagstaff, Walton Ferguson, Jr., Reginald Halliday, Charles Toy, Ezra Fitch, E.R. Wilbur, Julian Bishop, David P. Earle and Mr. Allen.

The first English Springer Spaniel Field Trial Association Specialty was held in October 1926 at Fisher's Island, New York. A. Allington arriv-

ed from England to judge an entry of 35. From 1930 until about 1945, the Specialties were held mostly in conjunction with all-breed shows in various parts of the United States from Westminster to events in Los Angeles and Chicago. Several specialties occurred at the Greenwich Kennel Club, the "home show" of Springer enthusiast, Joe Quirk.

In the mid-1940's, the Specialties were discontinued due to lack of interest. Then the suggestion was put forth for a "traveling National" sponsored by the E.S.S.F.T.A. but "hosted" by Regional Specialty clubs. This proved highly successful, and the first such event took place in August 1956 at Grosse Point, Michigan. The latest, as this was written, was in 1981 in Hempstead, Long Island. These events have continued without interruption now for the past 25 years.

Current officers of the English Springer Spaniel Field Trial Association (at the time of this writing) are E.H. Whitaker, President; Mrs. Frederick D. Brown, John Buoy and George Sokup, Vice Presidents; Joseph W. Angelovic, Treasurer; and Joan M. Ross, Secretary, P.O Box 274, Ingleside, Illinois 60041.

Left: Ch. Melilotus Royal Oak was the first Springer to win Best in Show at the American Spaniel Club Specialty and at the first National Specialty (English Springer Spaniel Field Trial Association) at Grosse Point, Michigan, in 1956. Mrs. R. Gilman Smith, now Mrs. Frederick D. Brown of St. Croix, Virgin Islands, was the owner.

Below: An interesting historical photograph of Melilotus Royal Oak winning his first blue ribbon at nine months old under Alva Rosenberg at the Eastern English Springer Specialty, Waterbury, Connecticut, October 9, 1949. Handling is the late Tom Lenfesty, who in 1956 judged the National Specialty at Grosse Pointe and selected Royal Oak, then 7½ years, for Best in Show.

186

Ch. Frejax Royalist Ambassador, by Ch. Frejax Royalist ex Ch. Frejax Supreme Challenge, was bred by Fred Jackson and owned by Catherine Donavan, Berkeley, California. Pictured taking Best of Breed from the classes at the 1960 National Specialty at the Ambassador Hotel, Los Angeles, California. Handler, K.M. McDonald; judge, Graham Head; trophy presenters, Mrs. R. Gilman Smith and Mr. John J. Breslin.

Am., Can. Ch. Geiger's Chief Geronimo, C.D., W.D., by Ch. Geiger's Winaway Duke, U.D., W.D.X., from Ch. Schwedekrest Lady Pamela, C.D., was born on November 21, 1959. He is pictured here at the Fifth National Specialty Show, in August 1960, taking first place in the Junior Puppy Sweepstakes and then going on to Reserve Winners Dog. This was Tillie Geiger's first National. She had been told that to enter in Sweepstakes one must enter in a regular class as well. Not knowing what to do, she asked an old-time fancier what class to put her new puppy in, and was told "open, of course," So she did!

Best of Breed winners at the National Specialty over the past 26 years:

1956   Champion Melilotus Royal Oak, Mrs. R. Gilman Smith

1957   Champion Oakhurst's Hi-Roc, Mr. and Mrs. Elmer J. Pion

1958   Champion Cartree Cosmic, P.J. Maher

1959   Champion Salilyn's Macduff, Mr. and Mrs. William J. Randall

1960   Champion Frejax Royalist Ambassador, Catherine M. Donavan

1961   Champion Wakefield's Black Knight, Mrs. W.J.S. Borie

1962   Champion Charlyle's Holdout, Charles R. Clement

1963   Champion Wakefield's Black Knight, Mrs. W.J.S. Borie

1964   Champion Debonair Dandy, Mrs. Vivian Diffendaffer

1965   Champion Muller's Blazing Kane, Arthur W. and Hazel Westlund

1966   Champion Charlyle's Fair Warning, Anne Pope

1967   Champion Beryltown Bold Crusader, Earl L. Taisey

1968   Champion Salilyn's Aristocrat, Mrs. F.H. Gasow

1969   Champion Salilyn's Aristocrat, Mrs. F.H. Gasow

1970   Champion Chinoe's Adamant James, Dr. Milton E. Prickett

1971   Champion Ramsgate's Scotch Mist, Richard A. and Janice C. Mau

1972   Champion Magill's Patrick, C.D., W.D.X., Wayne and Phyllis McGill

At the 1968 National Specialty, judge A. Peter Knoop awards honors in the Stud Dog Class to Ch. Salilyn's Aristocrat, shown with his son Overlord and daughter Sophistication. All owned by Mrs. Julie Gasow, Salilyn Kennels.

1973	Champion Salilyn's Classic, Mrs. F.H. Gasow and Barbara J. Gates
1974	Champion Loujon Executor, JoAnn Larsen
1975	Champion Salilyn's Classic, Salilyn Kennels
1976	Champion Salilyn's Hallmark, Salilyn Kennels
1977	Champion Salilyn's Classic, Salilyn Kennels
1978	Aspengrove Dubonet, Dr. Patrick and Barbara Baymiller
1979	Champion Prelude's Echo, Julie Gasow
1980	Champion Sellier's Quarterback Sneak, Edward Sellier, Jr.
1981	Champion Salilyn's Private Stock, Robert Gough and Julie Gasow

A stunning picture of Ch. Salilyn's Classic winning the National Specialty Best of Breed in 1975. Dick Cooper is handling for Mrs. Julie Gasow.

Ch. Filicia's Liberty Belle of Sulo is owner-handled by Anne Pope to First in the 6-9 Month Puppy Sweepstakes at the English Springer Spaniel Field Trial Association, July 1977.

Looking over the field with puppy on lead is E.H. (Ed) Whitaker of Downingtown, Pennsylvania, president of the parent club, the English Springer Spaniel Field Trial Association, and a highly successful amateur handler.

Best of Breed at the 1962 Potomac English Springer Spaniel Specialty goes to the magnificent dog on the right, Ch. Wakefield Black Knight, owned by Mrs. W.J.S. Borie and handled by Laddie Carswell. Best of Opposite Sex is Ch. Another Star of Pequa, owned by Mr. and Mrs. A.W. Matson and handled by Patty Matson Alston. Black Knight was the first of his breed to gain Best in Show at the Westminster Kennel Club.

189

Dungarvan's Right On at 1½ years age flushes a pigeon in Puppy Stake at Bushy Hill Club trial where she won second. Owner, Kathleen Cande; trainer, Ray Cacchio.

CHAPTER NINE

Evelyn Monte Van Horn Discusses English Springer Spaniel Field Trials

Pheasant Run Jil, English Springer Spaniel owned by Robert McLean, is shown at the Connecticut Spaniel Field Trial, Saybrook, Connecticut, in November 1938. Ed Knight, writing in *Popular Dogs,* said of Jil, "She had the finest nose of any gun dog of any breed ever seen in a lifetime of judging." Photo courtesy of Evelyn Monte Van Horn.

Author's Note

It is with great pride that we present Evelyn Monte Van Horn, noted judge and authority on Springers in Field Trial work, as author of our section on this subject. Mrs. Van Horn's accomplishments with her own dogs and as a judge are widely known and admired. She has officiated at our most prestigious events, and her opinions are well respected.

A.K.N.

Field Trials are outdoor contests in which individual dogs are given the opportunity to show their qualities under actual or simulated hunting conditions. Competitions vary according to the breed and the specialty of the breed or breeds.

Field Trials for Springers have been in existence since the earliest days of the breed in America. The Canadian fancier, Eudore Chevrier, is credited with the establishment of the first Springer club on this continent. The sole purpose of that club, the English Springer Spaniel Club of Canada, was to hold Field Trial meetings. The first meeting took place on September 30, 1922 in wild hunting country north of Winnipeg where the dogs could show their prowess in the field on prairie chicken, ruffed grouse and hare. Freeman Lloyd, British-born New York journalist and Sporting dog authority, was one of the judges and became a strong and articulate advocate of "the new gun dog breed." After the trial, he made a speech in which he predicted, in his booming voice, that the "Springer Field Trial movement would spread and spread until it reached every quarter of North America."

While perhaps not precisely as predicted, Springer Field Trials have indeed grown and flourished. Close to 50 clubs regularly hold championship point trials, and they range from Washington and California on the Pacific Coast to the Midwest, including Colorado and Texas, and to the Northeast. At the time of this writing five new clubs were in the process of starting trials.

The first Springer Field Trial in the United States took place at Fisher's Island, New York in October 1924. It was a 40-minute boat trip from the New London, Connecticut railroad station to the Island, where rolling fields and wooded areas bristling with briar patches provided a haven for game. Pheasants abounded, and it wasn't really necessary to plan a water test. Often the fall of a shot bird would be off the rugged shore into rough water and waves, a ready-made water retrieve. In those days, the term "ordinary day's shoot" was well founded.

Springer Spaniels can be and are used for hunting other game birds and many are used mainly for waterfowl, but they seem to be specialists on pheasants. For one thing, a spaniel uses both ground and body scent in seeking game and is talented in trailing, a feat that often has to be performed on a wily, skulking, maneuvering or running wounded pheasant.

Pheasants are the game used in formal Field Trials. In England, where it is possible to hold trials on native game, anything the Springer flushes, whether partridge, woodcock, pheasant or hare, is part of the action. In this country the days of wild pheasants are long past, but birds are of chief importance. Without game, there's no way to establish the basics of competition. For Field Trials, pheasants are released on the course or beats. These are pen-raised birds, raised in large ground-covered pens of sufficient height so the birds can be exercised and develop into vigorous and strong-winged flyers, as near as possible to those in the wild.

The late Dr. Samuel Milbank of Earlsmoor Kennels, noted for handling his own dogs in field trials with great success, is shown here with his Field Champion Rivington Countryman, famed as a contender and as a producer. Judges are Evelyn Monte Van Horn and the late Henry P. Davis.

Dr. Samuel Milbank handles Rivington Countryman to his championship at the Moraviana Spaniel Field Trial Club in 1956. Judges are Evelyn Monte Van Horn and Chuck Goodall.

The Springer is primarily a hunting dog. He began that way and, largely through the interest in Field Trials, is kept that way. It's the only breed with the distinction of having a "Field Trial Association" as the Parent Club. The title was determined by the sportsmen who fostered the breed in the beginning, who imported dogs from the British Isles and who wanted to emphasize the importance of Field Trials and of the Springer as a gun dog.

To hold an A.K.C.-licensed or member club Championship point trial, clubs must first qualify by applying for and holding at least two A.K.C.-sanctioned trials. Most budding clubs, even many established clubs, hold various types of informal trials in which pigeons are used. These are called "fun trials" or training trials or, in weather too warm for land work, water trials or retrieving tests. The organizers of such events can establish their own standard of performance subject only to local laws on the use of game and guns. They may hold "prospect" stakes for puppies, novice, even novice handler stakes. Attending or better still participating in these events is a good way for a "green beginner" to get the feel of a real Field Trial.

In order for a Springer to become a field champion, it must win two Open All-Age Stakes, each with at least 10 starters, at different trials. In recent years, a point system was approved by the A.K.C. so that winning one first place and points adding up to 10 in other Open All-Age Stakes qualify a dog for the title. The same qualifications hold for the title of Amateur Field Champion, except that the wins and points must be gained in Amateur All-Age Stakes.

The point rating system is as follows: second place, three points; third place, two points; fourth place, one point. The sole difference in wins and points acquired for the amateur title is that they must be won in the Amateur All-Age and, of course, handlers must be amateurs. In both cases, the dog also must have passed a water test.

The National Championships, all season, are the goal of every dedicated field trialer and to "get qualified" is the ambition at every season's regular trials. In order to qualify for entry in the National, a dog must win a first, second, third or fourth placement in an Open All-Age Stake during the calendar year. The first National Championship was held at the Crab Orchard Lake area near Marion, Illinois on the second weekend in December 1947. Of the 41 dogs that qualified, 34 were entered. It prompted such enthusiasm and interest that a new organization, the National English Springer Spaniel Field Trial Association, was formed the following year, and ever since has been responsible for this one annual event. Support comes from voluntary dues from the majority of clubs that hold trials. By contrast to that first "National," the catalogue for the 1980 trial held in Benton, Illinois shows 95 dogs qualified and 63 entered.

A gentleman who did much for this breed, Robert McLean, was photographed in 1949 at the National Springer Trial.

Ch. Geiger's Winaway Duke, U.D., W.D.X., sired by Ch. Royal Squire of Rexford ex Raggedy Ann, bred by Lloyd Herriman, owned by Robert C. Geiger. Duke (born May 1957, died April 1965) was top winning in obedience. Bob Geiger bought him as a hunting dog from Ken Jones, who hunted his show champions.

During the 1950's, interest in the Amateur All-Age Stakes had grown tremendously and the idea of having an amateur field championship took root. And rightly so, for many amateur owner-trainer-handlers were as good as professionals with their dogs on the same basis as the "open" dogs. Direct action soon followed. The late Robert McLean was president of the Parent Club, a post he held for many fruitful years, and at the 1960 meeting of the delegates to the National, he appointed an organization committee to plan for an amateur field championship. As a result of the committee's recommendation, the A.K.C. adopted changes in its rules to provide for Amateur All-Age Stakes to carry points towards the title "Amateur Field Champion."

The inaugural National Amateur Championship was held November 30–December 2, 1963 in Wilmington, Ohio. The qualifications for entry in the National Amateur are the same as those for the National Open except that wins or placements must be in Amateur All-Age Stakes. The National Amateur is run and supported by the Parent Club. The purpose of the Nationals is to determine the outstanding Springer of that year in each category. To accomplish this the Nationals are run under customary Field Trial procedure but spread over more series to reduce the element of luck as much as possible. It also brings into focus the stamina and durability of the dogs under the stress of repeated tests under various conditions of terrain, wind and weather. No unusual tests are permitted in the minimum of five land-series and two water-series that are run, and conditions approximate those of a day's shooting adjoining water. Dogs must complete all series to be eligible for a placement or award.

A.F.C., F.C. Julet Ski Hi, known as "Thumper," and A.F.C. Hi Tor's Ripper, owned by B.B. and Evelyn Flick, McMurray, Pennsylvania. The Flicks are true representatives of the stalwarts in field trials. As breeder, amateur trainer and handler, and a frequent judge, Bus Flick is a long time firm supporter of the sport.

Greatfield Kim of Hardthill bringing in the bird at the Connecticut Spaniel Field Trial Association, November 1953. Kingsley Kunhardt, owner, Greenwich, Connecticut.

195

Left: This very famous Springer, N.F.T.C., N.A.F.T.C., N.C.F.T.C. Saighton's Skud, whose titles indicate that he holds Amateur National Championship, National Open Championship, and Canadian National Championship, gained all these honors owner-handled. Skud belongs to Dr. and Mrs. C.A. Christensen, Cornelius, Oregon.

Below: Typical "from gallery" scene at a field trial. The "bird boy" (at right) is wearing the type of basket used for carrying dead birds. Photo courtesy of Evelyn Monte Van Horn.

Right: F.T.C., N.A.F.T.C. Misty Muffet, age nine years, belongs to Dr. and Mrs. C.A. Christensen of Cornelius, Oregon. A longer tail is needed for field trial work than for showing, as it makes it easier for a person to follow the dog's motion. This lovely National Amateur Field Trial Champion illustrates that feature well.

Below: National Champion Ludlovian Bruce of Greenfair, winner of the National Championship in 1954 and 1955, owned by the late Joseph C. Quirk and always handled by Larry MacQueen. Photo courtesy of Evelyn Monte Van Horn.

Left: 1967 National Field Champion Brackenbriar Snapshot, owned by the Brackenbriar Kennels of Greenwich, Connecticut, and handled by Dave Lorenz of Ingleside, Illinois.

Below: Left to right are Candy Lorenz; her father, Dave Lorenz, with F.C. Rivington Joe; Mrs. Philip D. (Julia) Armour, Jr. (the first lady ever to win the National), with her owner-handled 1960 National Champion Carswell Contessa; and the late Elmore Chick with his F.C., A.F.C. Carswell Bedelia.

Right: Dr. Christensen, with his National Field Trial Champion Dewfield Bricksclose Flint, won the 1969 National Open.

Below: Prominent Illinoisians and famous dogs of the 1960s are, left to right, E.W. Wunderlich, of Joliet, with National Champion Brackenbriar Snapshot; Julia Armour, of Chicago, with her National Champion Carswell Contessa; and the late John T. Pirie, Jr., of Lake Forest, with Field Champion Rivington Joe. Photo courtesy of Dave Lorenz.

Left: A beautiful delivery by Lily of the Valley, a top quality Ludlovian Socks daughter. Owned by E.D. Porges, Highland Park, Illinois; handled by Dave Lorenz.

Below: John T. Pirie, Jr., with his 1964 and 1965 National Field Champion Gwibernant Ganol and handler Dave Lorenz. This is one of many field champions and national winners trained by Mr. Lorenz.

Right: The highly successful owner-handler, Dr. C.A. Christensen, is shown with his National Field Trial Champion Dewfield Bricksclose Flint.

Below: At the 1971 Pittsburgh English Springer Spaniel Field Trial Club Open All Age Stake are left to right, A.F.C. Julet Ski Hi, owned and handled by B.B. Flick; Pam's Smarty of Camden, owned by David S. Ingalls, Jr., and handled by Lew Craig; Lord of Ardoon, owned by Col. R.R. Constable and handled by Stanley McQueen; and A.F.C. Saighton's Standard, owned and handled by Al Hric, now a professional trainer at Amherst, Ohio.

Field Trial Procedure

For at least two series, the Field Trial is carried on by two dogs running and hunting simultaneously on parallel courses or beats, each under one of the two judges. The dogs are listed in the catalogue by number and they are called up in numerical order to fill each vacancy as dogs are taken up by one or the other of the judges.

At the conclusion of the first series (it is no rule, but customary for each dog to be given a chance to show work on two birds and, if possible, a retrieve in the first and second series), each judge selects from the dogs that have run under him those he considers worthy of continuing and passes these numbers on to the other judge. Of

Ru-Char's Rocky Creek was a winner in the Amateur All Age Stake at the LASHA Trial, November 1979. Mrs. Charles W. (Ruth) Greening of Mahwah, New Jersey, is the breeder-trainer-handler-owner of many leading Field Trial Springers and creator of the LASHA, the original Ladies Amateur Spaniel Handlers Association, now Ladies Amateur Spaniel Handlers Association of Greater New York, an official club to which only ladies who have handled in recognized AKC point trials are eligible. Members range from coast to coast.

John Buoy, one of the most expert, popular, and successful amateur trainers in the nation, handled his imported Saighton's Ty Gwyn Slicker to the National (Open) Championship in 1974 and 1976, to third place in 1977, and second in 1978.

course, a dog that breaks (is not steady at the flush or wing or shot) is immediately "out." Other misdemeanors that may eliminate a dog are interference with a bracemate, lack of control or failure on a retrieve. The exchange of dogs from one to the other of the judges allows for each dog to be down separately under both judges. In the third series, the dogs are customarily run singly, one at a time, followed by both judges. In the National Open and National Amateur Championships with additional land series being run, each dog, unless eliminated early, is down twice under each judge.

The steward of the beat is in charge of the course and the placing or "planting" of the released birds. The shooting is done by official guns who may be two, three or usually more. The gun guides himself by the handler of the dog, moving forward when he moves, stopping when he stops and keeping himself in position to shoot without danger to those around him or to the gallery. The steward stays behind the judges and in front of the gallery, to which he and any additional stewards keep from moving up too close or from straggling off to the side. This can cause interference with the dog's work or that of the gun.

There is a captain of the guns who designates the position each gun should take and the time each gun will perform. Usually there is a center gun who walks between the two parallel beats, and two wing guns, one on each outer side. The gun is the silent partner, the good right arm of the handler. Usually the judges and/or the captain of the guns confer with the guns at the beginning of a trial for any possible special instructions. Experienced guns are extremely important to a trial. A gun that shoots in a sportsmanlike manner and kills cleanly, consistently and at a distance that enables a dog to show his ability to mark and retrieve, instills confidence in the handler, the judge and even the dog.

It is considered that the most efficient gun and load is a well-choked 12-gauge double gun and a load of not less than three-and-one-quarter drams of smokeless powder or equivalent and one and one-eighth ounces of number five, six, seven or seven-and-one-half shot.

F.T.C. Meadowrock's Rowdy Roger, 3rd in the 1979 National Championship, talks it over with trainer-handler Ray Cacchio. Ray is a grandson of Herman Mellenthin, a famous breeder of Cocker Spaniel show dogs, notably the great Best in Show winning Ch. My Own Brucie. This picture was taken at a training session, not at a field trial where nothing can be worn except clothes and a whistle. (A lead must be carried in a pocket so that none of it shows.)

F.T.C., N.A.F.T.C. Saighton's Signal, another of the famous National Amateur Champions owned by Dr. and Mrs. C.A. Christensen, Cornelius, Oregon.

This is Ray Cacchio's young son, Alex, with "Binnie," the Springer he often handled at water trials, patiently awaiting their turn.

Comparatively new to the sport and already dedicated, Mrs. Don (Kathleen) Cande, Locust Valley, New York, with her Nilo Heir of Sizzler, a son of John Olin's double National Field Trial Champion Saighton's Sizzler and Dungarvan's Right On. This dog has been winning well in the Open Stakes handled by Don Cande, amateur handler who also often serves as a judge or gun.

The Purpose of Field Trials

The purpose of a spaniel Field Trial is two-fold—to demonstrate the performance of a properly trained spaniel in the field, and to determine the dog with the finest qualities among those entered in each stake. Good judging is very important. Positive, constructive judging, not negative judging, affects the breeding plans of the future.

Judging of Field Trials

Paragraph seven in the official A.K.C. Rules and Standard Procedure for spaniel Field Trials sums it all up rather well:

In judging a spaniel's work, judges should give attention to the following points, taking them as a whole throughout the entire performance rather than giving too much credit to a flashy bit of work: Control

After a retrieve is completed, the handler always gives the bird to the judge, demonstrated here by professional trainer Ray Cacchio and judge James Stewart. This traditional act is to permit the judge to examine the bird to see if any damage has been done by the dog. If the bird has been chewed, torn or crushed presumably by the dog (indicating a hard mouth, an extreme rarity in Springers), the judge quietly tells the bird boy to keep the bird aside until later when he can discuss it with the other judge. Photo by Don Cande.

at all times and under all conditions. Scenting ability and use of wind. Manner of covering ground and briskness of questing. Perseverance and courage in facing cover. Steadiness to flush, shot and command. Aptitude in marking fall of game and ability to find it. Ability and willingness to take hand signals. Promptness and style of retrieve and delivery. Proof of tender mouth.''

Where facilities exist and water tests are held, such tests should not exceed in their requirements the conditions met in an ordinary day's rough shoot adjoining water. Land work is the primary function of a spaniel, but where a water test is given, any dog that does not complete the water test shall not be entitled to any award.

Summary

A Springer is a hunting dog that is also a retriever. He must seek, find and flush game and do it with desire, drive and eagerness. Then he must mark well the fall of game, persevere on the trail if the bird is wounded and running, and retrieve promptly to hand.

Hunting and game finding are essential. Staying within gun range is an absolute requirement because the spaniel is handled from foot. When game is flushed (sprung into the air), the trained spaniel must "hup," sit, or stop promptly and remain so until sent by his handler, who is first so instructed by the judge) to retrieve. "Hup," incidentally, is an old English word, short for "bird is up."

There are other times when a dog must "hup." The trained dog stops when he hears the sound of a shot at any time or when there is a bird in the air that he sees overhead. In a trial, when a bird is flushed and shot, the dog on the opposite beat should stop or "hup" automatically and thus honor the shot. He may then be called in close to his handler to wait until started again. The honor, of course, is to prevent interference with the retrieve being made by the other dog and also for the dog to stop hunting and thus not find and flush a bird while the action is taking place on the other beat.

Bob Geiger with two "young hopefuls" (Tiger Chief and a sister) in the field on a hunting trip in Eastern Washington. Ch. Chief Geronimo looks on. Photo by Tillie Geiger.

To the hunter and Field Trial enthusiast there is no more beautiful sight than a Springer bounding across the fields in that typical, exciting spaniel action, using the wind and hitting the cover, and driving in unerringly on the scent of game; then a sharp, tense "hup" at the flush; watching and marking intently; and then, at command, complete all action by a swiftly accomplished retrieve to hand.

All this takes training. A puppy may show great promise and natural ability, but it is proper training that brings out and develops his potential. Puppy Stakes in trials are normally run on pigeons and a Springer is eligible to run in Puppy Stakes up to the age of two years. Most Springers, however, are pretty well along in training by then and just about ready for the All-Age Stakes.

Lew Craig has sent in this photo of a future field trial "star." Pam's Bullet of Camden already is an expert at retrieving at the age of eight weeks.

Evelyn Monte in 1968 with her Field Champion and A.F.C. Hardthill's Toto (in foreground), one of the top winning Field Trial Springers in the 1960s and high point winner (field) in the country for 1967.

CHAPTER TEN

Evelyn Monte Van Horn Explains the Working Certificates

"Over the meadow and through the woods" go Chris, Harley, and Sin. Owned by Debra Valvo, Sure-Wyn Kennels.

There is a vast difference between a pup that may make a satisfactory shooting companion and one that is worth training for the highly competitive sport of Field Trials. Top-flight Field Trial dogs are dedicated animals, in love with their work. They are tough dogs with astonishing speed, nose and endurance—plus a touch of genius. There are, however, many Springers that are good hunting dogs, not flashy or strikingly brilliant or even very finished in performance, but with an inborn hunting instinct that enables them to do creditable work in a day's shooting.

The purpose of Working Certificates was an attempt to cooperate with the numerous breeders and exhibitors who desire to foster the hunting instinct of the Springer in their show stock and encourage others to do so. The names of dogs tested are entered on special entry forms, supplied on request, by the Chairman of the Working Certificate Committee. Dogs are run singly, but a minimum of three must be entered and present to make the test official. It is not competitive. Pigeons are the usual choice of game, but clubs or groups also have a choice of pheasant or chukars.

Started in 1978, due to requests, entries of all flushing spaniels are now accepted for these tests and the Parent Club of whichever breed is concerned issues the certificate. In the case of Springers, their certificates are issued by the English Springer Spaniel Field Trial Association. When you see the letters "W.D." or "W.D.X." following a dog's name, you will know those letters indicate the dog's having passed the necessary test to gain a Working Dog or Working Dog Excellent Certificate. A dog that has passed has shown he is not gun shy, can find a bird and will retrieve on land and from water.

For the land test, one live bird for each dog is "planted" on the course or beat, at least 60 to 80 feet ahead of the starting line, so that there is an opportunity for the dog to demonstrate ground coverage and hunting ability. There should be suitable cover in the form of stubble, grass, brush, etc.

For the water test, a shot is fired into the air and a dead bird is thrown, either from shore or from a boat, into the water, so as to fall at a distance that requires the dog to swim in order to make the retrieve.

N.F.T.C., A.F.T.C., C.F.T.C. Dewfield Bricksclose Flint, belonging to Dr. and Mrs. C.A. Christensen, is distinguished in both American and Canadian field trials.

A person to shoot a "gun" or two "guns" (one on either side) should accompany the handler; or, if the handler prefers, he may do his own shooting, always keeping the rules of safe gun-handling in mind.

Following is a resume of Working Certificates and their requirements:

In the Land Test, the dog 1) Should sit or stay beside the handler, at the starting line, unleashed, until the judge instructs the handler to proceed. The handler then "sends" his dog and

One of the Lleda Springers at work in the field. Owned by Ray and Estelle Adell, Huntington, New York.

walks behind, directing the dog on the course. 2) Should show fairly reasonable, not necessarily immediate, response to a whistle and/or a command, and reasonable quartering of his ground. He should not, for example, be completely out of control, although leniency and time should be given the handler to collect his dog. 3) Should *not* be required to be steady in flush or shot. 4) Should demonstrate sufficient hunting ability to find and put up game in a workmanlike manner, without undue urging, and should show no evidence of "pottering." 5) Should retrieve game to hand or within reasonable distance so that the handler can take or pick up the bird without chasing down the dog. The handler may direct the dog to the fall if the dog has not marked it. 6) Should avoid "Hard-mouth" which is a serious fault. When a dog delivers a damaged bird (by damaged is meant a bird that has been chewed or crushed by the dog's jaws, not damage done by the gun shot) that is not suitable for the table or cannot be used in a training session for another dog, he will be disqualified, even though this dog has fulfilled all other requirements satisfactorily on his Working Dog Tests.

In the Water Test, the dog 1) Should *not* be required to sit or stay on the line unleashed. He may be held on leash until the handler is directed by the judge to send the dog. 2) Should retrieve to hand or within reasonable distance so that the handler can take or pick up the bird without wading out into deep water or chasing the dog on land.

The following procedure is used in awarding Working Certificates by the judge or judges:

1) A dog that completes all parts of the test in a creditable manner will be awarded the Working Dog Certificate.

2) If, however, in the opinion of the judge or judges, the dog performs in an *excellent* manner in *all* the tests (not just part of them) he will be awarded the W.D.X. Certificate. Thus, a dog earning a W.D.X. must have *all* marks in the *excellent* column of the judges' report.

Chairman or Secretary of the officiating club or group shall, within one week of the tests, send all completed entry forms (whether the dogs qualified or not) signed by the judge or judges to Miss Tillie Geiger, Chairman—Working Certificates, English Springer Spaniel Field Trial Association, 41312 S.E. 130th Street, North Bend, Washington 98045.

Dungarvon Right On, owned by Mrs. Kathleen Cande, Locust Valley, New York, completes a retrieve to her handler, Ray Cacchio, at the 1980 National (Open) Championship, Benton, Illinois. Ray is wearing the arm band signifying the dog's number; such arm bands always are worn at the National. Photo by Don Cande.

Highest Scoring
in Regular Classes

G.C.E.S.S.A.,inc
April 23,1977

Judge
Mrs Betty Mac Regan

All set to go! Obedience Trial Champion Ruleon's Dandy of Belmar, 1980 National Obedience Springer of the Year, is pictured with trainer-owner-handler Steve Dreiseszun of Phoenix, Arizona.

Opposite: Accepting a 1977 award are Steve Dreiseszun and Obedience Trial Champion Ruleon's Dandy of Belmar.

Lady Dustin, C.D., is the first Springer at the Windfall Kennels of Mrs. Connie Mitchon, Springfield, Illinois. This lovely bitch completed her Obedience Title when 7½ years old. She is photographed with her young master, Mrs. Mitchon's son Brian.

Pequa's Pericles of Sunnykay, C.D., winning Highest Scoring Dog in Trial on a rainy day, is owned by Matthew Weingarten, Huntington Station, New York.

Am., Can. Ch. Perri's Timothy Von Zuda, C.D., an all-breed Best in Show winner and a Specialty Best of Breed winner, belongs to Donahan Springers, Donald and Carol Callahan, Prineville, Oregon. Don Callahan, handler; Everett Metzger, judge.

Opposite: Am., Can. Ch. Bushlo's Ephor, T.D., is by Ch. Winacko's Classic Replay, C.D., ex Highcliffe's Here Am I of Penhope; bred by Candace Johnson, owned by Howard Yost, Winston Salem, North Carolina. Although shown very little, this lovely dog is a Best in Show winner with several Sporting Group Firsts to his credit.

GROUP 1ST
LUMBERTON
KENNEL CLUB INC
KLEIN   OCT 1980

This handsome Best in Show and Specialty winning Springer, Ch. Jester's Jack In The Box, is a champion in the U.S.A., Canada, Colombia, Uruguay, Puerto Rico, and a South American International. Jester was sired by Ch. Winacko's Editor's Choice, C.D., ex Ch. Venetian Jester's Jypsi; bred by Andrea Glassford, owned by German Garcia y Garcia at the time of this picture, now owned by Mr. and Mrs. James Butt of Sporting Fields Kennels.

These two handsome Springers are Am., Can. Ch. Salilyn's Cameo of Trulu and Ch. Sunnykay's September Song. Sharon Weingarten, Huntington Station, New York.

Am., Can. Ch. Winackos Classic Replay, C.D., is the winner of three Bests in Show, sixteen times first in the Sporting Group, on the lists for Top Ten Springers, All Systems, in 1974, 1975, and 1976, Best of Breed at the English Springer Spaniel Club of Michigan in 1977, Best of Breed at the American Spaniel Club 1980 and the Potomac Valley English Springer Spaniel Club 1980 (from the Veteran's Class on the latter two occasions). Owned by Kathleen Reiss Lorentzen, Ocoee Springers, Saginaw, Michigan.

Opposite: Chuzzlewit's Pentimento, C.D., with points toward her championship, is a daughter of Ch. Winacko's Editor's Choice ex Canarch Contemplation. Owned by Francie Nelson, Fanfare Kennels, Minneapolis, Minnesota.

Ring-A-Ding's My Sin, C.D., goes over the jumps. Owned by Debby Valvo, Sure-Wyn Kennels, Middletown, Connecticut.

Opposite: Ch. Lleda's Spartacus of Sunnykay is coming at you. Barbara Weingarten and Karen Adell Garetano, owners.

Ch. Chuzzlewit's Polonaise, co-owned by Liz Hansen and Francie Nelson, was sired by Ch. Coventree's Allegro ex Canarch Contemplation.

Opposite: Two lovely Springers from Sunnykay Kennels, owned by the Weingartens.

Ch. Danaho's Hedy Tondelayo takes Best of Breed under Arlene Thompson at the SCVESS Association Specialty in an entry of 135, February 1981, aged 3 years. By Ch. Foyscroft Signed Edition ex Ch. Danaho's Ballet Russe.

CHAPTER ELEVEN

Selection of Your English Springer Spaniel

One of the Sunnykay puppies waits to see what will happen next. Barbara Weingarten, owner.

Once you have decided that the English Springer Spaniel is the breed of dog you wish to own, your next important step is to begin your education on selection of exactly the right puppy or dog to satisfy your needs. Do you prefer to start out with a young puppy or a grown dog? Would you prefer a male or a female? And what type of Springer do you wish: for show, for breeding, for obedience or field work; or as a pet and household companion? A decision should be reached about these matters prior to contacting breeders, in order to help them offer you something suitable. Remember, with any breed of dog, or for that matter with any major purchase, the more care and forethought you invest when planning, the greater the satisfaction and pleasure you are likely to receive.

Referring to a dog as a "major investment" might seem strange to you. It is an accurate description, however, for not only is a sizable sum of money involved, particularly if you are buying a show dog, but also, you are accepting the responsibility for a living creature and taking on all the moral obligations this involves. Assuming that everything will go well, the dog you purchase will be a member of your family for a dozen years or longer, sharing your home, your daily life and your interests. Whether these years will be happy and enjoyable for you, as they should be, or filled with irritation and frustration, or terminated because of disappointment or dissatisfaction, depends largely on the knowledge and intelligence that goes into the start of the relationship.

Certain ground rules apply to the purchase of a dog, regardless of your intentions for its future. Foremost among these rules is the fact that no matter what your plans for the dog may be, you must buy him from a reputable source where you can be confident that the puppy's health and well-being are of primary concern. In the case of a pet, this can be either a conscientious pet shop dealer who is known to you and has been especially well recommended by people whose opinion you respect, or a private breeder.

Breeders are usually dedicated people who raise dogs as part of a breeding program with the ambition of producing dogs of show quality and for improvement of the breed. Thus when you buy from one of them, you are getting a dog that has been the result of parents very carefully selected for both conformation and temperament and freedom for hereditary weaknesses. A breeder of this type has, as a goal, the production of sound, beautiful, high quality Springers, and since it is seldom feasible to keep all the dogs from every litter, fine young stock thus becomes available for sale. Puppies with flaws which in no way affect their strength or future health are sold as pets. In many cases, these faults, which would hamper the dog in show competition, are so minor as to be hardly noticed by the layman. In buying a dog of this type from a reliable breeder, you are getting all the advantages of good bloodlines and good temperament, careful rearing, and the happy well adjusted environment which puppies need to start life in order to be of sound temperament as adults.

Ch. Melilotus Highland Cream (Ch. Frejax Royal Salute ex Ch. Tranquillity of Melilotus) was owned by Mrs. John W. Mann, Hamilton, Massachusetts. Photo courtesy of Mrs. Frederick D. Brown.

If you are looking for a show dog, everything I have said about buying from a breeder applies, but with greater emphasis. Show-type puppies are bred from show-type dogs of proven producing lines and are the result of serious thought and planning. They do not just happen, and they are not likely to "crop up" in commercially raised litters.

Throughout the pages of this book, you will learn the names and locations of dozens of reputable and reliable English Springer Spaniel breeders. Should it happen that no one has puppies for sale at the moment you inquire, it would be far wiser for you to place your name on the waiting list and see what becomes available when a new litter arrives than to be impatient and rush off to buy someplace where the puppies may be less desirable. After all, we do not want you to repent at leisure and become a disappointed Springer owner or a former one, all because you made a bad choice.

Springer charm at an early age. This one is from Hillcrest Kennels, Henriette Schmidt, Brookfield, Wisconsin.

Willowbank Springer puppies from a 1960s litter. Mr. and Mrs. Alexander B. Merriman, Blairstown, New Jersey, are the owners.

When you start to think about purchasing a Springer, it makes sense to look at, observe and study as many members of the breed as possible prior to taking the final step. Familiarize yourself with correct type, soundness and beauty *before* making your purchase. Since you are reading this book, you have already started on this route. Now add to your learning opportunities by visiting some dog shows if you can. Even if you are not looking for a show dog, it never hurts to become aware of how such a dog appears and behaves. Perhaps there you will meet some breeders from your area who you can visit and with whom you can discuss the breed.

If you are buying a Springer as a pet, a puppy is preferable as you can teach him the ways of your own household, familiarize him with your schedule and start his training earlier. Two months is an ideal age at which to introduce the puppy into your home or as soon thereafter as possible. Older puppies may have already established habits which you may not approve of and which you may find difficult to change. Besides, puppies are such fun that it is great to enjoy every possible moment with them as they grow up.

Whether you select a male or a female is a matter of personal preference; however, Springers of either sex make devoted, thoroughly satisfactory and wonderful pets. The males are perhaps more likely to wander than the females, which are usually, by nature, "home bodies" and less inclined to roam. Frequently one finds that females make neater house dogs, are easier to train and in almost all cases make ideal childrens' pets. The principal objection to having a bitch, in the eyes of some pet owners, is the periodic coming "in season." There are sprays and chlorophyll tablets available in these modern times that can cut down on the nuisance of visiting canine swains stampeding your front door. Of course I advocate spaying bitches that will not be used for show or breeding purposes. Even those bitches should be spayed whose careers in competition or in the whelping box have come to a close. Bitches that have been spayed remain in better health when they become older as this operation eliminates almost entirely the possibility of breast cancer. Spaying also puts an end to the messiness and spotting of rugs and furniture that normally accompanies the female's estrous cycle.

An appealing baby Springer from Hillcrest Kennels.

When you are ready to buy, make appointments with as many Springer breeders as you have been able to locate in your area for the purpose of visiting their kennels, discussing the breed with them and seeing their dogs. This is a marvelous learning experience and you will find that the majority of breeders are willing, even happy, to spend time with you IF YOU HAVE ARRANGED THE VISIT IN ADVANCE. Kennel owners are busy people with full schedules, so do be considerate about this courtesy and make that telephone call before you appear.

If you have a choice of several kennels where it is possible to see the dogs and puppies, do take advantage of the opportunity rather than just buy the first puppy you see and like. You may return to your first choice but will do so with greater satisfaction and authority if you have seen the others that are available too. When you look at pet puppies, be aware that the one you should buy looks sturdy and big boned, bright and alert, with an inquisitive friendly attitude. The puppy's coat should look clean and glossy, and the eyes should be clear and clean. Do not buy a puppy that seems listless or dull or one that is strangely hyperactive. Do not buy a puppy that looks half sick, or one whose surround-

ings are dirty and ill kept. The conditions of the premises where the puppies are raised is of great importance, as you want a pup that is free of parasites.

One of the advantages of buying at a breeding kennel you can visit is that you are afforded the opportunity to see at least the dam of the puppies and, possibly the sire if he, too, belongs to the breeder. Be sure to note the parents' temperament, looking especially for any indication of emotional instability which might reflect in the puppies as they mature.

If there are no Springer breeders within your traveling range, or if what you have seen on your visits hasn't impressed you, do not hesitate to contact others who are recommended to you, even if the kennels are at a distance, and to purchase from one of them if you are favorably impressed with what is offered. The shipping of dogs is done with regularity nowadays, has become a recognized practice and is reasonably safe, so this should not present a problem. If you are contacting a well-known, recognized breeder, the puppy should be described and represented to you fairly. Breeders of this caliber want you to be satisfied, both for the puppy's sake and yours. They take pride in their kennel's reputation, and they make every effort to see that their customers are pleased. In this way, you are deprived of seeing your dog's parents but even so, you can buy with confidence when dealing with a specialized breeder. To them, it is the satisfied customer, not the sale, that is important.

Everything we have said about careful selection of your pet puppy and the place where it should be purchased applies, with even greater emphasis, when you start out to select a show dog or foundation stock for a breeding kennel. You look for everything I have already mentioned to begin with, but on a far more sophisticated level with many more factors to be taken into consideration. The Standard of the English Springer Spaniel should become your guide and it is essential that you know and understand not only the words of this Standard but also their application to the actual dogs *before* you are in a position to make a wise selection. Even then, if this is your first venture with a show-type Springer, listen well and heed the advice of the breeder. If you have clearly and honestly stated your ambitions and plans for the dog, you will find that breeders will cooperate by offering you something with which you should be successful.

There are several different degrees of show dog quality. There are dogs that should become top-flight winners which can be campaigned for "Specials" (Best of Breed competition) and with which you can strive for Sporting Group placements. There are dogs of championship quality which should gain their titles for you but do not have that little extra something to make them "Specials" potential. Then there are dogs that perhaps may never finish to championship but which should do a bit of winning for you in the classes—a blue ribbon here and there, perhaps Winners or Reserve occasionally but probably nothing too spectacular. Obviously, the hardest and most expensive to obtain are those in the first category, the truly top grade dogs. These are never plentiful, as they are what most breeders are aiming to produce for their own kennels and with which they are loath to part.

A dog of championship quality is easier to find and less expensive, although it still will bring a good price. The least difficult to obtain is a fair show dog that may do a bit of winning for you in the classes, or one with which your youngsters may enjoy working in Junior Showmanship or one with potential as an obedience dog.

Obviously, if you want a show dog you must make it a habit of attending dog shows. Now, this becomes a type of schooling rather than just a pleasant occupation. Much can be learned at the Springer ringside, if one truly concentrates on what one sees. Become acquainted with the various winning exhibitors. Watch the judging thoughtfully. Try to understand what it is that causes some Springers to win and others to lose. Note carefully the attributes of the dogs (decide for yourself which ones you like), giving particular attention to temperament as well as conformation, and close your ears to the ringside "know-it-alls" who have only derogatory remarks to make about each one and everything that happens inside the ring. You need to develop independent thinking at this stage and should not be influenced by the often entirely uneducated comments of the ringside spoilsports. Make an especially careful note of which exhibitors are campaigning winning home-breds —not just an occasional successful "star" but a series of consistent quality dogs. All this takes time and patience, but this is the period during which to "make haste slowly" as mistakes can be expensive.

Salilyn made one try at field breeding, Ch. Salilyn Good Omen bred to F.T.C. Ludlowian Scamp of Greenfair, and these are the pups. Julie Gasow, owner.

While making inquiries among various breeders regarding the purchase of a show dog or show prospect, keep these things in mind: show prospect puppies are less expensive than fully mature show dogs. The reason for this is that, with a puppy, there is the element of chance and one never can be certain how the puppy will develop. A mature dog, on the other hand, stands before you as a finished product, all set to step out and win. He is not liable to change except in such areas as weight and condition, which depend on the care and expertise which you as the new owner will provide.

There is always a risk involved with the purchase of a supposedly show-type puppy. Sometimes all goes well, but many a swan has turned into an ugly duckling as time passes, and it is far less likely that the opposite will occur. So weigh this well and balance all the odds before you decide whether a puppy or a mature dog would be your better investment. There are times when one actually has no choice in the decision if no mature show dogs are available for sale. Then one must either wait awhile or gamble on a puppy. But please be aware that GAMBLING IS WHAT YOU ARE DOING.

A quality litter of young hopefuls at Lleda Kennels, Huntington, New York.

If you do take a show-type puppy, be guided by the breeder's advice in choosing from among what is offered. The person accustomed to working with a particular strain or bloodline has the best chance of predicting correctly how the puppies will develop. Do not trust your own guess on this but rely on the experience of the breeder.

Although initially more expensive, a grown show dog in the long run often proves to be the far better bargain. Here you buy what you see, thus avoiding any element of chance. Another advantage, if you are a novice and about to become an exhibitor, is that a grown show dog usually has been trained for the ring; therefore, an inexperienced handler will find such a dog easier with which to work.

This is how a future "star" looks at eight weeks old. Ch. Sunnykay's Summer's Fantasy, taking first in the 2-4 months class at a puppy match, is owned by Michael Amato and Barbara Weingarten.

If you plan to have your dog campaigned by a professional handler, let the handler help you locate and select a future winner. Through their numerous clients, handlers usually have access to a variety of interesting show dogs. The usual arrangement is that the handler buys the dog and re-sells it to you for the price paid while at the same time making an agreement with you that the dog shall be campaigned by this handler throughout the dog's show career.

If the foundation of a future kennel is what you have in mind as you contemplate getting into Springers, concentrate on one or two really excellent bitches. Not necessarily top *show* bitches, but those representing the finest producing Springer bloodlines. A proven matron which has already produced show-type puppies is, of course, the ideal answer here. But, as with a mature show dog, she is more difficult to obtain and more expensive since no one really wants to part with so valuable an asset. You just might strike it lucky though in which case you are off to a flying start. If you do not find such a matron available, do the next best thing: select a young bitch of outstanding background representing a noted producing strain, one that is herself a decent type and free of glaring faults.

Great attention should be paid to the background of the bitch from which you intend to breed. If this is not already known to you, find out all you can about the temperament, character and conformation of her sire and dam. A person just starting out is wise to concentrate on a fine collection of bitches and to raise a few litters sired by leading *producing* sires. The practice of buying a stud dog and then breeding everything you have to that dog does not always work out—better to take advantage of the splendid available stud dogs for the first few litters.

In summation, if you want a "family dog," it is best to buy it young and raise it according to the habits of your household. If you are buying a show dog, the nearer it is to being fully mature, the better. If foundation for a kennel is the goal, bitches are better, and proven matrons from top producing bloodlines are ideal.

Now about prices. For Springers, as with other breeds, the price usually increases with the puppy's age as the breeder daily invests more money into his rearing (i.e., inoculations, worming, etc.). For a show prospect puppy, at least several hundred dollars would be the cost depending on the potential shown. For a mature show prospect, probably double that would be the cost at least. For a proven winner, the price can run well into four figures, depending on the circumstances of the sale, the winning the dog may have done, and other such considerations. Prices will, of course, vary from town to town, from state to state and from one part of the country to another.

Salilyn's Action Afield, owned by Julie Gasow, Troy, Michigan.

Puppy love! Sure-Wun's Black Magic with a friend. Debby Valvo, owner, Sure-Wyn Springers, Middletown, Connecticut.

When you buy a purebred dog which you are told is eligible for American Kennel Club registration, you must be given an A.K.C. application form that has been properly filled out by the seller. You must then complete this application and submit it, along with the necessary registration fee, to the American Kennel Club. In return, you will receive in the mail an A.K.C. registration certificate four to six weeks later. In some cases, the breeder may already have registered the puppy or dog you are buying. Then you will receive a registration certificate at the time of purchase. This must be signed on the back by both you and the breeder and used to transfer the registered dog into your name. NEVER accept a verbal promise that the registration application will follow, and never pay for a dog until you are certain that you are getting the registration in exchange. The seller should provide you with a pedigree of at least three generations of your puppy or dog and this should be delivered at the time of purchase.

This youthful Springer comes from Hillcrest Kennels of Miss Henriette Schmidt.

CHAPTER TWELVE

Advance Preparation for Your Springer Puppy's Arrival

The younger generation at Filicia's Kennels, owned by Anne Pope.

The moment you decide to become the new owner of a Springer puppy is not too soon to start planning for his arrival. The new family member (and you) will find the transition period easier if your home is geared for him in advance.

The first thing you will need, as you begin preparation, is a bed for the puppy and a place where you can pen him up for rest periods. I am a firm believer that every dog should have a crate of his own right from the very beginning. This will solve both of the above requirements and the puppy will come to know and love this crate as his special haven. It is an ideal arrangement for, when you want him to be free, the crate stays open. At other times, you securely latch it and know that the puppy is safe from harm, comfortable and out of mischief. If you plan to travel with your dog, the crate comes along in the car, and, of course, in order to travel by plane, the dog must be in the crate. If you show the dog, chances are he will be in the crate at the show a good deal of the day. No matter how you look at it, a crate is a very sensible, sound investment for your puppy's comfort, well being and safety— not to mention your own peace of mind.

The crates I recommend are the wooden ones with removable side panels. These are ideal for cold weather, with the panels in place, and equally useful for hot weather, when the panels are removed, allowing for better air circulation through the wiring. Crates made entirely of wire are all right in the summer but they provide no protection from winter chill or drafts. I intensely dislike aluminum crates, due to the manner in which aluminum reflects surrounding temperatures. If it is cold, so is the metal of the crate; if hot, that too reflects sometimes, so much so that one might burn one's fingers. For this reason, I consider them unsuitable.

When you select your puppy's crate, be certain that it is roomy enough not to be outgrown as he matures. There should be sufficient height so that, as a grown dog, he can stand up and sufficient area for him to stretch out full length when relaxed. When the puppy is young, first give him shredded newspapers as his bed, then next a mat or turkish towel. Carpet remnants are great for the bottom of the crate as they are inexpensive and, in case of accidents, can be easily replaced.

233

Eleven-week old Springer puppies at Fidelis Kennels, owned by Nancy S. Cowley, Woodstock, Connecticut.

Sharing importance with the crate is a safe area where the puppy can exercise and play. If you have a yard of your own, then part of it should be fenced in so that the dog can be outside safely. Springers need outdoor activity since they are Sporting dogs and if, at all possible, the fenced-in area should be ready and waiting for

Pictured below is a portion of the kennel area showing Salilyn Springers at home in Troy, Michigan. Owned by Mrs. Julie Gasow.

your Springer pup upon his arrival to your home. It does not need to be a vast area but it needs to be comfortable, safe and secure and in a shady location. If you have close neighbors, stockade fencing works well so the neighbors are less aware of the dog and so the dog cannot see everything that passes that would cause him to bark up a storm. If you are out in the country with lots of space between you and the neighbors, then regular chain link fencing is fine. Incidentally, if you only have one dog, do not feel that he will get sufficient exercise just sitting in his fenced-in area (which is what most of them do out there alone). Two or more dogs will play and move around in the process but just watch a single dog walk leisurely around examining everything and then sit down. You must include a daily walk or two in your plans if your puppy is to develop well both physically and mentally. One more word about the fenced-in area. Have it attended to promptly when you decide to get a puppy—do not wait until a sad accident has taken place.

As an absolute guarantee that a dog cannot dig his way out under the fence, an edging of cinder blocks tight against the inside bottom of the fence is very practical. Also, if there is an outside gate, provide a padlock for it and a key which SHOULD BE USED. You do not want anyone opening the gate and either removing the dog or setting him free. The ultimate convenience in this regard is, of course, a door from the house around which the fenced area can be enclosed, so all you have to do is open it and let him in or out. This is a much safer method (you need no outside gate) and a much easier one (in bad weather you can send the dog out without accompanying him). Such an arrangement is not always possible but whenever it can be managed, it is great.

The puppy will need a collar (one that fits *now*, not one into which he'll grow) and a lead, from the moment you take possession of him. These should be of an appropriate weight and type for a Springer. Also needed are water and food dishes, preferably made of unbreakable material and shaped so that the puppy's ears will stay out of his food and drink. Your local pet supplier should have a good line of dishes from which to choose. You will also need grooming tools suitable for a Springer as his coat needs simple care right from the start. The puppy's breeder should be able to recommend the proper tools to use.

Your local pet supply store has food and water dishes in a variety of sizes, styles, and materials.

Toys with which your Springer pup can keep himself amused and entertained are important. Avoid plastic and rubber toys, particularly any with squeakers. If you want a ball for the dog so that you can play with him, select one made for that purpose, one of very hard construction, as Springers have strong jaws. Even then, do not leave him alone with the ball; take it with you when the game is over. There are also some "tug of war" toys which are fun when you and the dog play together, but again, do not leave them with the dog.

The best treat of all is a beef leg or knuckle bone (the type you can purchase as a soup bone) cut to an appropriate size. These are absolutely safe and serve as great exercise devices during the puppy's teething period. Chewing on these bones helps to get the puppy's set of baby teeth out of the way quickly.

Nylabone® is the perfect chewing pacifier for young dogs in their teething stage and even for older dogs to help satisfy that occasional urge to chew. Unlike many other dog bones on the market, Nylabone® does not splinter or fall apart; it will last indefinitely and as it is used it frills, becoming a doggie toothbrush that cleans teeth and massages gums.

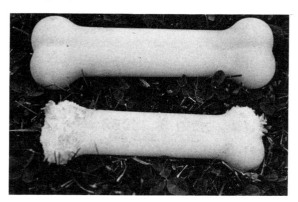

Too many changes all at once can be difficult and upsetting for a puppy; therefore, no matter what the method, keep him on the food and the feeding schedule to which he is accustomed for at least the first few days you have him. Find out ahead of time from the breeder what brand of food was used for the puppies, and how frequently and at what times they were fed. Be prepared to follow suit by having a supply of that food on hand when the puppy comes home, plus whatever supplements the breeder has been using and recommends.

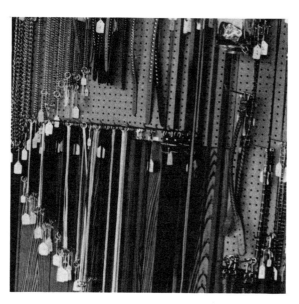

As you can see by this display, photographed at a pet supply store, there are many collars and leashes from which to choose.

One of the most important things that should precede the puppy's arrival is the selection of a veterinarian. If the breeder from whom you bought the puppy is located in your immediate area, ask for recommendations. If you have friends in the vicinity who are dog owners, get their opinions and find out what experiences they may have had with various veterinarians in the locality. Choose someone who several of your friends regard highly, then contact him about the puppy. If you too like him, make an appointment to stop there en route from the breeder's place to your home. Be sure to obtain from the breeder the puppy's health record which includes information on the shots, worming, etc., that the puppy has had to date.

With these things attended to, you are now prepared and ready to bring home and enjoy your new Springer.

Here's one of the handsome Springers from Hillcrest Kennels, Henriette Schmidt, Brookfield, Wisconsin.

CHAPTER THIRTEEN

Your Springer Spaniel Puppy Joins the Family

Springers have feline friends, too. Sure-Wyn's Black Magic trades secrets with the family cat, both owned by Debby Valvo, Sure-Wyn Kennels.

Remember, exciting and happy as it is for you, the puppy's move from his place of birth to your home can be a traumatic experience for him. His mother and littermates will be missed. He will perhaps be slightly frightened or awed at the change of surroundings. The person he trusted and depended on will be gone. Thus, everything should be planned to make smooth going for him, to give him confidence, to help him realize that yours is a pretty nice place to be after all.

Never bring a puppy home on a holiday. There is just too much going on, with people and gifts and excitement. If he is honoring "an occasion," work it out so that his arrival will be a few days before or perhaps, even better, a few days after the big event, when there will be normal routine and when you can give him your undivided attention. Try not to bring the puppy home in the evening. Early morning is the ideal time as then he has plenty of time to get acquainted and the first strangeness wears off before bedtime. You will find it a more peaceful night that way, I am sure. Allow the puppy to investigate his surroundings under your watchful eye. If you already have a pet in the household, keep a wary watch to see that things are going smoothly between them. If both pets are left unattended, the relationship may get off to a bad start and you may have a lasting problem. Much of their future attitude towards each other will

depend on what takes place that first day, so keep your mind on what they are doing and allow your other activities to "take a back seat" for the time being. Be careful not to let your older pet become jealous by paying more attention to the puppy than to him.

If you have a child, here again it is important that the relationship with the new puppy start out well. Hopefully you will have had a talk with the youngster in advance about puppies so that it will be understood that pets are not playthings but living creatures to be treated with kindness and consideration—not to be hurt, teased or mauled. Gentleness from the child towards the puppy should reflect in the dog's attitude towards the child as both mature. Never permit your child's playmates "to let loose" on the puppy (as I have frequently seen happen), tormenting the puppy until it turns on the children in self defense. Children often do not realize how rough is too rough. You, as a responsible adult, are obligated to assure that your puppy's relationship with children is pleasant.

A note of caution: do not start out by spoiling your puppy. They are usually pretty smart and what you had considered to be "just for tonight" may be accepted by the puppy as "for keeps." So be firm with him, adopt a routine and stick to it. The puppy will learn more quickly this way and everyone will be happier as a result.

Paul Valvo and "Pepsi" (Sure-Wyn's Forever Autumn), a most promising baby Springer, were snapped informally in May 1980 at Sure-Wyn Kennels in Connecticut.

Socializing and Training Your Springer

Socializing and training of your new puppy should begin the day he arrives in your home. Always address the puppy by his name and you will be amazed at how swiftly he will learn and respond to it. Avoid elaborate call names. A short, simple one is the easiest to teach him as it catches the dog's attention more quickly. Always address the dog by the same name, not a whole series of pet names that will confuse him.

Call the puppy over to you, using his name clearly, when you see him awake and wandering about. When he comes, make a big fuss over his being such a good dog. He will soon associate the sound of his name with coming and with pleasure.

Several hours after his arrival is not too soon for the puppy to become accustomed to the feel of a light collar. Either he may hardly notice it or he may struggle, roll over, and try to rub it off his neck. If the latter happens, divert his attention and before you know it, he won't even notice this strange new thing around his neck. The next step in training involves the lead, but not until the puppy is showing complete lack of concern for the collar. At that time, attach a light lead, then take the puppy immediately outdoors where there will be interesting diversions such as places to sniff and new things to see. He will probably resist the lead at first and struggle to free himself. Try not to pull him, but coax him along instead. In a few moments, interest and curiosity about his surroundings should take precedence over resentment, making him forget about fighting to escape the lead. Then he will start to wander about, and at first you should just follow along until he has become completely relaxed and seems unaware that the lead is there. Now try coaxing him to follow you. Don't be rough or jerk him with the lead; this will only increase any resentment he may feel for it. Just tug gently in the direction you wish him to take and encourage him if necessary with some sort of treat he enjoys, holding this just ahead of his reach. Once he has accepted the lead, the next step will be to teach him to follow on your left-hand side or to "heel." Of course, all of this will not be accomplished in one day—maybe not even in several days—but it should be a gradual process, one that makes him feel that this is fun. The exact length of time will vary with each puppy.

During the housebreaking period, you will need to take your puppy out frequently and at regular intervals, such as the first thing in the morning, immediately after meals, after the puppy has been napping or when you notice that the puppy is looking for a spot. Try to choose the same place each time for your puppy to relieve himself so that a pattern will be established. If he does not go immediately, do not return him to the house as chances are he will go the moment he is inside the door. Stay out with him until you get results; then praise him mightily and return indoors. If you catch the puppy having an accident, grab him up firmly and rush him outside with a sharp "NO" as you pick him up. If you do not see the accident occur, there is little point in doing anything beyond cleaning it up as once it has happened and been forgotten, the puppy most likely will not even realize why he is being punished.

Your Springer puppy should form the habit of spending a certain amount of time in his crate even when you are at home. Sometimes they will do this voluntarily but, if not, they should be taught to do so. This is accomplished by leading the puppy by the collar, then gently pushing him inside the crate while firmly saying "down" or "stay" as you fasten the door. Whatever command you use, always make it the same word each time for each act. Repetition is most important in training as is associating a word with what the dog is expected to do. When you mean "sit," always say exactly that. "Stay" should mean only that the dog should remain where he received the command. "Down" means something else again. Do not confuse the dog by shuffling the commands, as you will create a problem for yourself by confusing the dog.

Travel with your Springer by car so that he will become used to and enjoy the ride and not become a victim of motion sickness as this can happen with a dog that seldom travels. Take him everywhere you go where you are certain he will be welcome, to visit friends and relatives (if they do not have housepets that will resent four-footed visitors), to busy shopping centers (always keeping him on the lead) or just walking around the streets of your town. If someone admires him (this always seems to happen under these circumstances) encourage that person to pet and talk to him. Socialization of this type brings out the best in your puppy and helps him grow up with a friendly, outgoing personality, liking the world and its inhabitants. The worst detriment to a puppy's personality occurs when he is overly sheltered and pampered. By always keeping him away from strange people and strange surroundings, you may turn him into a nervous, neurotic dog—so don't do it!

Make obedience training a game with your puppy while he is still extremely young. Try to teach him the meaning of and expected response to such basics as "come," "stay," and "sit," "down" and "heel," along with the meaning of "NO." Even though he is still too young for formal training at this point, you will be pleased and proud of his good manners. These are intelligent dogs, so take advantage of this fact right from the beginning.

Feeding Your English Springer Spaniel

There was a time when providing good, nourishing food for our dogs involved a far more complicated routine and time-consuming process than people now feel is necessary. The old belief was that the daily rations should consist of fresh beef, vegetables, cereal, egg yolks and cottage cheese as basics, with such additions as brewer's yeast and other vitamin supplements.

During recent years, however, many minds have been changed regarding the necessity or even the desirability of this procedure. We still include eggs, cheese and supplements in the diet, but the basic methods of feeding dogs have become quite different—definitely for the better, in the opinion of many an authority. The current school of thought is that you are doing your dogs a definite service when you feed them on some of the fine commercially prepared dog foods in preference to your own home cooked concoctions.

This future star at four weeks of age is from Shinnecock Kennels, owned by Maureen Brady and Patty Alston.

The reasoning behind this new outlook is easily understandable. The dog food industry has grown to major proportions and some of the best known, most highly respected names of food manufacturers do turn out excellent products for dogs. As a result, people are feeding their canine friends these preparations with confidence, and the dogs are thriving, prospering and staying in top condition. What more could we want?

It is very easy to see the devotion between this lovely Springer and her owner. Several times Obedience Springer of the Year Bal-Lakes Lady Patricia, U.D., looks adoringly at her master, Ed Bahr of Edmonds, Washington.

There are at least half a dozen absolutely excellent dry foods that are to be mixed with water or broth and served to your dog in the amount and manner directed on the package. There are all sorts of canned meats, both 100% meat to be mixed with kibble or complete dinners already prepared in the can. There are several kinds of "convenience foods" in packets which can be opened and poured into the dog's dish. It is just that simple. The latter-mentioned convenience foods are neat and easy when you are traveling, but generally speaking, we personally prefer to use a dry food mixed with hot water or soup, to which is added either leftover meat scraps, ground beef or canned meat. Actually we feel that the canned meat with its added fortifications is more beneficial to the dogs than the fresh meat; however, the two can be used alternately or, if you prefer, and your dogs do well on it, by all means use ground beef.

The dogs enjoy variety regarding the meat part of their diet, and fortunately many types of canned meats are available including beef (chuck, ground, stew, etc.), lamb, chicken, liver and numerous concoctions of several of these meats blended together.

Springers are great dogs with youngsters. Just ask Anne and Carrie Merriman, pictured here with their friend, Ch. Willowbank's Make It Snappy, C.D., owned by Mrs. Alexander B. Merriman, Blairstown, New Jersey.

Fleishman's Spectacular, U.D., owned by Mr. and Mrs. Al Fleishman of Grant's Pass, Oregon, was the first winner (in 1959) of the Parent Club's Annual Obedience Springer of the Year Award.

There is also prepared food geared to every age bracket of your dog's life, from puppyhood through old age, with special additions or modifications to make it especially nourishing and beneficial under special as well as usual conditions. Our grandparents' generation and even our parents' generation never had it so good where the canine dinner is concerned because the foods developed today are tasty and prepared in such a way as to meet with the dog's gastronomical approval. Additionally, contents and nutrients are clearly listed on the labels as are careful instructions for feeding exactly the right amount for the size and weight of each dog.

With these foods, we personally do not feel that the addition of vitamins is necessary, but if you do, there are several excellent kinds that, besides being beneficial, serve as taste treats. Your local pet shop carries a full array of them.

Nancy S. Cowley's three Springer "girls" in their favorite sleeping position. Left to right, Velvet Heather, Estrellita de Avril, and Champion Felicia's Fidelis of Sulo.

Home-cooked meals, on the other hand, are perfectly alright for your Springer, but as already mentioned, it seems unnecessary when such truly satisfactory rations are commercially available.

How often you feed your Springer is a matter of how it works out best for you. Many owners prefer to do it once a day. I think that smaller quantities, twice a day, are more satisfying and better for the dog's digestion. What *is* important is that you DO NOT OVERFEED. That is the shortest route to all sorts of problems.

From the time that your puppy is fully weaned until he is about 12 weeks old, he should be fed three times daily. For the morning and evening meals, a Springer needs three-quarters to one full cup of puppy kibble soaked in about three-quarters of a cup of water, broth or soup and mixed with about one-half of a can of beef or one-half of a pound of ground raw beef. At noon-time, offer two-thirds of a can of evaporated milk mixed with an equal amount of water to which one-half cup of dry kibble has been added.

As your pup grows older, from three to six months, cut back to two meals and increase the kibble to about two cups with one cup of hot water or broth; double the amount of meat with each meal. From six months to a year, the puppy can switch to one meal daily if you wish, although most people prefer to continue with the two meals until the pup reaches a year old. After that, they may cut back to just one daily feeding. If you do feed just once a day, do so by early afternoon at the latest and give the dog some biscuits or other snack at bedtime.

Remember that plenty of fresh, cool water always should be available to your dog. This is of utmost importance in order to ensure good health throughout his lifetime.

Springer relay races held at the 1976 Springer National are shown in this photo, courtesy of Art Stewart.

Ch. Waiterock Firebow, a son of Ch. Waiterock Strongbow, was the first Springer Spaniel W.D. (Working Dog) in the United States. He was handled in field and show ring by breeder-owner Juanita Waite Howard, Lafayette, California.

CHAPTER FOURTEEN

Elliot More Discusses Grooming the English Spring Spaniel

Everything one could look for in a gorgeous Springer is found in Ch. Filicia's Etching, noted winner belonging to the Robert Goughs and Anne Pope.

English Springer Spaniels require frequent brushing and periodic grooming to keep their skin and coat in healthy condition. In this chapter we will deal with the step-by-step preparation of Springers for the show ring. Although this process may appear rather involved, it must be recognized that keeping your pet Springer looking neat and clean is really not that difficult.

Before getting into the actual mechanics of grooming, it should be pointed out that you will be more successful if, before starting, you have a picture in mind of what you are trying to achieve. There is no substitute for having a "good eye"; to develop one, you should read the breed standard carefully, look at pictures of show Springers in the various publications and go to shows to watch the better exhibitors (both professional and amateur) present their dogs.

The object of show trimming is to enhance your dog's appearance without creating a "barbered" or overtrimmed look; consequently, clipper or scissor marks should be avoided com-

pletely. Below is a list of tools required for preparing your Springer for the show ring.

Nail clipper and Quik-Stop (styptic powder)
Nail grinder (optional)
Tooth scaler
Electric clipper with #15 blade and #10 blade
Scissors: straight, seven and a half inch
       tapering (46 teeth, single edge thinning shears)
       regular thinning (double edge)
Combs: regular
      fine-tooth
Brushes: pin brush
      slicker
      bristle brush
Stripping knife: medium-fine to coarse
Towelling towel and pins (blanket or kilt pins)

Maintenance

Whether or not your Springer is being shown every weekend, there are certain things that should be done at least every other week.

Brushing

How often your dog should be brushed varies according to the length and texture of the coat. Dogs with a thick, softer coat will require more frequent brushing, and dogs undergoing a coat change or shedding will need extra brushing to remove the dead coat before it mats. If your Springer has been out hunting or running in the woods, any foreign matter such as sticks or burrs should be removed from the hair immediately, before they cause tangles and matting.

If you are trying to grow coat on your Springer, the following precautions should be taken: Before brushing, lightly dampen the coat, using a fine spray of water or conditioner to avoid damaging the ends as you brush. If the dog is particularly dirty and sticky, you will do less damage to the hair if the dog is first bathed and then brushed while the coat is still wet. Get rid of fleas and ticks. Fleas in particular will cause scratching and chewing that can ruin a coat overnight.

You will notice that certain areas of the Springer's coat tend to mat more quickly than others. These areas, or anywhere the feathering grows, may be "put in oil" to help protect the coat. Coat oils are commercially available and may be sprayed on the feathering or applied as a rinse after bathing. Instructions on the product should be followed carefully as too much oil, or oil left on the dog too long, can cause skin problems which in turn may adversely affect the coat.

During the summer, some liver Springers have a tendency to sunburn. To avoid this, try to keep the dog out of direct sunlight. There is also a sunscreen spray available for dogs.

Stripping

To keep the topcoat in good shape, it should be "dragged" with a stripping knife once every week or two. Properly used, a stripping knife will pull out the undercoat while leaving the glossier, harder topcoat intact.

Pet shops sell many different grooming tools, some very specialized and some having an almost universal utility. Below are representative examples of some of the tools available.

A—small animal clipper. B—seven-inch scissors. C—nail clipper. D—steel comb with two widths of teeth. E—carder or slicker brush. F—hound glove or mitt. G—bristle brush with wire center. H—rake. I—bristle brush. J—steel comb. K—dresser. L—stripping knife.

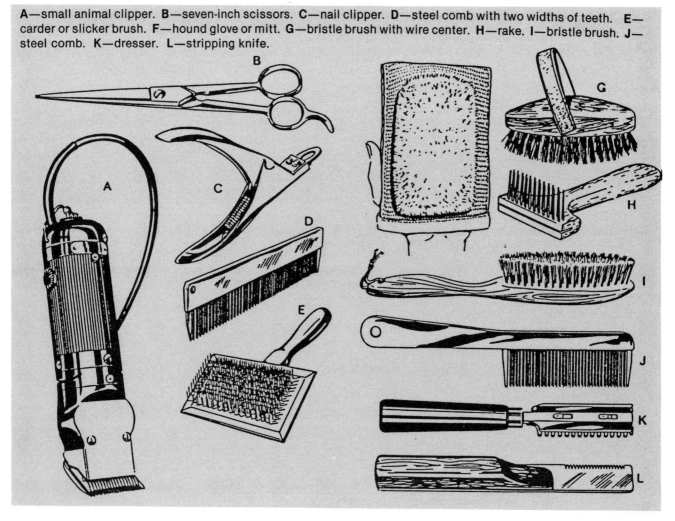

The knife should be held approximately parallel with the skin surface for maximum efficiency. If held too upright, it may scratch the skin. A brand new stripping knife is quite sharp at first and may cut some topcoat but the more it is used, the duller it becomes, thus making it more effective at pulling out the undercoat.

The type of knife to use varies according to your Springer's coat texture and thickness. Generally, the thicker the coat, the coarser the knife used. There are many such knives available in both right and left handed models, and you may have to try a few before you find the one most suited to yourself and your dog. Keep in mind that the knives get better with continued use.

Nails, Teeth and Ears

Nails should be cut and teeth and ears cleaned before the show; however, all of this should be done at least every other week, whether going to a show or not. The grooming tools you will need to trim the nails and to clean the teeth and ears are available in most pet shops.

Cutting or grinding the nails once a week helps to keep them short, and short nails contribute to properly compact feet. If the nails are kept back close to the quick, the quick will be prevented from growing. If the nails are left to grow, however, the quick will also grow, and at this point the only way to achieve the desired short nails is to cut into the quick. This is a messy and painful process, especially for the dog. Obviously, cutting or grinding the nails once a week is the preferred alternative. Always have some Quick Stop powder on hand to stop any bleeding that might occur.

To clean the tartar off all the teeth, use a tooth scaler. It is important to remove tartar in order to keep the teeth white and the gums healthy and ultimately to prevent the premature loss of any teeth.

The ears too must be cleaned regularly. Your veterinarian might assist you in choosing the right preparations to use.

Bathing

Before bathing your Springer, you should protect the dog's eyes and ears from the shampoo. This can be easily accomplished by placing a drop of mineral oil in each eye and cotton balls in the ears.

If your dog's skin is dry or flaky, a medicated shampoo may be beneficial. In any case, use a good quality shampoo and rinse thoroughly. A cream rinse or hair conditioner may now be applied. Most of these products should be at least partially rinsed out of the coat or they will leave it looking greasy.

Now the dog may be allowed to shake itself; then any excess water can be absorbed with a towel. Do not rub the topcoat with the towel. With the dog still wet, stand him on your grooming table and brush out his feathering with the pin brush, followed by a comb, to remove any tangles. It is important to keep your Springer's topcoat flat to help present a smooth outline through the neck, shoulders and topline.

Use a towel large enough to wrap entirely around the dog's middle but small enough so that the dog can move around without tripping over the ends. With the animal still wet from being bathed, use the slicker brush to straighten the topcoat by brushing it the way it would lie naturally. Take a towel of the proper width and fold it lengthwise to cover the dog from head to tail. Place the towel on the dog, being careful to keep the hair straight and flat. Now fold the towel back from the dog's head to make a collar, and pin the towel tightly under the dog's chin. Then, from the rear, pull the towel tight and pin it firmly underneath the dog behind his last rib, being careful not to catch any hair in the pin.

Am., Can. Ch. Willowbank's Second Look, liver and white, belongs to the Willowbank Springers, Mr. and Mrs. Alexander B. Merriman, Blairstown, New Jersey.

Clipper Work

It is usually advisable to do the clipper work on your Springer at least a couple of days before he is to be shown. This gives any clipper marks a chance to fill in. Clipper marks can be caused by any number of reasons, such as dull or dirty blades or too much pressure being exerted while clipping. Thus, clippering should be done carefully and evenly, with occasional stops to clean the blade.

A number 15 blade may be used on the face and neck. Clip in the same direction that the hair grows. The neck should be clipped down to a point slightly above the breastbone and back to the cowlick which extends down the neck from the base of each ear. Do not clip beyond this.

A number 10 blade may be used to trim the top of the head in the same direction that the hair grows, from the eyebrows to the base of the skull. The ears may be trimmed with the same blade against the natural growth of the hair, about one-third of the way down on both sides.

While you have the clippers, the bottoms of the feet may be "scooped out" with the number 15 blade. This helps to prevent infection and makes the feet easier to trim.

Scissor Work

It is now time to do the scissor work. Before you start, remember, scissoring is a process of neatening and smoothing out natural body lines, not just trimming the dog down as tightly as possible all over. Proceed slowly and make a habit of standing back every now and then to study the dog from different angles (especially the same angles from which the judge will view the dog) to make sure the desired effect is being created. This will help you avoid accidentally making "holes" in the coat from concentrating too much on one spot without considering the rest of the dog. As always, while working, keep in mind the picture you are trying to create.

With a little practice and patience, the methods described below will produce the desired result. Don't expect perfection from your first attempts!

Using fine thinning or tapering shears (46 teeth), smooth out the cowlick running down each side of the neck. Brush the cowlick vertically with the slicker, using a downward stroke, thus causing the hair to stick out. With the tapering shears held upright, thin the hair until it no longer sticks out.

The hair behind the cowlick must now be trimmed to blend in with the clippered front of the neck. Assuming the topcoat has been stripped as described earlier, this blending can be achieved by "backcombing." Use a regular comb to lift the hair up and out by running it through the coat against the growth of the hair, holding the comb in your left hand if you are right-handed. At the same time, while holding the tapering shears in your right hand parallel to the coat, thin the hair that sticks out beyond the comb as it is run through the coat. If you are left-handed, reverse the hands. This may be repeated as many times as necessary. Use the slicker to brush the hair back in place at frequent intervals during this procedure in order to monitor your progress. If necessary, this backcombing process may be continued moderately around the back of the neck and shoulder area to smooth out any bumps. At this point it might be necessary to take the hair directly behind the cowlick down a little tighter and also to blend the hair growing close and to either side of the top of the bib. Using double-edge thinning shears, go in against the growth of the hair and thin lightly until you have achieved the desired effect. This completes the trimming of the neck and shoulder area. A properly maintained topcoat should require little scissor work.

Standing by the grooming table is one of the Adells' puppies from Lleda Springers, Huntington, New York.

A Springer's tail usually grows hair profusely and it must be trimmed down to its natural shape. Use tapering shears to trim the hair underneath the tail rather tightly. The hair on the sides and top of the tail should be trimmed so it appears to taper slightly from its base to the tip. You may wish to leave a little hair at the tip of the tail, if it was docked short or if there is a bald spot on the end.

If the hair on the rump, or croup, is thick enough to detract from the dog's outline even after stripping and towelling, you may wish to backcomb and thin there so that the hair will lie in better.

If the dog's rear feathering (skirts) is particularly full, you may wish to thin it towards the top. When viewed in profile, the skirts should not stick out at the top as this will detract from the natural outline of the dog and make him appear longer than he actually is. Similarly, when viewed from behind, particularly in motion, the skirts should not bush way out on either side or grow excessively below the hock joint. Again, use thinning shears to neaten the skirts without leaving any chop marks.

The feet should be trimmed in the following manner. If the bottom of the foot has already been "scooped" with the clipper, use straight scissors to cut off any hair growing between the pads on the bottom of the feet. The hair between the toes should be combed out with the fine-tooth comb. Using tapering shears and cutting downward the way hair grows, thin the hair tight to the foot (with the feet standing in a natural position). The edges may be neatened carefully with straight shears. The object is to achieve a round or slightly oval, compact and deep foot without leaving any scissor marks and without making the feet appear unnecessarily flat.

The leg feathering behind the front feet may be tapered below the pastern to emphasize a strong pastern. You may wish to taper the hair a little higher and tighter for outdoor shows on grass rather than for indoor shows.

The hair on the rear metatarsus (the area below the hock joint and above the rear feet) should be neatened with the tapering shears so that the hocks look parallel when viewed from the rear.

On dogs that grow a long coat, it may be necessary to trim the body coat, again using tapering shears to avoid leaving scissor marks.

Ch. Kay N Dee Geoffrey (by Salilyn's Classic ex Ch. Judge's Pride Jennifer, C.D.) is owned by Dr. Mary B. Gibbs, Spencerville, Maryland.

You may just need to trim a little of the long hair behind the last rib to produce a slight tuck-up effect. When doing this, aim towards the front of the rear leg and cut at a slight upward angle. If this is not enough, cut some more but do just a little at a time. Likewise, if any of the remaining feathering needs to be shortened, use the tapering shears and do a little at a time.

Finishing

When your trimming is complete, the dog should be bathed and towelled the day before the show. You will probably need to touch up your trimming the day of the show.

Remember, proper presentation of your Springer includes good handling as well as good grooming. The judge has only a very short time to compare your dog with the competition and your dog must make the proper impression from the minute he walks in the ring. The preceding guidelines on trimming should provide you with a good start. Good luck!

Ch. Holly Hill's Honey Locust (Ch. Charlyle's Fair Warning ex Ch. Kaintuck Fortune Huntress), bred and owned by Alice Semke, Malvern, Pennsylvania. This was the full sister, later litter, to famous champions Kaintuck Tolstoy, Kaintuck Svetiana, and Kaintuck Serendipity. Photo courtesy of Dana Hopkins.

CHAPTER FIFTEEN

Responsibilities of Springer Owners and Breeders

Ch. Toprock Todd of Spennymoor (Ch. Spennymoor Burnet ex Sweet Talk of Spennymoor), bred by Mrs. John G. Fletcher, owned by Dana Hopkins, Los Angeles, California.

Everyone contemplating the purchase of a dog should be aware of the fact that, along with the dog he is acquiring, are certain responsibilities both to the dog and to the community in which he resides. Anyone not willing to assume these obligations really should not own a dog.

To your community, you owe the responsibility of not permitting your dog to become a nuisance. Dogs should be kept on their owner's property or else on a leash. They should not be permitted to roam free, annoying others who perhaps are not dog lovers (and will become even less so if you permit them to be aggravated by your pet). Even if they do like dogs, they may not be enthusiastic over the destruction of their lawns, the ransacking of their garbage cans and the digging up of their flower beds and shrubs. Imagine the dog that is turned loose in the morning and makes a beeline for the neighbor's property. He digs around a bit, investigates the garbage for tasty morsels, perhaps chases the neighbor's cat up a tree or teases that person's properly fenced-in dog into outraged barking. Then, to add insult to injury, he relieves himself! This is certainly not the way for you or for your dog to win a popularity contest. Before you acquire your Springer, have a suitable fenced-in area ready and let him remain there whenever he is outside the house, unless you are walking him on a lead or personally playing with him on your property.

A dog permitted to run loose is in danger every moment of the time no matter how high your ideals are on "allowing him to enjoy his freedom." Do not forget that this enjoyment of freedom can and often does lead to being hit by cars, becoming lost or being stolen. Do not kid yourself with the idea that your dog is too smart for any of those eventualities and that he can take care of himself because that simply is not true. Permitting your Springer to run loose is irresponsible not only to your neighbors but to your dog as well.

A dog should not be left fenced in or tied up outside hour after hour during your absence from home. Here again it is unfair to the neighbors since under these circumstances the dog is very likely to do a bit of barking. Other dog lovers will feel sorry for him; however, even they may become cross if this is repeated often. So leave your dog *indoors* when you are away; he will be safer and better off there anyway.

Another responsibility which you owe to your dog (or dogs)—one that is often overlooked—is to make provisions for his (or their) safety and welfare in the event of an emergency or your death. Even the youngest and healthiest of us should have a will prepared in which our dogs (be they pets, show dogs or breeding stock) are provided for specifically and in detail, should they suddenly be left alone. Do not believe that your family or relatives will take over as though

249

you are still there, as this may be entirely impracticable. If the dogs are a family project which you, your spouse and/or your children share with equal enthusiasm, perhaps then you may feel safe knowing that everything will be handled well. If, however, you are the only family member who is "doggy," and your next of kin is someone who knows absolutely nothing about the care, needs and potential of your dogs to the Fancy, it is really unfair to expect such a person to know how things should be handled. We do not want our dogs turned over to some Humane Society who "will, of course, find homes for them." We do not want our canine friends turned over to people who have no idea of how to properly care for a pet or protect its safety, nor do we want them to end up producing for "puppy mills." All of this may seem far-fetched to you as you are reading this, but, believe me, it is not.

It is also hoped that you will find some better provision to make for your dogs (especially those of middle-age or less that are well and enjoying life) other than simply to instruct that they be put to sleep. It is egocentric to feel that your dogs could not possibly enjoy life without you. If there is any way at all of managing it, they should have the opportunity to live out their lives with other loving, responsible owners.

Ch. Danaho's Firebird, by Ch. Filicia's Anlon Patriot ex Ch. Danaho's Ballet Russe, was bred and is owned by Dana Hopkins.

Please give all of this very serious thought, then sit down and write out exactly what you wish to have done and by whom, should any misfortune remove you from the care of your dogs. Your lawyer should have instructions regarding this matter and all pertinent information should be incorporated in your will in order to avoid the possibility of someone else taking over without your consent. *Never* leave your dogs to anyone, or in their charge, without first having received their agreement and permission for you to do so. A close friend or relative who feels as you do about the dogs should be asked to assume the responsibility and then the entire matter should be thoroughly discussed between you. Preferably this should be a person familiar with your dogs, one who knows each of them and who frequently sees them.

The name and address of the person to be called, should your dogs need their care and protection, should be prominently posted on your desk, in your kennel office and if you travel with the dogs to any extent in your car, van or motor home. In our own case, we have done this; there is a notation in our van so that in the event of an emergency or an accident the person whose name, address and phone number are located over the windshield is to be contacted immediately. That person has a signed blank check with which to purchase airline tickets (so as to get them promptly to the scene of the accident) or whatever might be needed in case something happens to us while we're away from home.

It always amazes me to see the number of dog lovers who have either one or several dogs completely dependent on them, yet who give not a thought as to what may become of the dog or dogs in case of an emergency or in the event of their (the owner's) death. People are very apt to feel that of course *they* will always be alive to look out for their pets or that *someone* will see to it that the dog or dogs will be alright. How heartbroken these people would be in many cases if they were to live to realize the fate that had befallen their dogs through lack of planning!

Such basics as proper feeding, shelter, inoculations, obedience training and the other aspects of being a good dog owner are covered in other chapters of this book. Those responsibilities which are covered in this section are of such tremendous and special importance that they are included in a chapter of their own. Please heed our advice!

The first responsibility of a person breeding English Springer Spaniels or, for that matter, any breed of dog, is to do so with restraint, careful planning, forethought and deliberation. It is pointless and inexcusable to breed promiscuously, adding to the Springer population dogs that are not truly needed. This is a selfish way of carrying on your show line or your program for perpetuation of your bloodlines. A responsible breeder NEVER causes a litter to be born if there are not definite plans and commitments for homes for the puppies where there will be people to assure their welfare and well-being. This means that a breeder should have a waiting list of purchasers, reliable clients who will act in the best interests of the breed and of the individual dog. True, this may cut down on the number of Springers born; however, it will also cut down on the numbers that may end up in animal shelters, experimental laboratories or on the streets. All of these are fates none of us would like to see befall our dogs.

An ideal breeding program is one in which no Springer bitch ever whelps a litter for which proper arrangements have not been made. If your bitch comes into season at a time when you have no definite prospects for sales and would not want to keep the entire litter yourself, it is better to skip her until a more favorable time than to find yourself with a batch of unwanted puppies. Certainly no Springer owner wants to find himself in the position of frantically searching for buyers, or even someone to whom a few puppies can be given. Often the latter is not a good idea as there are many people who will accept free anything offered to them, whether they really want it or not. These same people usually lose interest when they find that care, time and expense are involved in keeping their free acquisition. Thus, the unfortunate puppy that is given away may end up passing from one home to another and consequently may develop temperament disorders or other problems along the way. So, for the sake of your dogs, and the breed, practice restraint when your bitches come in season and do not breed them unless the time and circumstances are right.

Do not sell a puppy to just anyone who may appear at your kennel without first learning something about the person, his ideas about a dog's place in the family, the facilities he has for keeping a dog and the purposes for which the dog is intended. I have tremendous admiration for those breeders who insist on "checking out" a prospective purchaser before turning over a puppy or dog to this person. People interested in purchasing a dog should realize that the seller who asks questions and checks out prospective customers is simply doing his duty in seeking to protect the dog against misuse, abuse or neglect.

Once a dog has been sold, a breeder should never abandon it. If the purchaser is unhappy with the dog, the breeder willingly should take it back and place it elsewhere. After all, what good is a dog in the hands of someone who does not like or want to keep it? Many a dog that does not fit well with one family works out quite differently in another environment. Remember, if problems arise regarding the sale of a dog, do not hesitate to ask for its return.

A further responsibility of the breeder is to assist their customers and offer advice, especially when problems arise. Many a new dog owner panics when things go wrong and it is comforting for them to know they may discuss their problems with their puppy's breeder. Incidentally, this is one of the great bonuses when one buys from a *breeder*, as they *do* care, and they *do* make every effort to assure you that your relationship and enjoyment with the dog they have sold you will be on the highest level. If you are a breeder or plan to breed in the future, please stand behind your puppies and do your best to help new owners in every way possible.

Ch. Kaintuck Dixie was owned by Marilyn Epstein and Dana Hopkins after the death of her breeder, Stuart M. Johnson.

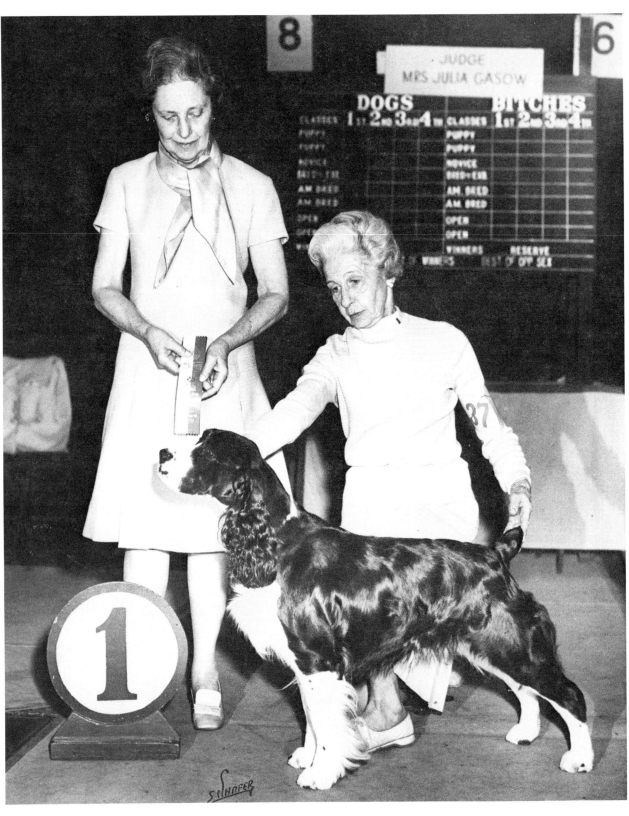

Ch. Dot's It of Mar-Len, owned by Mary Ellen Bates and handled by Dorothy Callahan, is pictured winning under judge Mrs. Julie Gasow in 1970.

CHAPTER SIXTEEN

Showing Your Springer Puppy

A promising Springer puppy nibbles at the corner of the book of Rules and Regulations. Torrey, age three months, is owned by Mrs. Julie Gasow's Salilyn Kennels, Troy, Michigan.

Match Shows

Your Springer's first experience in show ring procedure should be in match shows, for several reasons. First of all, this type of event is intended as a learning experience for both the puppies and the exhibitors; thus, you should feel no embarrassment if your puppy "acts up" or if your own handling techniques are awkward. There will be many others in that same position. What is most important is that the two of you learn what it is like to compete against other dogs for the approval of the judge.

Another reason for starting out in match shows is because only on rare occasions is it necessary to enter them in advance of the actual event. Even those with a "pre-entry" policy will usually accept dogs at the door, as well as prior to judging time; therefore, you need not plan several weeks in advance in order to get your entries in, as you must do with the point shows.

A third reason is basically economic. There is a considerable difference in the cost of entering at the two types of competition. Match show entry fees are usually around two to three dollars, while the average point shows charge anywhere from 11 to 15 dollars, making them rather expensive training grounds! So take advantage of the less expensive method until you feel that you and the puppy are ready to hold your own with at least a decent performance, before entering the more rigid point shows.

As with training classes, you can find out about match show dates, locations, etc., from breeders in your area, from your local kennel club if there is one, or from your veterinarian. Of course, if you belong to a training class, the person running it will be able to supply you with this information.

One of the principal benefits of match shows, from the new owner's point of view, is that many of them are judged by professional handlers whom you will find willing to discuss your dog and your own handling with you, following the close of their assignment. Making inquiries is to be expected, and you can obtain great help if you take advantage of this. The point show judges are usually working on too full a schedule to talk with you beyond just a word or two, but it is considered part of the day's work in match show judging, so do not hesitate to ask. Such advice and comments will be greatly beneficial in preparing you for entry into the sophisticated world of point shows.

Entering a Point Show

As previously mentioned, entries for American Kennel Club point shows must be made in advance. This must be done on an official entry blank of the show-giving club, then filed either personally or by mail with the show superintendent in time to reach the latter's office prior to the published closing date. If the show is limited in the number of entries, filing must be made prior to the filling of the quota. These entries should be written out carefully and signed by the owner of the dog or the owner's agent (your professional handler). They must be accompanied by the entry fee; if they're not, they will not be accepted. Remember, it is not when the entry leaves your hands that counts, but the date and time of its arrival at its destination. If you are relying on the postal system, bear in mind that it is best not to wait until the last moment. With the delays with which the mails are frequently beset these days, keeping right on the expected schedule does not always happen.

As a new exhibitor, be sure to add the new book, *Successful Dog Show Exhibiting*, written by this same author, to your library. Published by T.F.H. Publications, it is available wherever you purchased this book and contains a wealth of useful information, particularly for those of you who are just getting started in this exciting phase of dog ownership.

A dog must be entered at a dog show in the name of the actual owner at the time of the entry closing date for that specific show. If a registered dog has been acquired by a new owner, it must be entered in the name of the new owner in any show for which the entries close, following the date of purchase and regardless of whether the new owner has actually received the registration certificate indicating that the dog is registered in his name. State on the entry form whether the transfer application has been mailed to the American Kennel Club. It goes without saying that the latter should be attended to promptly when you purchase a registered dog.

In filling out your entry blank, be sure to type, print or write clearly. Pay particular attention to the spelling of names, registration number, etc., and sign your name as owner exactly as it is, or will be, registered. For example, if you sign your name Jane Doe one time, do not use Jane C. Doe or Mrs. John Doe on other occasions. Always sign your name the same way to avoid confusion.

At a Springer Match Show, photo courtesy of Estelle Adell. Note the care with which these three are being posed.

Match shows make excellent training grounds for ring careers. Here Bud DiDonato is proudly setting up his puppy, future Group winning Ch. Bryden's Marque on Maidenhead, in the Sporting Group at a match held on the Trenton Kennel Club Show Grounds when "Ben" was but three months old. He won that Sporting Group, then went on to take Best in Match.

Croft Harbor's Cabocharde, by Ch. Rube's Sportin' Life of Lleda ex Ch. Lleda's Legacy to Croft Harbor, is pictured winning Best of Opposite Sex to Best Puppy in Match at the English Springer Spaniel Club of Long Island Puppy Match (from the 2-4 month class). Owner is Lisa Berbit, Huntington, New York.

In selecting the class in which to enter your Springer, take the following into consideration.

Puppy Classes are for dogs or bitches that are six months of age and under 12 months, that were whelped in the United States and that are not champions. The age of a puppy shall be calculated up to and inclusive of the first day of a show you are entering. For example, a dog whelped on January first is eligible to compete in a Puppy Class at a show the first day of which is July first of the same year, and he may continue competing in Puppy Classes up to and including a show the first day of which is December 31 of the same year. A dog or bitch is *not* eligible to compete in a Puppy Class at a show the first day of which is January first of the following year.

The Puppy Class is the first one in which you should enter your puppy, for several reasons. To begin with, a certain allowance for behavior is made in view of the fact that they *are* puppies. A puppy that is immature, or displays less than perfect ring manners, will not be penalized as heavily as he would be in one of the more competitive classes, such as Open. Also, it is quite likely others in the Puppy Class will be suffering from the same problems as your puppy, since they are pretty much on equal footing where age and ring assurance are concerned. A puppy shown in the same class with the fully matured show-wise dogs or bitches looks all the more young and inexperienced, and is far less likely to appeal to the judge than if he or she is shown in a class competing with his or her peers. There are many judges who will take a smashing good puppy right on through to Winners, but more often than not, this puppy started the day where it belonged—in the Puppy Class, instead of bucking all the top showmen in Open.

A word of caution on the Puppy Class. Some shows, especially the larger ones, are apt to divide the classification so that the six to nine month group and the nine to 12 month youngsters each compete separately rather than in just one huge Puppy Class. Be sure to check your premium list carefully, under "classification," to ascertain whether this is the case; then be sure that you get your puppy into the correct group for the age he or she will be at the time of the show.

Shinnecock Tumbleweed is shown winning Best in Match at 10 weeks over 85 dogs of all ages. Handled by Maureen Brady, Shinnecock Springers, Flanders, New York.

The *Novice Class* is for dogs six months of age and over, that were whelped in the United States or in Canada, and which, PRIOR TO THE OFFICIAL CLOSING DATE FOR ENTRIES have NOT won any of the following: three first prizes in the Novice Class; a first prize in the Bred-by-Exhibitor, American-bred or Open Classes; or one or more points towards championship. The provisions for this class are confusing to many people (which is probably the reason it is less frequently used than should be the case). A dog may win an unlimited number of first prizes in the Puppy Class and still retain eligibility for Novice. He may place second, third or fourth not only in Novice, on an unlimited number of occasions, but in Bred-by-Exhibitor, American-bred or Open, while still remaining eligible for Novice. A dog or bitch may no longer be shown in Novice when he or she has won either three blue ribbons in that class, one blue ribbon in Bred-by-Exhibitor, American-bred or Open or a single championship point.

In determining whether your dog is eligible for the Novice Class, keep in mind that previous wins are calculated according to the official closing date of the entries for that particular show, not by the date on which you may have actually made the entry. If you have sent in your entry ahead of the published closing date, and between the time of your having done so and the published date your dog makes a win, causing it to become ineligible for the Novice Class, contact the Show Superintendant IMMEDIATELY to change the class of entry. If you show your Springer as a Novice, once it has become ineligible to compete therein, any win you may make will be cancelled.

The Novice Class always seems to have the fewest entries of any class (undoubtedly due to all these specifications); therefore, it is a splendid "practice ground" for a young dog. In addition, entering the Novice Class provides you with the added opportunity (should your dog take first prize) to gain a "warm up" before meeting the stiff competition of the Winners Class. And yes, dogs from the Novice Class can, and upon occasion, do continue on to take the points that day, if they are deserving.

The *Bred-by-Exhibitor Class* is for dogs whelped in the United States or, if individually registered with the American Kennel Club Stud Book, for dogs whelped in Canada. They must be six months of age or over, they must not be champions and they must be owned wholly or in

Anne Pope is with Ch. Filicia's Coronation at 11 months. Winners Bitch at Keystone, Michigan, and Potomac Specialties from the Puppy Class; Best in Sweepstakes at the National Specialty. Truly an exciting way in which to start a show career.

Ch. Waiterock Trident (black, white, and tan tricolor dog) finished his championship from the American-bred Class while waiting for his coat to grow for entry in Open! Owned by Janice M. Dunn of Lafayette, California; bred by Juanita Waite Howard; whelped February 1964.

part by the person or by the spouse of the person who was the breeder or one of the breeders on record. Dogs entered in Bred-by-Exhibitor must be handled in the class by the owner or by a member of the immediate family of the owner. Members of an immediate family for this purpose are husband, wife, father, mother, son, daughter, brother and sister. This is the class which is really the "breeders' showcase", and one which breeders should enter with special pride to show off their achievements.

The *American-bred Class*, as its name indicates, is for all dogs, except champions which are six months of age or older, that were whelped in the United States by reason of a mating which took place in the United States. Even though they may actually have been whelped in the United States, dogs born from a mating which took place in another country are NOT considered to be American-bred.

The *Open Class* is for any dog, six months of age or older, with no further restrictions. Dogs with championship points compete in it (as they do in all of the regular classes, with the exception of Novice), dogs which are finished champions are entitled to enter if their owners wish, dogs which are imported are entered in this one, as are dogs whelped in the United States. For some strange reason, this class is the favorite of exhibitors, who rush like sheep to enter it. It is not at all unusual to find the breed's entire entry, for both dogs and bitches, all in the Open Classes. The reasoning must be that the exhibitor feels by entering in Open, he is telling

the judge he considers his dog to be of Winners quality. In my opinion, this is foolish psychology. It makes more sense to place your dog in one of the less competitive classes where you have a better chance of winning. Many a good dog has been completely lost in a large Open Class because of the huge number of entries among which the judge has had to divide his attention. Such a dog might have fared better had the exhibitor been smart enough to enter an easier class to win, then be afforded the opportunity of a second chance.

One does not enter a dog or bitch in the *Winners Class*. One's dog or bitch earns the right to compete in it by winning first prize in Puppy, Novice, Bred-by-Exhibitor, American-bred or Open. No dog defeated in any of these classes is eligible to compete for Winners, and every dog that has been a blue ribbon winner in one of them, *must* do so. Following the selection of the Winners Dog or the Winners Bitch, the dog or bitch receiving that award leaves the ring. Then the dog or bitch that placed second in the class to that winner, unless already defeated by having competed in more than the one class and being beaten by a different dog, returns to the ring to compete against the remaining first prize winners for the award known as Reserve Winners. The latter means that the dog or bitch receiving it is standing "in reserve," should, through any technicality when the awards are reviewed at the American Kennel Club, the one that was chosen for Winners be disqualified. In that case, the one having placed Reserve is moved up to Winners.

Ch. Waiterock Arrow, by Ch. Salilyn's Aristocrat ex Ch. Waiterock Marchita (daughter of Elmer Brown) completed his title at the Santa Clara Valley Springer Club. Breeder-owner is Juanita Waite Howard, Lafayette, California.

Winners Dog and *Winners Bitch* are awarded championship points based on the number of dogs and bitches actually in competition on a given day. These points are scaled one through five, the latter being the greatest number available to any dog or bitch for any one ring-appearance. Three, four or five point wins are considered to be what are known as "majors." In order to become a champion, a dog or bitch must have won two "majors" under two different judges, plus at least one point from a third judge, and the additional points necessary to bring the total to 15. When your dog has gained 15 points as described above, a Certificate of Championship will be issued to you by the American Kennel Club, and your Springer's name will be published in the *American Kennel Gazette—Pure Bred Dogs*, the official publication of the American Kennel Club.

The scale of championship points for each breed is worked out by the American Kennel Club and is reviewed annually. At the time of review, the number of dogs and the number of bitches required in competition (in order to gain between one and five points) may be raised, lowered or remain the same, depending upon entry trends in that breed and geographic area. The scale of championship for all breeds is published annually in the *Gazette*, and the current ratings for each breed within that area is published in every dog show catalogue.

When a dog or bitch is adjudged *Best of Winners*, its championship points for that show are compiled on the basis of which sex had the entry to merit the greater number of points. If, for example, there are two points in dogs and four in bitches and the dog is awarded Best of Winners, then he too will receive four points. Under those

Ch. Lou Jon's Femininity wins Best of Opposite Sex under breeder-judge Ray Adell at the American Spaniel Club, with Patty Alston handling.

Here is Ch. Sunnykay's Summer's Fantasy, Best of Winners and Best of Opposite Sex at the 1980 Newtown Specialty, taking Best of Winners at Kennel Club of Northern New Jersey in 1981. Michael Amato and Barbara Weingarten, owners.

circumstances, *both* dog and bitch receive the greater number of the two. Should the Winners Dog or the Winners Bitch continue on to win Best of Breed over Springers that are competing for "Best of Breed Competition Only," additional points will be gained according to the number of "Specials" (as dogs or bitches thus entered are called) in competition. Should your Springer that has taken Winners Dog or Winners Bitch continue on to Best of Opposite Sex, an additional point or points will be credited, according to the number of additional dogs or bitches thus defeated. These points are then added to the points already won for Winners or Best of Winners as the case may be.

A Springer winning the *Variety Group* from the classes (i.e., having been entered originally in one of the regular classes, the first prize winner of which competed in the Winners Class) will receive the greatest number of championship points awarded to any dog of any breed included in that Variety Group at that show. By gaining Best in Show under these circumstances, the same is true, but now applies to the greatest number of points awarded to any breed in the entire show.

Best of Breed competition consists of the Winners Dog and the Winners Bitch which automatically compete on the strength of these awards, plus whatever dogs and bitches have been entered specifically for this class. Also, dogs and bitches, which, according to their owners' records, have completed the requirements for championship after closing of the entries for the show, but whose championships are unconfirmed, may be transferred from one of the regular classes to the Best of Breed competition. THIS TRANSFER, HOWEVER, MUST BE MADE BY THE SHOW SUPERINTENDENT OR SHOW SECRETARY ONE HALF HOUR PRIOR TO THE START OF ANY JUDGING AT THE SHOW.

This latter has proven to be an extremely popular new rule, as under it a dog can finish on Saturday, then be transferred to "Specials" and compete as such on Sunday. Note those words of caution, though: The change must be made *prior to the start of the day's judging*, which means prior to the start of *any* judging at the show, not just of your individual breed.

English Springer Spaniel Best of Breed winners are entitled to compete in the *Sporting Group*. This is not mandatory, but it is a privilege which exhibitors value. The dogs winning first in each of the seven Variety Groups (Sporting, Hound, Working, Terrier, Toy, Non-Sporting, and Herding) *must* compete for *Best in Show*.

Ch. Arel's Deuce, C.D.X., gaining his first points toward the title by going Best of Breed.

In this 1965 photo from the American Spaniel Club, Anne Pope is winning Best Brace in Show with her Springers, Ch. Filicia's Uncle Tom and Melilotus Stonewall, under judge Mrs. Mildred Imrie.

Non-Regular Classes are sometimes included at the all-breed shows and almost invariably at Specialty Shows. These include *Stud Dog Class* and *Brood Bitch Class*, which are judged on the basis of the quality of the offspring accompanying the sire or dam. The quality of the latter is beside the point in these classes; it is the youngsters that count. The quality of both the progeny is to be averaged to decide which sire or dam is the best and most consistent producer, as that is the point of this competition.

Then there is the *Brace Class*, the winner of which (at all-breed events) moves up to competi-tion for Best Brace in each of the Variety Groups, then Best Brace in Show. These dogs are judged on the similarity and evenness of their appearance; in other words, the pair (or brace) of Springers should look like identical twins with regard to their size, color, markings and type, and they should move together almost as a single dog (one person handling them) with precision. The same applies to the *Team Class*, which is infrequently seen nowadays. The difference between Brace and Team is that four dogs are involved in the latter, and if necessary, two handlers are present.

The *Veteran's Class* is for the older dogs, and usually seven years is the minimum entry age. The dogs and bitches in this class are judged for their quality, as is the case with all other classes in which the winners meet to compete for higher honors, and these veterans are eligible for Best of Breed competition. It is not the oldest dogs, but the most excellent specimen according to the breed Standard, that the judge looks for.

Then there are the *Sweepstakes Classes*, which are sponsored by many Specialty Clubs, sometimes as part of their Specialty shows and sometimes held separately from them, and the *Futurity Stakes*, of which the latter also is true. The difference between these is that Sweepstakes entries usually include dogs from six to 18 months of age, and entries are made at the usual time as the others for the same show. For a Futurity, the bitch is nominated at the time of breeding; thus her puppies are eligible to be entered as soon as they are born.

Ch. Arel's Deuce winning Veteran Dog at the Eastern English Springer Spaniel Club in June 1979. Ardella and Noel Pease, owners.

Judging the Sweepstakes Class for Puppy Bitches, 3-6 months, at an English Springer Spaniel Club of Long Island Match Show in June 1972. Photo courtesy of Estelle Adell, Huntington, New York.

Another lovely Joan Ludwig headstudy, this one is of Ch. Danaho's Firebird (Ch. Filicia's Anlon Patriot ex Ch. Danaho's Ballet Russe), owned and bred by Dana Hopkins, Los Angeles, California.

CHAPTER SEVENTEEN

Pre-show Preparation for You and for Your Springer

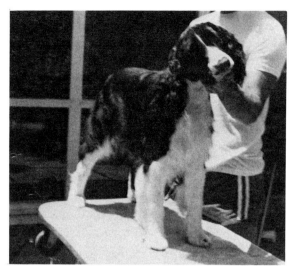

Filicia's Captain Lightfoot at 10 months. Anne Pope, owner.

As an English Springer Spaniel exhibitor, getting together the things you will need for a show should not be left until the last moment. You will be far more relaxed if you plan several days ahead of the show,

The importance of having a crate for your Springer has already been discussed (see the chapter entitled "Advance Preparation For Your Springer Puppy's Arrival"), and we assume that it has long since been in use. Of equal importance is the grooming table, which, it is hoped, you have acquired by now. These folding tables with ribbed rubber topping are useful for "doing up" your Springer both at home and at the show. If you have not yet purchased one, you should. You will find it an invaluable aid and the ideal place from which to work on your Springer, as the rubber top prevents the dog from slipping. These tables are manufactured specifically for this purpose; however, if you have not been able to find out where they are sold, there will probably be a concession stand at the show which stocks them.

Another necessity is a sturdy tack box in which to carry your grooming tools, leads (leashes) and other miscellaneous items. The grooming tools should include: brushes, combs, scissors, nail clippers, cotton, swab sticks, a turkish towel or two, first aid essentials and anything else you are in the habit of using on your dog.

Be sure to bring a large thermos jug or a cooler of ice in the summer (the biggest one you can accommodate) for use by both you and your Springer. Take along a jug of water (there are lightweight, inexpensive containers available wherever sporting goods or camping equipment are sold) and a water dish. If you plan to feed your dog at the show, or if you will be away from home for more than the one day, bring dog food from home so that your Springer will be sure to have the brand to which he is accustomed. You should also plan to supply some well-cooked, dried out liver, or any of the small packaged "dog treats" your dog likes, for "baiting him" to be alert in the show ring.

You may or may not want to purchase an exercise pen. Personally, I think this is a must, even if you travel with only one dog. While the shows do provide ex-pen areas for the dogs to use, these are among the worst places for your Springer to be since he will come into contact with whatever viruses may be currently going around. I feel that keeping one's dog away from these community exercise pens is an important preventive measure towards keeping your dog healthy. Also, since the exercise pen you provide is roomier and allows your Springer more freedom than the crate, it serves as a place for your dog to relax. You will find it an especially handy piece of equipment at outdoor shows in the hot weather, at rest areas, at motels or wherever you wish to exercise your dog safely and without leaving a mess behind.

You will also need a pair of "pooper-scoopers" with which to clean up after the dog when he is inside or out of the exercise pen. Several grocery bags or plastic bags, in which to deposit the dog's excrement and other trash, should also be included with your dog show provisions.

Ch. Lleda's Syncopation (by Ch. Welcome Great Day ex Ch. Clancy's Erin of Packanack), born in 1973, was bred by the Adells and belongs to Don Rockefeller and Karen Adell Garetano.

Ch. Shinnecock's Tumbleweed, handled by Maureen Brady to Best of Winners at the Long Island English Springer Spaniel Club Specialty in 1980. Bred and owned by Maureen Brady and Patty Alston.

It is important to remember your own comfort as well as your Springer's. Be sure to bring folding chairs for the members of your party, unless you all are fond of standing, as very few shows provide any seating nowadays. Remember to place your name on each chair with some permanent marker such as indelible ink, crayon or nail polish to discourage others from "borrowing" them. Bring along whatever you and your family enjoy for drinks and snacks in a picnic basket or cooler. While there are exceptions, dog show food for people, generally speaking, is expensive and indigestible. Keep your car, van or motor home equipped with rain coats, rain hats and boots, and always have an extra coat or sweater handy should the weather turn cold. This happens especially at the outdoor shows when one never knows exactly what to anticipate. You should include with your gear at least two pairs of shoes and a smock or big apron to wear when grooming your dog. In your tack box or overnight case, include a small sewing kit for emergency repairs, headache and indigestion remedies and any medications or toiletries you normally use.

In your car, there should be maps of the area in which the show is being held and also an assortment of motel directories. Be careful to note what motels will accept dogs when you select one of these. We have found that most Holiday Inns, Sheratons, Ramadas and Howard Johnsons will permit dogs overnight. Best Westerns frequently have a "no pets" policy as do the majority of privately owned motels. Some of the smaller chains will take dogs—others will not— so be sure to check this out when making advance reservations.

Before you retire the night before the show, have everything ready for an early departure in the morning. Your clothes should have been selected for the day. If there is any question in your mind as to what you wish to wear, try things on and make the decision before that morning. If you are taking sandwiches or snacks, have them ready in the refrigerator. Be certain that the dog's identification and your judging program are in your purse or briefcase. Work out the best route for reaching the show *before* leaving home, not while you are driving, and remember to allow a bit of extra time for traffic and emergencies. As you near the show grounds,

Ch. Canamer Blue Ribbon, T.D., making a nice Best of Breed win for owners Jim and Irene Eadie, Park Ridge, Illinois.

Ch. Lleda's Majestic Mr. J., shown here in another attractive informal pose, is owned by Dave Schwartz of Atlanta, Georgia. Bred by the Adells.

traffic may become extremely slow and congested. More often than not, access to the show is hardly adequate to handle the early morning rush, as everyone seems to "pile in" at the same time.

A final word about what you will wear: *Do not overdress.* It is your dog, not you, that is to be the focus of attention. Wear comfortable, low heeled shoes so that you can keep pace with the dog as you gait him. Your shoes should have rubber soles for safety's sake, as wet grass at the outdoor shows and some types of flooring at indoor shows can be extremely slippery.

You and Your Springer on the Dog Show Day

From the moment of your arrival at the show grounds until after your Springer has been judged, keep this fact foremost in your mind: *he* is the reason for your being there. You will need to arrive well in advance of the judging to put last minute touches on your dog so that he will enter the ring looking his handsome best. Exercise him before entering the ring and play with him a bit so that he will be in good spirits, alert, and will show well for you.

Ch. Anastasia of Berclee, sired by Ch. Charlyle Fair Warning, photographed in the mid-1960s.

When you reach ringside, request your arm card from the ring steward and anchor it firmly into place with the elastic provided for this purpose. Make sure that you are there and ready to enter the ring immediately when your class is called. Incidentally, the fact that you have picked up your number does not guarantee, as some seem to think, that the judge will wait for you to make a tardy arrival. If you are not there when the class starts, the most the judge will do is to permit you to enter it if he has not yet lined up his winners. In this case, you are short-changing yourself, since your dog misses out on the important "first impression" by the judge who initially views the class (those dogs in the ring) when it opens.

Even though you may be nervous, assume an air of cool, collected calm. Remember, this is a hobby to be enjoyed, so approach it in that state of mind. The dog will show better, too, as his attitude is quick to reflect that of his handler.

If you make mistakes in presenting the dog, don't worry about it; next time you'll do better. Do not be intimidated by the presence of more expert and experienced exhibitors. Remember, they too once were beginners.

Always show your Springer with an air of pride. An apologetic "I don't know what I'm doing here" attitude on the part of the exhibitor looks stupid and does little to help the dog win.

Obviously you consider him worth showing or you would not be doing so. Make that attitude apparent in your general demeanor.

The judging routine starts when the judge requests that the dogs be moved around the ring in as large a circle as space permits. During this period he is noting each dog's style, topline, reach and drive, head and tail carriage, all in addition to general balance. Keep your mind and eye on your dog, moving him at his most becoming gait, and keep your place in line without running in too close on the dog and exhibitor ahead of you. Always keep your dog on the inside of this circle, between yourself and the judge, so that the judge has an unobstructed view of the dog.

Calmly pose your dog when requested to set him up for examination. If you are at the head of the line and several dogs are behind you, go all

Teri and Karen Adell are readying a Springer for the Junior Showmanship ring. Lleda's Something Special is the dog, and the preparations were for the 1969 Westminster for which Teri, aged 10 years, had qualified. This show marked Karen's last appearance in Junior Showmanship at the Garden, as she had reached 16 years of age, and she was awarded the 1968 Top Junior Handler Trophy there. It was Teri's first appearance, after having gained six victories in short order when she reached the minimum age of 10 years. She also qualified in 1969 and 1970, becoming one of the finalists on the latter occasion.

the way to the end of the ring before starting to "stack" yours. Do not stop halfway down and begin setting up there, leaving insufficient room for the others to do as the judge has requested. Also, space the dogs so that the judge has room in which to examine them from all angles, as he will need to do. Time is important when you are setting up your Springer, since you want him to look just *right* when the judge first comes upon him. Practice for dexterity and speed in front of a full length mirror at home until you become accustomed to "getting it all together" correctly in the shortest possible length of time. When you set up your Springer, keep these ideas in mind: you want forelegs well under the dog, feet directly below the elbows, toes pointing straight ahead; the hindquarters should be extended cor-

rectly, not overdone (stretched too far behind) or with the hind feet more forward than they should be. It is customary to remove a Sporting dog's lead when setting him up for examination, holding his head high with your fingers on the inner back corner of his lips. When the judge has finished examining the dog's head, you move in front of the dog and smooth his ears forward along the muzzle with your hands, steadying the dog for the judge to examine the dog's neck, forequarters, topline, body and rear. You want the overall picture of your Springer to be a short-backed dog with the head well carried on a good length of neck; the hindquarters nicely angulated; the front, straight and true; the dog standing firmly on his feet; and the tail, a wagging extension of the topline.

Ch. Salilyn's Joy of Phylwayne wins Best of Opposite Sex under Ludell Beckwith, owner-handled by Wayne Magill, Kent, Washington.

Listen carefully when the judge instructs as to the manner in which he wishes the dog to be gaited, whether it is straight down and back, down the ring, across the back or in a triangle; lately, from what I have observed, the latter has become the most popular pattern with judges and when you are told to gait your dog "in a triangle," it is intended that you should move the dog down the indicated side of the ring, across the end of the ring and back to the center diagonally to the judge. When you do this pattern, do not break each time you reach a corner to twirl the dog around you and start in the next direction, as this breaks the dog's stride and does not give nearly as good an impression as if you and the dog were to move smoothly along in an *uninterrupted* triangle.

In moving your Springer for the judge, do not gallop or race around the ring with the dog. The greatest mistake exhibitors make is moving their dogs too fast. It is not a race; speed is unattractive when overdone, as generally the dog lopes

Ch. Kay N Dee Charlie My Luv, by Ch. Kay N Dee Geoffrey ex Ch. Kay N Dee Lil Luv. This fine home-bred finished in 1979 for Dr. Mary B. Gibbs, Spencerville, Maryland.

This lovely Springer bitch is the newest champion from Joanne DeBoth's Sandhaven Kennels at Green Bay, Wisconsin. Ch. Kung-O-Vik Misty Moonlite completed her title in August 1981, handled by Dick Cooper. A Dave Andre photo.

or jumps at the same time and completely ruins the picture. Considerable thought and study should be given to discovering your dog's most becoming gait, and once you have done so, that is how he should be moved. Get a friend to move him for you so that you can see how he would look in the ring at different speeds. You want a steady, sure gait at a *moderate* speed so that the dog's reach and drive can be seen to full advantage. A Springer should travel smoothly with his head held high, his topline level and his tail wagging, reaching well out before him as his hindquarters propel him with strength and power.

Do not allow your Springer to sidetrack, flop, jump up at you or weave from side to side as you gait him. The show ring is not the place for this, and you should work at home with him until any such tendencies have been overcome.

In baiting your dog, do so in a manner that will not disturb others in the ring or cause problems for exhibitors in classes which follow. Liver and other treats are fine to use in baiting, but DO NOT leave even one of them lying around on the floor or ground to excite or throw off another exhibitor's dog. It is important, on your way out of the ring, to pick up any pieces you have strewn about.

When the awards have been made, accept yours courteously no matter how you may feel about it. To argue with a judge is unsportsmanlike and will not change the decision. Be gracious, congratulate the winners if your dog has been defeated and try not to show your disappointment. By the same token, please be a gracious winner too, which sometimes seems to be even more difficult!

Ch. Canarch Cardinal's Lancer, one of the many fine Springers owned by the Canarch Kennels, Mr. and Mrs. Charles F. Hendee, Barrington, Illinois. Photo taken in June 1980.

Ch. Filicia's Custom Maid, co-owned by the Robert Goughs and Anne Pope, is by Can., Am. Ch. Tara's Aquarius ex Ch. Filicia's Liberty Belle of Sulo.

Mrs. Charles F. Hendee is the owner of Ch. Canarch Exchequer, 4W Dog, handled by Clint Harris in this 1977 photograph.

Ch. Penny's Clown Prince of Lleda finishes his ti-
tle at the Eastern English Springer Spaniel Club
Specialty in June 1972. Breeder-judge is Joan
Ross.

Ch. Clancy's Erin of Packanack finishing her
championship in 1972. Lleda Kennels, Huntington,
New York.

Our thanks to Anne Pope for this picture of Ch. Salilyn's Classic winning the Michigan Specialty in 1973, with his
four-month old son, future Champion Filicia's Etching, set up behind him.

Right: Ch. Welcome Lleda's Delegate, by Ch. Welcome Great Day ex Ch. Clancy's Erin of Packanack, taking Winners Dog at the Sir Francis Drake Kennel Club, 1975, at the age of one year. A Specialty winner, Delegate is pictured with owner-handler Mary Jo Hosteny. Co-owned by Estelle Adell.

Below: Ch. Filicia's Etching on the way to the title at Providence, 1974. Anne Pope, owner-handling; Peter Knoop, judging.

BEST
OF
WINNERS
SHAFER PHOTO

Left: Ch. Anastasia of Berclee, owned by Bernice Roe, winning Best of Breed with Dorothy Callahan handling at Capital City Kennel Club. Anastasia was later campaigned by Bill Trainor to finish her title in Canada and in Bermuda.

Below: Ch. Salilyn's Hallmark has more than 12 champion get, making him a second generation Top Producer. In 1976 he won the Quaker Oats Award for Top Sporting Dog. By Ch. Salilyn's Classic out of the Aristocrat daughter, Ch. Salilyn's Welcome Edition. Mrs. Julie Gasow, owner.

This lovely liver-and-white bitch is Ch. Salilyn's Lyra, owned by Mrs. Julie Gasow of Troy, Michigan.

Fun with the garden hose for a Shinnecock Springer owned by Patty Alston and Maureen Brady, Flanders, New York.

Right: Ch. Jester's Southwind Twister, owner-handled by Andrea Glassford, taking the 6-9 month Puppy Class at the Pittsburgh Springer Specialty. Jester Springers are at Ashtabula, Ohio.

Below: Admiring the tulips is the handsome young Springer, Sure-Wyn's Black Magic, from Debra Valvo's Sure-Wyn Kennels in Connecticut.

Ch. Waiterock Adam's Apple is a liver-and-white Springer dog sired by Ch. Waiterock Arrow ex Waiterock Christmas Holly, bred by Juanita Howard, owned by Janice M. Dunn and Juanita Howard of Lafayette, California.

Ch. Chuzzlewit's Courier, a black-white-tan male, is by Ch. Winacko's Editor's Choice, C.D., ex Canarch Contemplation, whelped November 1976, owned by Frances Nelson, Fanfare Springers. George Alston handled him to Best of Winners at Bucks County, 1979.

Ch. Maginna's Royal Heiress, pictured here winning Best of Breed, is the first homebred champion from Maginna Kennels, owned by Helen M. Maginnes of Exeter, New Hampshire. The liver-and-white bitch is by Ch. Cricket's Rhody Mac ex Ch. Loujon Maginna's Victoria.

Maginna's Sir Sandringham is a black-and-white son of Am., Can. Ch. Veron's Marco Polo ex Ch. Loujon Maginna's Victoria, whelped July 26, 1979. Here he is taking Reserve Winners at the Eastern English Springer Spaniel Specialty in June 1980, handled by Kathy Kirk. Owned by Helen H. Maginnes, Maginna Kennels, Exeter, New Hampshire.

Future champions, these are Chuzzlewit's Courier and Chuzzlewit's Editorial (10th Top Springer in America, Phillips System for 1980) at 14 weeks. Owned by Francie Nelson, Fanfare Kennels.

Charming Springer pups photographed by Joan Ludwig, these are double grandchildren of Ch. Kaintuck Tolstoy, being by Ch. Tara's Aquarius ex Danaho River Birch Gilda. On the left is Danaho's Excaliber Trifle, and on the right is Danaho's Excaliber Goldcoast. Danaho Springers belong to Dana Hopkins, Los Angeles, California.

Ch. Torlin's Spellbinder is by Ch. Winacko's Classic Replay, C.D., ex Ch. Torlin Pequa Mischief Maker, bred and owned by Ray and Linda Beyrer of New York. It is interesting now when solid blanket markings are in vogue that this handsome black-and-white dog took on tough Eastern competition with his 16-year-old handler, Eileen Beyrer, and finished at 13 months, thus proving an open colored dog still can win when quality is present.

An ideal Springer head and expression is depicted here by the seven-year-old Schwedekrest Sorceress, by Ch. Cartref Cosmic ex Loujon Joy of Watch-A-Kee. Owners are Helen and Ray T. Ebert. Thanks to Dana Hopkins for this photo.

Anne Pope is pictured with Ch. McDerry's Cameo, by Ch. Filicia's Anlon Patriot ex Welset Dawn, a Top Bitch in 1980. Lillian Gough looks on as Anne Clark makes the award.

Debbie Weingarten takes first place among Junior handlers at the Eastern English Springer Club Specialty, June 1978, with Ch. Lleda's Spartacus of Sunnykay, co-owned by Barbara Weingarten and Karen Adell Garetano.

Ch. Excaliber's Royal Maiden with her owner Peggy Howard is pictured winning a Junior Showmanship Class under judge James Edward Clark. She is one of the fine tri-color Springers from Triagain Kennels at Cockeysville, Maryland.

Ann Roberts, owner of the Chinoe Springers, is shown with her Ch. Chinoe's Applause, a Best in Show winning liver-and-white dog.

Ch. Lleda's Athena of Sunnykay takes Best of Breed for Sharon Weingarten and Karen Adell Garetano as Ch. Lleda's Keeps Comin' On, her brother, goes Best of Opposite Sex for Karen Adell Garetano and Estelle Adell in May 1976. Arleen Thompson is the judge. These two outstanding Springers are by Ch. Veron's Marco Polo ex Ch. Clancy's Erin of Packanack, and were bred by Karen Adell.

Right: Ch. Lleda's Athena of Sunnykay (Ch. Veron's Marco Polo ex Ch. Clancy's Erin of Packanack) is pictured at a 1976 event. Bred and handled by Karen Adell Garetano, who co-owns this excellent Springer with Sharon Weingarten of Sunnykay Springers.

Below: Ch. Salilyn's Lyra, whelped November 1, 1974, was in 1977 a current top Group and Specialty Best of Breed winner. By Ch. Salilyn's Classic ex an Aristocrat daughter. Among her important successes was Best of Breed over many "specials," at the American Spaniel Club Specialty. Mrs. Julie Gasow, owner.

Karen Adell Garetano looks proudly at her Junior Showmanship ribbons.

CHAPTER EIGHTEEN

Junior Showmanship with Springers

Karen Adell Garetano is pictured winning in Junior Showmanship with Ch. Randhaven's Lleda Sue (Ch. Mister Tamridge of Stage Run ex Ch. Daphne of Recess).

If there is a youngster in your family between the ages of 10 and 17, I cannot think of a more rewarding hobby than having a dog to show in Junior Showmanship. This is a truly super activity for young people, as it teaches many things: sportsmanship; the fun of competition where one's own skill is the deciding factor of success; the proper care of a pet; and how to socialize with one's peers. Junior Showmanship also allows its participants to experience the thrill of winning and the satisfaction of striving to do something well. It is a time-consuming hobby which keeps those involved on a very busy schedule working with the dog and attending shows, and it can be a family project with one or both parents active in the dog show world too. Members of the Fancy often comment on how seldom one hears of dog show kids getting into trouble or serious scrapes, as do so many teenagers with no constructive hobbies these days, because they have an exciting and satisfying interest taking up their time and occupying their thoughts.

Through the years, the English Springer Spaniel has always seemed an especially popular breed with Junior Showmanship-minded youngsters. Being of a moderate size and good temperament, they are agreeable dogs for the youngsters to work with, and judging by the success of Springers with their young handlers in the Junior Showmanship ring, these dogs are well suited for this type of competition.

Eligibility for entry in Junior Showmanship Classes ranges from 10 to 17 years of age. Classification is as follows:

Novice For boys and girls who are at least 10 and under 17 years old on the day of the show, and who, at the time the entries close, *have not* won three first place awards in a Novice Class at a licensed or member show.

Open For boys and girls who are at least 10 and under 17 years old on the day of the show, and who *have* won three first place awards in a Novice Junior Showmanship Class at a licensed or member show. The winner of a Novice Class shall automatically become eligible to enter and to compete in the Open Class at the same show, provided that the win is his third first place award in Novice, and provided that there are one or more junior handlers competing in the Open Class.

Junior and Senior Classes Either or both of these regular classes may be divided by age into junior and senior classes, provided that the division is specified in the premium list. A Junior class shall be for boys and girls who are at least 10 and under 13 years old on the day of the show. A Senior class shall be for boys and girls who are at least 13 and under 17 years old.

Classes For Boys and Girls Any or all of these regular classes may be divided by sex to provide a class or classes for boys and a class or classes for girls, provided the division is specified in the premium list.

Best Junior Handler A club offering Junior Showmanship may offer a prize for the Best Junior Handler, provided the prize is offered in the premium list. The junior handler placing first in each of the regular Junior Showmanship Classes, if undefeated in any other Junior Showmanship Class at that show, shall automatically be eligible to compete for this prize.

Each dog handled in a regular Junior Showmanship Class must be entered and shown in one of the breed or obedience classes at that show OR must be entered for Junior Showmanship *only*. Each dog must be owned or co-owned by the junior handler, or by the junior handler's parent(s), grandparent(s), aunt or uncle, brother or sister, including the corresponding step- and half-relations. Every dog entered for Junior Showmanship must be eligible to compete in dog shows or in obedience trials. At a Specialty show, each dog must be of the breed for which the show is held.

A dog that has been excused or disqualified by a bench show committee may still be handled in Junior Showmanship if eligible to compete in obedience trials. A dog that has been rejected, dismissed or excused under the dog show rules for the protection of the dog excused or of the other dogs at the show may not be handled in Junior Showmanship.

Above is a resume of excerpts from the American Kennel Club rules covering Junior Showmanship Classes. There are many youngsters who also enjoy showing in the regular conformation classes as well as in the formal Junior competition. There are no age restrictions to showing a dog in breed competition. A youngster may start at an age his parents think suitable; of course, much depends upon the individual child.

Junior Showmanship Classes are judged entirely on the skill and ability of the junior handling the dog. The question is not which dog most closely conforms to the Standard of the English Springer Spaniel; it is which youngster does the best job with the dog that is under consideration. Juniors get a double opportunity for success when they have a dog they can enjoy in both Junior Showmanship and conformation classes, plus the advantage of twice getting into the ring and working with the dog.

The first and third prize winners here are both from Sunnykay Kennels, owned by the Weingartens. Springers are great for Junior Showmanship!

Ch. Arel's Deuce gained the final leg on his C.D. with Jane Alston at this National Specialty in 1975. On the same day Jane won high-scoring Junior Handler, making it a very thrilling occasion for George and Patty Alston's young daughter.

The high point of each year's Junior Showmanship competition is when those talented juniors, who qualify, compete in these classes at the Westminster Kennel Club Dog Show in Madison Square Garden, New York City each February. The privilege of doing so is gained by the number of classes won during the preceding year, and the qualifications are explained in detail on the Westminster entry blank.

Some of our best known professional handlers, breeders and owner-handlers of Springers have come up through the Junior Showmanship ranks. Patty Matson Alston, for example, was in there as a youngster with her parents' Pequa Springers. Now Patty and George Alston's daughter, Jane, is carrying on the family tradition. Dr. Gibbs's daughters, Debbie and Kathy Kirk, had Springers in the Junior rings en route to the present, when all are now involved with Kay N Dee successes. On Long Island we find, among others, the Adell sisters, Karen Adell Garetano and Teri Adell, who have gained fame as juniors and are now successfully breeding and handling at leading Eastern shows.

Karen Adell Garetano began her Junior Showmanship career when she was 11 years old at the 1963 Eastern English Springer Spaniel Club Specialty with her nine-month-old puppy, Scotch Mist of Pequa. Neither she nor "Scotty" knew very much about the show ring at that

time. As they entered the Junior Showmanship Novice Class (pre-entry was not necessary in those days), someone told Karen to hold the lead in her left hand—the only bit of instruction that she had received on what to do when she got in there. Being the lone entry in the Novice Class, Karen came away the winner and thus was thrown into Open competition, at a time when she still knew little of what she should be doing.

Karen did lots of practice work that year but did not enter many shows, preferring to learn a bit more first. Then, in 1964, Scotty, now Champion Scotch Mist of Pequa, and she started out with a bang, winning five Open Classes to qualify for Junior Showmanship competition at the Westminster Kennel Club, which is every junior competitor's dream.

Another successful Junior Handler is Tommy Alston, shown here with "Soc" as he beats his Mom for Best of Breed at Naugatuck Valley in July 1977.

From 1964 through 1968, Karen competed in Junior Showmanship, and for all five years she qualified for Westminster. She was considered to be one of the top junior handlers in the East, and in 1968 was awarded the *Dog World* trophy for Top Junior Handler of the Year on the strength of having won the greatest number of classes in Open Juniors during that period. Karen was also the first junior to be presented with an award from the English Springer Spaniel Field Trial Association (the Parent Club), an award which has now become an annual feature.

Teri Adell winning a Junior Showmanship Class.

Karen's younger sister, Teri Adell, also distinguished herself as a junior handler, qualifying for Westminster in three consecutive years, 1968, 1969 and 1970. In 1968, Mr. and Mrs. Adell must have been proud parents indeed, as *both* of their daughters qualified for Westminster that year—the only two members of the same family to do so. When Karen became 17 that year, however, she was no longer eligible to compete. Teri went on to become a finalist in the 1970 Westminster Junior Showmanship competition, really carrying on the family tradition.

Karen Adell has these words to say on the subject of Junior Showmanship:

> Today's junior competitor is the breeder and exhibitor of the future. Junior Showmanship is an integral part of dog shows, and it has played a very important role in my own dog career. I feel that what I learned and achieved during my years of competition as a junior has made me a better sportsman and competitor in the dog world today.

Another junior competitor with an outstanding career is Lisa Berbet of Croft Harbor Springers. It was in 1979 that Lisa determined to try for the wins necessary to qualify for Westminster, since this was the last year she would be eligible. She started off by winning at the American Spaniel Club, then went on to win the Junior Classes at such events as Northern New Jersey, the Potomac Valley Specialty, Huntington Valley, the Eastern Specialty, Riverhead and New Brunswick. She was selected Best Junior Handler at each of these shows that offered the award. Lisa finished with seven of the now required eight wins—so close and yet so far! Her last five shows through December 1979 saw her place second on four occasions. Despite the disappointment about Westminster, Lisa was proud of her accomplishments, as they had brought her to the position of Number two Junior Handler of Springers during 1979. She also is proud of having won the English Springer Spaniel Club of Long Island award for Junior Showmanship three years in a row. Lisa says, "I am glad that I became involved in junior handling, for it taught me how to work hard at presenting my dogs in the best way that I could and how to deal with defeat as well as the joys of victory." Lisa comments on the help that she received from Karen Adell Garetano in getting started with her dogs. To quote her, "Without Karen's guidance, my role in dog shows would be non-existent and non-productive. She was an 'upper' when I was down, and a fan when I won."

Lleda's Legacy to Croft Harbor with her owner, Lisa Berbit, pictured winning the Open Senior Class for Junior Handlers at the Eastern English Springer Spaniel Club in 1979.

Betty Bates is still another youngster who fared well in Junior Showmanship. She competed for five years and, in the last three, was a finalist at Westminster. Betty started showing in Junior Showmanship at age 12, and in her very first summer in competition, she won four Open Classes. At 13, she trained and handled one of her mother's Springers to a C.D. title, doing likewise with another one the following year. Additionally, she has been highly successful in conformation competition with Springers, including winning at least one Specialty Best of Breed.

Karen Adell with Ch. Scotch Mist of Pequa. As with so many of the younger Springer enthusiasts, Karen was keenly involved in Junior Showmanship, and she and Scotty were a highly successful team in these competitions.

Jane Alston, third generation Springer fancier, wins Best Junior Handler.

Just a few more of the many Junior Showmanship ribbons in the collection of Karen Adell Garetano.

Obedience Trial Champion Chuzzlewit's Favorite Son, the first OTCH Springer and the 1977 National Obedience Springer of the Year. Owned by Patricia and Clayton Berglund, Bloomington, Minnesota.

CHAPTER NINETEEN

You, Your Springer and Obedience

Obedience Trial Champion Ruleon's Sir Dandy of Belmar, 1980 National Obedience Springer of the Year, with owner-trainer-handler Steve Dreiseszun, both smiling happily following one of their numerous High Score in Trial Awards.

All dogs, at the very least, should learn to recognize and obey the commands "come," "heel," "down," "sit" and "stay," for their own protection and safety. The dog's recognition of these commands might sometime save his life, and in less extreme circumstances, will certainly make him a better behaved, more pleasant member of society. If you are patient and enjoy working with your dog, study some of the excellent books available on the subject; then personally teach your Springer these basic manners. If you need the stimulus of working with a group, find out where obedience training classes are being held (usually your veterinarian, your dog's breeder if located in or near your area, or a dog owning friend might tell you) and either you and your Springer can enroll, or you can send the dog to class with someone else to do the training. The latter arrangement is the least rewarding method as you give up the opportunity to work with your own dog.

If you do plan to train your dog yourself, here are some basic rules: You must remain calm and confident in attitude. Never lose your temper and frighten or punish your dog unjustly. Never resort to cruelty. Be quick and lavish with praise each time a command is correctly followed. Make it fun for your dog and he will respond by

eagerness to please you. Repetition is the keynote, but it should not be continued (without recess) to the point of tedium. Limit the training sessions to 10- or 15-minute periods at a time.

Formal obedience training can be followed (and frequently is) by entering the dog in obedience competition to work towards an obedience degree, or several degrees, depending on the dog's aptitude and your own enjoyment. Obedience trials are held in conjunction with the majority of all-breed conformation dog shows and Specialty shows and also as independent events. To acquire a list of these trials, if you are working alone with your dog, contact those people already mentioned with regard to locating obedience training classes, or write to the American Kennel Club, 51 Madison Avenue, New York, New York 10010. The A.K.C.'s official publication, a monthly magazine called *Pure-Bred Dogs, American Kennel Gazette* carries a current listing of all member or licensed dog shows and obedience trials in the United States. Subscription to this is really a *must* for anyone wishing to keep abreast of what is taking place.

If you have been working with a training class, you will find information regarding dates and locations of scheduled trials readily available there.

Ch. Kaintuck's Pixie, C.D., gained the latter title at 11 years of age. Who says you cannot teach an older dog new tricks? Anne Pope, owner, Filicia Springers.

The goals for which one works in formal A.K.C. obedience trials are as follows: Companion Dog (C.D.), Companion Dog Excellent (C.D.X.) and Utility Dog (U.D.). These degrees are earned by receiving three "legs" (qualifying scores of 170 to a possible 200 points at each level) for each. The degrees must be earned in order; for example, Novice Class (C.D.) completed prior to Open Class (C.D.X.) and Open Class prior to Utility (U.D.). The ultimate title possible to attain in obedience is Obedience Trial Champion (O.T.Ch.). To gain this one, dogs that are holders of the U.D. degree must receive the required 100 points by wins which include a first place in Utility (or Utility B if divided), with at least three dogs in competition;

a first place in Open B, with at least five dogs in competition; and a third first place, in one or the other of these classes. The three first placements must have been gained under three different judges. Only dogs that have completed their Utility degrees are eligible to compete for an Obedience trial championship.

When you see the letters C.D. following a dog's name, you will know that the dog has satisfactorily completed the following six exercises in the Novice Class: heel on leash, stand for examination, heel free, recall, long sit and long down. C.D.X. indicates that the dog has completed the Open Class consisting of the following seven exercises: heel free, drop on recall, retrieve on flat, retrieve over high jump, broad jump, long sit and long down. U.D. indicates that all of the above has been accomplished in addition to the Utility Class tests, which include hand signal exercises, two scent discrimination tests (leather articles and metal articles), directed retrieve, directed jumping and group examination.

There is also a Tracking Dog title (T.D.), as well as the new, more difficult title, Tracking Dog Excellent (T.D.X.), which are earned at tracking trials.

The letters T.D. indicate that a dog has been trained and passed the tests to follow the trail of a stranger along a path whose trail was laid between 30 minutes and two hours previously.

Sure-Wyn's Black Magic takes the high jump, dumbbell in mouth, for owner Debra Valvo, Middletown, Connecticut.

Along this trail there must be more than two right angle turns, at least two of which are well out in the open where no fences or other boundaries exist for guidance to the dog or the handler. The dog wears a harness and is connected to the handler by a lead 20 to 40 feet in length. At the end of the track is an article, usually a glove or a wallet, which has been inconspicuously dropped, and which the dog is expected to locate and the handler is expected to pick up.

In obedience competition, the dog's conformation does not count. In fact, even dogs that might be disqualified under A.K.C. rules, including spayed bitches and neutered dogs, are eligible to compete in obedience.

Distinguished Obedience Springers and Their Owners

We are pleased to bring you a resume of the Springers which have distinguished themselves by gaining the Obedience Springer of the Year award. This award has been offered by the Parent Club since its inception in 1959, through 1980. Also included are photographs of a number of these dogs, and some facts about them and their owners. For this we are indebted to Stephen G. Dreiseszun of Phoenix, Arizona who compiled this list for our use and who also helped to furnish the information and pictures featured on obedience.

"Over the jumps" goes Ring-A-Ding's My Sin, C.D., owned by Debra Valvo.

This is Pussy Willow Sir Skeeter, Obedience Springer of the Year for 1961, owned by R.G. "Bud" Leonard of Adrian, Michigan.

Obedience Springers of the Year 1959–1980

1959 Fleishman's Spectacular, U.D.
Mr. and Mrs. A.H. Fleishman
Grant's Pass, Oregon

1960 Pussy Willow Sir Skeeter
R.G. Leonard
Adrian, Michigan

1961 Bal Lakes Lady Patricia, U.D.
Edson Bahr
Edmonds, Washington

1962 (same)
1963 (same)
1964 (same)

1965 Loujon Deuce of Charlemar, C.D.X., W.D.
(TIE) *Karen Prickett*
South Lyon, Michigan

and

La Belle Don Mitzi
Judy Lundbeck
Louisville, Nebraska

Bal Lakes Lady Patricia, U.D., and her owner, Ed Bahr, receiving some of the honors won by this very talented Springer.

1966 Champion Walpride Karrie of Charlemar, C.D.X., W.D.
(TIE) Loujon Deuce of Charlemar
   Both owned by Karen Prickett
1967 La Belle Don Mitzi, C.D.X.
   Judy Lundbeck
1968 (same)
1969 Tigaria Pamper, U.D.
   Ruth Wallace
   Lake Forest, Illinois
1970 Loujon Lord Kelvin, U.D.
   Theresa Luley
   Carmel, Indiana
1971 Champion New Dawn of Marjon, U.D.
   (gained C.D., C.D.X. and U.D. within one year)
   Kitty Wray
   Annapolis, Maryland
1972 Nancy's Fancy Lady, U.D.
   Larry Libeu
   Garden Grove, California
1973 Naia's Molly Malone, U.D.
   Larry Libeu
1974 (same)
1975 (same)

Bal Lakes Lady Patricia, U.D., was Obedience Springer of the Year several times in the early to mid 1960s. She belonged to Mr. and Mrs. Ed Bahr and their family at Edmonds, Washington.

Left to right are Jessica Imp of Whimsy, U.D.; Manchester Lord Bernard, C.D.X.; and Willowbank's Brookside Ajax, C.D.X. All are fine representatives of Martha Leonard's Whimsy Kennels, Montclair, New Jersey.

1976 Marjon's Happy Thing, U.D.
(TIE) *Art and Sharon Stewart*
Irvine, California
and
Endeavor's White Frost, U.D.
Doris Peppers
Broomfield, Colorado
1977 Chuzzlewit's Favorite Son, U.D.
Patricia and Clayton Berglund
Bloomington, Minnesota
1978 Ruleon's Sir Dandy of Belmar, U.D.
Steve Dreiseszun
Phoenix, Arizona
1979 Jessica Imp of Whimsey, U.D.
Martha Leonard
Montclair, New Jersey
1980 Obedience Trial Champion Ruleon's Sir
Dandy of Belmar
Steve Dreiseszun

For those of our readers unfamiliar with the Obedience Springer of the Year award offered by the Parent Club (the English Springer Spaniel Field Trial Association), qualifications for it are as follows: All dogs with five or more qualifying scores during the fiscal year shall be eligible to compete. Of those eligible, the average of the five best scores of each dog shall be determined, and the one with the highest average will be named Best Obedience Springer of the Year. The number of qualifying scores for eligibility may vary from year to year, if, in the opinion of the Committee, the number of eligible dogs is too small. In this case, the number of qualifying scores may be lowered.

These Springer "stars" of the obedience world are Jessica Imp of Whimsy, U.D., on the right, and Manchester Lord Bernard, C.D.X., left. Both of these talented dogs are owned by Martha Leonard, Whimsy Kennels.

How gracefully OTCH Ruleon's Dandy of Belmar goes over the jumps during an obedience trial! The National Obedience Springer of the Year, 1980, belongs to Steve Dreiseszun of Phoenix, Arizona.

The first Springer ever to have gained this award in 1959 was Fleishman's Spectacular, owned by Mr. and Mrs. Al Fleishman of Grant's Pass, Oregon. This dog, by Champion Schwedekrest High Regards ex Cindy's Triumph, was bred by Howard E. Hill of Seattle, Washington. At the age of eight-and-one-half months, Spectacular entered his first show and in six shows, earned his C.D. and C.D.X. degrees. Winning three consecutive legs with a score of 195 or better, "Spec" qualified for the Will Judy Award of Canine Distinction presented by *Dog World* Magazine.

Spectacular finished his C.D.X. at the age of 13 months, then went on to add Utility to his titles in short order.

For 10 years, Spec hunted for his master, along with some of Mr. Fleishman's buddies. At times he kicked up and retrieved for as many as five hunters in the field at one time, retrieving ducks and geese in various rivers and lakes where the men hunted. Of this lovely Springer Mr. Fleishman writes, "Spec was the one dog that a man is privileged to have during his lifetime. His congenial disposition made him a perfect family dog and all-around companion. Our two children, aged five and seven years, could dress him up in doll clothes or have him sit at their small table and play tea party with them. Once when I had to be out of town during an A.K.C. obedience trial in Spokane, my wife Jean showed Spec. He worked so well for her that he came away with a score of 199½, although he was not accustomed to having her as his handler."

Spec sired several litters of purebred Springers because people wanted to show in obedience or wanted to hunt or just wished to have beautiful family dogs.

A very showy dog in appearance, Spec was nicely marked with a dark saddle and he had white in all of the perfect places. He was liver-and-white. Although he was not a bench show champion, he was a regal dog and showed very well in the obedience ring. He was a real "ham" because he loved going to shows, and he knew exactly what he was to do when he arrived there.

This is Fleishman's Spectacular, U.D., owned by the Al Fleishmans of Grand Pass, Oregon, surrounded by some of his trophies. "Spec" was the Parent Club's Obedience Springer of the Year in 1959, the first time this award was offered.

Spec's grandsire was Champion Melilotus Little Acorn; his great-grandsire was Champion Melilotus Royal Oak. Of course these dogs go back to Champion Frejax Royal Salute, a line from which many noted bench show champions have been produced.

Mr. Fleishman retired Spectacular from the obedience trials in 1963, primarily because of lack of competition available within the area. He then turned his own attention to conducting training classes county-wide, starting a program for 4-H children and judging at A.K.C. obedience matches.

When Spec died at the age of 11, his owners truly felt that they had lost a member of the family. They have had other dogs since that time, including Springers, Labrador Retrievers and at present a Golden Retriever, but to quote them, ". . . all lovely dogs, but we have never had one that replaced 'Spec' in our hearts."

The Parent Club's Obedience Springer for the year 1960 was Pussy Willow Sir Skeeter. His owner, Ralph G. Leonard, and Skeeter were to gain still further honors from the National, as Sir Skeeter also won the National's Open Class award in 1963 for having earned his C.D.X. degree with the highest average of any Springer in the country that year. We understand there were 15 C.D.X. degrees awarded during 1963 and of these, Skeeter's was first with an average of 198.5, an achievement in which to take pride.

Ralph G. Leonard, or "Bud" as he is known to his friends, owned Skeeter and trained and worked him. They made an impressive team, racking up high honors and important victories during Skeeter's exciting career. Bud Leonard and his friend Tom Chute, a Cocker enthusiast and owner, for more than 20 years conducted obedience classes on a regular schedule in their hometown of Adrian, Michigan. Bud also owned another noted Springer, Wonderland Scorch, on which he gained a C.D.X. This dog was the son of Field Trial Champion Kansan. Additionally, at the time of this writing, Darktown Strutter, a son of Author, was being readied for competition later in 1981.

Regarding Springers in obedience, Mr. Leonard comments, "It takes a special team effort of dog and trainer to bring about the top working performance necessary to win the high scores. Springers are fun loving, willing workers but cannot be trained on hard, rigid or rough methods. Each dog must be developed in line with his personality as some are soft and others are able to take stronger corrections." Proof positive of Mr. Leonard's statement was Skeeter, a dog that really loved to work and a "performer" in every sense of the word.

Bal Lakes Lady Patricia, or "Patty" as everyone called her, was the four-time winner of the prestigious Obedience Springer of the Year award (1961–1964). Born June 17, 1959, Patty lived on a farm with goats, horses and cattle for more than three months until her eventual owners, Bonnie and Ed Bahr, of Edmonds, Washington "discovered" her. The Bahrs were looking for a Springer, and it was Bonnie Bahr who noticed and fell in love with Patty out of the litter of eight pups romping around them at the farm. Ed Bahr wanted the big male, but Bonnie

kept insisting that "this one was special." So Patty came home with the Bahrs and proved Bonnie's prediction to have been correct, for she grew up to become an excellent hunter, an ideal family dog and a supreme obedience dog.

It was the Bahr's son and daughter, Bob and Sandra, along with their mother, who were instrumental in training Patty for obedience trials. At five months, Patty was ready for Novice A. Her scores in Novice were respectable, but when she had advanced into the Open Class, they became spectacular. At the 1961 National Springer Specialty, Patty won the award as First Springer in the Open Class. At the 1962 Specialty, she topped all others as the Obedience Springer of the Year with a truly fantastic record. She rolled up a total of 21 qualifying

Bal Lakes Lady Patricia, U.D., with owner-handler Ed Bahr, is in a dignified pose as her talents are rewarded.

scores in Open and Utility, and the average of her five best scores for the year was 199.6, including one perfect 200 in Utility. In addition, she had been Highest Scoring Dog in Trial seven times. She repeated as Obedience Springer of the Year in 1963 and 1964. Sadly, Patty died of cancer in 1965, and she is missed right until the present time, for she was a Springer that truly became a member of the family.

Loujon Lord Kelvin, C.D.X., U.D., owned and handled by Terry Luley, receives the trophy for Highest Scoring Dog in Trial at Terre Haute, March 29, 1969. "Kelly" was the Parent Club Obedience Springer of the Year in 1970.

Loujon Lord Kevin, U.D. was the English Springer Spaniel Field Trial Association Obedience Springer of the Year in 1970. Competing in 44 A.K.C. recognized obedience classes from February 1967 to September 1970, he qualified on 39 of these occasions and earned 28 scores above 195 and only two below 190. His winnings included eight firsts, eight seconds, three thirds and six fourths, and on four occasions, he was named Highest Scoring Dog in Trial. This is an impressive record indeed and one which must bring enormous pleasure to his owner, Theresa A. Luley, D.V.M., of Carmel, Indiana.

From the time that she was less than 10 years old, Dr. Luley recalls that her overwhelming desire was to own a show dog, particularly one with which she could compete in obedience. Her family owned a series of mixed breed dogs over the years and as a little girl, Dr. Luley spent endless hours grooming and training her "champions." When she was 15, the 4-H dog obedience program started in Indianapolis. Not having a dog in her own family at the time, our young friend made the rounds in her neighborhood until she located a Beagle whose owner wished to have her trained. The Beagle was an apt pupil, and a summer's patient training resulted in a third prize ribbon at the state fair. The next year, Theresa trained two Poodles, one of which was A.K.C. registered, for other neighbors. With the owner's permission, she continued working with this dog (the registered one) until that became her first C.D. winner. This was followed by a Welsh Corgi.

Then, while attending a show, Theresa noticed a young lady showing Springers and doing very well in obedience. She loved the breed on sight, wanted one for herself and became acquainted with this exhibitor. The latter was Karen Crisanti, now Karen Prickett, who was at that time manager of the Loujon Kennels which belonged to Mr. and Mrs. John S. Greene of New Richmond, Ohio. Finally, in May of 1966, as a graduation gift from her parents, Theresa received her dreamed-of Springer puppy. This was "Kelly"—Loujon Lord Kelvin—bred by Karen Prickett from her Champion Walpride Karrie of Charlemar, U.D., W.D. (a star obedience dog in her own right) by the Greene's Champion Loujon Beau of Drewry Lane C.D. Kelly was selected with an obedience career in mind, and the following years proved him to have been an excellent choice.

In November 1966, Kelly was taken to his first match and won the Novice Class and Highest Scoring Dog in Trial. His show career started in February 1967 in Muncie, where a second in Novice A was gained with a score of 197½. Kelly was able to compete in seven Novice Classes before receiving his C.D. that spring. All scores were above 195, and so Kelly earned the *Dog World* award for winning his C.D. in the first three trials with scores over 195. He had three firsts and four seconds and capped his Novice competition in Cincinnati, in June 1967, with a Highest Scoring Dog in Trial.

Open training progressed through the summer and fall of 1967, with a few times out to compete in Graduate Novice Classes "just for fun." Kelly earned his C.D.X. in three shows in the Spring of 1968 with scores of 190½, 195½ and 197½.

Theresa Luley was accepted into the Veterinary School at Purdue University and began her professional studies in September 1968. It was necessary to leave her Springer at home as she was living in a dormitory on campus. She did manage to get home almost every weekend, however, and to compete, with Kelly, in Open B that year. She even won two High Scoring Dog in Trial Awards. Utility training was shelved for awhile.

During Theresa's second year, Kelly went to Purdue too. Theresa took an apartment with another student so as to be able to have her dog with her. Kelly and his mistress found time to "study" for a utility degree and helped to launch a new Obedience Training Club in Lafayette, a club of which Dr. Luley later became director of training. Kelly earned his U.D. in the spring of 1970 with scores of 196, 193 and 191.

The high point of their career in obedience for Dr. Luley (Theresa) and Loujon Lord Kelvin (Kelly) came at the 1970 Springer National Specialty, where Kelly was High Scoring Dog in Trial and received his Obedience Springer of the Year Award.

Of her dearly loved Springer, Dr. Luley says, "Kelly was an intelligent, loyal dog and we shared the type of relationship on which story books are based, a feeling that will probably never be recaptured. He loved to go to shows, and he was a consistent, dependable worker; although he was never as quick and flashy as some dogs, he was very accurate, and we hardly ever left the ring without a sincere round of applause from the spectators."

Catherine Wray of Annapolis, Maryland is the owner and trainer of a very distinguished Springer, Champion New Dawn of Marjon, U.D., the 1971 National Obedience Springer of the Year. Mrs. Wray has been involved with Springers and obedience since 1960 when, as a young mother of two children, working hard at two jobs and helping her husband through college, she felt a strong need to have some special interest for herself. Although she knew next to nothing about dogs, she wanted very much to own one. There was an encyclopedia in the family with pictures of all the breeds, and after studying it, Mrs. Wray felt the English Springer Spaniel to be the most outstanding in appearance. She stretched the budget for $35.00, found a seller in the local paper and that was the beginning of her association with this breed.

The puppy, as we might guess, never won in conformation, but she opened an exciting new chapter in Mrs. Wray's life. At six months of age, Duchess of Thistle, as she had been named, and her new owner were fortunate enough to have joined the Southwest Obedience Club of Los Angeles. Duchess became the High Scoring Dog for that club's team for two years in a row at the Top Ten Competition of Southern California, when she placed first with over 35 clubs represented. She was also one of the first Springers to have earned a Will Judy *Dog World* award for her C.D.X.—not bad for a first venture!

Mrs. Wray has owned other Springers since that time, three bench champions among them, but obedience is her first and greatest love.

Ch. New Dawn of Marjon, U.D., owned by Catherine Wray, Annapolis, Maryland, was the Parent Club Obedience Springer of the Year in 1971, with the extraordinary accomplishment of having gained C.D., C.D.X., and U.D. titles within one year.

From 1968–1980 Mrs. Wray owned Champion New Dawn of Marjon, U.D., a bitch that was bred by Peggy and Vern Johnson of Marjon Kennels. "Tisha" was entirely owner-handled by Mrs. Wray through her breed championship, as well as through obedience, and she earned her first "major" the first time she was shown at a Specialty. She earned her C.D., C.D.X. and U.D. titles within seven-and-one-half months, and she produced Champion Crack O'Dawn that Mrs. Wray owner-handled to his title from Bred-by-Exhibitor. Besides being proud of Tisha's accomplishments, Mrs. Wray says she was an "A-1" companion. To quote Mrs. Wray, "I couldn't have asked more of one dog—she did it all so well."

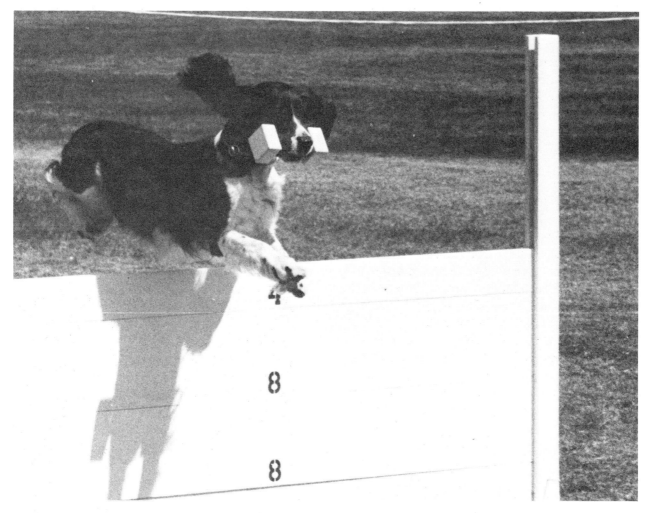

Marjon's Happy Thing, U.D., performs with authority for owners Sharon and Art Stewart, Irvine, California. One of the Parent Club's Obedience Springers of the Year 1976.

Through showing in the breed ring, Mrs. Wray became interested in grooming, and she was lucky enough to have apprenticed under two handlers who owned a pet grooming shop. Today Mrs. Wray herself owns two pet grooming salons and with her husband, Tim, operates The Maryland School of Dog Grooming in Silver Springs, Maryland.

For the past 15 years, Mrs. Wray has conducted obedience classes. She started the 4-H program for Anne Arundel County, and has been active in obedience classes for the 4-H for the past eight years.

Mrs. Wray says of obedience training, "If I could give three pieces of advice to a novice, this is what they would be: 1) Search out and start with the best instructor within your reach. 2) Be able to correct without anger and praise with genuine pleasure each time. 3) Stay with the basics, even with an old timer."

Mr. and Mrs. Laurence J. Libeu of Garden Grove, California can well take pride in their accomplishments in the world of English Springer Spaniels. Our first attention to their dogs was prompted by finding that two of them, Nancy's Fancy Lady, U.D. and Naia's Molly Malone, U.D., gained the National award for Obedience Springer of the Year, the former in 1972, the latter in 1973, 1974 and 1975. This is certainly impressive; however, as one reads further, one becomes even more admiring of these fanciers and of their accomplishments in the Springer world.

It was in 1963 that the Libeus purchased their first Springer, Kenlor California, a liver-and-white sired by Champion Stokely Toreador ex Champion Loresta's Gay Temptress. "Cal" was trained and shown by the Libeus in both obedience and conformation, and he earned his C.D. in three shows and his C.D.X. in five shows. Next came Nancy's Fancy Lady in 1966, a black-and-white bitch by Green Branch Juggernaut ex Lady Susan of Chadwick. She too was owner-trained and handled. In 1967, she won the National Novice Springer award, the *Dog World* award and earned her C.D. in three trials. In 1968, she was the southern California Obedience Council Novice Top Dog; in 1969, she earned her C.D.X., and the National award for Open and the Gateway Cities' Obedience Springer of the Year were hers; in 1972, she earned her U.D., the National Utility award and the National Obedience Springer of the Year award. We understand this bitch is the only Springer to date that has earned all four of the Parent Club awards and the Southern California Obedience Council Top Dog award.

Naia's Molly Malone was the Libeu's third Springer, a home-bred by Kenlor California, C.D.X. ex Nancy's Fancy Lady, U.D. She has moved right along in the Libeu family tradition, earning her C.D. in 1970 in three trials, her C.D.X. in 1972 and her U.D. in 1973. She became the Gateway Cities' Obedience Springer of the Year in 1970 and repeated this award in 1972, along with winning the *Dog World* award for having completed her C.D.X. in three trials. In 1973, she was the National Obedience Springer of the Year, the National Utility Springer and again the Gateway Cities' Obedience Springer of the Year. In 1974 and 1975, she was again National Obedience Springer and the Gateway Cities' Obedience Springer the latter year. Several times during her career, Molly was High Scoring Dog in Trial. Her lifetime qualifying score was 1948, the total of 48 scores.

Other Springers with which the Libeus have been successful include American and Mexican Champion Marjon's Miss Abigail Doolittle, C.D., P.C. This liver-and-white bitch was bred by Peggy and Vern Johnson and whelped in 1972. She was owner-handled to U.S.A. Championship at two years of age and shown as a "Special" for about a year, during which time she won many Best of Opposite Sex ribbons. She earned her C.D. in three trials with two seconds and one third for an average score of 194.67, and she gained her Mexican championship in seven shows and her P.C. obedience title in three shows with an average score of 197.33.

"Abby" had one litter which produced Champion Marjon's Tumbleweed, a Best in Show and Specialty winner; American and Mexican Cham-

pion Albert Tilbury, Esq. of Marjon, a Group winner; and Champion Marjon's Give Em Hell Harry, W.D.X., a Best of Breed winner from the classes.

Mr. Libeu enjoys many facets of the Springer Fancy. A long-time member of the Gateway English Springer Spaniel Association, he has held the offices of President, Vice President, Director and Obedience Chairman. He is also the Obedience Chairman of the Bench Show Committee for the English Springer Spaniel Field Trial Association and he is active in the Santa Ana Valley Kennel Club where he has held various offices, including Sporting Dog Director and Obedience Director. In addition, he belongs to, and works on behalf of, the Dog Obedience Instructors and Trainers Association and the Western Obedience Judges Association. Currently he is licensed by the American Kennel Club to judge the Novice and Open Classes.

With his Springers, Mr. Libeu has earned 10 A.K.C. obedience degrees, three A.K.C. bench show championships, three Mexican Championships and one Mexican P.C. (Perro Companelo) obedience title. He and Mrs. Libeu are breeders of a litter containing three U.S.A. champions, including a Best in Show winner, two Group winners, one U.D.X. and two Mexican champions.

Here is another view of Marjon's Happy Thing, U.D., the distinguished obedience winner belonging to Sharon and Arthur Stewart.

A tie for the 1976 National Obedience Springer of the Year award was between Endeavor's White Frost, U.D., owned by Doris Peppers of Broomfield, Colorado, and Marjon's Happy Thing, U.D., owned by Art and Sharon Stewart of Irvine, California.

Endeavor's White Frost, U.D., W.D. was born on November 24, 1971 and started life in the Peppers's home as a family pet and hunting dog. It was decided that she needed some obedience training, so Larry the Peppers son, who was 14 years old at the time, took her through a course in basic obedience. They did so well that the instructor suggested White Frost be shown in obedience competition. At that point, the Peppers had never seen or attended a dog show, so they did a bit of research, then entered two fun-matches, followed by an A.K.C. show. White Frost, handled by Larry Peppers, gained her Novice degree in three shows with scores of 198, 192½ and 196½. Larry started losing interest at about this time, so his mother took over. She and White Frost gained the Open title in four shows and Utility in seven shows. "Susie" retired with 54 points towards an obedience trial championship.

Endeavor's White Frost, U.D., owned by Doris Peppers of Broomfield, Colorado, was one of the National's Obedience Springer of the Year Award winners for 1976.

Again we present Marjon's Happy Thing, U.D., National Obedience Springer of 1976 (in a tie for the award).

Marjon's Happy Thing, U.D., the other winner of the 1976 National Obedience Springer of the Year award, was bred by Peggy and Vern Johnson, by Champion Marjon's Black Is Beautiful ex Marjon's Samantha. She was purchased as a show prospect that was to have become Sharon Stewart's "project" but in short order became "Art's dog," and as Art Stewart has little interest in conformation competition, he and his dog headed for obedience school. "Happy" earned her C.D. during 1971 in straight shows with an average of 194, going on to complete C.D.X. in September 1972 with an average of 193. Next came Utility, where again Happy distinguished herself with a 192 average.

On Happy's list of credits are such honors as High Scoring Dog in Trial (her highest score was 198½ in utility), Gateway Cities' English Springer Spaniel Club's Obedience Springer of the Year in 1972 and 1976 and the National Utility Springer of the Year award in 1976. The exciting pinnacle of her career, according to her owners, was the National Specialty in 1977, where she captured High Scoring Dog in Trial, plus being presented with her Obedience Springer of the Year 1976 award for which she had tied. This was certainly a day to be remembered!

In addition to Happy, the Stewarts own her son, the black-and-white tri-color Champion Arron Benwood.

In speaking of obedience, Art Stewart says that he has no special training techniques. He uses the tried and true methods of consistency, well-deserved praise from a sincere handler and prompt correction. He feels that obedience should be made part of a dog's life with its owner and feels this enhances the dog's performance in the ring, as it helps to demonstrate the value of a dog as a companion to its master.

Obedience Trial Champion Chuzzlewit's Favorite Son, belonging to Patricia and Clayton

This is Obedience Trial Champion Chuzzlewit's Favorite Son, the first Springer to have attained this most prestigious title which was created by the American Kennel Club only a short time ago. Patricia and Clayton Berglund of Bloomington, Minnesota, own this lovely dog that was the National Obedience Springer of the Year in 1977.

Berglund of Bloomington, Minnesota, was the Parent Club's Obedience Springer of the Year 1977. He also boasts an additional very distinguishing honor; he was the first O.T.Ch. (Obedience Trial Champion) for his breed when that highly prestigious award was created a few years ago by the American Kennel Club.

"Sonny," bred by Frances Nelson, is by Champion Chinoe's Eminent Judge, C.D.X. from Willowbank's Best Regards. He boasts a lifetime cumulative average score of 194.966. Out of 74 qualifying scores, he earned 36 placements, of which 15 were first place wins. He has won High Scoring Dog in Trial on six occasions.

Martha Leonard of Montclair, New Jersey is the trainer-owner of Jessica Imp of Whimsey, the 1979 National Obedience Springer of the Year. This black-and-white bitch is described by her owner as having been a precocious puppy. At the age of 10 months, she completed her C.D., scoring 196½, 198½ and 198½, thus earning a *Dog World* award. She tied the score for Top Novice Springer of 1975 for the National Club's award and went on to get her C.D.X. with scores of 191, 195½, 197½ and 197, winning two firsts in the process. At the 1977 Gaines' Eastern Regionals, she was Sunday's High Scoring Open Dog, topping the division with a 198. In 1979, for her Utility Dog title, Jessica averaged 194 with multiple class placements, and in that same year, she was the 1979 Top Utility Springer.

During her obedience career, Jessica has many times taken the High Scoring Springer and High Scoring Sporting Dog awards. She has accounted for four Highest Scoring Dog in Match honors and seven High in Trial, including the 1978 National Specialty, the 1979 American Spaniel Club and five all-breed trials. In 1981, she retired the American Spaniel Club's George E. Bennett Memorial Trophy, a sterling silver challenge trophy. In March of 1981, she won the Open B Class at the Bronx County Kennel Club with a score of 199, then topped the Utility Class winner in a run-off for High in Trial. Jessica has placed either first, second or third among the Top Ten Obedience Springers on all rating systems for the past two years, as of June 1981. At the time of this writing, Jessica passed the "magical 100" and became the third Springer and the first Springer bitch ever to attain the difficult and very special Obedience Trial Champion title. Congratulations!

Jessica Imp of Whimsy, U.D., Sunday's High Scoring Open Dog with a score of 198 at the 1977 Gaines Eastern Regionals, belongs to Martha Leonard, Whimsy Springers, Montclair, New Jersey.

Martha Leonard's Whimsey Kennel is a small but extremely active one. Since the early 1970's, this enthusiastic fancier has campaigned, in addition to her obedience Springers, two Group placing champion Field Spaniels, the Number one Welsh Springer bitch of 1978 and a *Dog World* award-winning Flat Coated Retriever bitch. The Springers, however, are the primary interest.

The first Whimsey Springer to enter the obedience ring was a liver-and-white male, Manchester Lord Bernard. "Bernie" earned his C.D. in three shows, averaging better than 193, and placed twice in the ribbons. He went on to his C.D.X. with a 192-plus average, winning two classes and placing third in a large class for his last leg. After a three-year retirement, Bernie was entered in Open B at the 1979 American Spaniel Club Specialty. Still working with style and flair, he placed second with 195 to kennelmate Jessie. More recently, Bernie has topped three Veteran Classes with scores of 195½, 196 and 199. He still is going strong at the age of nine years.

Whimsey's next obedience Springer was Willowbank's Brookside Ajax, owned and handled by John Leonard. This liver-and-white dog earned his C.D. in four straight shows, scoring 194½, 196½, 191 and 195. Along the way, he won two classes and had several High Scoring Springer awards. Ajax excelled in Open, attaining his title with four class placements, including a first (197½) and averaging 195. Although now retired from the ring, he is still a beloved house pet and companion.

Jessie, Bernie and Ajax have done much to promote the English Springer Spaniel in obedience. All three are people-loving, outgoing dogs, demonstrating in their work the key words in the obedience regulations preamble—"enjoyment" and "willingness." They love to please and be praised, they are quick to learn and they revel in applause and attention. To see Bernie at the age of nine, thundering in on the recall, brown ears flapping, always makes owner Martha Leonard think of how greatly she enjoys working with her dogs and training them to compete in the exciting sport of obedience.

Obedience Trial Champion Ruleon's Sir Dandy of Belmar, bred by Billie and Elmer Marlin and owner-handled by Stephen G. Dreiseszun of Phoenix, Arizona, was born on September 29, 1974. He was sired by Ruleon's Tobruk ex Ruleon's Fancy. Sir Dandy was the National Obedience Springer for 1980. He is Steve Dreiseszun's first dog and the first dog this young fancier has trained in obedience. Although Steve's family had always owned dogs while he was growing up (his mother had trained her Boxers in obedience), he had never come into contact with the sport of showing and was totally unaware that obedience was anything more than the simple training received in local parks. As he says, "Boy, did I learn in a hurry!"

Steve's mother became interested in Springers when their old farm Collie was killed by a hit-and-run driver. When their new Springer bitch's first litter arrived, Steve was given an early pick for his first dog, hoping to select the next prodigy for the conformation ring. Actually, Dandy ended up picking him when Steve could not decide between two of the puppies. Dandy was the one that climbed into Steve's lap and would not leave.

Soon some "simple" obedience work started as Steve and Dandy enrolled for classes advertised in the newspaper. Steve learned that they were training "novice" work, which seemed reasonable since he (Steve) certainly felt like a novice. As training progressed, Dandy showed incredible enthusiasm to please, and the instructors began to educate Steve in the basics of the show ring. At the end of the first training course, a "trial" was held for graduation, in which Dandy placed first. Steve became hooked and continued to work for the opportunity to exhibit his dog in an A.K.C. trial.

For relaxation, Obedience Trial Ch. Ruleon's Sir Dandy of Belmar enjoys a game of Frisbee. He is the 1980 Phoenix City Canine Catch and Fetch Champion. Steve Dreiseszun owner.

The instructors had prepared them well, as Dandy and Steve scored 198½ placing second, 197½ and 194-plus placing second in their first three trials. Dandy was High Scoring Springer twice in these trials, and he received the *Dog World* award for his Novice work. All told, Dandy placed five of the six times shown in the Novice class prior to age 13 months. He and Steve went on to Open where Dandy's enthusiasm was multiplied by the addition of retrieving and jumping. He completed his C.D.X. title with a 193 placing first, 194½ and 192½ placing third.

Utility presented a more difficult challenge, requiring total patience to communicate each part of the directive and discriminating exercises. Dandy seemed to put together the enthusiasm he had had in Novice and Open on his third leg in Utility, scoring 192½ and placing third in the class. At the age of two years, he had become a Utility Dog, completing his C.D., C.D.X. and U.D. in 12½ months.

A dedicated Frisbee dog, Ch. Ruleon's Sir Dandy of Belmar displays his championship form.

The newly formulated obedience trial championship brought a new challenge which Dandy completed with a flourish one could only dream about. He began 1980 at the 67 point level and needed 33 points to reach the necessary 100. Dandy "shifted into overdrive" on the Mission Circuit in California, placing first in Open B with 196½ at Antelope Valley. The following day, he scored a 199 in Utility B for first place in San Francisco and was High Scoring Dog in Trial.

Coming back to Arizona with 79 points certainly must have felt wonderful; however, there were only two more shows ahead before the heat of summer wilted everything, including the dog's enthusiasm.

Flagstaff Kennel Club, June 7, 1980, brought Dandy a second place Utility score of 197-plus and four more points towards his championship. The following morning found Dandy and Steve in Prescott, Arizona with the heat becoming really intense. In spite of this, Dandy responded with a Utility score of 197, good for first place and 14 points. His final class of the day, Open B, brought him 197½ and his second first placement of the day. To top it off, he received six points to complete his championship and was awarded High Scoring Dog in Trial. Adding a special note to the happiness of that day, Miss Nancy Pollack, the same judge who awarded Dandy his first leg towards his C.D. when he was just starting out, also awarded his final points for the championship.

This dog's enthusiasm for working, his desire to please, his love of performing, his grace of movement and balance in jumping are all attributes which have made his and Steve's career together a total pleasure. These also are attributes reflective of the breed and what make Springers so fulfilling indeed.

We feel that our readers should find these stories of some of the most highly successful obedience Springers, and the people working with them, both interesting and helpful. You will note that in many cases these accomplishments were achieved by "one dog owners" who started out as total novices in the Fancy, but who have come to succeed and to know and enjoy the pleasure of competition, comradeship and working with their dogs. You, too, can achieve these things with your Springer. All it takes is willingness to give time and patience.

In addition to the C.D., C.D.X. and Utility Dogs in this chapter, you will find these titles following the names of a large number of Springer bench champions as well. It is not unusual for the show kennels to compete in both conformation and obedience, as you will note in reading our kennel stories and picture captions throughout the book.

Right: A beautiful head-study of Ch. Willowbank's Make It Snappy, C.D., owned by Willowbank Springers, Mrs. and Mrs. Alexander B. Merryman, Blairstown, New Jersey.

Below: Ch. Starfoot Shawnee Prince, C.D., being handled by Laddie Carswell to a win under Clark Thompson. Owned and bred by Harold L. Hall, Prince was sired by Ch. Kaintuck Tolstoy ex Ch. Starfoot Seneca Gypsy.

W.D.

photo by Gilbert

Ch. Danaho'e Lalique of Stanton, liver and white, by Ch. Filicia's Anlon Patriot ex Ch. Danaho's Ballet Russe, a fine example of the quality Springers from Anne Pope's Filicia strain.

CHAPTER TWENTY

The English Springer Spaniel Brood Bitch

The handsome Springer bitch Ch. Melilotus Love Song (Ch. Melilotus Royal Oak ex Ch. Melilotus Woodelf), dam of Ch. Melilotus Shooting Star and Ch. Melilotus Bright Bouquet. Owned by Mrs. R. Gilman Smith, now Mrs. Frederick D. Brown.

In a previous chapter, we discussed buying a puppy. One of the most important purchases you will make in dogs is the selection of the brood bitch (or bitches) on which you plan to establish your breeding program. She should be a bitch of marvelous bloodlines and should possess very good qualities herself.

You will not want to breed your bitch until at least her second heat—sometimes even later, if she starts early and comes in for the first time promptly at six months, then again at a year. Under these circumstances, I would recommend waiting until her third heat.

Meanwhile, you should be watching alertly for that perfect mate for her. Attend dog shows with this in mind. Also subscribe to the dog magazines so that dogs in other areas, of which you may not have heard, will not be overlooked. Be sure to watch for a stud dog strong in any points where your bitch may be lacking, watching for his get at the shows and in the magazines to see if he succeeds in passing along these qualities you need. Make a particular note of what he has sired from bitches of background similar to your own. Be sure to contact the various stud owners to request a pedigree of their dogs for your perusal.

When a tentative decision has been reached, get in touch with the stud's owner and make all of the necessary arrangements regarding stud fee (whether it is to be in cash or a puppy), approximate time the bitch should be ready, etc. Find out, too, what requirements the stud owner has, such as health certification, tests, etc. Make all necessary airplane reservations if you plan to ship your bitch by air.

The airlines have certain requirements such as, in some cases, temperature limits in extremely hot or cold weather and what type of crates they will accept. Also, find out how far in advance of flight time (usually about two hours) they will need to have the bitch there. Most of the airlines have available their own crates which may be purchased for a nominal fee, if you do not have a suitable one. They are made of fiberglass and are the safest type for shipping. Normally you must notify the airline several days in advance for a reservation for the bitch as they can accommodate only a limited number of dogs on each flight. Plan to ship the bitch on about the eighth or ninth day of her cycle, and be careful not to ship on a weekend as some flights do not run then and some freight offices are closed on Saturday and Sunday. Whenever it can possibly be arranged, ship dogs on a DIRECT flight. This avoids the danger of a dog being left behind during the transfer from one plane to another or some other such occurrence.

A big day for these two lovely littermates! Ch. Penny's Crown Prince of Lleda, C.D., and Ch. Clancy's Erin of Packanack (Top Producing Dam with seven champions), by Ch. Beryltown Virginian of Pequa ex Clancy's Copper Penny of Lleda, here are taking Winners Dog and Winners Bitch, Best of Winners and Best of Opposite Sex at the 1972 Specialty of the Eastern English Springer Spaniel Club. Bred by Karen Adell and Marie Clancy, they are owned by Ray and Estelle Adell of Huntington, New York.

If you plan on hand-delivering your bitch to the stud dog, it is simpler in the long run. Some people fear that the trauma of being shipped may occasionally prevent the bitch from conceiving. Be sure to allow enough time for breeding her at the proper time, usually anywhere from the 10th through the 14th day, and if you want the bitch bred twice, you must allow one day in between. Do not expect the stud owner to put you up during your visit to his area. Check out what good motels are nearby, see if they take dogs and make a reservation for yourself.

Just prior to your bitch's season, you should take her to your veterinarian. Have her checked for worms, see that she is up-to-date on all her shots, and take care of any other tests the stud owner has requested. The bitch may act and be perfectly normal up until her second or third week in whelp, but it is better to have any tests or shots attended to ahead of time. If she is a lit-

tle overweight, right now is when you should get those excess pounds off her. She should be in good hard condition, neither fat nor thin.

The day you've been waiting for finally arrives and you notice the swelling of her vulva, followed within a day or two, by the appearance of color. Call the stud owner to finalize arrangements immediately, advising whether you will be shipping or bringing her, the exact day and time, etc. Advise the stud owner of the flight number, the time of departure and time of arrival as soon as you know this information. If you are shipping the bitch, the check for the stud fee should be mailed now. There will probably be an additional charge for the stud owner's trip to the airport, both to pick up the bitch and to send her home again, if the airport is not quite close to the owner's home. You should include this fee now (if you know it) or send it immediately when you know the amount.

On the day you ship your bitch, if that is how she will make the trip, do not feed her but be sure that she has a drink of water and is well exercised before you put her in the crate. Several layers of newspaper plus some torn newspapers will make a good bed and can be discarded at the end of her trip. Rugs and towels are not suitable as she may soil them and they will have to be washed when she reaches her destination. Remember to have her at the airport approximately two hours ahead of her flight time, as previously mentioned.

If you are driving, be sure that you will arrive at a reasonable time of day. If you are coming from a distance and get in late, have a good night's sleep and contact the stud owner in the morning. If possible, leave the children and relatives at home, as they will only be in the way. Most stud owners object to having many people around during the actual breeding.

Once the breeding has been completed, first take the bitch out to the car and put her in her crate; then, if you wish to sit and chat, do so.

Dave Andre, Brillion, Wisconsin, is the photographer who has so beautifully captured the Springer excellence of Ch. Kung-O-Vik Misty Moonlite (by Ch. Charlyle's Late Edition ex Chardon Love Affair) and her son by Debonairs Marksman. Both are owned by Joanne DeBoth, Sandhaven Springers, Green Bay, Wisconsin.

Ch. Canarch Inchidony Brook, famous bitch belonging to Mr. and Mrs. Charles F. Hendee, Barrington, Illinois. Clint Harris is handling.

Remember, she should not urinate for at least an hour following the breeding. If you have not already done so, pay the stud fee now, and get your copy of the stud certificate and the stud dog's pedigree.

Now all you need to do is to wait in happy anticipation for the puppies to arrive.

This is the foundation bitch of Judy and Bud DiDonato's Springers, purchased in 1971. Maidenhead's Bineski Koda finished in short order, and quickly taught her owners the fun of being involved in the world of pure-bred dogs.

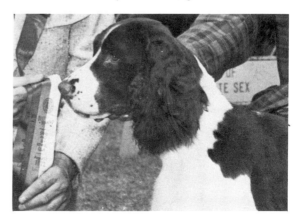

This is Ch. Tranquillity of Melilotus, the top matron from the highly successful Melilotus Kennels at Bethel, Connecticut whose contribution to her breed was inestimable.

The great producing bitch Ch. Lou Jon's Femininity winning the Brood Bitch Class at the 1979 National Specialty in Colorado for Patty Alston and Maureen Brady, is shown with her offspring, Ch. Shinnecock's Tumbleweed and Ch. Salilyn's Selection; handled by Patty Alston, Maureen Brady, and Dick Cooper.

Danaho's Nightshade, C.D., at 13 months of age, by Ch. Kaintuck Tolstoy ex Bonny Belle of Merry-L. This dam of champions was bred by Mary Jane Wilkerson and is owned by Ruth and Bill Kirby of Florida. Photo courtesy of Dana Hopkins.

Left: Ch. Canarch Carillon, T.D., here is going Best of Winners and Best of Opposite Sex, Milwaukee Kennel Club 1976. Judge, Roy Ayers; handler, Gwen Hendee; owners, Canarch Kennels, Reg.

Below: The consistent winning Springer, Ch. Salilyn's Continental, owned by Patricia A. Cabot and Karen A. Jenkins, handled by Houston Clark here to a Sporting Group First under judge Michele Billings. "Lincoln," a son of Ch. Salilyn's Continental ex Ch. Salilyn's Sophistication, was the Quaker Oats Award Sporting Dog winner for 1978. His show record totals 36 Bests in Show and 114 Group Firsts.

Ch. Salilyn's Explosion, by Ch. Prelude's Echo ex Gh. Salilyn's Pirate Queen, a Best in Show winner. Mary Ann Alston is handling for Lillian and Robert Gough.

Ch. Rube's Sportin' Life of Lleda, by Ch. Somerset-Sage's Sirius ex Ch. Lleda's Aegena of Rube, is owned by Estelle Adell, Lleda Kennels, Huntington, New York.

Lleda's Heaven Sent, by Ch. Rube's Sportin' Life of Lleda ex Ch. Lleda's Ariana, takes Best of Opposite Sex at the Eastern English Springer Spaniel Club Futurity in June 1980. Owned by the Adells.

Ch. Kay N Dee's Reginna's Gibson Girl, C.D., taking first in Sweepstakes at the Greater Pittsburgh Specialties 1980 for Dr. Mary B. Gibbs.

We are indebted to Dana Hopkins for this very important picture of Martha Borie with that well-known sire behind so many winning Eastern dogs, Ch. Runor's Deacon (Ch. Rufton Breeze ex Ch. Audley Farm Judy). Deacon's owners were Mr. and Mrs. Atha Whitaker, Ambler, Pennsylvania.

CHAPTER TWENTY-ONE

The English Springer Spaniel Stud Dog

Ch. Salilyn's Inchidony Banquo, sired by Ch. Salilyn's Macduff, a three times Best in Show winner, with 20 Sporting Group Firsts. He is the sire of ten champions, including four offspring with National Specialty points; his son, Ch. Canarch Jupiter Five, is a Best in Show and Group winner. Mrs. Julie Gasow, owner.

Choosing the right stud dog to best complement your bitch is no easy task. The principal factors to be considered are the stud's quality and conformation and his pedigree. The pedigree lists the ancestry of the stud dog and the various bloodlines involved. If you are a novice in the breed, I would suggest you seek advice from some of the more experienced fanciers who are old-timers and who would be able to discuss with you some of the various dogs behind the one to which you are planning to breed your bitch. Many times such people remember well the dogs you need to know about and perhaps they even have access to photos of them. In addition, be sure to carefully study the photos in this book which most likely will include some, if not all, of the ancestors.

It is extremely important that the stud's pedigree be harmonious with that of your bitch. Do not rush to breed to the latest winner with no thought of whether or not he can produce well. Take time to check out the stock being sired by the dog or dogs you have under consideration. A dog that has not sired quality litters for other people probably will do no better for you (unless of course he is a young stud just starting out that may not have yet had the opportunity to do so). Ask yourself, "Do I want to waste my bitch's time on an unknown quantity, or would I prefer to use a dog with a good producing record?"

Breeding dogs is not a money-making proposition. By the time you pay a stud fee, take care of the bitch during gestation, whelp the litter and raise and care for the puppies until they reach selling age, you will be lucky if you break even on the cost of the litter; therefore, it is foolish to skimp on the stud fee. Try to breed to the dog that seems best suited to your bitch, the one with the best producing record regardless of the cost. Remember that raising mediocre pups is just as expensive as raising good ones. You will fare better financially if you have some show prospects to sell rather than if they are all pets. If the latter is true, you may be forced to let them go at far smaller prices than you had anticipated. So, in choosing the stud to use, bear in mind that by breeding to the most suitable one, a proven, consistent producer of quality, you really are making the wisest investment.

You will have to decide among three choices in planning your breeding strategies. They are: inbreeding, line-breeding and out-crossing. *Inbreeding* is normally considered to be the mating of father to daughter, mother to son, brother to sister. *Line-breeding* involves combining two dogs that belong to the same original family of Springers, i.e., they are descended from the same ancestors such as half brother to half sister, niece to uncle, etc. *Outcross* breeding means a dog and a bitch of completely dissimilar bloodlines with no, or only a few, mutual distant ancestors are used.

Each of these methods has its fans and its detractors. I would say that line-breeding is probably the safest for the novice breeder and, generally speaking, it is the most popular method. In-breeding should be left to the experienced, very sophisticated breeder who knows the line extremely well, who is in a position to pre-evaluate the probable results. Outcrossing is normally done when you are trying to bring in a specific trait, such as shortening up backs, achieving better head type or more correct action, etc. Everyone sincerely interested in breeding dogs wants to develop a line of their own but this is not accomplished overnight. It takes at least several generations before you can consider yourself successful in having achieved this. Close study of bloodlines is essential, along with getting to know and truthfully evaluating the dogs with which you are working in order to preserve the best in what you have while at the same time eliminating weaknesses.

As a novice breeder, your safest bet is to start by acquiring one or two bitches of the finest quality and background you can buy. In the beginning, it is really foolish to own your own stud dog as you will make out better in the long run paying a stud fee to use one of the outstanding producing Springers available to service your bitch. A stud dog attractive to breeders must be well known, at least a champion (and usually one that has attracted some attention in "Specials" competition), and he must have winning progeny in the ring. He represents a good deal of time and money before he becomes a dog that will bring in returns on your investment. So start out by paying a stud fee a few times to use such a dog or dogs, keeping the best bitch out of your first several litters before you consider owning a stud of your own. By that time you will have gained the experience to recognize exactly what sort of dog you need for this purpose.

Ch. Filicia's Anlon Patriot, Top Sire All Breeds 1980, winning at Elmira in 1977 under Ed Bracy, handled by Jane Kamp Forsyth for Anne Pope.

This is the highly successful sire, Ch. Veron's Marco Polo, by Salilyn's Morning Breeze ex Salilyn's Dolly Veron, owned by G. Westlake, from Michigan. This photograph, loaned to us by Estelle Adell, was taken at Columbus, Ohio, in 1973, when Marco Polo was just under three years old.

A future stud dog should be selected with the utmost care and great consideration. He must be of very high standard as he may be responsible for siring many puppies each year. Ideally, he should come from a line of excellent dogs on both his sire's and dam's side. His pedigree should contain good dogs all the way through and the dog himself should be of high quality, to hold his own in top competition in his breed. He should be robust, virile, a keen stud dog proven and able to transmit his best qualities to his puppies. Do not use on your bitch, or anyone else's, an unsound dog or a dog with an outstanding or major fault. Not all champions can pass on their splendid quality, and by the same token, occasionally one will find a dog that has never finished but that *does* sire puppies better than himself PROVIDED THAT HIS PEDIGREE IS OUTSTANDING IN TOP PRODUCING DOGS AND BITCHES. Remember, too, that the bitch also has great influence on the quality of her litter. No stud dog can do it all.

If you are the proud owner of a promising young stud dog, either one you have bred from your own litters, or one that you have purchased, do not allow him to be used for the first time until he is about a year old. The first time he is bred, it should be to a bitch that is a proven matron (experienced at being mated) so as to make his first encounter easy and enjoyable. He could be put off breeding forever by a maiden bitch that gives him a bad time until he gets to "know the ropes." Also, his first breeding should be done in quiet surroundings with only you and one other person present to hold the bitch. Don't make a circus of it, as this first time will determine his attitude and feelings about breeding from then on.

Your young stud must allow you to help with the breeding, as later there will be bitches that will not be cooperative and he then needs to be in the habit of accepting assistance. If right from the beginning you are there helping and praising him, he will expect and accept this help. Before you introduce the dogs, be sure to have ready things you might need. K-Y Jelly is the only lubricant that should be used to facilitate copulation and either a stocking or a length of gauze with which to muzzle the bitch should be on hand, if that becomes necessary.

Ch. Kaintuck Tolstoy, shown here at five years of age, sired many champions and became an important winning Springer for Dana Hopkins, Danaho Kennels, Los Angeles, California.

Ch. Salilyn's Colonel's Overlord is a many-time Best in Show and Group winner, 1969 Top Winning Springer, and second only to Ch. Chinoe's Adamant James in 1970, sired a number of champions. Owned by Mrs. Julie Gasow, Troy, Michigan.

The stud fee is due to be paid at the time of breeding and generally is figured on the basis of the price of a show prospect puppy. Normally a return service is offered, should the bitch fail to produce; however, you should check to see that this has been made clear in the contract. Usually one live puppy is considered to be a litter. It is a good idea to have a stud certificate printed up which both you and the owner of the bitch should sign. It should spell out all the conditions of the breeding as well as the dates of mating. Also at this time you should provide the owner of the bitch with a pedigree of your stud dog.

Sometimes a pick-of-the-litter puppy is taken instead of a cash stud fee, and this should be noted on the stud·certificate, as well as stating how old the pup should be when picked up by the owner of the sire, and whether it is to be a dog puppy, a bitch puppy or just a "pick puppy." All of this should be clearly stated to avoid misunderstandings later on.

In almost every case, the bitch must come to the stud dog for the breeding. Once the owner of the bitch decides where the breeding will occur, and to what stud dog the bitch hopefully will be bred, he should contact the owner of the stud dog immediately to discuss the stud fee, terms, approximate time the bitch is due in season and whether she will be shipped or brought to the stud owner. Then, as soon as the bitch comes into season, another phone call must be made to finalize the arrangements. I have personally experienced times when the bitch's owner has waited until the last moment to contact the stud's owner, only to meet with disappointment at the owner's not being home. So do not waste a moment; when you find that the bitch definitely will be ready soon, pass along this information.

It is important for the stud owner to have proper facilities to house the bitch while she is there. Nothing can be more heartbreaking than to have a bitch misbred or, still worse, get away and become lost. Unless you can provide proper care for visiting bitches, DO NOT offer your dog at public stud.

Owning a stud dog is no easy way to riches, as some seem to think. Making the dog well-known is expensive and time-consuming and one must spend a considerable amount of money in the acquisition and campaigning of good dogs before coming up with such a celebrity. Be selective in the bitches you permit to be bred to your dog. It takes two to make the puppies and an inferior bitch from a "nothing" sort of background will probably never produce well, no matter how splendid the dog to which she is bred. Remember that those puppies will be advertised as sired by your stud dog and you do not want any that will embarrass you or him!

Ch. Waiterock Bodkin is one of the more than forty champions sired by Am., Can. Ch. Waiterock Elmer Brown. Breeder-owner Juanita Waite Howard, Lafayette, California.

I do not feel that we need to go into the actual breeding here as the experienced breeder already knows what is involved and the novice should not attempt to try it for the first time by reading directions in a book. If breeding is new to you, plan to have a breeder or handler friend help you until you are accustomed to handling such matters with ease; if this is not possible, it is very likely that your veterinarian can arrange to help or to get someone on his staff to assist you.

If a complete "tie" is made, actually that one breeding is all that is really necessary. On a maiden bitch, however, or one that has missed in the past, most people like to give a second breeding, leaving one day in between.

Once the "tie" has been completed and the bitch and stud have released, be sure that the male's penis goes completely back into his sheath. He should be allowed a drink of water and a short walk. Then put him in his kennel or somewhere alone where he can settle down. Do not allow him to be with other dogs for awhile (especially if there are other males around) as he will have the odor of the bitch about him, and this could result in a fight. The scent of a bitch in season will excite the other males.

The bitch, however, should not be allowed to relieve herself for at least an hour. In fact, many people feel she should be "up ended" (hindquarters held off the ground) for several minutes after the breeding to allow the sperm to travel deeper into the vagina. She should be crated and kept quiet in any case.

Ch. Waiterock Annie Oakley is typical of the progeny of Ch. Waiterock Elmer Brown (ex Ch. Waiterock Oak Branch). Sturdy, fast moving, trained for hunting, and of gentle temperament; bred and owned by Juanita Waite Howard, Waiterock Springers.

Ch. Lleda's Athena of Sunnykay, by Ch. Veron Marco Polo ex Ch. Clancy's Erin of Packanack, was bred by Karen Adell Garetano and Estelle Adell, and is co-owned by Barbara Weingarten and Karen Adell Garetano. Athena won four points at the Keystone English Springer Spaniel Club Specialty in 1976 en route to her title.

There are no standard rules governing the conditions of a stud service. They are whatever the owner of the stud chooses to make them. The stud fee is paid for the act, not for the litter, and if a bitch fails to conceive, this does not automatically call for a return service unless agreement for such has been included in the contract. This is a courtesy, not something that can be regarded as a right.

When a bitch has been given one return service, then misses again, that ends the stud dog owner's responsibility, even among the most lenient of breeders. It is unreasonable for owners of a bitch, under these circumstances, to expect more than the one free return breeding.

The management of a stud dog and his visiting bitches is difficult and time-consuming and the stud owner has usually well earned the fee when one service has been achieved, let alone having repeated visits by the same bitch. Usually, a bitch that has missed twice by a reliable stud dog is the one at fault and very well may never conceive, no matter how frequently she is bred. This is *her* owner's problem, not that of the stud dog owner.

Am., Can. Ch. Geiger's Chief Geronimo's first Stud Dog Class, with Kurt Meuller as the judge at Puget Sound English Springer Spaniel Club Specialty Show in 1969. The progeny are Ch. Magill's Patrick, C.D., W.D.X.; Ch. Geiger's Royal Princess, C.D.; Am., Mex. Ch. Muller's Blazing Kane; and Geiger's Winaway Geronimo, C.D., W.D.X. These dogs illustrate well the high quality Springers produced by the Geigers and other breeders in the Puget Sound area.

329

Ch. Canarch Inchidony Brook, black and white bitch, taking Best of Winners at Chattanooga on March 12, 1966. Brook was the foundation bitch at Chinoe Kennels, owned by Ann Roberts; bred by Mrs. Roberts' sister, Mary Lou Hendee. Clint Harris is handling.

CHAPTER TWENTY-TWO

Your English Springer Spaniel's Gestation, Whelping and Litter

The Adells' Ch. Daphne of Recess with a litter of newly born puppies.

When your bitch has been bred and is back at home, be reminded to remain ever watchful that no other male gets to her until at least the 22nd day of her season. Prior to that time, it will still be possible for an undesired breeding to take place, which at this point would be catastrophic. Remember that she actually can have two separate litters by two different dogs, so take care.

In all other ways, she should be treated quite normally. It is not necessary for her to have any additives to her diet until she is at least four to five weeks pregnant. Also, it is unnecessary for her to have additional food. It is preferable not to overfeed the bitch this early as the puppies do not strain her resources until the final stages of her pregnancy.

Controlled exercise is good and necessary for the bitch. She should not be permitted to just lie around. At about seven weeks along, this should be slowed down to several walks daily, not too long and preferably on the lead.

In the fourth or fifth week of pregnancy, calcium may be added to the diet and at seven weeks, the one meal a day may be increased to two meals with some nutritional additives in each. Canned milk may be added to her meals at this time.

One week before she is due to whelp, your Springer bitch should be introduced to her whelping box so that she will have accustomed herself to it and will feel at home there by the time the puppies arrive. She should be encouraged to sleep there, but permitted to come and go as she pleases. The box should be roomy enough for her to lie down and stretch out but not too large or else the pups will have too much room in which to roam and may get chilled if they move off too far from the mother. Be sure that there is a "pig-rail" for the box which will prevent the puppies from being crushed against the side of the box. The room where the box is placed, either in the home or the kennel, should be free from drafts and should be kept at about 70°F. In winter, it may be necessary to have an infrared lamp in order to maintain sufficient warmth; however, guard against this being placed too low or too close to the puppies.

Keep a big pile of newspapers near the box. You'll find that you never have enough when you have a litter. Start accumulating them ahead of time. Also, keep a pile of clean towels, a pair of scissors and a bottle of alcohol on hand. Have all this ready at least a week before the bitch is due to whelp, as you never know when she may start.

Ch. Lleda's Springhill April Fool, by Ch. Point-Spar's Gay Star ex Ch. Daphne of Recess, winning a "major" on the way to the title. Bred, owned, and handled by Karen Adell Garetano.

The day or night before she is due, the bitch will become restless, moving in and out of her box and in and out of the door. She may refuse food, and at this point her temperature will start to drop. She will start to dig at and tear up the newspapers in her box, shiver and generally look uncomfortable. You alone should be with the bitch at this period. She does not need an audience. This is not a "side show," and several people hovering over the bitch may upset her to the point where she might hurt the puppies. Stay nearby but do not fuss too much over the bitch. Eventually she will settle down in her box and begin to pant, very shortly thereafter start to have contractions and soon a puppy will start to emerge, sliding out with one of the contractions. The mother immediately should open the sac and bite the cord and then clean up the puppy. Permit her to eat the placenta. Once the puppy is cleaned, it should be placed next to the bitch, unless she is showing signs of having another one immediately. The puppy should start looking for a nipple on which to nurse. You should make certain that the puppy is able to latch on to the nipple successfully.

If a puppy is a breech, i.e., born feet first, then you must watch carefully to see it is completely delivered as quickly as possible and that the placental sac is removed immediately, so that the

puppy does not drown in the amniotic fluid. Sometimes, even a normally positioned pup will seem extremely slow in coming. Should this occur, you might take a clean towel and pull the puppy out, gently and with great care, as the bitch contracts. If once the puppy is delivered it shows little sign of life, take a rough (turkish) towel and rub him quite briskly back and forth, massaging the chest. Continue this for about 15 minutes and be sure that the mouth is free of liquid. It may be necessary to try mouth-to-mouth breathing. This is done by first pressing open the puppy's jaws and using a finger to depress the tongue which may be stuck to the roof of the mouth. Then blow hard down the puppy's throat. Bubbles may pop out of its nose, but keep on blowing. Rub with the towel again across the chest and try artificial respiration, pressing the sides of the chest together slowly and rhythmically, in and out, in and out. Keep trying one method or the other for *at least 15 minutes* before giving up. You may be rewarded with a live puppy that otherwise would not have made it.

Such a puppy should not be put back with the mother immediately but it should be kept extra warm for awhile. Put it in a cardboard box and place the box near the stove or on an electric pad. If it is the time of year for your heat to be on, place the box near a radiator. Using any of these methods, keep the puppy warm until the rest of the litter has been born. Then it can go back in the whelping box with the others.

The bitch may go for an hour or more between puppies, which is fine, so long as she seems comfortable and is not straining or contracting. I would not allow her to remain unassisted for more than an hour if she does continue to contract. Now is the time to call your veterinarian (who you should have alerted ahead of time so that he could be somewhere within reach if you needed him). He may want the bitch brought to his office so that he can examine her and perhaps give her a shot of Pituitrin. In some cases, the veterinarian will find that a Caesarean operation is necessary, if there is a puppy lodged inside the mother making normal delivery impossible. This sometimes occurs due to size of a puppy or sometimes the puppy has turned in the wrong position. If the bitch does require a section, the puppies already born must be kept warm in the manner described above, i.e., in a cardboard box with a heating pad under the box.

Once the veterinarian has checked the bitch or performed the Caesarean section (if this was necessary), the mother and her pups should be returned home. Once home, do not attempt to put the pups in with the bitch until she is at least fairly conscious as she may inadvertently hurt them. Do get them back together with the dam as soon as possible so they can start nursing. If the mother lacks milk at this point, hold each puppy at the mother's teats in order to stimulate and encourage the secretion of milk. With adequate stimulation, the milk should start to flow shortly. If it does not, continue this procedure several times a day until there are positive results. In the meantime, the puppies will have to be hand-fed.

Assuming that there has been no problem and the bitch has whelped naturally, you should insist that she go outside to exercise, staying just long enough to make herself comfortable. Offer her a bowl of milk and a biscuit, then allow her to settle down with her family. Be sure to clean out the whelping box and change the newspapers so that she will have a fresh bed. Actually, unless some problem occurs, there is little you must do for the puppies until they become three to four weeks old, other than to keep the box clean with new newspapers. When the pups are a couple of days old, towels should be tacked down to the bottom of the box so that the puppies will have traction when they move. Do not interfere unless the mother is unable to care for her puppies in the normal manner.

If you should be so unfortunate as to lose the bitch, or if anything happens which prevents her from performing her maternal duties, then you must promptly take over. For example, if the bitch has difficulties with her milk supply, then you must be prepared to either hand feed or tube feed the puppies if they are to survive. Newborn puppies must be fed every three to four hours around the clock and they must be kept warm during these feeding periods. I personally prefer the tube feeding method as it is so much faster and easier. Ask your veterinarian to show you how it's done. After each feeding, you will have to gently rub each puppy's abdomen with wet cotton in order to make it urinate; the rectum should be rubbed gently in the same manner to open the bowels. Interestingly, newborn puppies cannot urinate or move their bowels without stimulation from their mother who licks the genital area.

After a normal whelping, the bitch will require additional food to enable her to produce sufficient milk. She should be fed twice daily now; additionally some canned milk should be offered several times during the day.

At two weeks old, you should clip the puppies' nails as they are needle-sharp at this stage and can hurt or damage the mother's teats and stomach as the pups hold on to nurse.

Between three and four weeks of age, weaning the puppies should begin. Scraped beef (prepared by scraping it off slices of beef with a spoon so that none of the muscle or gristle is included) may be offered in very small quantities a couple of times daily for the first few days. Then, by the third day, mix in ground puppy chow with warm water as directed on the package, offering it four times daily. By now the mother should be kept away from the puppies and out of the box for several hours at a time until, when they reach five weeks, she is left in with them only overnight. By the time they are six weeks old, the puppies should be entirely weaned and the mother should check on them occasionally.

A tisket, a tasket, Springers in a basket! These puppies are from Hillcrest Kennels, owned by Henriette Schmidt.

Most veterinarians recommend a temporary DHL (Distemper, Hepatitis, Leptospirosis) shot when the puppies are six weeks of age. This remains effective for about two weeks. Then, at eight weeks, the series of permanent shots begins for the DHL prevention. It is also a good idea now, since the prevalence of the dreaded new Parvo virus, to discuss the advisability of having these shots too for your puppies. Each time the pups go to the vet for shots, you should bring stool samples to be checked for worms, even though the previous ones may have proved negative. Worms go through various stages of development and may be present although they do not appear positive each time checked.

The puppies should be fed four times daily until they are three months old. Then cut back to three feedings daily. By six months old, two meals daily are sufficient. Some people feed their dogs twice daily throughout their lifetime, while others cut to one meal daily when the puppy reaches one year of age.

The ideal time for puppies to go to their new homes is between eight and 12 weeks old, although some do so successfully at six weeks. Be certain that they go to their future owners accompanied by a diet list and schedule of the shots they have received and those they will still need. These should be included with the registration applications and copies of pedigrees.

Bud DiDonato looks proudly at his birthday present (on December 1, 1975) from Ch. Salilyn's Bravo ex his Wakefield Cinderella. Future Ch. Maidenhead's Remembrance is among these puppies at Maidenhead Kennels, Lawrenceville, New Jersey. Cindy's pedigree is reproduced on the next page.

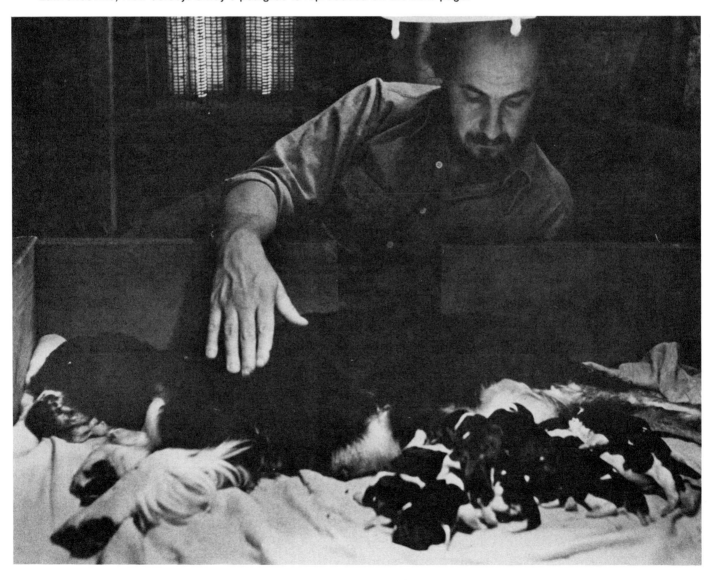

Certified Pedigree

Cindy
CALL NAME

REGISTERED WITH

Wakefield's Cinderella
REGISTERED NAME OF DOG

BREED English Springer Spaniel DATE WHELPED February 5th, 1969 SEX Female

BREEDER _____ ADDRESS _____

OWNER _____ ADDRESS _____

Black and white
GENERAL DESCRIPTION

SIRE

Ch.Kaintuck Ulysses

REG. NO. ....

- Ch.Kaintuck Winston
  - Ch.Kaintuck Christmas Carol
    - Ch.Kaintuck Beau Brummel
      - Beau Geste of Sandblown Acre
      - Kaintuck Roxane
    - Ch.Cartref Spring Chime
      - Ch.Frejax Prince Peter
      - Cartref Cae of Bittersweet
  - Kaintuck Diana
    - Ch.Kaintuck Beau Brummel
      - Beau Geste of Sandblown Acre
      - Kaintuck Roxane
    - Ch.Kaintuck Kate
      - Ch.Kaintuck Marc Anthony
      - Ch.Syringa Sue
- Salilyn's Kaintuck Julie
  - Ch.Salilyn's Macduff
    - Ch.King William of Salilyn
      - Firebrand of Sandblown Acre
      - Salutation of Salilyn
    - Shercliffe's Lady Debbie
      - Ch.Sir Lancelot of Salilyn
      - Candy Kisses of Konana
  - Kaintuck Jude
    - Ch.Kaintuck Beau Brummel
      - Beau Geste of Sandblown Acre
      - Kaintuck Roxane
    - Ch.Kaintuck Kate
      - Ch.Syringa Marc Anthony
      - Ch.Syringa Sue

DAM

Ch.Atha's Olivia of Wakefield

REG. NO. ....

- Ch.Wakefield's Sir Galahad
  - Ch.Kaintuck Beau Brummel
    - Beau Geste of Sandblown Acre
      - Chuck of Sandblown Acre
      - Deb of Sandblown Acre
    - Kaintuck Roxane
      - Ch.Melilotus Royal Oak
      - Kaintuck Aunt Clara
  - Ch.Wakefield's Fanny
    - Ch.Melilotus Royal Oak
      - ACCh.Frejax Royal Salute
      - Ch.Tranquillity of Melilotus
    - Judy of Gwynedd
      - Ch.Runor's Deacon
      - Victoria of Gwynedd
- Ch.Syringa Claudette
  - Ch.Kaintuck Marc Anthony
    - Ch.Kaintuck Prince Hamlet
      - Ch.Amos of Melilotus
      - Kaintuck Aunt Clara
    - Kaintuck Roxane
      - Ch.Melilotus Royal Oak
      - Kaintuck Aunt Clara
  - Ch.Syringa Sue
    - Ch.Runor's Deacon
      - ACCh.Rufton Breeze of Rob Roy
      - Ch.Audley Farm Judy
    - Ch.Her Ladyship of Melilotus
      - ACCh.Frejax Royal Salute
      - Ch.Tranquillity of Melilotus

A rare photo of the great 1949 English National Champion Rivington Glensaugh Glean, progenitor of many field trial "stars" in the United States. Photo courtesy of Dave Lorenz.

Ch. Chuzzlewit's Courier, by Ch. Winacko's Editor's Choice ex Canarch Contemplation, is one of the magnificent Springers belonging to Francie Nelson, Fanfare Kennels, Minneapolis, Minnesota.

Ch. Loujon Maginna's Victoria, by Ch. Salilyn's Encore ex Ch. Loujon Heritage, is the foundation brood bitch at Maginna Kennels, owned by Helen H. Maginnes, Exeter, New Hampshire. Karen Prickett, handler.

Opposite: Ch. Salilyn's Classic, born in 1971, is the sire of at least 75 champions, including six Best in Show winners. Owned by Mrs. Julie Gasow, Troy, Michigan.

Ch. Maitre's Dawn of Maidenhead, invaluable in the whelping box, has so far produced four champions, including the Group winner, Ch. Bryden's Marque of Maidenhead, with at least three from the same litter sure to finish. From the Maidenhead Kennels of Judy and Bud DiDonato, Lawrenceville, New Jersey, she is shown here winning a highly competitive (eight entries) brood bitch class at a Springer Specialty judged by Derek Rayne.

Opposite: This lovely portrait is of Champion Loujon Maginna's Victoria, the foundation bitch at Maginna's Springers.

Ch. Lilley's Holiday Cheer, C.D.X., is the foundation bitch of Donahan Springers owned by Don and Carol Callahan. She is Dam of five champions and grand-dam of two Best in Show winners; she is handled here by Don Callahan to win under judge Bob Waters.

Opposite: Ch. Filicia's Anlon Patriot was Top Sire All Breeds, 1980. By Ch. Filicia's Etching ex Ch. Kaintuck Pixie, he is owner-handled here by Anne Pope at the Eastern Futurity, 1976.

EASTERN ENGLISH SPRINGER
SPANIEL CLUB
JUNE 19, 1976
FUTURITY
1ST PLACE
PUPPY DOG
12-18 MONTHS

Van de Merlen

These newly born Springer puppies are from Fanfare Kennels, Francie Nelson, Minneapolis, Minnesota. Photographed by Joyce Kleven.

A very dignified Ch. Lou Jon's Femininity, after the arrival of her first litter, seems well aware that she has started something big on the road to becoming a Top Producer. This great bitch is behind many of the champions proudly wearing the Shinnecock prefix to their names. Patty Alston and Maureen Brady, owners.

Ch. Salilyn's Touch of Mink, photographed at 9 years, a daughter of Ch. Salilyn's Colonel's Overlord ex Ch. Salilyn's Something Special, was bred by Mrs. Julie Gasow and belongs to Cecil and Nancy Kemp of Las Vegas, Nevada.

The foundation bitch at Kalyn Springers is Pokohaven's Howling Success, owned by Kathy and Lynn Freese, Burdett, New York.

Ch. Danaho's Lalique of Stanton (by Ch. Filicia's Patriot ex Ch. Danaho's Ballet Russe, daughter of Ch. Kaintuck Tolstoy) is owner-handled here by Anne Pope.

Opposite: Ch. Danaho's Firebird, by Ch. Filicia's Anlon Patriot ex Danaho's Ballet Russe.

One might say that Ch. Lleda's Majestic Mr. J. is resting on his laurels in this attractive photo. A son of Ch. Veron's Marco Polo ex Ch. Clancy's Erin of Packanack, Mr. J. was bred by Karen Adell Garetano and Estelle Adell and is owned by Dave Schwartz of Atlanta, Georgia.

Opposite: This is Duncan, a son of Ch. Veron's Marco Polo ex Ch. Clancy's Erin of Packanack, in an informal pose with a member of his family. Lleda Springers, Huntington, New York.

Two young Springers with a future, four-and-a-half months old when photographed, have grown up to become Ch. Willowbank's Trendsetter and Willowbank's Largesse. The latter hates the show ring but makes beautiful puppies, several of which are now out and winning. Owned by Mr. and Mrs. Alexander R. Merriman, Willowbank Kennels, Blairstown, New Jersey.

Pedigrees—The Background of a Breeding Program

The pedigree certificate for Ch. Fortune's Regina lists several famous English Springer Spaniels.

To anyone interested in the breeding of dogs, pedigrees are the basic tool with which this is successfully accomplished. It is not sufficient to just breed two nice looking dogs to one another, then sit back and await outstanding results. Chances are they will be disappointing as there is no equal to a scientific approach in the breeding of dogs if quality results are the ultimate goal.

We have selected for you pedigrees of dogs and bitches that either themselves are great producers or that come from consistently outstanding producing lines. Some of these dogs are so dominant that they have seemed to "click" with almost every strain or bloodline. Others need to be carefully linebred for best results. The study

of breeding is a challenging and exciting occupation. For those fanciers who desire additional information on the subject of breeding, we recommend *Dogs and How to Breed Them* by Hilary Harmar and *Dog Breeding For Professionals* by Dr. Herbert Richards. Both books are published by T.F.H. Publications.

Even if you have no plan of involving yourself in breeding but just in owning and loving a dog or two, it is fun to trace back the dog's pedigree into earlier generations to learn about the sort of dogs behind yours. You will find many pictures throughout this book of dogs whose names are in these pedigrees, and these will enable you not only to trace the names in the background of your own dog but to see what the ancestors looked like too.

SALILYN KENNELS
English Springer Spaniels
4031 COOLIDGE — TROY, MICHIGAN
Certified Pedigree of

Name: Ch. *Salilyn's Touch of Mink*   Whelped: *Feb. 12 - 1969*   Breeder: *Mrs. F.H. Gasow*

A.K.C. No.: *SA - 674664*   Litter No.: *SL-317367*   Sex: *Female*   Color: *Black + White*

Grand Parents	Great Grand Parents	Great-Great Grand Parents

Sire: CH. SALILYN'S COLONEL'S OVERLORD (andy) — A.K.C. No. SA 559477

- Sire: CH. SALILYN'S ARISTOCRAT (Rocky)
  - Sire: CH. INCHIDONY PRINCE CHARMING
    - Sire: CH. SALILYN'S CITATION II
    - Dam: CH. SALILYN'S CINDERELLA II
  - Dam: CH. SALILYN'S LILY OF THE VALLEY
    - Sire: SALILYN'S ROYAL CONSORT
    - Dam: SALILYN'S GLENDA
- Dam: CH. SALILYN'S RADIANCE
  - Sire: SALILYN'S GOOD FORTUNE
    - Sire: CH. SALILYN'S COCKTAIL TIME
    - Dam: CH. SALILYN'S GOOD OMEN
  - Dam: CH. RANDALANES BRIGHT CHIPS
    - Sire: CH. SALILYN'S MAC DUFF
    - Dam: CH. ASCOT'S LIBBY

Dam: CH. SALILYN'S SOMETHING SPECIAL (Reule) — A.K.C. No. S.A. 448569

- Sire: CH. INCHIDONY PRINCE CHARMING
  - Sire: CH. SALILYN'S CITATION II
    - Sire: CH. SALILYN'S SENSATION C.D.
    - Dam: SALILYN'S PRINCESS MEG
  - Dam: CH. SALILYN'S CINDERELLA II
    - Sire: CH. KING PETER OF SALILYN
    - Dam: A.C. CH. WALPRIDE GAY BEAUTY
- Dam: CH. SALILYN'S LILY OF THE VALLEY
  - Sire: SALILYN'S ROYAL CONSORT
    - Sire: CH. SALILYN'S CITATION II
    - Dam: CH. ASCOT'S ESTRALITA
  - Dam: SALILYN'S GLENDA
    - Sire: CH. KING WILLIAM OF SALILYN
    - Dam: CH. SALILYN'S GOOD OMEN

CERTIFIED PEDIGREE

BREED: Eng. Springer Spaniel   COLOR AND/OR MARKINGS: Liver & White   SEX: Female   DATE WHELPED: May 5, 72

CALL NAME: _____   BREEDER: Cecil Kemp   ADDRESS: 4825 E. Van Buren, Las Vegas, Nev

REG. NAME: _____   A.K.C. REG. No.: _____   SELLER: _____

- **Ch. Salilyn's Aristocrat** (Sire)
  - Ch. Inchidony Prince Charming (Sire)
    - Ch. Salilyn's Citation II (Sire)
      - Sire: Ch. Salilyn's Sensation CD
      - Dam: Salilyn's Princess Meg
    - Ch. Salilyn's Cinderella II (Dam)
      - Sire: Ch. King Peter of Salilyn
      - Dam: AC Ch. Walpride Gay Beauty
  - Ch. Salilyn's Lilly of the Valley (Dam)
    - Salilyn's Royal Consort (Sire)
      - Sire: Ch. Salilyn's Citation II
      - Dam: Ch. Ascots Estralita
    - Salilyn's Glenda (Dam)
      - Sire: Ch. King William of Salilyn's
      - Dam: Ch. Salilyn's Good Omen
- **Ch. Salilyn's Touch of Mink** (Dam)
  - Ch. Salilyn's Colonels Overlord (Sire)
    - Ch. Salilyn's Aristocrat (Sire)
      - Sire: Ch. Inchidony Prince Charming
      - Dam: Ch. Salilyn's Lilly of the Valley
    - Ch. Salilyn's Radiance (Dam)
      - Sire: Salilyn's Good Fortune
      - Dam: Ch. Randalanes Bright Chips
  - Ch. Salilyn's Something Special (Dam)
    - Ch. Inchidony Prince Charming (Sire)
      - Sire: Ch. Salilyn's Citation II
      - Dam: Ch. Salilyn's Cinderella II
    - Ch. Salilyn's Lilly of the Valley (Dam)
      - Sire: Salilyn's Royal Consort
      - Dam: Salilyn's Glenda

I hereby certify that this Pedigree is true to the best of my knowledge _____

Signed

At the English Springer Spaniel Club of Michigan, 1974, Mrs. Elaine Mathis is judging. Ch. Salilyn's Aristocrat is on the left; his son, Ch. Salilyn's Colonel's Overlord, is on the right. Both dogs may be found as sires in the pedigrees on the facing page.

Ch. Salilyn's Colonel's Overlord, photographed at 7 years old, is a black and white son of Ch. Salilyn's Aristocrat ex Ch. Salilyn's Radiance, whelped November 24, 1967. Bred by Forrest Andrews, co-owned with Julie Gasow. All three of the Springers mentioned appear in the pedigrees reproduced on the facing page.

Ch. Jester's Southwind Twister, liver and white, is shown taking Best of Winners from the Puppy Class, handled by Tom Glassford for Mrs. Andrea Glassford at Wyoming Valley Kennel Club, 1981. His pedigree and that of Jester's Jack-in-the-Box are shown on the facing page.

Ch. Jester's Jack-in-the-Box is pictured winning under Doris Wilson at Trumbull County in May 1980, handled by Tom Glassford. Jester was bred by Andrea Glassford and recently sold to Sporting Fields Kennels, Mr. and Mrs. James Butt.

Jester Springers

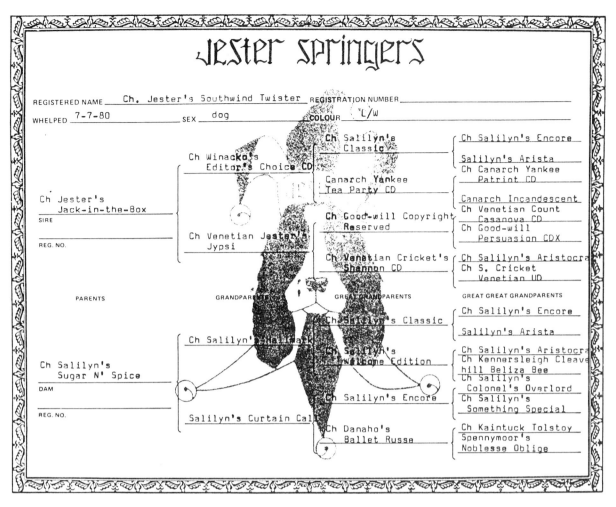

REGISTERED NAME __Ch. Jester's Southwind Twister__ REGISTRATION NUMBER _____

WHELPED __7-7-80__   SEX __dog__   COLOUR __L/W__

PARENTS	GRANDPARENTS	GREAT GRANDPARENTS	GREAT GREAT GRANDPARENTS

Ch Jester's Jack-in-the-Box
SIRE
REG. NO.

- Ch Winacko's Editor's Choice CD
  - Ch Salilyn's Classic
    - Ch Salilyn's Encore
    - Salilyn's Arista
  - Canarch Yankee Tea Party CD
    - Ch Canarch Yankee Patriot CD
    - Canarch Incandescent
- Ch Venetian Jester's Jypsi
  - Ch Good-will Copyright Reserved
    - Ch Venetian Count Casanova CD
    - Ch Good-will Persuasion CDX
  - Ch Venetian Cricket's Shannon CD
    - Ch Salilyn's Aristocrat
    - Ch S. Cricket Venetian UD

Ch Salilyn's Sugar N' Spice
DAM
REG. NO.

- Ch Salilyn's Hallmark
  - Ch Salilyn's Classic
    - Ch Salilyn's Encore
    - Salilyn's Arista
  - Ch Salilyn's Welcome Edition
    - Ch Salilyn's Aristocrat
    - Ch Kennersleigh Cleave hill Beliza Bee
- Salilyn's Curtain Call
  - Ch Salilyn's Encore
    - Ch Salilyn's Colonel's Overlord
    - Ch Salilyn's Something Special
  - Ch Danaho's Ballet Russe
    - Ch Kaintuck Tolstoy
    - Spennymoor's Noblesse Oblige

Jester Springers

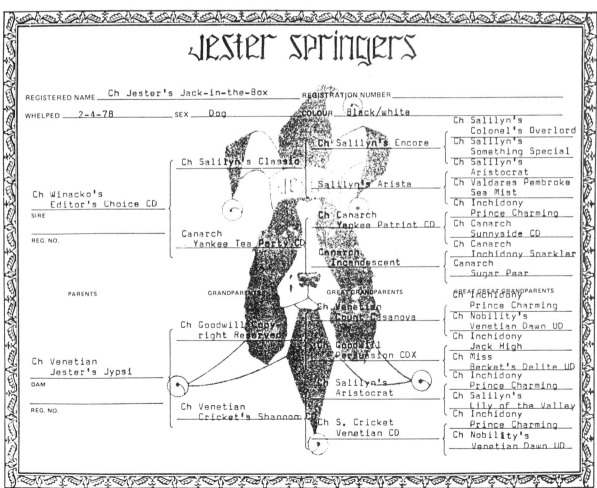

REGISTERED NAME __Ch Jester's Jack-in-the-Box__ REGISTRATION NUMBER _____

WHELPED __2-4-78__   SEX __Dog__   COLOUR __Black/white__

PARENTS	GRANDPARENTS	GREAT GRANDPARENTS	GREAT GREAT GRANDPARENTS

Ch Winacko's Editor's Choice CD
SIRE
REG. NO.

- Ch Salilyn's Classic
  - Ch Salilyn's Encore
    - Ch Salilyn's Colonel's Overlord
    - Ch Salilyn's Something Special
  - Salilyn's Arista
    - Ch Salilyn's Aristocrat
    - Ch Valdares Pembroke Sea Mist
- Canarch Yankee Tea Party CD
  - Ch Canarch Yankee Patriot CD
    - Ch Inchidony Prince Charming
    - Ch Canarch Sunnyside CD
  - Canarch Incandescent
    - Ch Canarch Inchidony Sparkler
    - Canarch Sugar Pear

Ch Venetian Jester's Jypsi
DAM
REG. NO.

- Ch Goodwill Copyright Reserved
  - Ch Venetian Count Casanova
    - Ch Inchidony Prince Charming
    - Ch Nobility's Venetian Dawn UD
  - Goodwill Persuasion CDX
    - Ch Inchidony Jack High
    - Ch Miss Becket's Delite UD
- Ch Venetian Cricket's Shannon CD
  - Ch Salilyn's Aristocrat
    - Ch Inchidony Prince Charming
    - Ch Salilyn's Lily of the Valley
  - Ch S. Cricket Venetian CD
    - Ch Inchidony Prince Charming
    - Ch Nobility's Venetian Dawn UD

Ch. Scotch Mist of Pequa, a Specialty Show winner with Best of Breed and Group placements, is taking First in the Sporting Group in the mid-1960s, handled by owner Ray Adell under judge Frank Foster Davis. Sired by Ch. Elk Groves Black Watch of Pequa ex Blairshinnock Cover Girl. See also the pedigree below.

LLEDA
English Springer Spaniels

16 LONGACRE DRIVE, HUNTINGTON, L.I., N.Y. 11743

REGISTERED NAME *Ch. Scotch Mist of Pequa* OFFICIAL REGISTRATION NO. _____ REGISTERED LITTER NO. _____

SEX *male* BORN *Sept 27, 1962* COLOR AND MARKINGS *Liver White*

SOLD TO _____ ADDRESS _____ *died 1979*

358

Ch. Lleda's Ariana, by Ch. Duncan's Fife ex Ch. Lleda's Athena of Sunnykay, is pictured taking a "major" from the Bred-by Exhibitor Class at Westbury at 10 months old. Shown here by Teri Adell, "Ara" finished with four "majors," two of them at Specialty Shows. Owned by the Adells; bred by B. Weingarten and Karen Adell Garetano. See the pedigree below, which also shows Ch. Scotch Mist of Pequa several generations back.

LLEDA
English Springer Spaniels

16 LONGACRE DRIVE, HUNTINGTON, L.I., N.Y. 11743

REGISTERED NAME Ch. Lleda's Ariana INDIVIDUAL REGISTRATION NO. _____ REGISTERED LITTER NO. _____

SEX female BORN _____ COLOR AND MARKINGS liver & white

SOLD TO Bred by B. Weingarten ADDRESS _____
& Karen Adell Garetano

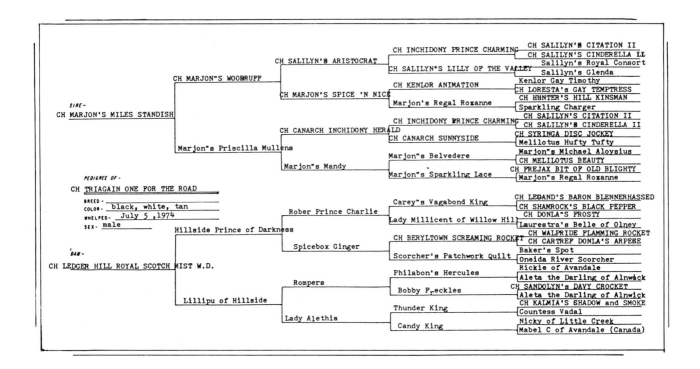

PEDIGREE OF -
CH TRIAGAIN ONE FOR THE ROAD
BREED -
COLOR - black, white, tan
WHELPED - July 5, 1974
SEX - male

SIRE -
CH MARJON'S MILES STANDISH

- CH MARJON'S WOODRUFF
  - CH SALILYN'S ARISTOCRAT
    - CH INCHIDONY PRINCE CHARMING
      - CH SALILYN'S CITATION II
      - CH SALILYN'S CINDERELLA LL
    - CH SALILYN'S LILLY OF THE VALLEY
      - Salilyn's Royal Consort
      - Salilyn's Glenda
  - CH MARJON'S SPICE 'N NICE
    - CH KENLOR ANIMATION
      - Kenlor Gay Timothy
      - CH LORESTA's GAY TEMPTRESS
    - Marjon's Regal Roxanne
      - CH HUNTER'S HILL KINSMAN
      - Sparkling Charger
- Marjon's Priscilla Mullens
  - CH CANARCH INCHIDONY HERALD
    - CH INCHIDONY PRINCE CHARMING
      - CH SALILYN'S CITATION II
      - CH SALILYN'S CINDERELLA II
    - CH CANARCH SUNNYSIDE
      - CH SYRINGA DISC JOCKEY
      - Melilotus Hufty Tufty
  - Marjon's Mandy
    - Marjon's Belvedere
      - Marjon's Michael Aloysius
      - CH MELILOTUS BEAUTY
    - Marjon's Sparkling Lace
      - CH FREJAX BIT OF OLD BLIGHTY
      - Marjon's Regal Roxanne

DAM -
CH LEDGER HILL ROYAL SCOTCH MIST W.D.

- Hillside Prince of Darkness
  - Rober Prince Charlie
    - Carey's Vagabond King
      - CH LEDAND'S BARON BLENNERHASSED
      - CH SHAMROCK'S BLACK PEPPER
    - Lady Millicent of Willow Hill
      - CH DONLA's FROSTY
      - Laurestra's Belle of Olney
  - Spicebox Ginger
    - CH BERYLTOWN SCREAMING ROCKET
      - CH WALFRIDE FLAMMING ROCKET
      - CH CARTREF DONLA'S ARPEBE
    - Scorcher's Patchwork Quilt
      - Baker's Spot
      - Oneida River Scorcher
- Lillipu of Hillside
  - Rompers
    - Philabon's Hercules
      - Rickie of Avandale
      - Aleta the Darling of Alnwick
    - Bobby Freckles
      - CH SANDOLYN's DAVY CROCKET
      - Aleta the Darling of Alnwick
  - Lady Alethia
    - Thunder King
      - CH KALMIA'S SHADOW and SMOKE
      - Countess Vadal
    - Candy King
      - Nicky of Little Creek
      - Mabel C of Avandale (Canada)

Ch. Triagain One For The Road at 14 months is winning his first point. The following year he finished with three 5-point "majors" in three consecutive days for a most exciting weekend. Sired by Ch. Marjon's Miles Standish ex Ch. Ledger Hill Royal Scotch Mist, W.D., this splendid tri-color Springer is owned by Susanne B. Howard and handled by George Alston. The pedigree for Triagain One For The Road is at the top of this page.

360

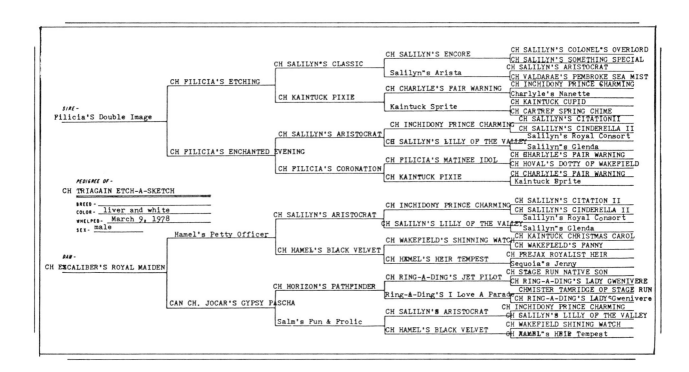

SIRE- Filicia'S Double Image					CH SALILYN'S COLONEL'S OVERLORD

Pedigree chart:

- **SIRE- Filicia'S Double Image**
  - CH FILICIA'S ETCHING
    - CH SALILYN'S CLASSIC
      - CH SALILYN'S ENCORE
        - CH SALILYN'S COLONEL'S OVERLORD
        - CH SALILYN'S SOMETHING SPECIAL
      - Salilyn's Arista
        - CH SALILYN'S ARISTOCRAT
        - CH VALDARAE'S PEMBROKE SEA MIST
    - CH KAINTUCK PIXIE
      - CH CHARLYLE'S FAIR WARNING
        - CH INCHIDONY PRINCE CHARMING
        - Charlyle's Nanette
      - Kaintuck Sprite
        - CH KAINTUCK CUPID
        - CH CARTREF SPRING CHIME
  - CH FILICIA'S ENCHANTED EVENING
    - CH SALILYN'S ARISTOCRAT
      - CH INCHIDONY PRINCE CHARMING
        - CH SALILYN'S CITATION II
        - CH SALILYN'S CINDERELLA II
      - CH SALILYN'S LILLY OF THE VALLEY
        - Salilyn's Royal Consort
        - Salilyn's Glenda
    - CH FILICIA'S CORONATION
      - CH FILICIA'S MATINEE IDOL
        - CH CHARLYLE'S FAIR WARNING
        - CH HOVAL'S DOTTY OF WAKEFIELD
      - CH KAINTUCK PIXIE
        - CH CHARLYLE'S FAIR WARNING
        - Kaintuck Sprite

PEDIGREE OF- CH TRIAGAIN ETCH-A-SKETCH

BREED -
COLOR- liver and white
WHELPED- March 9, 1978
SEX- male

- **DAM- CH EXCALIBER'S ROYAL MAIDEN**
  - Hamel's Petty Officer
    - CH SALILYN'S ARISTOCRAT
      - CH INCHIDONY PRINCE CHARMING
        - CH SALILYN'S CITATION II
        - CH SALILYN'S CINDERELLA II
      - CH SALILYN'S LILLY OF THE VALLEY
        - Salilyn's Royal Consort
        - Salilyn's Glenda
    - CH HAMEL'S BLACK VELVET
      - CH WAKEFIELD'S SHINNING WATCH
        - CH KAINTUCK CHRISTMAS CAROL
        - CH WAKEFIELD'S FANNY
      - CH HAMEL'S HEIR TEMPEST
        - CH PREJAX ROYALIST HEIR
        - Sequoia's Jenny
  - CAN CH. JOCAR'S GYPSY PASCHA
    - CH HORIZON'S PATHFINDER
      - CH RING-A-DING'S JET PILOT
        - CH STAGE RUN NATIVE SON
        - CH RING-A-DING'S LADY GWENIVERE
      - Ring-A-Ding's I Love A Parade
        - CH MISTER TAMRIDGE OP STAGE RUN
        - CH RING-A-DING'S LADY Gwenivere
    - Salm's Fun & Prolic
      - CH SALILYN'S ARISTOCRAT
        - CH INCHIDONY PRINCE CHARMING
        - CH SALILYN'S LILLY OF THE VALLEY
      - CH HAMEL'S BLACK VELVET
        - CH WAKEFIELD SHINING WATCH
        - CH HAMEL'S HEIR Tempest

Ch. Triagain Etch A Sketch (Filicia's Double Image ex Ch. Excaliber's Royal Maiden) was three times Best of Breed from the classes en route to the title. Susanne B. Howard, owner, Triagain Kennels, Cockeysville, Maryland; George Alston, handler. At the top of this page is the pedigree for this dog. Notice that the name of Ch. Salilyn's Aristocrat appears four times.

Ch. Schwedekrest Lady Pamela, C.D., the dam of Am., Can. Ch. Geiger's Chief Geronimo, C.D., W.D.X., is pictured taking Best of Opposite Sex at the Puget Sound English Springer Spaniel Association, 1959. Owned by Tillie Geiger.

Ch. Geiger's Winaway Duke, U.D., W.D., the sire of Ch. Geiger's Chief Geronimo, making one of his many splendid wins for owners Bob and Tillie Geiger, North Bend, Washington. See also the pedigree on the facing page.

Ch. Geiger's Chief Geronimo, C.D., and daughter Ch. Geiger's Royal Princess winning under judge Harvey Gates at Lewiston, Idaho, in 1965. Tillie and Bob Geiger, owners.

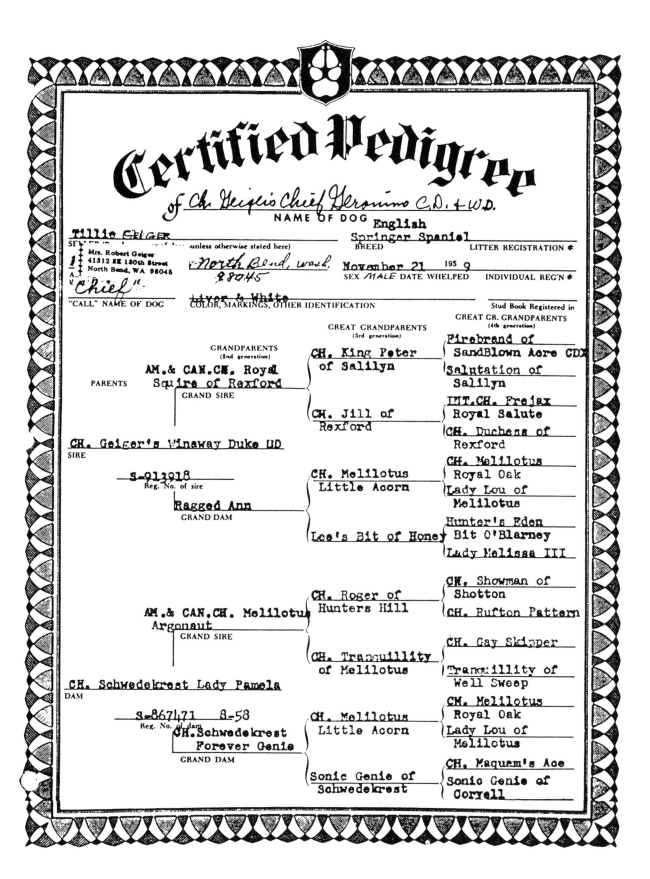

Certified Pedigree

of *Ch. Geiger's Chief Geronimo C.D. & W.D.*

NAME OF DOG

Tillie GEIGER

SF... .... (unless otherwise stated here)

Mrs. Robert Geiger
41312 SE 130th Street
North Bend, WA 98045

North Bend, wash.
98045

"Chief"

"CALL" NAME OF DOG

English
Springer Spaniel

BREED   LITTER REGISTRATION #

November 21 195 9

SEX *MALE* DATE WHELPED   INDIVIDUAL REG'N #

Liver & White

COLOR, MARKINGS, OTHER IDENTIFICATION

Stud Book Registered in

PARENTS	GRANDPARENTS (2nd generation)	GREAT GRANDPARENTS (3rd generation)	GREAT GR. GRANDPARENTS (4th generation)
CH. Geiger's Winaway Duke UD SIRE	AM.& CAN.CH. Royal Squire of Rexford GRAND SIRE	CH. King Peter of Salilyn	Firebrand of SandBlown Acre CDX
			Salutation of Salilyn
		CH. Jill of Rexford	INT.CH. Frejax Royal Salute
			CH. Duchess of Rexford
	S-913918 Reg. No. of sire Ragged Ann GRAND DAM	CH. Melilotus Little Acorn	CH. Melilotus Royal Oak
			Lady Lou of Melilotus
		Lee's Bit of Honey	Hunter's Eden Bit O'Blarney
			Lady Melissa III
CH. Schwedekrest Lady Pamela DAM	AM.& CAN.CH. Melilotus Argonaut GRAND SIRE	CH. Roger of Hunters Hill	CH. Showman of Shotton
			CH. Rufton Pattern
		CH. Tranquillity of Melilotus	CH. Gay Skipper
			Tranquillity of Well Sweep
	S-867471 8-58 Reg. No. of dam CH.Schwedekrest Forever Genie GRAND DAM	CH. Melilotus Little Acorn	CH. Melilotus Royal Oak
			Lady Lou of Melilotus
		Sonic Genie of Schwedekrest	CH. Maquam's Ace
			Sonic Genie of Coryell

This is a very famous English Springer Spaniel bitch, Am. and Can. Ch. Alynn's Green Beret, C.D., W.D.X., pictured as a youngster taking Best of Opposite Sex in the 1970 National Futurity. Owned by Lynn Benson of Issaquah, Washington, Beret three times from the puppy class was Winners Bitch, took the pictured B.O.S. at the National when 13 months old, shortly thereafter gained 5 points at the Puget Sound Specialty, then on a three-day weekend at consecutive shows gained her Canadian title and went first in group (all owner-handled). Her C.D. title was earned in three shows, including first in Novice B at the 1973 National Specialty. Bred to seven different sires, she has produced excellent temperament, soundness, and type in each of her litters.

Green Beret was sired by Ch. Geiger's Chief Geronimo, C.D., W.D., from Am., Can. Ch. Alynn's Miss Midnight Frost, W.D.X., a Ch. Ruleon's Duffson daughter. Chief Geronimo also may be found listed twice in the pedigree shown below.

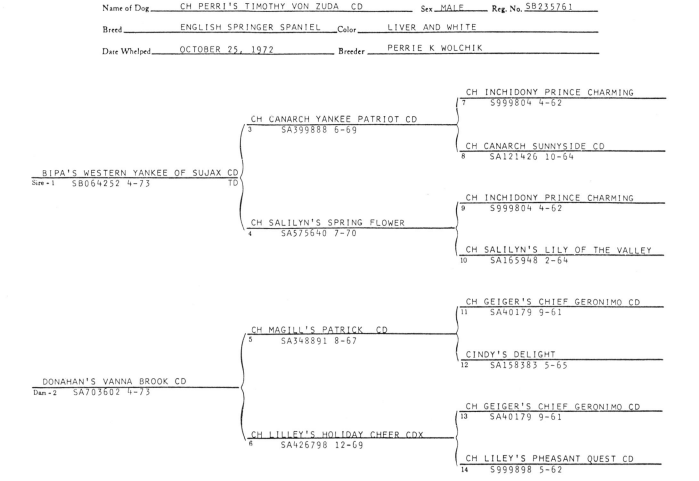

Name of Dog_____CH PERRI'S TIMOTHY VON ZUDA CD_____ Sex __MALE_____ Reg. No. SB235761 _____

Breed_____ENGLISH SPRINGER SPANIEL__Color_____LIVER AND WHITE_____

Date Whelped_____OCTOBER 25, 1972_____ Breeder_____PERRIE K WOLCHIK_____

CH INCHIDONY PRINCE CHARMING
7   S999804 4-62

CH CANARCH YANKEE PATRIOT CD
3   SA399888 6-69

CH CANARCH SUNNYSIDE CD
8   SA121426 10-64

BIPA'S WESTERN YANKEE OF SUJAX CD
Sire - 1   SB064252 4-73   TD

CH INCHIDONY PRINCE CHARMING
9   S999804 4-62

CH SALILYN'S SPRING FLOWER
4   SA575640 7-70

CH SALILYN'S LILY OF THE VALLEY
10   SA165948 2-64

CH GEIGER'S CHIEF GERONIMO CD
11   SA40179 9-61

CH MAGILL'S PATRICK CD
5   SA348891 8-67

CINDY'S DELIGHT
12   SA158383 5-65

DONAHAN'S VANNA BROOK CD
Dam - 2   SA703602 4-73

CH GEIGER'S CHIEF GERONIMO CD
13   SA40179 9-61

CH LILLEY'S HOLIDAY CHEER CDX
6   SA426798 12-69

CH LILEY'S PHEASANT QUEST CD
14   S999898 5-62

364

N.F.T.C., N.A.F.T.C. Dansmirth's Gunshot retrieves a bird. Bred, owned, trained, and handled by Daniel Langhans, Harvard, Illinois. The pedigree shown below is for Dansmirth's Gunshot; it lists the dam as N.F.T.C. Brackenbriar Snapshot, pictured in Chapter Nine.

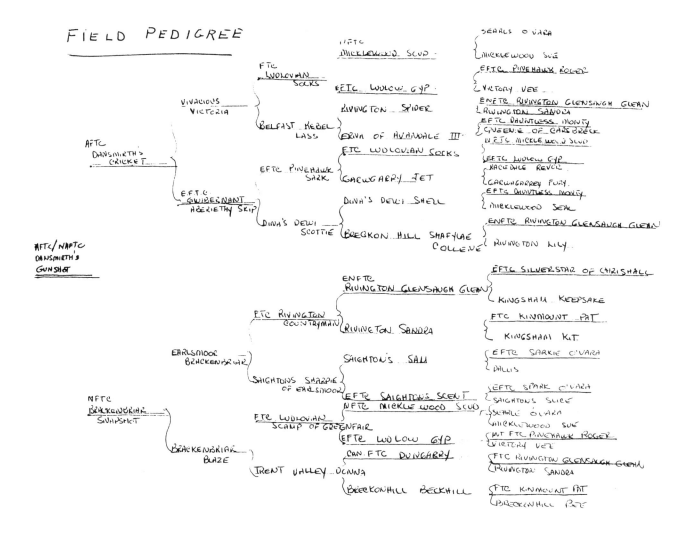

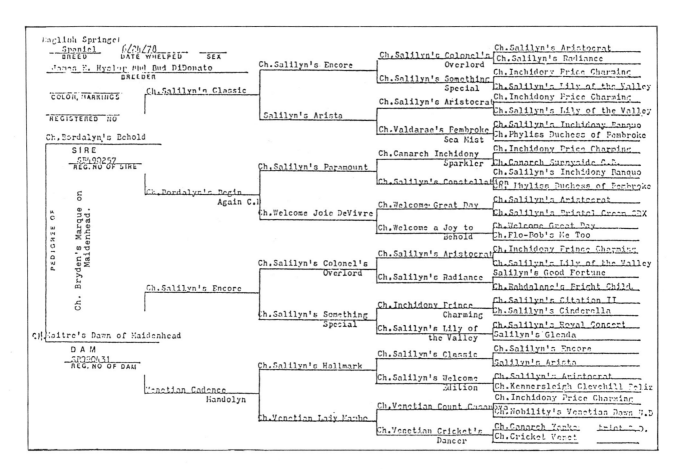

English Springer
Spaniel   6/26/78
BREED   DATE WHELPED   SEX

James E. Hyslop and Bud DiDonato
BREEDER

COLOR, MARKINGS

REGISTERED NO

PEDIGREE OF

Ch. Bryden's Marque on Maidenhead.

SIRE
Ch. Bordalyn's Behold
SR199257
REG. NO OF SIRE

DAM
Ch. Maitre's Dawn of Maidenhead
SR280431
REG. NO OF DAM

	Ch.Salilyn's Encore	Ch.Salilyn's Colonel's Overlord	Ch.Salilyn's Aristocrat
Ch.Salilyn's Classic			Ch.Salilyn's Radiance
		Ch.Salilyn's Something Special	Ch.Inchidony Price Charming
			Ch.Salilyn's Lily of the Valley
	Salilyn's Arista	Ch.Salilyn's Aristocrat	Ch.Inchidony Price Charming
			Ch.Salilyn's Lily of the Valley
		Ch.Valdarae's Pembroke Sea Mist	Ch.Salilyn's Inchidony Banquo
			Ch.Phyliss Duchess of Pembroke
Ch.Bordalyn's Begin Again C.D.	Ch.Salilyn's Paramount	Ch.Canarch Inchidony Sparkler	Ch.Inchidony Price Charming
			Ch.Canarch Sunnyside C.D.
		Ch.Salilyn's Constellation	Ch.Salilyn's Inchidony Banquo
			Ch.Phyliss Duchess of Pembroke
	Ch.Welcome Joie DeVivre	Ch.Welcome Great Day	Ch.Salilyn's Aristocrat
			Ch.Salilyn's Bristol Cream CDX
		Ch.Welcome a Joy to Behold	Ch.Welcome Great Day
			Ch.Flo-Bob's Me Too
Ch.Salilyn's Encore	Ch.Salilyn's Colonel's Overlord	Ch.Salilyn's Aristocrat	Ch.Inchidony Prince Charming
			Ch.Salilyn's Lily of the Valley
		Ch.Salilyn's Radiance	Salilyn's Good Fortune
			Ch.Rahdalane's Bright Child
	Ch.Salilyn's Something Special	Ch.Inchidony Prince Charming	Ch.Salilyn's Citation II
			Ch.Salilyn's Cinderella
		Ch.Salilyn's Lily of the Valley	Ch.Salilyn's Royal Concert
			Salilyn's Glenda
Venetian Cadence Mandolyn	Ch.Salilyn's Hallmark	Ch.Salilyn's Classic	Ch.Salilyn's Encore
			Salilyn's Arista
		Ch.Salilyn's Welcome Edition	Ch.Salilyn's Aristocrat
			Ch.Kennersleigh Clevehill Feliz
	Ch.Venetian Lady Maybe	Ch.Venetian Count Casanova	Ch.Inchidony Price Charming
			Ch.Nobility's Venetian Dawn W.D
		Ch.Venetian Cricket's Dancer	Ch.Canarch Yankee Print C.D.
			Ch.Cricket Veret

Ch. Bordalyn's Behold winning the Stud Dog Class at the Eastern English Springer Spaniel Club Specialty in June 1979. Mary Ann Alston handled for owner Susan Ritter. The progeny are Champion Bryden's Marque of Maidenhead (pedigree information above) and Champion Maidenhead Memory at Croyden, winners of their Puppy Classes on the day.

Field Ch. Rumson Blackjack, owned by Evelyn Monte Van Horn of Southbury, Connecticut, is pictured "ready to go." His background is given in the pedigree certificate reproduced below.

CERTIFIED PEDIGREE

Name of Dog __FLD CH RUMSON BLACKJACK__   Sex __MALE__   Reg. No. __SB072229__

Breed __ENGLISH SPRINGER SPANIEL__   Color __LIVER & WHITE__

Date Whelped __AUGUST 11 1971__   Breeder __MRS DORIS E BRENNAN__

			RIVINGTON COUNTRYMAN (UNITED	RIVINGTON GLENSAUGH GLEAN
			15 S658988 12-55 KINGDOM)	31 1924AF 104570/48
		EARLSMOOR BRACKEN BRIAR		RIVINGTON SANDRA
		7 S888443 4-60		32 1974AH 70162/50
			SAIGHTON'S SHARPIE OF EARLS-	SAIGHTON'S SAM
			16 S747351 10-56 MOOR (UNITED	33 1925AG 75632/49
	BRACKENBRIAR BOULDER		KINGDOM)	SAIGHTON'S SCENT
	3 SA86280 7-64			34 2158AH 89166/49
			FLD CH LUDLOVIAN SCAMP OF	MICKLEWOOD SCUD
			17 S717676 8-56 GREENFAIR	35 S588501 6-54
		BRACKENBRIAR BLAZE		LUDLOW GYP
		8 SA6469 5-61		36 2095AG 58952/49
			TRENT VALLEY DONNA (CANADA)	DUNGARRY
			18 S866048 11-59	37 333636
JULET PEPPY				BRECKONHILL BECKFOOT
SIRE-1 SA260867 6-72				38 338637
			SAIGHTON'S SAM	SARKIE O'VARA
			19 1925AG 75632/49	39 360AD
		SAIGHTON'S SENTRY OF HARDIHILL (UNITED	DALLIS
		9 S759054 8-56 KINGDOM)	40
			SAIGHTON'S SCENT	SPARK O'VARA
			20 2159AH 89166/49	41 954AD
	JULET'S BREEZE			SAIGHTON'S SLICE
	4 S836061 12-59	(UNITED KINGDOM)	42 2238AG
			FLD CH GREATFORD KIM OF HARDT-	HARPERSBROOK APETHORPE TEAZLE
			21 S610326 9-54 HILL	43 2378AF 68417/46
		WANGUNK SNOW		BOBBIE OF ROTHWELL
		10 S688433 12-56		44 20106/46
			HARDTHILL'S SHOOTING STAR	FLD CH NIMROD TOM OF FAIRVIEW
			22 S445506	45 S191572
				FLD CH HARDTHILL'S GIN
				46 S65160
				FLD CH LUDLOVIAN SOCKS
			PINEHAWK SARK	47 1390AM
			23 1745AQ 99781/56	GARNGAAREG JET
		FLD CH RILSON OF RANSCOMBE (UNITED	48
		11 S944195 2-63 KINGDOM)	SILVERSTAR OF CHRISHALL
			RILLA OF RANSCOMBE	49 679AD
			24 53528/51	REVERIE OF RANSCOMBE
FLD & AMTR FLD CH BETHSAIDA'S BINOCULARS				50 464AF
5 SA134141 12-69			FLD CH RIVINGTON COUNTRYMAN	RIVINGTON GLENSAUGH GLEAN
			25 S659988 12-55 (UNITED KING-	51 1924AG 104570/48
		AMTR FLD CH JULET'S CINDY DOM)	RIVINGTON SANDRA
		12 SA5606 11-61		52 1974AH 70162/50
			JULET'S BREEZE	SAIGHTON'S SENTRY OF HARDIHILL
			26 S836061 12-59	53 S759054 8-56
				WANGUNK SNOW
				54 S688433 12-56
				FLD CH RIVINGTON COUNTRYMAN
COUNTRY GIRL OF RUMSON			EARLSMOOR BRACKEN BRIAR	55 S658988 12-55
DAM-2 SB035321 6-72			27 S888443 4-60	SAIGHTON'S SHARPIE OF EARLS-
		FLD CH BRACKENBRIAR BONFIRE		56 S747351 10-56 MOOR
		13 SA86281 3-67		FLD CH LUDLOVIAN SCAMP OF
			BRACKENBRIAR BLAZE	57 S717676 8-56 GREENFAIR
			28 SA6469 5-61	TRENT VALLEY DONNA
	TRANQUILLITY'S THREE ALARM			58 S866048 11-59
	6 SA446054 12-69			SAIGHTON'S SENTRY OF HARDTHILL
			FLD CH RIPPLES OF GUNNERHAVEN	59 S759054 8-56
			29 S825365 3-60	WANGUNK SNOW
		GUNNER RIP'S GIN SLING		60 S688433 12-56
		14 SA304716 3-67		FLD CH JOHNNY RINGO
			TOODRY GIN	61 S931526 10-60
			30 SA67392 9-63	JULET'S BREEZE
				62 S836061 12-59

The Seal of The American Kennel Club affixed hereto certifies that this pedigree has been compiled from official Stud Book records.

Date Issued __3-27-80 SH__

367

Fidelis Halls of Montezuma, when three months, shown at a Fun Match by a young friend under judge Mrs. Tiederman in 1979. Mrs. Nancy S. Cowley, owner, Woodstock, Connecticut. His pedigree is reproduced below.

Certified Pedigree
ENGLISH SPRINGER SPANIEL

Reg. Name __Fidelis' Halls of Montezuma__ A.K.C. No. __SC578388__ Sex __Male__

Whelped __November 7, 1978__ Litter No. __SL807497__ Color __B/W__

Breeder __Nancy S. Cowley__ Address _____

Owner _____ Address _____

Grand Parents	Great Grand Parents	Great-Great Grand Parents

Sire __Ch. Foyscroft Signed Edition__
A.K.C. No. __SB074606__

Sire __Ch. Salilyn's Signature__

Sire __Ch. Inchidony Prince Charming__
- Sire __Ch. Salilyn's Citation__
- Dam __Ch. Salilyn's Cinderella__

Dam __Salilyn's Glenda__
- Sire __Ch. King William of Salilyn__
- Dam __Ch. Salilyn's Good Omen__

Dam __Ch. Kaintuck Pixie C.D.__

Sire __Ch. Charlyle's Fair Warning__
- Sire __Ch. Inchidony Prince Charming__
- Dam __Charlyle's Nanette__

Dam __Kaintuck Sprite__
- Sire __Ch. Kaintuck Cupid__
- Dam __Ch. Cartref Spring Chime__

Dam __Ch. Filicia's Fidelis of Sulo__
OFA EN-1173-T CERF-202/78-17
A.K.C. No. __SC155359__

Sire __Ch. Filicia's Anlon Patriot__

Sire __Ch. Filicia's Etching__
- Sire __Ch. Salilyn's Classic__
- Dam __Ch. Kaintuck Pixie C.D.__

Dam __Ch. Filicia's Westcot Joy of Anlon__
- Sire __Ch. Salilyn's Aristocrat__
- Dam __Ch. Kaintuck Pixie C.D.__

Dam __Ch. Filicia's Black Magic of Solo__

Sire __Ch. Filicia's Bequest__
- Sire __Ch. Salilyn's Classic__
- Dam __Ch. Kaintuck Pixie C.D.__

Dam __Ch. Filicia's Coronation__
- Sire __Ch. Filicia's Matinee Idol__
- Dam __Ch. Kaintuck Pixie C.D.__

A promising youngster, Ch. Filicia's Dividend is pictured at ten months of age. Filicia Springers are owned by Anne Pope. See the pedigree below for background information.

Certified Pedigree

SEX __Ch. Filicia's Dividend__ COLOR _____ DATE WHELPED _____

REGISTERED WITH _____ DATE OF PURCHASE _____ NAME OF PURCHASER _____

Ch. Salilyn's Private Stock
- Ch. Filicia's Bequest
  - Ch. Salilyn's Classic
    - Ch. Salilyn's Encore
    - Salilyn's Arista
  - Ch. Kaintuck Pixie, C.D.
    - Ch. Charlyle's Fair Warning
    - Kaintuck Sprite
- Ch. Salilyn's Sonnet
  - Ch. Salilyn's Aristocrat
    - Ch. Inchidony Prince Charming
    - Ch. Salilyn's Lily of the Valley
  - Salilyn's Pirate Queen
    - Ch. Angladales Mocha Bandit
    - Ch. Salilyns' Something Special

Ch. Danaho's Lalique of Stanton
- Ch. Filicia's Anlon Patriot
  - Ch. Filicia's Etching
    - Ch. Salilyn's Classic
    - Ch. Kaintuck Pixie, C.D.
  - Ch. Filicia's Wescot Joy
    - Ch. Salilyn's Aristocrat of Anlon
    - Ch. Kaintuck Pixie, C.D.
- Ch. Danaho's Ballet Russe
  - Ch. Kaintuck Tolstoy
    - Ch. Charlyle's Fair Warning
    - Ch. Kaintuck Fortune Huntess
  - Spennymoor's Noblesse Oblige
    - Ch. Spennymoor's Doc's Boy
    - Billet Doux of Spennymoor

I HEREBY CERTIFY THAT TO THE BEST OF MY KNOWLEDGE AND BELIEF THE ABOVE PEDIGREE IS TRUE AND THAT ALL ANCESTORS NAMED ABOVE ARE OF THE SAME BREED.

SIGNED THIS _____ DAY OF _____ 19 _____

SIGNATURE _____ ADDRESS _____

BORDALYN
ENGLISH SPRINGER SPANIELS

CERTIFIED PEDIGREE OF
BORDALYN'S KEVRIETT CHARISMA

F	L&W		5/30/76	*Crissy* ~~Star~~
Sex	Color	Reg. No.	Date Whelped	Call Name

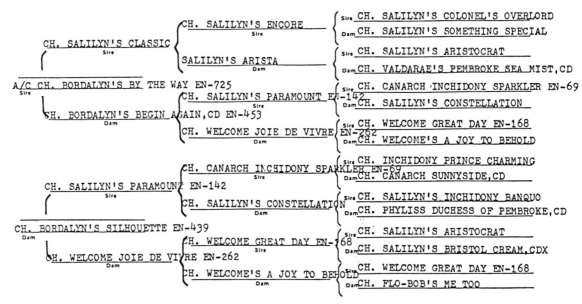

```
                                                        ┌ Sire CH. SALILYN'S COLONEL'S OVERLORD
                             CH. SALILYN'S ENCORE      ┤
                                    Sire                └ Dam CH. SALILYN'S SOMETHING SPECIAL
        CH. SALILYN'S CLASSIC  ┤
               Sire                                     ┌ Sire CH. SALILYN'S ARISTOCRAT
                             SALILYN'S ARISTA          ┤
                                                        └ Dam CH. VALDARAE'S PEMBROKE SEA MIST,CD
A/C CH. BORDALYN'S BY THE WAY EN-725 ┤
        Sire                                            ┌ Sire CH. CANARCH INCHIDONY SPARKLER EN-69
                             CH. SALILYN'S PARAMOUNT EN-142 ┤
                                    Sire                └ Dam CH. SALILYN'S CONSTELLATION
        SH. BORDALYN'S BEGIN AGAIN,CD EN-453 ┤
               Dam                                      ┌ Sire CH. WELCOME GREAT DAY EN-168
                             CH. WELCOME JOIE DE VIVRE EN-262 ┤
                                    Dam                 └ Dam CH. WELCOME'S A JOY TO BEHOLD

                                                        ┌ Sire CH. INCHIDONY PRINCE CHARMING
                             CH. CANARCH INCHIDONY SPARKLER EN-69 ┤
                                    Sire                └ Dam CH. CANARCH SUNNYSIDE,CD
        CH. SALILYN'S PARAMOUNT EN-142 ┤
               Sire                                     ┌ Sire CH. SALILYN'S INCHIDONY BANQUO
                             CH. SALILYN'S CONSTELLATION ┤
                                    Dam                 └ Dam CH. PHYLISS DUCHESS OF PEMBROKE,CD
CH. BORDALYN'S SILHOUETTE EN-439 ┤
        Dam                                             ┌ Sire CH. SALILYN'S ARISTOCRAT
                             CH. WELCOME GREAT DAY EN-168 ┤
                                    Sire                └ Dam CH. SALILYN'S BRISTOL CREAM,CDX
        SH. WELCOME JOIE DE VIVRE EN-262 ┤
               Dam                                      ┌ Sire CH. WELCOME GREAT DAY EN-168
                             CH. WELCOME'S A JOY TO BEHOLD ┤
                                    Dam                 └ Dam CH. FLO-BOB'S ME TOO
```

I hereby certify that this Pedigree is true to the best of my knowledge _____

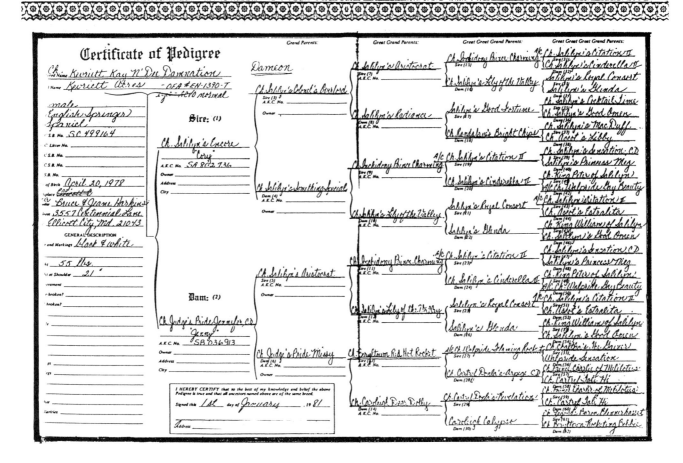

Right: Ch. Bordalyn's By The Way, W.D.X., is handled to Best of Breed by Mary Ann Alston for his breeder, Bonita Bosley. Bordalyn's Kevriett Charisma was sired by this champion dog, as shown in the pedigree at the top of the facing page.

Below: Ch. Judge's Pride Jennifer, C.D., by Ch. Salilyn Aristocrat ex Ch. Judge's Pride Missy, was Top Producing Springer Bitch in 1979, four of her progeny having finished that year. At the time of this writing, she had a total of seven champions to her credit. She is pictured placing in the Veterans Class at the English Springer Spaniel Field Trial Association, August 1980, handled by Debbie Kirk for Dr. Mary B. Gibbs, Spencerville, Maryland. See also the pedigree at the bottom of the opposite page, which lists Jenny as dam.

Ch. Filicia's Bequest, sire of many champions, including two Best in Show winners, by Ch. Salilyn's Classic ex Ch. Kaintuck Pixie, C.D., is owned by Mrs. Julie Gasow, bred by Anne Pope. Below is the pedigree of Connie Mitchon's Ch. Telltale Windfall, sired by Ch. Filicia's Bequest, whose name also appears in the pedigree on the following page.

REGISTERED NAME	REG. NO.	COLOR	SEX
CH Telltale Windfall	IDENTACODE NO.	Liver / white	F
KENNEL NAME	BREED	MARKINGS	WHELPED
Windfall			11-22-78

GREAT GRANDPARENTS

GREA

GRANDPARENTS

SIRE CH Filicia's Bequest

CH Salilyn's Classic
- CH Salilyn's Encore
- Salilyn's Arista

CH Kaintuck Pixie CD
- CH Charlyles Fair Warning
- Kaintuck Sprite

INDICATE MARKINGS IN COLOR

DAM CH Telltale Rambling Heart

CH Salilyn's Aristocrat
- CH Inchidony Prince Charming
- CH Salilyn's Lily of the Valley

Telltale Victoria
- CH Salilyns Classic
- Canarch Triple Crown

372

SEX Ch. Filicia's Custom Maid   COLOR _____ DATE WHELPED _____

REGISTERED WITH _____ DATE OF PURCHASE _____ NAME OF PURCHASER _____

Tara's Acquarius

  Ch. Kaintuck Tolstoy

    Ch. Charlyle's Fair Warning

      Ch. Inchidony Prince Charming

      Charlyle's Nanette

    Ch. Kaintuck Fortune's Huntress

      Ch. Kaintuck Vicar of Wakefield

      Ch. Fortune's Dorsue Diana of Day

  Ch. Fortune's Judy Belle

    Ch. Kaintuck Vicar of Wakefield

      Ch. Kaintuck Christmas Carol

      Ch. Wakefield's Fanny

    Ch. Fortune's Dorsue Dianna of Day

      Ch. Syringa Disc Jockey

      Ch. Fortune's Lucky Penny

Ch. Filicia's Liberty Belle of Sulo

  Ch. Filicia's Anlon Patriot

    Ch. Filicia's Etching

      Ch. Salilyns' Classic

      Ch. Kaintuck Pixie, C.D.

    Ch. Filicia's Wescot Joy of Anlon

      Ch. Salilyn's Aristocrat

      Ch. Kaintuck Pixie, C.D.

  Ch. Filicia's Black Magic of Sulo

    Ch. Filicia's Bequest

      Ch. Salilyn's Classic

      Ch. Kaintuck Pixie, C.D.

    Ch. Filicia's Coronation

      Ch. Filicia's Matinee Idol

      Ch. Kaintuck Pixie, C.D.

The subject of the above pedigree is future Champion Filicia's Custom Maid, pictured at 4 weeks of age, one of the many fine Springers from Anne Pope's Felicia Kennels.

Am., Can. Ch. Tara's Aquarius, sire of Felicia's Custom Maid as well as of many other champions, was bred by Lillian and Robert Gough and owned by Dr. and Mrs. C.J. and Mara Lo Paro.

In this scene from the 1960s, Ch. Syringa Sue takes Winners Bitch and Best of Opposite Sex at six years of age (and after several litters) at an Eastern English Springer Club Specialty, judged by Mrs. Mary Scott of Yorkshire, England. Handled by Dorothy Callahan and owned by Dorothy and Jim Fortuna of Fortune Kennels, Sue was the start of a line of excellent producing bitches that carried down through at least several generations.

Ch. Syringa Sue appears in the breeding lines of both sire and dam of Ch. Fortune's Dorsue Diana of Day.

Ch. Kaintuck Prince Hamlet
Ch. Kaintuck Marc Anthony
Kaintuck Roxane
Ch. Syringa Disc Jockey
Ch. Runor's Deacon
Ch. Syringa Sue
Ch. Her Ladyship of Melilotus

CH. FORTUNE'S DORSUE DIANA OF DAY

Ch. Cartref Beau Brummel
Ch. Kaintuck Christmas Carol
Ch. Cartref Spring Chime
Ch. Fortune's Lucky Penny
Ch. Runor's Deacon
Ch. Syringa Sue
Ch. Her Ladyship of Melilotus

Ch. Syringa Sue also can be found in the background of Am., Can. Ch. Winacko's Classic Replay, C.D., although you will have to look several generations back in order to locate her.

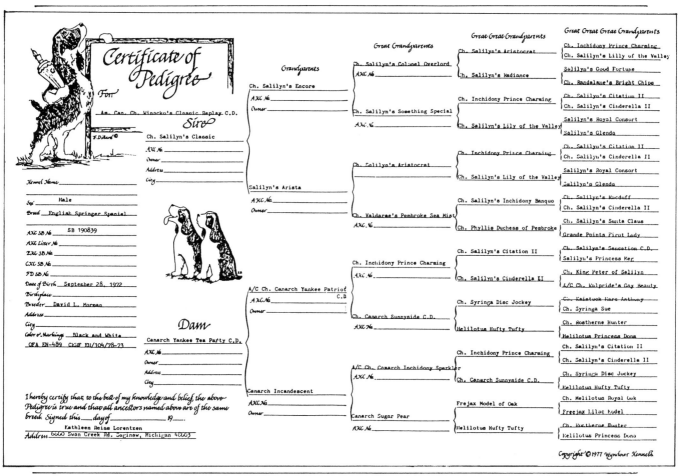

CH. SALILYN'S SENSATION CD
— AM. & CAN. CH. FREJAX ROYAL REQUEST
— QUEEN VICTORIA OF SALILYN

CH. SALILYN'S CITATION II

SALILYN'S PRINCESS MEG
— CH. KING PETER OF SALILYN
— CH. SALILYN'S ANIMATION

CH. INCHIDONY PRINCE CHARMING

CH. KING PETER OF SALILYN
— FIREBRAND OF SANDBLOWN ACRE CDX
— SALUTATION OF SALILYN

CH. SALILYN'S CINDERELLA II

AM. & CAN. CH. WALPRIDE GAY BEAUTY
— CH. CHALTHA'S THE GAINER
— WALPRIDE SENSATION

SIRE
CH. SALILYN'S SIGNATURE

FIREBRAND OF SANDBLOWN ACRE CDX
— TRAVELER OF SANDBLOWN ACRE
— DAWN'S ELF OF SANDBLOWN ACRE

CH. KING WILLIAM OF SALILYN

SALUTATION OF SALILYN
— AM. & CAN. CH. FREJAX ROYAL SALUTE
— NANCY OF SALILYN

SALILYN'S GLENDA

CH. CARTREF BOB BOBBIN
— CH. CARTREF TALISMAN
— CARTREF FIRE OF BITTERSWEET

CH. SALILYN'S GOOD OMEN

SALILYN'S SURPRISE
— CH. SALILYN'S SENSATION CD
— SALUTATION OF SALILYN

CH. SANDOLYN'S DAVY CROCKETT
— AM. & CAN. CH. WALPRIDE FLAMING ROCKET
— CH. SANDOLYN'S BALLERINA

CH. LEGEND'S BARON BLENNERHASSET

CH. MELILOTUS WINTER STARLIGHT
— CH. PRINCE CHARMING OF MELILOTUS
— CH. MELILOTUS EMILY GRAY

AM. & CAN. CH. CAREY'S LUCKY KNIGHT CD

AM. & CAN. CH. WALPRIDE FLAMING ROCKET
— CH. CHALTHA'S THE GAINER
— WALPRIDE SENSATION

CH. SHAMROCK'S BLACK PEPPER CD

CH. UPLAND MERRIE SUNSHINE
— CH. SIR LANCELOT OF SALILYN
— SUE'S DONNA OF SANDBLOWN ACRE

DAM
CH. CAREY'S DUSTY ROSE

CH. KAINTUCK MARC ANTHONY
— CH. KAINTUCK PRINCE HAMLET
— KAINTUCK ROXANE

CH. CAREY'S PRINCE MICHAEL UDT WDX

BONNIE MINX OF LAKELAND CD
— JOY'S DURMONT NED
— GLENWOOD'S AUGUSTA

CH. CAREY'S SWEET SUE

CAREY'S ROYAL BILL
— CH. CHRISRICK STARFLIGHT
— TRANT'S SHEILA

CH. CAREY'S BROWN BETTY CD

LAURESTRA'S ROYAL BEAUTY
— CH. FREJAX ROYAL COMMAND
— FREJAX VIRGINIA MISS

Additional pedigrees of interest are reproduced here and on the following page.

Certificate of Pedigree

	Grand Parents:	Great Grand Parents:	Great Great Grand Parents:	Great Great Great Grand Parents

Registered Name TELTALE VALLEYBROOK SECRET , T.D.

Kennel Name HEATHER

Sex Female

Breed ENGLISH SPRINGER SPANIEL

A.K.C.S.B. No. SB 471653

C.K.C. No. 894177 EQ

E.K.C.S.B. No.

C.K.C.S.B. No. EQC 312

F.D.S.B. No.

Date of Birth August 17,1973

Birthplace St. Thomas, Ontario Canada

Breeder Howard Northey

Address RR 8

City St. Thomas, Ontario Canada

GENERAL DESCRIPTION

Color and Markings Liver and White

Weight

Tracking Degree May 12,1974 at 8 months
Canadian tracking degree Nov.2,1974

Feather Tattoo number
ZBR-9-E

Sire: (1)
CH Telltale Prime Minister
A.K.C.No. SB 157218
Owner Delores Streng
Address 32534 Shady Ridge Dr
City Farmington, Michigan 48024

CH. SALILYN'S CLASSIC
A.K.C.No. SB 001920

Canarch Triple Crown
A.K.C.No. SA 644286

CH. Salilyn's Encore
A.K.C.No. SA 802736

CH. Salilyn's Arista
A.K.C.No. SA 660451

CH Inchidony Prince Charming
A.K.C.No. S 999804

Canarch Paddock C.D.
A.K.C.No. SA 396087

Dam: (2)
C.CH Valleybrook U.E. Loyalist
C.K.C.No. 894177
Owner Howard Northey
Address RR 8
City St. Thomas Ontario Canada

C.CH. Canarch Minute Man
A.K.C.No. SA 737008
C.K.C. 849911

C.CH. Valleybrook Petite Jeannette
C.K.C. 766839

CH Canarch Yankee Patriot C.D.
A.K.C.No. SA 399688

Canarch Incandescent
A.K.C.No. SA 565234

C.CH. Linbar's Great Samson C.D.
C.K.C. 635232

C.CH. Tammie of Vu Tower
C.K.C. 589093

CH. Salilyn's Colonel's Overlord
CH. Salilyn's Something Special SA 448569
CH. Salilyn's Aristocrat SA 309120
CH Valdagae's Pembroke Sea Mist
CH. Salilyn's Citation II S 896979
CH. Salilyn's Cinderella II S857656
CH Salilyn Inchidony Banquo SA 105640
CH. Canarch Inchidony Brook SA 260608
CH Inchidony Prince Charming S999804
CH. Canarch Sunnyside
A. & C.CH Canarch Inchidony Sparkler
Canarch Sugar Pear
CH Salilyn Inchidony Banquo SA105640
A. & C.CH Salilyns Morning Star
C.CH Toror - Vu's Hedge Runner
Ginbars Lady Jane

SA 559477
CH. Salilyn's Aristocrat
CH Inchidony Radiance
CH. Inchidony Prince Charming
CH. Salilyns Lily of the Valley
CH. Inchidony Prince Charming
CH. Salilyns Lily of the Valley
CH. Salilyn Inchidony Banquo SA105640
CH Phyllis Duchess of Pembroke
CH Salilyns Sensation
Salilyns Princess Meg
CH King Peter of Salilyn
A. & C.CH Walpride Gay Regents
CH Salilyns MacDuff
CH Salilyns Cinderella II S857656
CH Inchidony Prince Charming
CH Canarch Sunnyside C.D.
CH Salilyns Citation II S896
CH Salilyns Cinderella II S857656
CH Springer Disc Jockey
Mellilotus Dufty Tufty
CH Inchidony Prince Charming S999
CH Canarch Sunnyside CD
Frejax Manul of Oak
Mellilotus Dufty Tufty
CH Salilyns MacDuff
CH Salilyns Cinderella II S857656
A. & C.CH Gay Beauties Action Award
CH Salilyns Good Omen
A. & C. CH Point Spa Royal Symbol
Orstrum Humds Ginger Judd
C.CH Gay Beauties Royal Commi
A. & C. CH Salilyns Morning Star

I Hereby Certify that to the best of my knowledge and belief the above Pedigree is true and that all ancestors named above are of the same breed.

Signed this ___ day of ___ 19__

Address ___

Certified Pedigree

SEX DOG   COLOR ___   DATE WHELPED ___

REGISTERED WITH ___   DATE OF PURCHASE ___   NAME OF PURCHASER ___

CH. GINGERBREAD BOY OF HILLCREST, C.D.
SIRE OF 23 CHS.!

Eng. CH. STUDLEY MAJOR

BOXER OF BRAMHOPE

PETER, BENEFACTOR
BRAMHOPE SUZETTE

BOUNTIFUL OF BEECHFIELD

GRAND LODGE
SOUBRETTE OF HAPPY DAZE

CH. ROSTHERNE HUNTER, WD

ROSTHERNE BEAUTY

GARRYDALE SKYMASTER

GRAND LODGE
SELECT OF HAPPEE DAZE

MOLLY

RUST
BEAUTY OF WESTBANK

CH BANNERET'S REGAL BRIGADIER.

CH. EBONY OF HILLCREST

Ch Co-PILOT OF SAND BLOWN ACRES
THIRTY ACRES LADY BELL

BANNERET, GAY FESTIVAL

Ch EBONY OF HILLCREST
HEYWOODS DELIGHT

CH. GINGER SNAP OF HILLCREST

ELK GROVE'S CONCHITA

CH. FREJAX FIREBRAND FLUFF

FIREBRAND OF SAND BLOWN ACRES CDX
FREJAX THE FLUFF

FAVORITE OF CAULIERS

Ch CAVALIER OF CAULIERS
PRINCESS OF CAULIERS

I HEREBY CERTIFY THAT TO THE BEST OF MY KNOWLEDGE AND BELIEF THE ABOVE PEDIGREE IS TRUE AND THAT ALL ANCESTORS NAMED ABOVE ARE OF THE SAME BREED.

SIGNED THIS ___ DAY OF ___ 19 ___

SIGNATURE ___   ADDRESS ___

An informal pose of Andrea Glassford's Ch. Venetian Jester's Jypsi saying "please." Jester Springers, Ashtabula, Ohio.

CHAPTER TWENTY-FOUR

The Veterinarian's Corner

by Joseph P. Sayres, DVM

Still looking and feeling prime in older years is Truly Fair of Merry-L, a well-cared for homebred belonging to Mary L. Hamann, Manhattan Beach, California. By Bingo of Merry-L ex Radiance of Merry-L. Photo courtesy of Dana Hopkins.

By way of introduction to this chapter concerning the medical aspects of the care of your Springer Spaniel, I think we should devote a few paragraphs to how to choose your veterinarian.

Until recent years, there has been a lot of misunderstanding and even animosity between veterinarians and breeders. Some distrust on the breeders' part arose because most veterinarians were not familiar with, or even interested in, learning about purebred dogs. Some of the problems encountered were peculiar to certain breeds, and some would crop up at inconvenient times. Veterinarians were then beset by breeders who thought that they knew more about the medical problems of their dogs than did the vets. The veterinarians very often were only called for emergencies, or when it was too late to save a sick dog that had been treated too long by people in the kennel. Another problem was that many breeders had never included veterinary fees in their budgets and were slow to pay their bills, if indeed they paid them at all.

Fortunately, these problems have been, to a large extent, solved. Education and better communication between breeders and veterinarians have eliminated most areas of friction.

Today, veterinary education and training have advanced to a point paralleling that of human standards. This resulted from advances in the field of Veterinary Science in the last two decades. Sophisticated diagnostic procedures, new and advanced surgical techniques and modern well-equipped hospitals all make for improved medical care for our dogs.

Educated breeders now realize that, while they may know more about the general husbandry of their dogs and the unique traits of the Springer Spaniel, they should not attempt to diagnose and treat their ailments.

In choosing your veterinarian, be selective. He or she should be friendly, should be interested in your dogs, and, in the case of breeders, should be interested in your breeding programs. Veterinarians should be willing to talk freely with you. Such things as fees, availability for emergencies and what services are and are not available should be discussed and understood before a lasting relationship with your veterinarian can be established.

You can expect your veterinarian's office, clinic or hospital to be clean, free of undesirable odors, well equipped and staffed by sincere, friendly personnel who willingly serve you at all times. All employees should be clean, neat in appearance and conversant with whatever services you require. You may also expect your dog to be treated carefully and kindly at all times by the doctor and his staff.

Your veterinarian should participate in continuing education programs in order to keep up with changes and improvements in his field. He should also be aware of his limitations. If he doesn't feel confident in doing certain procedures, he should say so and refer you to qualified individuals to take care of the problem. Seeking second opinions and consultation with specialists on difficult cases are more the rule than the exception nowadays. That is as it should be.

You will know that if your veterinarian is a member of the American Animal Hospital Association, he and his facility have had to measure up to high standards of quality and are subjected to inspections every two years. Many excellent veterinarians and veterinary hospitals, by choice, do not belong to the American Animal Hospital Association. You can satisfy your curiosity about these places by taking guided tours of the facilities to learn by first hand observation about the quality of medicine practiced at these hospitals.

So far we have discussed only what you should expect from your veterinarian. Now, let's discuss what the veterinarian expects.

Most of all, he expects his clients to be open and frank in their relations with him. He doesn't like to be double-checked and second-guessed behind his back. He also wants you to handle your pet so that he, in turn, can examine him. He also expects you to leash your dog, to control him and keep him from bothering other pets in the room. He expects to be paid a fair fee and to be paid promptly for services rendered. Fees in a given area tend to be consistent, and variations are due only to complications or unforeseen problems. Medicine is not an exact science; therefore, things unpredictable can happen.

If you are dissatisfied with the services or fees, then ask to discuss these things in a friendly manner with the doctor. If his explanations are not satisfactory or he refuses to talk to you about the problem, then you are justified in seeking another doctor.

The veterinarian expects to provide his services for your animals during regular hours whenever possible. He also realizes that in a kennel or breeding operation, emergencies can occur at any time, and that his services will be needed at off hours. You should find out how these emergencies will be handled and be satisfied with the procedures.

No veterinarian can be on duty 24 hours of every day. Today, cooperative veterinarians group together to take turns covering each other's emergency calls. Some cities have emergency clinics that operate solely to take care of those catastrophes that usually seem to happen in the middle of the night or on weekends.

My conclusion, after 30 years of practice, is that most disagreements and hard feelings between clients and veterinarians are a result of a breakdown in communications. Find a veterinarian that you can talk to and can be comfortable with, and you'll make a valuable friend.

In using veterinary services to their best advantage, I believe that you will find that prevention of diseases and problems is more important than trying to cure these things after they occur. In other words, an ounce of prevention is worth a pound of cure.

Springer Spaniels have their share of congenital defects. From the publication, *Congenital Defects in Dogs*, published by Ralston Purina Company, as well as other reliable sources, the following conditions are listed as congenital defects in Springer Spaniels:

A. FACTOR XI DEFICIENCY

A deficiency in the blood clotting mechanism which results in minor bleeding episodes and severe prolonged bleeding postsurgically.

B. EHLERS-DANLOS SYNDROME (Hyperextensibility and Fragility of Skin)

Severe lacerations in skin from minimal trauma, lax skin, very fragile skin.

C. PROGRESSIVE RETINAL ATROPHY

Affecting dogs three to five years old. Causes loss of central vision with resulting difficulty in seeing stationary objects, and sight is best in dim light. Retinal Displasia.

D. UNILATERAL OR BILATERAL CRYPTORCHIDISM

Nondescent of the testicles.

By proper and vigilant vaccination programs, the following contagious diseases can be eliminated: distemper, hepatitis, leptospirosis, rabies, parainfluenza and parvovirus enteritis. With proper sanitation and the guided use of insecticides and vermifuges, the following conditions can be made extinct or of only minor importance: roundworm infestation, hookworm infestation, whipworm infestation, tapeworm infestation, coccidiosis, fleas, ticks and lice. These problems will be dealt with individually as our chapter progresses.

The following vaccination schedule should be set up and strictly followed to prevent infectious diseases:

Disease:	Age of Vaccinate:
Distemper	Six to eight weeks old. Second inoculation to be given at 12 to 16 weeks of age; revaccinate annually.
Hepatitis (adenovirus)	Same as distemper.
Parainfluenza (kennel cough)	Same as distemper.
Leptospirosis	Give first vaccine at nine weeks old; revaccinate with second D.H.L.P. (distemper, hepatitis, leptospirosis, parainfluenza) at 12 to 16 weeks of age; revaccinate annually.
Parvovirus	Give first vaccine at six to eight weeks old; second vaccine two to four weeks later; duration of immunity from two injections established at only four months at the time of this writing; revaccinate annually; revaccinate before going to dog shows or going to boarding kennels if more than six months have elapsed since the last shot.
Rabies	First inoculation at three to four months old, then revaccinate when one year old and at least every three years thereafter; if dog is over four months old at the time of the first vaccination, then revaccinate in one year and then once every three years thereafter.

Vaccines used are all modified live-virus vaccines except for leptospirosis which is a killed bacterium and parvovirus vaccine which is a killed or modified live strain of feline distemper vaccine. New and improved vaccines to immunize against parvovirus will appear shortly.

Other communicable diseases for which no vaccines have been perfected as yet are: canine brucellosis, canine coronavirus and canine rotavirus.

Infectious Diseases

Distemper

Distemper is caused by a highly contagious airborne virus. The symptoms are varied and may involve all of the dog's systems. A pneumonic form is common, with heavy eye and nose discharges, coughing and lung congestion. The digestive system may be involved, as evidenced by vomiting, diarrhea and weight loss. The skin may show a pustular type rash on the abdomen. Nervous system involvement is common with convulsions, chorea (twitches and incoordination) and paralysis as persistent symptoms. This virus may have an affinity for nerve tissue and may cause encephalitis and degeneration of the spinal cord. These changes for the most part are irreversible and death or severe crippling ensues.

We have no specific remedy or cure for distemper, and recoveries when they occur can only be attributed to the natural resistance of the patient, good nursing care and control of secondary infections with antibiotics.

That's the bad news about distemper. The good news is that we rarely see a case of distemper in most areas today because of the efficiency of the vaccination program. This is proof that prevention by vaccination has been effective in almost eradicating this dreaded disease.

Hepatitis

Another contagious viral disease affecting the liver is hepatitis. This is not an airborne virus, and it can be spread only by contact. Although rarely seen today because of good prevention by vaccination programs, this virus is capable of producing a very acute, fulminating, severe infection and can cause death in a very short time. Symptoms of high temperature, lethargy, anorexia (loss of appetite) and vomiting are the same as for many other diseases. Careful evaluation by a veterinarian is necessary to confirm the diagnosis of this disease.

The old canine infectious hepatitis vaccine has been replaced by a canine adenovirus type-two strain vaccine which is safer and superior. The new vaccine seems to be free of post-vaccination complications such as blue eye, shedding of the virus in the urine and some kidney problems.

Leptospirosis

This is a disease that seriously affects the kidneys of dogs, most domestic animals and man. For this reason, it can become a public health hazard. In urban and slum areas, the disease is carried by rats and mice in their urine. It is caused by a spirochete organism (a type of bacteria) which is very resistant to treatment. Symptoms include fever, depression, dehydration, excessive thirst, persistent vomiting, occasional diarrhea and jaundice in the latter stages. Again, it is not always easy to diagnose, so your veterinarian will have to do some laboratory work to confirm it.

We see very few cases of leptospirosis in dogs, and then, only in the unvaccinated ones. The vaccine is generally given concurrently with the distemper and hepatitis vaccinations. Preventive inoculations have resulted in the almost complete demise of this dreaded disease.

Parainfluenza

This is commonly called kennel cough. It is caused by a throat-inhabiting virus that causes an inflammation of the trachea (wind pipe) and larynx (voice box). Coughing is the main symptom and fortunately it rarely causes any other systemic problems. The virus is airborne, highly contagious and is the scourge of boarding kennels. A vaccine is available that will protect against this contagious respiratory disease and should be given as part of your vaccination program, along with the distemper, hepatitis, leptospirosis and parvovirus shots. Pregnant bitches should not be vaccinated against parainfluenza because of the possibility of infecting the unborn puppies. As there may be more than one infectious agent involved in contagious upper respiratory disease of dogs, vaccination against parainfluenza is not a complete guarantee to protect against all of them.

Rabies

This is a well-known virus-caused disease that is almost always fatal and is transmissible to man and other warm-blooded animals. The virus causes very severe brain damage. Sources of the infection include foxes, skunks and raccoons, as

A portion of Mrs. Julie Gasow's well-kept Salilyn Kennels, Troy, Michigan.

well as domesticated dogs and cats. Transmission is by introduction of the virus by saliva into bite wounds. Incubation in certain animals may be from three to eight weeks. In a dog, clinical signs will appear within five days. Symptoms fall into two categories depending on what stage the disease is in when seen, the *dumb* form and the *furious* form. There is a change of personality in the furious form; individuals become hypersensitive and over react to noise and stimuli, and they will bite any object that moves. In dumb rabies, the typical picture of the loosely hanging jaw and tongue presents itself. Diagnosis is confirmed only by a laboratory finding the virus and characteristic lesions in the brain. All tissues and fluids from rabid animals should be considered infectious, and you should be careful not to come in contact with them. Prevention by vaccination is a must because there is no treatment for rabid dogs.

Contagious Canine Viral Diarrheas

A) Canine Coronavirus (C.C.V.): This is a highly contagious virus that spreads rapidly to susceptible dogs. The source of infection is through infectious bowel movements. The incubation period is one to four days, and the virus will be found in feces for as long as two weeks. It is sometimes hard to tell the difference between cases of diarrhea caused by coronavirus and parvovirus. Coronavirus generally is less severe or causes a more chronic or sporadic type of diarrhea. The fecal material may be orange in color and may have a very bad odor. Occasionally it will also contain blood. Vomiting sometimes precedes the diarrhea, but loss of appetite and listlessness are consistent signs of the disease. Fever may or may not be present. Recovery is the rule after eight to 10 days, but treatment with fluids, antibiotics, intestinal protectants and good nursing care are necessary in the more severe watery diarrhea cases. Dogs that survive these infections become immune but for an unknown length of time.

To control an outbreak of this virus in a kennel, very stringent hygienic measures must be taken. Proper and quick disposal of feces, isolation of affected animals and disinfection with a 1:30 dilution of Clorox are all effective means of controlling an outbreak in the kennel.

There is no vaccine yet available for prevention of canine coronavirus. Human infections by this virus have not been reported.

Ch. Salilyn's Design, by Ch. Salilyn's Classic ex Ch. Salilyn's Applause, the latter a Ch. Salilyn's Hallmark daughter. Design is from Classic's last litter, and is a 1981 winner from Mrs. Julie Gasow's Salilyn Kennels.

B) Canine Parvovirus (C.P.V.): This is the newest and most highly publicized member of the intestinal virus family. Cat distemper virus is a member of the same family but differs from canine parvovirus biologically. It has been impossible to produce this disease in dogs using cat virus as the inducing agent, and conversely, canine parvovirus will not produce the disease in a cat; however, vaccines for both species will produce immunity in the dog. The origin of C.P.V. is still unknown.

Canine parvovirus is very contagious and acts rapidly. The main source of infection is contaminated bowel movements. Direct contact between dogs is not necessary, and carriers such as people, fleas, medical instruments, etc., may carry and transmit the virus.

The incubation period is five to 14 days. The symptoms are fever, severe vomiting and diarrhea, often with blood, depression and dehydration. Feces may appear yellowish gray streaked with blood. Young animals are more severely affected, and a shock-like death may occur in two days. In animals less than six weeks old, the virus will cause an inflammation of the heart muscle, causing heart failure and death. These pups do not have diarrhea. A reduction in the number of white blood cells is a common finding early in the disease.

Ch. Kay N Dee Classic Lady, by Ch. Salilyn's Classic ex Ch. Judge's Pride Jennifer, C.D., finished in 1979 to help make Jennifer Dam of the Year. Owned by Dr. Mary B. Gibbs, Spencerville, Maryland.

The virus is passed in the feces for one to two weeks and may possibly be shed in the saliva and urine also. This virus has also been found in the coats of dogs. The mortality rate is unknown. Dogs that recover from the disease develop an immunity to it, but the duration of this immunity is unknown.

Control measures include disinfection of the kennels, animals and equipment with a 1:30 dilution of Clorox and isolation of sick individuals. Treatment is very similar to that for coronavirus, namely, intravenous fluid therapy, administration of broad-spectrum antibiotics, intestinal protectants and good nursing care. Transmission to humans has not been proved.

Clinical studies have proved that vaccination with two injections of the approved canine vaccine given two to four weeks apart will provide good immunity for at least four months and possibly longer, as future studies may show. At present, puppies should be vaccinated when six to eight weeks old, followed with a second injection two to four weeks later. Full protection does not develop until one week following the second injection. The present recommendations are for annual revaccinations, with an additional injection recommended before dog shows or boarding in kennels if a shot has not been given within six months.

C) Canine Rotavirus (C.R.V.): This virus has been demonstrated in dogs with a mild diarrhea, but again, with more severe cases in very young puppies. Very little is known about this virus. A milder type diarrhea is present for eight to 10 days. The puppies do not run a temperature and continue to eat. Dogs usually recover naturally from this infection. There is no vaccine available for this virus.

Canine Brucellosis

This is a disease of dogs that causes both abortions and sterility. It is caused by a small bacterium closely related to the agent that causes undulant fever in man and abortion in cows. It occurs worldwide.

Symptoms of brucellosis sometimes are difficult to determine, and some individuals with the disease may appear healthy. Vague symptoms such as lethargy, swollen glands, poor hair coat and stiffness in the back legs may be present. This organism does not cause death and may stay in the dog's system for months and even years. The latter animals, of course, have breeding problems and infect other dogs.

Poor results in your breeding program may be the only indication that brucellosis is in your kennel. Apparently, normal bitches abort without warning. This usually occurs 45 to 55 days after mating. Successive litters will also be aborted. In males, signs of the disease are inflammation of the skin of the scrotum and shrunken or swollen and tender testicles. Fertility declines and chronically infected males become sterile.

The disease is transmitted to both sexes at the time of mating. Other sources of infection are aborted puppies, birth membranes and discharge from the womb at the time of abortions.

Humans can be infected, but such infections are rare and mild. Unlike its presence in the dog, the disease in humans responds readily to antibiotics.

Diagnosis is done by blood testing, which should be done carefully. None of the present tests are infallible and false positives may occur. The only certain way that canine brucellosis can be diagnosed is by isolating the organism B. canis from blood or aborted material, and for this, special techniques are required.

Treatment of infected individuals has proven ineffective in most cases. Sterility in males is permanent. Spaying or castrating infected pets should be considered, as this will halt the spread of the disease and is an alternative to euthanasia.

At present, there is no vaccine against this important disease.

Our best hope in dealing with canine brucellosis is prevention. The following suggestions are made in order to prevent the occurrence of this malady in your dogs.

1) Test breeding stock annually and by all means breed only uninfected animals.

2) Test bitches several weeks before their heat periods.

3) Do not bring any new dogs into your kennel unless they have two negative tests taken a month apart.

4) If a bitch aborts, isolate her, wear gloves when handling soiled bedding and disinfect the premises with Roccal.

5) If a male loses interest in breeding or fails to produce after several matings, have him checked.

6) Consult your veterinarian for further information about this disease, alert other breeders and support the research that is going on at the John A. Baker Institute for Animal Health at Cornell University.

External Parasites

The control and eradication of external parasites depends on the repeated use of good quality insecticide sprays or powders during the warm months. Make a routine practice of using these products at seven-day intervals throughout the season. It is also imperative that sleeping quarters and wherever the animal commonly stays be treated also.

Fleas

These are wingless brown insects with laterally compressed bodies and strong legs; they are blood-suckers. Their life cycle comprises 18 to 21 days from egg to adult flea. They can live without food for one year in high humidity but die in a few days in low humidity. Able to multiply rapidly, they are more prevalent in the warm months. They can cause a severe skin inflammation in those individuals that are allergic or sensitive to the flea bite or saliva of the flea, and they can act as a vector for many diseases and do carry tapeworms. Control measures must

Ch. Kaintuck Pixie, C.D., owner-handled by Anne Pope at Trenton Kennel Club in 1970.

Ch. Bordalyn's Behold, handled by Mary Ann Alston for Debbie Ritter, Chesapeake, Virginia.

include persistent, continual use of flea collars, flea medallions, sprays or powders. The dog's bedding and premises must also be treated because the eggs are there. Foggers, vacuuming or professional exterminators may have to be used. All dogs and cats in the same household must be treated at the same time.

Ticks

There are hard and soft species of ticks. Both types are blood-suckers and at times cause severe skin inflammations on their host. They act as vectors for Rocky Mountain spotted fever, as well as other diseases. Hibernation through an entire winter is not uncommon. The female tick lays as many as 1,000 to 5,000 eggs in crevices and cracks in walls. These eggs will hatch in about three weeks and then a month later become adult ticks. Ticks generally locate around the host's neck and ears and between the toes. They can cause anemia and serious blood loss if allowed to grow and multiply. It is not a good idea to just pick ticks off the dogs because of the danger of a reaction in the skin. Simply apply the tick spray directly on the ticks, which then die and fall off eventually. Affected dogs should be dipped every two weeks. The premises, kennels and yards should be treated every two weeks during the summer months, being sure to apply the insecticide to walls and in all cracks and crevices. Frequent or daily grooming is effective in finding and removing ticks.

Lice

There are two kinds of lice, namely the sucking louse and the biting louse. They spend their entire life on their host but can be spread by direct contact or through contaminated combs and brushes. Their life cycle is 21 days, and their eggs, known as nits, attach to the hairs of the dog. The neck and shoulder region, as well as the ear flaps, are the most common areas to be inhabited by these pesky parasites. They cause itchiness, some blood loss and inflammation of the skin. Eradication will result through dipping or dusting with methyl carbonate or Thuron once a week for three to four weeks. It is a good idea to fine-comb the dogs after each dip to remove the dead lice and nits. Ask your veterinarian to provide the insecticides and advice or control measures for all of these external parasites.

Healthy Springer babies, owned by Francie Nelson, Fanfare Kennels. Photo by Joyce Kleven.

Internal Parasites

Worms

Puppies should be tested for worms at four weeks of age and then six weeks later. It is also wise to test them again, six weeks following their last worm treatment, to be sure the treatments have been successful. Annual fecal tests are advisable throughout your dog's life. All worming should be done only under the supervision of your veterinarian.

Ascarids

These include such things as roundworms, puppyworms, stomachworms, milkworms, etc. They can be difficult to eradicate. Puppies become infested shortly after birth and occasionally even before birth. When passed in the stool or thrown up, the worms look somewhat like cooked spaghetti when fresh or like rubber bands when they are dried up. Two treatments at least two weeks apart will eliminate ascarids from most puppies. An occasional individual may need more wormings according to where in its life cycle the worm is at the time of worming. Good sanitary conditions must prevail, and immediate picking up of bowel movements is necessary to keep this worm population down.

Hookworms

This is another troublesome internal parasite that we find in dogs. They are blood-suckers and also cause bleeding from the site of their attachment to the lining of the intestine when they move from one site to another. They can cause a blood-loss type of anemia and serious consequences, particularly in young puppies. Their life cycle is direct, and their eggs may be ingested or passed through the skin of its host. Yards and runs where the dogs defecate should be treated with 5% sodium borate solution, which is said to kill the eggs in the soil. Two or three worm treatments three to four weeks apart may be necessary to get rid of hookworms. New injectable products (administered by your veterinarian) have proved more effective than remedies used in the past. Repeated fecal examinations may be necessary to detect the eggs in the feces. These eggs pass out of the body only sporadically or in showers, so it is easy to miss finding them unless repeated stool testing is done. As with any parasite, good sanitary conditions in the kennel and outside runs will help eradicate these worms.

Whipworms

These are a prevalent parasite in some kennels and in some individual dogs, where they cause an intermittent mucous diarrhea. As they live only in the dog's appendix, it is extremely difficult to reach them with any worm medicine given by mouth. Injections seem to be the most effective treatment, and these have to be repeated several times over a long period of time to be effective. Here again, repeated fresh stool samples must be examined by your veterinarian to be sure that this pest has been eradicated. Appendectomies are indicated in only the most severe chronic cases. To repeat, cleanliness is next to godliness and most important in getting rid of these parasites.

Tapeworms

These are another common internal parasite of dogs. They differ in their mode of transmission, as they have an indirect life cycle. This means that part of their cycle must be spent in an intermediate host. Fleas, fish, rabbits and field mice all may act as intermediate hosts for tapeworms. Fleas are the most common source of tapeworms in dogs, although dogs that live near water may eat raw fish, and hunting dogs that eat the entrails of rabbits may get them from those sources. Another distinguishing feature of the tapeworms is the suction apparatus, the part of the head that enables the tapeworm to attach itself to the lining of the intestine. If, after worming, just the head remains, it has the capability of regenerating into another worm. This is one reason why they are so difficult to get rid of. It will require several treatments to get all of the tapeworms out of a dog's system. These worms are easily recognized by the egg-containing body segments which break off and appear on top of a dog's bowel movement or stick to the hair around the rectal area. These segments may appear alive and mobile at times but most often are dead and dried up when found. They look like flat pieces of rice and may be white or brown when detected. Elimination of the intermediate host is an integral part of any plan to rid our dogs of these worms.

Before leaving the topic of internal parasites, it should be stressed that all worming procedures be done carefully and only with the advice and supervision of your veterinarian. The medicants used to kill the parasites are, to a certain extent, toxic, so they should be used with care.

Ch. Lleda's Keeps Comin' On is Best of Breed at the 1979 Keystone English Springer Spaniel Club Specialty. Owned by Ray and Estelle Adell and Karen Adell Garetano.

Heartworm Disease in Dogs

We have all been alerted to the dangers of heartworm disease in most sections of the United States. This chapter would not be complete without a comprehensive report on this serious parasitic disease.

Just as the name implies, this disease is caused by an actual worm that goes through its life cycle in the blood stream of its victims. It ultimately makes its home in the right chambers of the heart and in the large vessels that transport the blood to the lungs. They vary in size from 2.3 inches to 16 inches. Adult worms can survive up to five years in the heart.

By its nature, this is a very serious disease and can cause irreversible damage to the lungs and heart of its host. Heart failure and lung pathology soon result in serious problems for the dog. The disease is transmitted and carried by female mosquitoes that have infected themselves after biting an infected dog; they then pass it on to the next dog that they come in contact with.

The disease has been reported wherever mosquitoes are found. It is most prevalent in warmer climates where the mosquito population is the greatest, but hotbeds of infection exist in the more temperate parts of the United States and Canada also. Rare cases have been reported in cats and in humans

Concerted effort and vigorous measures must be taken to control and prevent this serious threat to our dog population. The most effective means of eradication, I believe, will come through annual blood testing for early detection, through the use of preventive medicine during mosquito exposure times and also through ridding our dog's environment of mosquitoes.

Annual blood testing is necessary to detect cases that haven't started to show symptoms yet and thus can be treated effectively. It also enables your veterinarian to prescribe safely the preventive medicine to those individuals that test negative. There is a 10 to 15% margin of error in the test, which may lead to some false negative tests. Individuals that test negative but are showing classical symptoms of the disease such as loss of stamina, coughing, loss of weight and heart failure, should be further evaluated with chest X-rays, blood counts and electrocardiograms.

Serious consequences may result when the preventive medication is given to a dog that has heartworm already in his system. That is why it is so important to have your dog tested annually before starting the preventive medicine.

In order to be most effective, the preventive drug diethylcarbamazine should be given in daily doses of 2.5 mg. per pound of body weight or 5 mg. per kilogram of body weight of your dog. This routine should be started 15 days prior to exposure to mosquitoes and be continued until 60 days after exposure. Common and trade names for this drug are Caricide, Styrid-Caricide and D.E.C. It comes in liquid and tablet forms.

This drug has come under criticism by some breeders and individuals who claim that it affects fertility and causes some serious reactions. Controlled studies have shown no evidence that this drug produces sterility or abnormal sperm count or quality. Long-term studies on reproduction, when the drug was given at the rate of 4.9 mg. per pound of body weight (three times the preventive dose level) for two years, showed no signs of toxic effects on body weight maintenance, growth rate of pups, feed consumption, conception rate, numbers of healthy pups whelped, ratio of male to female pups, blood counts and liver function tests. It is reported as a well-tolerated medication, and many thousands of dogs have benefited from its use. From personal experience, I find just an occasional dog who will vomit the medicine or get an upset stomach from it. The new enteric coated pills have eliminated this small problem.

However, if you still don't want to give the preventive, especially to your breeding stock, an alternative procedure would be to test your dogs every six months for early detection of the disease, so that it can be treated as soon as possible.

Heartworm infestation can be treated successfully. There is a one to five percent mortality rate from the treatment. It can be expected that treatment may be completed without side effects, if the disease hasn't already caused irreversible problems in the heart, lungs, kidneys, etc. Careful testing, monitoring and supervision are essential to success in treatment. Treatment is far from hopeless these days, and if the disease is detected early enough, a successful outcome is more the rule than the exception.

In conclusion, remember that one case of heartworm disease in your area is one too many, especially if that one case is your dog. By following the steps mentioned, we can go a long way in ridding ourselves of this serious threat to our dogs.

Other Parasites

Less commonly occurring parasitic diseases, such as demodectic and sarcoptic mange, should be diagnosed and treated only by your veterinarian. You are wise to consult your doctor whenever any unusual condition in your dog's coat and skin occurs and persists. These conditions are difficult at best to diagnose and treat, so that the earlier a diagnosis is obtained, the better the chances are for successful treatment. Other skin conditions such as ringworm, flea bite allergy, bacterial infections, eczemas, hormonal problems, etc., all have to be considered.

The great Ch. Filicia's Etching, by Ch. Salilyn's Classic ex Ch. Kaintuck's Pixie, handled by George Alston for co-owners Mr. and Mrs. Robert Gough and Anne Pope.

Home Remedies and First Aid

You have repeatedly read here of my instructions to call your veterinarian when your animals are sick. This is the best advice I can give you. There are a few home remedies, however, that may get you over some rough spots while trying to get professional help.

I think it is a good idea to keep some medical supplies on hand, for example, a first aid kit. The kit should contain the following items: a roll of cotton, gauze bandages, hydrogen peroxide, tincture of metaphen, cotton applicator swabs, B.F.I. powder, a rectal thermometer, adhesive tape, boric acid crystals, tweezers and a jar of petroleum jelly.

A word here on how to take a dog's temperature may be in order. Always lubricate the thermometer with petroleum jelly and carefully insert it well into the rectum. Hold it in place for two to three minutes and then read it. The thermometer should be held firmly so that it doesn't get sucked up into the rectum.

The multi-Best of Breed bitch, Ch. Sunnykay's September Song, by Ch. Lleda's Spartacus of Sunnykay ex Ch. Salilyn's Cameo of Trulu. Barbara Weingarten co-owns her with Sharon Weingarten of Huntington Station, New York.

Stopping vomiting

Mix one tablespoon of table salt to one pint of water and dissolve the salt thoroughly. Then give one tablespoonful of the mixture to the patient. After waiting one hour, repeat the procedure and skip the next meal. The dog may vomit a little after the first dose, but the second dose works to settle the stomach. This mixture not only provides chlorides, but also acts as a mild astringent, and many times, in mild digestive upsets, will work to stop the vomiting.

Giving Medicines

To administer liquid medicines to dogs, simply pull the lips away from the side of the mouth, making a pocket for depositing the liquid. Tilt the dog's head slightly upward, and he will be able to swallow the liquid properly. Giving liquids by opening the mouth and pouring them directly on the tongue is an invitation to disaster because inhalation pneumonia can result. Putting it in the side of the mouth gives the dog time to hold it in his mouth and then swallow

Tablets are best administered by forcing the dog's mouth open and pushing the pill down over the middle of the tongue into the back of his mouth. If put in the right place, a reflex tongue reaction will force the pill down the throat to be swallowed. There is also no objection to giving the pills in favorite foods as long as you carefully determine that the medicine is surely swallowed with the food.

Diarrhea

In the case of adult Springer Spaniels, give three or four tablespoons of Kaopectate or milk of bismuth every four hours. Use one fourth of this dosage for puppies. Skip the next meal, and if the bowels persist in being loose, then start a bland diet of boiled ground lean beef and boiled rice in the proportions of half and half. Three or four doses of this medicine should suffice. If the diarrhea persists and, particularly, if accompanied by depression, lethargy and loss of appetite, your veterinarian should be consulted immediately. With all these new viral-caused diarrheas floating around, time is of the essence in securing treatment.

A Mild Stimulant

Dilute brandy half and half with water, add a little sugar and give a tablespoonful of the mixture every four to five hours. For puppies over three months old, reduce the dosage to a teaspoonful of the mixture every four to five hours.

A Mild Sedative

Dilute brandy half and half with water, add a little sugar and give a tablespoon of the mixture every 20 to 30 minutes until the desired effect is attained. For puppies over three months old, reduce the dosage to a teaspoonful of the mixture every 20 to 30 minutes.

Using brandy for both sedation and stimulation is possible by varying the time interval between doses. Given every four to five hours it's a stimulant, but given every 20 to 30 minutes it acts as a sedative.

Treatment of Minor Cuts and Wounds

Cleanse them first with soap and water, preferably tincture of green soap. Apply a mild antiseptic, such as Bactine or tincture of metaphen, two or three times daily until healed. If the cut is deep, fairly long and bleeding, then a bandage should be applied until professional help can be obtained.

Whenever attempting to bandage wounds, apply a layer or two of gauze over the cleaned and treated wound, then a layer of cotton and then another layer or two of gauze. The bandage must be snug enough to stay on but not so tight as to impair the circulation to the part. Adhesive tape should be applied over the second layer of gauze to keep the bandage as clean and dry as possible until you can get your dog to the doctor.

Tourniquets should be applied only in cases of profusely bleeding wounds. They are applied tightly between the wound and the heart, in addition to the pressure bandage that should be applied directly to the wound. The tourniquets must be released and reapplied at 15 minute intervals.

Burns

Application of ice or very cold water and compresses is the way to treat a skin burn. Apply cold packs as soon as possible, and take the dog immediately to your vet.

Frost Bite

The secret in treating this uncommon condition is to restore normal body temperature gradually to the affected parts. In other words, use cold water and then tepid water to thaw out the area slowly and restore circulation. In cases of severe freezing or shock due to bitterly cold temperature, take the animal to the veterinarian as soon as possible.

Ch. Sunnykay's Sir Winston Cromwell, by Ch. Lleda's Spartacus of Sunnykay ex Ch. Salilyn's Cameo of Trulu, belongs to Peter Guinta and Barbara Weingarten, and is shown taking Best of Breed at Perkiomen Valley Kennel Club in 1980.

Abscesses and Infected Cysts

Obvious abscesses and infected cysts that occur between the toes may be encouraged to drain by using hot boric acid packs and saturated dressings every few hours until professional aid can be secured. The boric acid solution is made by dissolving one tablespoon of crystals in one pint of hot water. Apply frequently to the swollen area. Further treatment by a veterinarian may involve lancing and thoroughly draining and cleaning out the abscess cavity. As most abscesses are badly infected, systemic antibiotics are generally indicated.

Heat Stroke or Heat Exhaustion

A word about the serious effects of heat on a dog is appropriate. It never ceases to amaze me how many people at dog shows have to be warned and advised not to leave their dogs in cars or vans on a warm day.

A dog's heat regulating mechanism is not nearly as efficient as ours; consequently, they feel the heat more than we do. Keep them as cool and as well ventilated as possible in hot weather. Another opportunity for shock is taking your dog out of a cool air-conditioned vehicle and exposing him immediately to the hot outdoors. Make the change as gradual as you can, because a rapid change can cause a shock-like reaction.

Three generations of Sunnykay Springers belonging to the Weingartens.

In cases of suspected heat stroke—which manifests itself with very high body temperatures (as high as 106-107-108°F. sometimes), severe panting, weakness, shaking and collapse—act quickly to get your dog into a cold bath or shower, or put ice cold compresses on his head. Then, without delay, rush him to the nearest veterinarian for further treatment. Prevention is the key here, and with a little common sense, heat stroke and exhaustion can be avoided.

Poisons

Many dogs are poisoned annually by unscrupulous people who hate dogs. Many others are victims of poisoning due simply to the careless use of rat and ant poisons, insecticides, herbicides, antifreeze solutions, drugs and so forth. Dogs also frequently insist on eating poisonous plants, either in the house or outdoors, which can lead to serious consequences. Common sources of these toxic products are named in the following section.

Plants that can be a source of poison for dogs are listed here. This list contains only the most common ones. Garden flowers: daffodil, oleander, poinsetta, mistletoe, philodendron, delphinium, monkshood, foxglove, iris and lily of the valley. Vegetables: rhubarb, spinach, tomato plants and sunburned potatoes can be harmful. Trees and shrubs: rhododendron, cherry, peach, oak, elderberry and black locust. Wild plants: Jack in the Pulpit, Dutchman's breeches, water hemlock, mushrooms, buttercups, poison hemlock, nightshade, jimson weed, marijuana, locoweed and lupine. Also, grain contaminants can exist in dog food. The most common ones are ergot, corn cockle and grotolaria.

Poisonous *animals* are such snakes as vipers, rattlesnakes, copperheads, water moccasins and the coral snakes. The only poisonous lizards are the Gila monster and Mexican beaded lizard, both deadly. Some toads, spiders, insects and fishes also are potential sources of trouble.

Chemicals comprise perhaps the largest and most common source of poisoning in our environment. These are hazards that our dogs may be exposed to every day. Careful handling and storage of these products are essential. Toxic materials are found in all of the following groups of materials: arts and crafts supplies, photographic supplies, automotive and machinery products (such as antifreeze and de-icers, rust inhibitors, brake fluids, engine and carburetor cleaners, lubricants, gasoline, kerosene, radiator cleaners and windshield washers), cleaners, bleaches, polishes, disinfectants and sanitizers all contain products that potentially are dangerous. Even health and beauty aids may contain toxic materials if ingested in large enough quantities. These include some bath oils, perfumes, corn removers, deodorants, antiperspirants, athlete's foot remedies, eye makeup, hair dyes and preparations, diet pills, headache remedies, laxatives, liniments, nail polish removers, sleeping pills, suntan lotions, amphetamines, shaving lotions, colognes, shampoos and certain ointments. Paints and related products also can be dangerous. Caulking compounds, driers, thinners, paints, paint brush cleaners, paint and varnish removers, preservatives and floor and wood cleaners all fit into the category. Pest poisons meant for birds, fungi, rats and mice, ants and snails all can be toxic and sometimes fatal to dogs. Miscellaneous items like fire extinguishers and non-skid products for slippery floors can be unsafe. Almost all solvents like carbon tetrachloride, benzene, toluene, acetone, mineral spirits, kerosene, and turpentine are bad.

In cases of suspected poisoning, one should be aware of what to do until professional help can be obtained.

a) Keep the animal protected, quiet, and warm.

b) If a contact is on the skin, eye or body surface, cleanse and flush the area with copious amounts of water. Do this also if the dog gets something in his eye. Protect him from further exposure.

c) Inducing vomiting may be dangerous and should be done only on the advice of a veterinarian. Giving peroxide may induce vomiting in some cases. It is better to allow the animal to drink as much water as he wants. This will dilute the poison. Giving milk or raw eggs whites is helpful many times to delay absorption of the toxic products.

d) Do not attempt to give anything by mouth if the patient is convulsing, depressed or unconscious.

e) Do not waste time. Get veterinary service as quickly as possible. Take any vomited material or suspected poisons and their containers with you to the vet. When the suspected product is known, valuable time can be saved in administering specific treatment. The suspected specimens should be uncontaminated and be put in clean containers.

A word to the wise should be sufficient. Keep away from your dog all products that in any way can harm him.

Bloat

One of the most serious and difficult problems and real emergency situations that can occur is that of bloat. Other names for this condition are torsion and acute indigestion. This condition generally occurs in larger breeds after the consumption of a large meal (usually dry feed), and then drinking a lot of water immediately after eating. Follow this with a vigorous exercise period, and the stage is set for bloat. The stomach, being pendulous and overloaded at this point, can become twisted or rotated. This, of course, cuts off the circulation to the stomach and spleen and may also interfere with the large blood vessels coming to and from the liver. A shock-like syndrome follows, and death may ensue shortly if heroic measures are not undertaken to save the stricken animal. If ever there was an emergency, this is truly one. Dry heaves, painful loud crying and abdominal enlargement take place in a very short time. Relief of the torsion requires immediate surgery to right the stomach to its normal position and to keep it there. Circulation may then return to normal. In cases of acute indigestion without torsion, the distress and bloat may be relieved by passing a stomach tube to allow the gas to escape. At the risk of being redundant, it must be said that this condition is very acute and requires *immediate* and heroic action to save the victim.

Preventive measures for bloat include dividing the dog's normal diet into three or four meals a day. Water should not be given for one hour before and one hour after each meal, and no exercise is advisable for an hour or two after eating.

With breeders and veterinarians becoming more aware of the bloat syndrome, I feel that more of these cases will be saved than in the past.

Whelping

We cannot leave the subject of emergencies without considering the subject of whelping. Most bitches whelp without any problems. It is wise, however, to watch them closely during this time. I feel that no bitch should go more than two hours in actual labor without producing a puppy. This includes the time before the first one as well as between puppies. If more than two hours elapse, then the dam should be examined by a veterinarian. It will then be determined if she is indeed in trouble or is just a slow whelper. This rule of thumb gives us time to find out if there is a problem, what it may be and time to save both dam and puppies in most cases.

It is good practice to have your bitches examined for pregnancy three and a half to four weeks after mating, as well as at term around the 58th or 59th day. These procedures will enable the veterinarian to discover any troubles that may occur during pregnancy, as well as alert him as to when the whelping is going to take place. Knowing this, he can plan to provide service if needed during off hours.

Sunnykay Springers relaxing after a busy day.

Bitches that are difficult to breed, miss pregnancies or have irregular reproductive cycles should have physical exams, including laboratory tests, to determine the cause of the trouble. These tests may be expensive, but a lot of breeding and sterility problems which are due to sub-par physical condition, hormonal imbalances or hypothyroidism can be corrected. If a valuable bitch is restored to her normal reproductive capacity, the reward more than offsets the medical costs.

Another important thing to remember about whelping and raising puppies is to keep them warm enough. This means a room temperature of 75° to 80°F. for the first 10 days to two weeks until the puppies are able to generate their own body heat. Be sure the dam keeps them close. Leave a light burning at night for the first week so she won't lose track of any of them or accidentally lie on one of them. Chilling remains the biggest cause of death of newborn puppies. Other causes are malnutrition, toxic milk, hemorrhage and viral and bacterial infections. Blood type incompatibilities have been discovered lately to be causes of trouble.

Consultation with your veterinarian concerning these and any other breeding problems you've had in the past may result in the solution of these problems. This may result in larger litters with a higher survival rate.

Approaching Old Age

Providing medical services from cradle to grave is the slogan of many veterinarians, and rightly so. The average life expectancy for our dogs these days is about 13 years. Sad to say, this is a short time compared to our life span. Larger breeds historically do not live as long as the medium-sized or smaller breeds. However, I think that, with proper care, your Springers should be expected to reach this maximum. This, then, is a good time to speak about approaching old age and some of the problems we can expect during that time. Arthritis, kidney disease, heart failure and cataracts are probably the most common ailments in older dogs. When our pet has trouble getting up in the morning, jumping up or going upstairs, you can bet that some form of a joint problem is starting. Giving two enteric coated aspirin tablets three times a day for five days very often will help these in-

Ch. Lleda's Aegina of Rube, Winners Bitch for a 5-point "major" at the Eastern English Springer Spaniel Club in 1976. By Ch. Welcome Great Day ex Ch. Clancy's Erin of Packanack. Estelle Adell, Lleda Springers, Huntington, New York.

dividuals. This dosage is for the older dogs. It is relatively free of side effects and as long as nothing else is wrong, your dog will get a bit of relief.

Signs of kidney weakness are excessive drinking, inability to hold urine through the night, loss of weight, lack of appetite and more than occasional bouts of vomiting and diarrhea. If any of these signs present themselves, it would be worthwhile for the dog to have a checkup. Very often corrective measures in diet and administering some medicine will prolong your dog's life.

Some form and degree of heart failure exists in a lot of older animals. Symptoms of chronic congestive heart failure consist of a chronic cough (especially after exercise), lack of stamina, lethargy, abdominal enlargement and labored breathing at times. If diagnosed and treated early in the disease, many heart patients live to a ripe old age.

Cataracts form in the lenses of most, if not all, old dogs. They are a part of the normal aging process. Total blindness from cataracts generally does not result for a long time, and distant and peripheral vision remain satisfactory for the expected life span of the dog. Rarely is total blindness produced by these aging cataracts before the dog's life expectancy is reached. There is no effective treatment for cataracts other than their surgical removal, which is not recommended in the older patient that has any vision at all left.

Hip Dysplasia

It is becoming more evident that most of the arthritis in older dogs in large breeds is the result of problems in bone growth and development when the individual was very young. Problems such as panosteitis, hip dysplasia, elbow dysplasia and osteochondrosis dessicans all are often precursors of arthritis. In Springer Spaniels, according to information from the Orthopedic Foundation for Animals, hip dysplasia is found in 27.3% of the cases presented to them.

At any rate, hip dysplasia seems to be a developmental condition and not a congenital anomaly. It is thought to be an inherited defect, with many genes being responsible for its development. Environmental factors also enter into the severity of the pathology in the hip joints. Nutrition during the growth period has been an important factor. Over-feeding and over-supplementation of diets have caused an abnormal growth rate with overweight puppies. These

Best of Breed at the English Springer Spaniel Specialty in conjunction with Old Dominion some years back went to Anne Pope with Ch. Blairschnock Faith, by Ch. Charlyle Fair Warning ex Blairschnock Echo.

individuals, if they were susceptible to hip dysplasia in the first place, show more severe lesions of hip dysplasia. Restricted feeding of growing dogs is necessary for normal bone growth and development.

Signs of hip dysplasia vary from one dog to another, but some of the more common ones are: difficulty in getting up after lying for awhile, rabbit-like gait with both rear legs moving forward at the same time when running, lethargy and walking with a swaying gait in the rear legs. In many cases, a period of pain and discomfort at nine months to one year old will resolve itself and even though the dysplasia is still there, most of the symptoms may disappear.

It is recommended that dysplastic individuals not be bred, that they not be allowed to become overweight and that they have moderate exercise. The selection of dysplastic-free individuals for breeding stock eventually will result in the production of sounder hip joints in affected breeds. This factor, of course, is only one consideration in the breeding and production of an overall better Springer Spaniel.

Above: Ch. Danaho's Hedy Tondelayo, by Ch. Foyscroft Signed Edition ex Ch. Danaho's Ballet Russe, was Best of Breed under Arleen Thompson at the Santa Clara Valley English Springer Spaniel Association Specialty in 1981 in an entry of 135 including 19 "specials." Handled by Dana Hopkins, breeder and co-owner.

Left: Ch. Croft Harbor's Triumph is pictured winning Best of Breed over Best in Show winning "specials" at Schooley's Mountain Kennel Club, handled by Karen Adell Garetano. Triumph, by Ch. Fortune's Terrible Ted of Lleda ex Marshall's Pixie of Chanel, is owned by Lisa Berbit of Croft Harbor Springers, Huntington, New York.

Ch. Rube's Sportin Life of Lleda, by Ch. Somerset Saga's Sirius ex Ch. Lleda's Aegina of Rube, taking Winners at Westbury for the Adells in September 1980.

Ch. Filicia's Black Magic, by Ch. Filicia's Bequest ex Ch. Filicia's Coronation, is owner-handled by Anne Pope.

John and Phyllis Buoy, Ingleside, Illinois, with their two-time National Champion Saighton's Ty Gwyn Slicker.

That magnificent liver-and-white dog, Ch. Chinoe's Adamant James, taking Best in Show at Beverly Hills Kennel Club in June 1971. Handled by Clint Harris, bred by Ann H. Roberts, owned by Dr. Milton Prickett, Adamant James in both 1971 and 1972 was Best in Show at the Westminster Kennel Club in New York, and gained 48 Bests in Show in one year, a record only recently broken.

Glossary

To the uninitiated, it must seem that fanciers of purebred dogs speak a special language all their own, which in a way we do. To help make this book more comprehensive to our readers, the following is a list of terms, abbreviations, and titles that you will run across which may be unfamiliar to you. We hope that they will lead to fuller understanding, and that they will also assist you as you meet and converse with others of similar interests in the world of purebred dogs.

A.K.C.—See American Kennel Club.

ALBINO—A deficiency of pigmentation causing the nose leather, eye rims and lips to be pink.

ALMOND EYE—The shape of the tissue surrounding the eye creating an almond-shaped appearance.

AMERICAN KENNEL CLUB—The official registry for purebred dogs in the United States. Publishes and maintains the Stud Book, handles all litter and individual registrations, transfers of ownership, etc. Keeps all United States dog show, field trial and obedience records; issues championships and other titles as earned; approves and licenses dog show, obedience trial and field trial judges; licenses or issues approval to all championship shows, obedience trials, field trials and recognized match shows. Creates and enforces the rules, regulations and policies by which the breeding, raising, exhibiting, handling and judging of purebred dogs in this country are governed. Clubs, not individuals, are members of the American Kennel Club, represented by a delegate chosen from their own membership for the purpose of attending the quarterly American Kennel Club Delegates'

Meetings, A.K.C. is the commonly used abbreviation of American Kennel Club. The address of the A.K.C. is 51 Madison Avenue, New York, N.Y. 10010.

ANGULATION—The angles formed by the meeting of the bones, generally referring to the shoulder and upper arm in the forequarters and the stifle and hock in the hindquarters.

APPLE HEAD—An exaggerated roundness of the topskull.

APRON—Frill of longer hair below the neck.

BAD BITE—One in which the teeth do not meet correctly according to the specifications of the breed Standard.

BAD MOUTH—Can refer to a wryness or malformation of the jaw or to incorrect dentition.

BALANCE—Symmetry and proportion. A well-balanced dog is one in which all the parts appear in correct ratio to one another: height to length, head to body, neck to head and body and skull to foreface.

BEEFY—Refers to over-musculation or over-development of the shoulders, hindquarters or both.

BEST IN SHOW—The dog or bitch chosen as the most representative of any dog in any breed from among the six Group winners at an all-breed dog show.

BEST OF BREED—The dog or bitch that has been adjudged the best of its breed in competition at a dog show.

BEST OF OPPOSITE SEX—The dog or bitch adjudged Best of Opposite Sex to the one adjudged Best of Breed when the latter award has been made.

BEST OF WINNERS—The dog or bitch selected as the better of the two between Winners Dog and Winners Bitch.

BITCH—The correct term for a female dog.

BITE—The manner in which the dog's upper and lower teeth meet.

BLOOM—A word used to describe coat in good, healthy condition.

BLUE RIBBON WINNER—A dog or bitch that has won first prize at an A.K.C. point show.

BONE—Refers to the substance and girth of a dog's leg bones. A dog that is "good in bone" has legs that are the correct girth for its breed and for its own general conformation.

BRACE—Two dogs, or a dog and a bitch, closely similar in appearance and moving together in unison.

BREED—Purebred dogs descended from mutual ancestors refined and developed by man.

BREEDER—A person who breeds dogs.

BREEDING PARTICULARS—Name of the sire and dam, date of breeding, date of birth, number of puppies in the litter, sex, name of the breeder and name of the owner of the sire.

BRISKET—The forepart of the body between the forelegs and beneath the chest.

BROOD BITCH—A bitch used primarily for breeding.

CACIB—A Challenge Certificate offered by the Federation Cynologique Internationale toward a dog's championship.

CANINES—Dogs, jackals, wolves and foxes as a group.

CANINE TEETH—The four sharp pointed teeth at the front of the jaws, two upper and two lower, flanking the incisors; often referred to as fangs.

CARPALS—Pastern joint bones.

CASTRATE—To neuter a dog by removing the testicles.

CAT-FOOT—A short-toed, round, tight foot similar to that of a cat.

CHAMPION—A dog or bitch that has won a total of 15 points including two "majors," the total under not less than three judges, two of whom must have awarded the "majors" at A.K.C. point dog shows. Ch. is the abbreviation of the word Champion.

CHARACTER—Appearance, behavior, and temperament considered correct in an individual breed of dog.

CHEEKY—Cheeks which bulge or are rounded in appearance.

CHEST—The part of the body enclosed by the ribs.

CHISELED—Clean-cut below the eyes.

CHOKE COLLAR—A chain or leather collar that gives maximum control over the dog. It is tightened or relaxed by the pressure on the lead caused by either pulling of the dog or tautness with which it is held by the handler.

CHOPS—Pendulous, loose skin creating jowls.

CLODDY—Thickset or overly heavy or low in build.

CLOSE-COUPLED—Compact in appearance. Short in the loin.

COARSE—Lacking in refinement and elegance.

COAT—The hair which covers the dog.

CONDITION—A dog said to be in good condition is one carrying exactly the right amount of weight, whose coat looks alive and glossy and who exhibits a general appearance and demeanor of well-being.

CONFORMATION—The framework of the dog, its form and structure.

COUPLING—The section of the body known as the loin. A short-coupled dog is one in which the loin is short.

COW-HOCKED—When the hocks turn inward at the joint causing the hock joints to approach one another with the result that the feet toe outward instead of straight ahead.

CRABBING—A dog moving with its body at an angle rather than coming straight on to you. Otherwise referred to as sidewheeling or sidewinding.

CREST—The arched portion of the back of the neck.

CROPPING—The cutting of the ear leather, usually performed to cause the ear to stand erect.

CROSSING ACTION—A fault in the forequarters caused by loose or poorly knit shoulders.

CROUP—The portion of the back directly above the hind legs.

CRYPTORCHID—An adult dog with testicles not normally descended. A disqualification; a dog with this condition cannot be shown.

CYNOLOGY—Study of canines.

DAM—Female parent of a dog or bitch.

DENTITION—Arrangement of the teeth.

DERBY—Field Trial competition for young novices generally one to two years of age.

DEW CLAWS—Extra claws on the inside of the legs. Should generally be removed several days following the puppy's birth. Required in some breeds, unimportant in others and sometimes a disqualification, all according to the individual breed Standard.

DEWLAP—Excess loose and pendulous skin at the throat.

DIAGONALS—The right front and left rear leg make up the right diagonal. The left front and right rear, the left diagonal. These diagonals move in unison as the dog trots.

DISH-FACED—The condition existing when the tip of the nose is placed higher than the stop.

DISQUALIFICATION—A fault or condition so designated by the breed Standard or by the American Kennel Club. Judges must withhold awards at dog shows from dogs having disqualifying faults, noting the reason in the Judges' Book for having done so. The owner may appeal this decision, but a disqualified dog cannot again be shown until it has been officially examined and reinstated by the American Kennel Club.

DISTEMPER TEETH—A condition so-called due to its early association with dogs having suffered from this disease. It refers to discolored, badly stained or pitted teeth.

DIVERGENT HOCKS—Frequently referred to as bandy legs or barrel hocks as well. The condition in which the hock joints turn outward, thus the exact opposite of cow-hocks.

DOCK—Shortening a tail by cutting it.

DOG—A male of the species. Also used to collectively describe male and female canines.

DOG SHOW—A competition in which dogs have been entered for the purpose of receiving the opinion of a judge.

DOG SHOW, ALL-BREEDS—A dog show in which classification may be provided, and usually is, for every breed of dog recognized by the American Kennel Club.

DOG SHOW, SPECIALTY—A dog show featuring one breed only. Specialty shows are generally considered to be the showcases of a breed, and to win at one is an especially coveted honor and achievement, competition at them being particularly keen.

DOMED—A condition of the top-skull by which it is rounded rather than flat.

DOUBLE COAT—A coat that consists of a harsh, weather resistant protective outer coat, with a short, soft undercoat providing warmth.

DOWNFACED—Describes downward inclination of the muzzle towards the tip of the nose.

DOWN IN PASTERN—A softness or weakness of the pastern causing a pronounced variation from the verticle.

DRAG—A trail that has been prepared by dragging a bag (generally bearing the strong scent of an animal) along the ground.

DRAWING—The selection by lot of dogs that decides in which pairs they will be run in a specific Field Trial.

DRIVE—The powerful action of the hindquarters which should equal the degree of reach of the forequarters.

DROP EAR—Ears carried drooping or folded forward.

DRY HEAD—One exhibiting no excess wrinkle.

DRY NECK—A clean, firm neckline free of throatiness or excess skin.

DUAL CHAMPION—A dog or bitch that has gained both Bench Show and Field Trial Championships.

DUDLEY NOSE—Flesh colored nose.

ELBOW—The joint of the forearm and upper arm.

ELBOW, OUT AT—The condition by which the elbow points out from the body rather than being held close.

EVEN BITE—Exact meeting of the front teeth, tip to tip with no overlap of the uppers or lowers. Generally considered to be less serviceable than the SCISSORS BITE, although equally permissible or preferred in some breeds.

EWE NECK—An unattractive concave curvature of the top area of the neckline.

EXPRESSION—The typical expression of the breed as one studies the head. Determined largely by the shape and placement of the eye. Should be soft and gentle in the Springer.

FAKING—The artificial altering of the natural appearance of a dog. A highly frowned upon and unethical practice which must lead, upon discovery by the judge, to instant dismissal from competition in the show ring, with a notation stating the reason in the Judges' Book.

FANCIER—A person actively involved in the sport of purebred dogs.

FANCY—Dog breeders, exhibitors, judges and others actively involved with purebred dogs comprise the Dog Fancy.

FEDERATION CYNOLOGIQUE INTERNATIONALE—A canine authority representing numerous countries, principally European, all of which consent to and agree on certain practices and breed identification. F.C.I. is the abbreviation.

FEET EAST AND WEST—An expression describing toes on the forefeet turning outward rather than pointing straight ahead.

FETCH—Retrieving of game by a dog, or the command for the dog to do so.

FIDDLE FRONT—Caused by elbows protruding from the desired closeness to the body, resulting in pasterns which approach one another too closely and feet turning outward, the whole resembling the shape of a violin.

FIELD CHAMPION—The title given to a dog or bitch that has defeated a specified number of dogs in specified competition at a series of A.K.C. licensed or member Field Trials. Field Ch. is the abbreviation, and this prefix is used before the dog's name.

FIELD TRIAL—A competition for specified Hound or Sporting breeds where dogs are judged according to their ability to and style of following a game trail or of finding and retrieving game.

FINISHING A DOG—Refers to completing a dog's championship, obedience title or Field Trial title.

FLANK—The side of the body through the loin area.

FLARE—A blaze that widens as it goes up the top skull.

FLAT BONE—Bones of the leg which are not round.

FLAT SIDED—Ribs that are flat down the sides rather than slightly rounded.

FLEWS—A pendulous condition of the inner corners of the upper lips.

FLUSH—To drive birds from cover; to spring at them; to force them to take flight.

FLYER—An especially promising or exciting young dog.

FLYING EARS—Ears correctly carried dropped or folded that stand up or tend to "fly" upon occasion.

FLYING TROT—The speed at which you should never move your show dog in the ring. All four feet actually leave the ground briefly during each half stride, making correct evaluation of the dog's normal gait virtually impossible.

FOREARM—The front leg from elbow to pastern.

FOREFACE—The muzzle of the dog.

FRONT—The forepart of the body viewed head-on, including the head, forelegs, shoulders, chest and feet.

FUTURITY—A competition at shows or Field Trials for dogs less than 12 months of age and for which puppies are nominated at or prior to birth. Usually highly competitive among breeders, with a fairly good purse for the winners.

GAIT—The manner in which a dog walks and trots.

GALLOP—The fastest gait. Never to be used in the show ring.

GAME—Animals or wild birds that are hunted.

GAY TAIL—Tail carried high.

GOOSE RUMP—Too sloping (steep) in croup.

GROOM—To bathe, brush, comb and trim your dog.

GROUPS—Refers to the six Variety Groups in which all breeds of dogs are divided.

GUN DOG—A dog or bitch that has been specifically trained to work with man in the field for purposes of retrieving game that has been shot and for locating live game.

GUNS—The persons who do the shooting during Field Trials.

GUN SHY—Fear of the sight or sound of a gun.

HACKNEY ACTION—High lifting of the forefeet in the manner of a hackney pony.

HAM—Muscular development of the upper hind leg. Also used to describe a dog that loves applause while being shown, really going all-out when it occurs.

HANDLER—A person who shows dogs in competition, either as an amateur (without pay) or as a professional (receiving payment for the service).

HARD-MOUTHED—A dog that grasps the game too firmly when retrieving, thus causing bites and tooth marks.

HARE FOOT—An elongated paw, like the foot of a hare.

HAW—A third eyelid or excess membrane at the corner of the eye.

HEAT—The period during which a bitch can be bred. Also referred to as "season."

HEEL—A command ordering the dog to follow close to the handler.

402

HIE ON—A command used in hunting or Field Trials which urges the dog to go further.

HINDQUARTERS—Rear assemblage of the leg.

HOCK—The joint between the second thigh and the metatarsus.

HOCKS WELL LET DOWN—Expression denoting that the hock joint should be placed low toward the ground.

HONORABLE SCARS—Those incurred as a result of working injuries.

INCISORS—The front teeth between the canines.

INTERNATIONAL CHAMPION—A dog awarded four CACIB cards at F.C.I. dog shows.

JOWLS—Flesh of lips and jaws.

JUDGE—Person making the decisions at a dog show, obedience trial or Field Trial. Must be approved and licensed by A.K.C. in order to officiate at events where points toward championship titles are awarded.

KENNEL—The building in which dogs are housed. Also used when referring to a person's collective dogs.

KNEE JOINT—Stifle joint.

KNITTING AND PURLING—Crossing and throwing of forefeet as a dog moves.

KNUCKLING OVER—A double-jointed wrist, sometimes accompanied by enlarged bone development in the area, causing the joint to double over under the dog's weight.

LAYBACK—Used in two different ways. A) As description of correctly angulated shoulders. B) As description of a short-faced dog where pushed-in nose placement is accompanied by undershot jaw.

LEATHER—The ear flap. Also the skin of the actual nose.

LEVEL BITE—Another way of describing an even bite, as teeth of both jaws meet exactly.

LEVEL GAIT—A dog moving smoothly, topline carried level as he does so.

LIPPY—Lips that are pendulous or do not fit tightly.

LOADED SHOULDERS—Those overburdened with excessive muscular development.

LOIN—Area of the sides between the lower ribs and hindquarters.

LUMBER—Superfluous flesh.

LUMBERING—A clumsy, awkward gait.

MAJOR—A dog show at which there are three or more points awarded the Winners Dog and/or Winners Bitch.

MATCH SHOW—An informal dog show where no championship points are awarded and entries can usually be made upon arrival, although some demand pre-entry. Excellent practice area for future show dogs and for novice exhibitors, as the entire atmosphere is relaxed and congenial.

MATE—To breed a dog and a bitch to one another. Litter mates are dogs which were born in the same litter.

MILK TEETH—The first baby teeth.

MISCELLANEOUS CLASS—A class provided at A.K.C. Point Shows in which specified breeds may compete in the absence of their own breed classification. Dogs not yet recognized by A.K.C. are permitted to compete in this class prior to becoming recognized and with their own classification.

MOLARS—Four premolars are located at either side of the upper and lower jaws. Two molars exist on either side of the upper jaw, three on either side below. The lower molars have two roots, the upper molars have three roots.

MONORCHID—A dog with only one properly descended testicle. This condition disqualifies from competition at American Kennel Club dog shows.

NICK—A successful breeding that results in puppies of excellent quality is said to "nick."

NON-SLIP RETRIEVER—A dog that merely walks at heel, marks the fall of a game bird then retrieves upon command. The dog is not expected to flush or to find the game.

NOSE—Describes the dog's organ of smell, but also refers to his talent at scenting. A dog with "a good nose" is one adept at picking up and following a scent trail.

OBEDIENCE TRIAL—A licensed obedience trial is one held under A.K.C. rules at which it is possible to gain a "leg" toward a dog's obedience title.

OBEDIENCE TRIAL CHAMPION—Denotes that a dog has attained Obedience Trial Championship under A.K.C. regulations, having gained a specified number of points and first place awards. O.T.Ch. is an abbreviation of this title.

OBLIQUE SHOULDERS—Shoulders angulated so as to be well laid back.

OCCIPUT—Upper back point of skull.

OCCIPITAL PROTUBERANCE—A prominent occiput noted in some of the Sporting breeds.

ORTHOPEDIC FOUNDATION FOR ANIMALS—This organization is ready to read the hip radiographs of dogs and certify the existence of or freedom from hip dysplasia. Board Certified radiologists read vast numbers of these films each year. O.F.A. is a commonly used abbreviation.

OUT AT ELBOW—When the elbows point away from the body instead of being held close to the body.

OUT AT SHOULDER—A loose assemblage of the shoulder blades.

OVAL CHEST—Deep with only moderate width.

OVERSHOT—Upper incisors overlap the lower incisors.

PACING—A gait in which both right legs and both left legs move concurrently, causing a rolling action.

PADDLING—Faulty gait in which the front legs swing forward in a stiff upward motion.

PADS—Thick protective covering of the bottom of the foot. Serves as shock absorber.

PAPER FOOT—Thin pads accompanying a flat foot.

PASTERN—The area of the foreleg between the wrist and the foot.

PERRO COMPANELO (P.C.)—A Mexican obedience title.

PIGEON CHEST—A protruding, short breastbone.

PIGEON-TOED—Toes which point inward, as those of a pigeon.

PILE—Soft hair making a dense undercoat.

PLUME—A long fringe of hair on the tail.

POACH—To trespass on private property when hunting.

POINT—The position assumed by a hunting dog which indicates the discovery and location of game.

POLICE DOG—Any dog that has been trained to do police work.

QUALITY—Excellence of type and conformation.

RACY—Lightly built, appearing overly long in leg and lacking substance.

RANGY—Excessive length of body combined with lack of depth through the ribs and chest.

REACH—The distance to which the forelegs reach out in gaiting, which should correspond with the strength and drive of the hindquarters.

REGISTER—To record your dog with the American Kennel Club.

REGISTRATION CERTIFICATE—The paper you receive denoting your dog's registration has been recorded with the A.K.C., giving the breed, assigned name, names of sire and dam, date of birth, breeder and owner, along with the assigned Stud Book number of the dog.

RESERVE WINNERS DOG OR RESERVE WINNERS BITCH—After the judging of Winners Dog and Winners Bitch, the remaining first prize dogs or bitches remain in the ring where they are joined by the dog or bitch that placed second in the class to the one awarded Winners Dog or Winners Bitch, provided he or she was defeated by that one dog or bitch only on the day. From these a Reserve Winner is selected. Should the Winners Dog or Winners Bitch subsequently be disallowed due to any error or technicality, the Reserve Winner is then moved up automatically to Winners in the A.K.C. records and the points awarded to the Winners Dog or Winners Bitch then transfer to the one which placed Reserve. This is a safeguard award, for although it seldom happens, should the winner of the championship points be found to have been ineligible to receive them, for Reserve dog keeps the Winner's points.

ROACH BACK—A convex curvature of the topline of the dog.

ROCKING HORSE—An expression used to describe a dog that has been overly extended in forequarters and hindquarters by the handler, the forefeet placed too far forward and the hind feet pulled overly far behind, making the dog resemble a child's rocking horse. To be avoided in presenting your dog for judging.

ROLLING GAIT—An aimless, ambling type of action correct in some breeds but a fault in others.

SADDLE BACK—Of excessive length with a dip behind the withers.

SCISSORS BITE—A bite in which the outer sides of the lower incisors touch the inner side of the upper incisors. Generally considered to be the most serviceable type of jaw formation.

SECOND THIGH—The area of the hindquarters between the hock and the stifle.

SEPTUM—The vertical line between the nostrils.

SET UP—To pose your dog in position for examination by the judge. Sometimes referred to as stacking.

SHELLY—A body lacking in substance.

SHOULDER HEIGHT—The dog's height from the ground to the withers.

SIRE—The male parent.

SKULLY—An expression referring to a coarse or overly massive skull.

SLAB SIDES—Flat sides with little spring of rib.

SOUNDNESS—Mental and physical stability. Sometimes used to denote the manner in which the dog gaits, denoting correct conformation of forequarters and hindquarters.

SPAY—To neuter a bitch by surgery. Once this operation has been performed the bitch is no longer eligible to enter the regular classes at A.K.C. shows.

SPECIAL—A dog or bitch entered only for best of breed competition at a dog show.

SPECIALTY CLUB—An organization devoted to sponsoring an individual breed.

SPRING—To flush game.

STAKE—A class in Field Trial Competition.

STANCE—The natural position a dog assumes in standing.

STANDARD—The official description of the ideal specimen of a breed. The Standard of Perfection is drawn up by the Parent Specialty Club, approved by its membership and by the American Kennel Club and serves as a guide to breeders and to judges in decisions regarding the merit or lack of it in individual dogs.

STIFLE—The joint of the hind leg corresponding to a person's knee.

STILTED—Refers to the somewhat choppy gait of a dog lacking rear angulation.

STOP—The step-up from nose to skull. An indentation at the juncture of the skull and foreface.

STRAIGHT BEHIND—Lacking angulation of the hindquarters.

STRAIGHT SHOULDERED—Lacking angulation of the shoulder blades.

STUD—A male dog that is a proven sire.

STUD BOOK—The official record kept on the breeding particulars of recognized breeds of dogs.

SUBSTANCE—Degree of bone size.

SWAYBACK—Weakness in the topline between the withers and the hipbones.

TAIL SET—Placement of the tail at its base.

T.D., T.D.X.—See Tracking Dog, Tracking Dog Excellent.

TEAM—Generally four dogs.

THIGH—Hindquarters from the stifle to the hip.

THROATINESS—Excessive loose skin at the throat.

TOPLINE—The dog's back from withers to tail set.

TRACKING DOG—A title awarded dogs that have fulfilled the A.K.C. requirements at licensed or member club tracking tests. T.D. is an abbreviation.

TRACKING DOG EXCELLENT—An advanced tracking degree. T.D.X. is an abbreviation.

TRAIL—Hunting by following a ground scent.

TROT—The gait in which the dog moves in a rhythmic two-beat action, right front and left hind foot and left front and right hind foot each striking the ground together.

TUCK-UP—A noticeable shallowness of the body at the loin, creating a small-waisted appearance.

TYPE—The combination of features which makes a breed unique, distinguishing it from all others.

U.D., U.D.T.—See Utility Dog, Utility Dog Tracking.

UNDERSHOT—The front teeth of the lower jaw overlap or reach beyond the front teeth of the upper jaw.

UPPER ARM—The foreleg between the forearm and the shoulder blade.

UTILITY DOG—Another level of obedience degree. U.D. is an abbreviation.

UTILITY DOG TRACKING—Indicates that the dog has gained both Utility Dog and Tracking Dog degrees. U.D.T. is an abbreviation.

WALK—The gait in which three feet support the body, each lifting in regular sequence one at a time off the ground.

WALLEYE—A blue eye, fish eye, or pearl eye caused by a whitish appearance of the iris.

WEEDY—Lacking in sufficient bone and substance.

WELL LET DOWN—Short hocks, hock joint placed low to the ground.

WET NECK—Dewlap or superfluous skin.

WHEEL BACK—Roached back with topline considerably arched over the loin.

WINNERS DOG OR WINNERS BITCH—The awards which are accompanied by championship points, based on the number of dogs defeated, at A.K.C. member or licensed dog shows.

WITHERS—The highest point of the shoulders, right behind the neck.

WRY MOUTH—When the lower jaw is twisted and does not correctly align with the upper jaw.

This Joan Ludwig headstudy of Ch. Kaintuck Tolstoy fully captures the dog's beautiful and typical nature. Sired by Ch. Charlyle's Fair Warning ex Ch. Kaintuck Fortune Huntress, Tolstoy was bred by Mr. Stuart Johnson and belongs to Dana Hopkins, Danaho Kennels, Los Angeles, California, who purchased him from Anne Pope.

Index

This index is composed of three separate parts: a general index, an index of kennels, and an index of names of persons mentioned in the text.

General Index

A

Abscesses, 391
Amateur All-Age-Stakes, 193
American-bred Class, 257
American Kennel Club, 21, 231, 253, 257, 292, 297
American Kennel Club Gazette, 22
American Kennel Gazette – Pure-Bred Dogs, 258
American Spaniel Club, 185
Animals (poisonous), 392
Arthritis, 394
Ascarids, 387

B

Baiting, 269
Bathing, 245
Bed, 233
Best of Breed, 259
Best of Breed Winners (list), 187-189
Best of Winners, 258
Bloat, 393
Boke of St. Albans, 11
Brace Class, 260
Bred by Exhibitor Class, 256
Breech puppy, 332
Breeding, 323, 327
Breeding program, 250
Brood bitch, 315-316
Brood Bitch Class, 260
Brucellosis, 384-385
Brushing, 244
Burns, 391

C

Caesarean operation, 332, 333
Canada, English Springer Spaniels in, 17-19
Captain of the Guns, 203
Cataracts, 395
Characteristics of English Springer Spaniels, 175-176
Chemical poisons, 392
Classes for Boys and Girls, 291
Clipper work, 246
Collar, 234
Congenital Defects in Dogs, 380-381
Contagious canine viral diarrheas, 383-384
Coronavirus, 383
Cost, 231
Crate, 233, 234
Cryptorchidism, 380
Cuts and minor wounds, 391
Cysts, 391

D

Demodectic mange, 389
Diarrhea, 390
Disqualifications, 172
Distemper, 381
Dog show day, 265-269
Dog World, 293, 301, 304, 307, 309, 311, 312,
Dogs and All About Them, 11
Dry foods, 240

E

Ears, 245
Ehlers-Danlos Syndrome, 380
English Dogges, 11
English Springer Spaniel
in Canada, 27
characteristics, 175
and children, 237
field trials, 191
grooming, 243
history, 11
obedience, 297
origin, 11
problem, 180
showing, 253
type, 177
in United States, 21
English Springer Spaniel Field Trial Association, 185-188, 208
English Springer Spaniel puppy
arrival, 233
and family, 237
selection, 237
English Springer Spaniels in America, 21
External parasites, 385-386

F

Factor XI deficiency, 380
Feeding, 239-241, 331
Fenced area, 234
Field & Stream, 17, 21
Field trials, 191-205
judging, 204
procedure, 202
purpose, 204
Finishing, 247
First aid, 390-395
First aid kit, 390
Fleas, 385-386
Frost bite, 391
Futurity Stakes, 261

G

Gestation, 331-334
Grooming, 243-247
Grooming tools, 243, 244

H

Hand-feeding, 333
Heart failure, 395
Heartworm disease, 388-389

Heat exhaustion, 391-392
Heat stroke, 391-392
Hepatitis, 381-382
Hip dysplasia, 395
History (English Springer Spaniel),
    11-15
Home remedies, 390-395
Hookworm, 387
Housebreaking, 238

I

Illini Search and Rescue Group, 52
Inbreeding, 323
Internal parasites, 387-389

J

Judging, 177-180
    field trials, 204
    posing, 267
    routine, 266
Junior Class, 291
Junior showmanship with Springers,
    291

K

Kennel Review, 82, 98, 119
Kennel Review Awards, 105
Kennel Review Hall of Fame, 105, 184
Kidney weakness, 395

L

Leashes, 235
Leptospirosis, 382
Lice, 386
Life expectancy, 394
Line-breeding, 323
Litter, 331-333

M

Match Shows, 253
Mating, 327
Meat in diet, 240
Medicine (administration), 390
Moving your dog, 268

N

Nails, 245
National Championship, 194
Non-Regular Class, 260
"Norfolk Spaniels," 12
Novice Class, 256
Nylabone, 235

O

Obedience, 297-313
Obedience Springers, 299-301
Old age, 394-395
Open All-Age Stakes, 193
Open Class, 257
Outcross, 323

P

Parainfluenza, 382-383
Parasites, 385-389
Parvovirus, 383-384
Pedigrees, 335, 353, 354, 358-361,
    363, 364, 370, 372-373, 375-377
Physical characteristics (type), 177
Pick-of-the-litter, 326
Plants (poisonous), 392
Point show, 253
Poisoning (first aid), 392-393
Poisons, 392-393
Pre-show preparation, 263-269
Problems of the breed, 180-183
Progressive retinal atrophy, 380
Puppy, 233-235
    arrival, 233
    and family, 237
    selection, 237
Puppy Class, 255
Puppy Stakes, 205
*Pure-Bred Dogs, American Kennel
    Gazette,* 68, 297

R

Responsibilities (breeder, owner). 249-
    251
Rocky Mountain spotted fever, 386
Rotavirus, 384
Rural Sports, 12

S

Sarcoptic mange, 389
Scissor work, 246
Sedative, 391
Selecting English Springer Spaniel,
    225-231
Senior Class, 291
Shots (for puppies), 334
Show dog awards, 258-259
Show dog classes, 253-261
Show dog qualities, 229
Showing, 253-261
    entering, 253
    junior showmanship, 291
    match shows, 253
    pre-show preparation, 263
    Springer Spaniel puppy, 253
Socializing and training, 238-239
Sporting Group, 259
Springer Review, 58
Standard (English), 13
Standard (AKC), 165-171
Stimulant, 390
Stripping, 244-245
Stud dog, 323-327
Stud Dog Class, 260
Stud fee, 326
Successful Dog Show Exhibiting, 254
Sweepstakes Classes, 261

T

Tapeworm, 387
Team Class, 260
Teeth, 245
Temporal lobe epilepsy 181, 182
Ticks, 386
Titles (obedience), 298-299
Toys, 235
Travel, 239

V

Vaccination, 381
Vaccines, 381
Variety Group, 259
Veteran's Class, 261
Veterinarian (choice of), 235
Veterinarian's corner, 379
Vitamins, 240
Vomiting, 390

W

Weaning, 33
Westminster Kennel Club Dog Show,
    293
Whelping, 331-334, 393-394
Whelping box, 331
Whipworms, 387
William Rauch III Memorial Trophy,
    163
Winners Bitch, 258
Winners Class, 257
Winners Dog, 258
Working certificate, 207, 208
Worms, 387-389

Index of Kennels

(page reference in bold face
indicates location of kennel story)

A

Abilene, 19, 24
Airiebrooke, 24
Allegheny, 24
Althea, 21
Aqualate, 13
Athadale, 29
Audley, 24, 99
Aughrim, 14
Avalon, 24
Avandale, 14, 18
Avendale, 14
Avondale, 18

B

Beechgrove (British), 13
Beechgrove (U.S.A.), 17, 24
Bellmoss, 18
Blue Leader, 24
Boghurst, 24, 146
Boisdale, 24
Brackenbriar, **49**, 198
Breeze, 23
Butternut, 24

C

Cairnies, 13
Caistor, 12
Camden, 50
Canamar, **51-52**
Canarch, **52-54**, 59, 67, 269, 320
Carey, **54-59**
Chadakoin, 24
Chinoe, **59-60**, 61, 330
Chrishall, 13
Chuzzlewit, 67
Clarion, 22, 146, 148
Cornfields, 14
Cornhuskers, 24
Croft Harbor, 396

D

Dalshangan, 15
Danaho, **61-63**, 281, 325, 406
Dansmith, **64**
Denne, 13
Deveron, 15
Donahan, **64-66**, 342
Dormond, 25
Dungarvan, 66

E

Earlsmoor, 25
Ellwyns, 14
Elwood, 25
Eskdale, 19

F

Falcon Hill, 21
Fanfare, 47, **66-68**, 132, 219, 280,
    337, 344, 380
Faskally, 15
Fidelis, **69-70**, 234
Filicia, **70-75**, 135, 136, 161, 182,
    183, 233, 298, 369, 373
Fintry, 15
Firenze, 25
Foremost, 25
Fortune, **76**, 89, 374
Frejax, 99

G

Gerwyn, 13
Green Valley, 23
Greenflint, 23

H

Hagley, 13
Hillcrest, **77-79**, 226, 228, 232, 236,
    333
Holiday, 64
Homestead, **79-80**, 131
Horizon, **80-81**
Horsford, 14, 22

I

Inveresk, 15

J

Jester, **82-83**, 378
Jonmunn, 25

K

Kalyn, **83-84**
Kay N Dee, **84-85**
Kevriett, **86-87**

L

Langtoun, 15
Lansdowne, 19
Laverstroke, 15
Leam, 14
Ledgeland, 22
Lleda, 37, **87-89**, 208, 230, 246,
    270, 304, 321, 351, 394

M

Maginna, **90**, 279, 339, 441
Maidenhead, 43, **92-93**, 334, 340
Maple Grove, 19
Marjon, 305
Marobar, 25
Matford, 15
Melilotus, **94-96**, 161, 318
Menhall, 25
Merlin, 15
Morewood, 21

N

Nor East, 23

O

Oaktree, 19
Ocoee, **96-97**
O'Vara, 15

P

Patrician, **98**
Pembroke, **99-101**
Pequa, 87
Phylwayne, **101-102**
Pride 'n' Joy, **102-103**

R

Ranscombe, 14
Rivington, 14
Rowcliff, 147
Roycroft, 146
Rufton, 22
Rumak, 150
Rustic Woods, 44

S

Saighton, 66
Salilyn, 19, 43, 99, **103-107**, 164,
    188, 234, 253, 382, 383
Sandblown, 150
Sandhaven, 268, 317
Sandyhill, 108
Scadbury, 15
Shalimar, **108-109**, 163
Shinnecock, 45, 74, **109-115**, 239,
    256, 345
Silverbow, **115-116**
Skegness, 15
Solway, 15
Sporting Fields, 216, 356
Stowmarket, 15
Stylish, 15
Sunny Kay, 223, 289, 292, 392, 393
Sure-Wyn, 47, **116-117**, 220, 231,
    237, 238, 275

T

Tamridge, 123
Tedwyn, 15
Trent Valley, 18
Triagain, **117-118**, 286, 361
Troquehain, 15
Tuscawilla, 24, 25

W

Waiterock, **118-122**, 327
Well Sweep, 148
Whimsey, 300, 301
Willowbank, **123-125**, 245, 313
Windfall, **125**, 212
Winnebago, 23, 145
Woodland, 18, 19

Index of People

A

Adell, Estelle, 43, 138, 140, 254, 261, 271, 288, 321, 394
Adell, Karen (*see also* Garetano), 88, 156, 266, 288, 295, 316
Adell, Ray, 258
Adell, Ray & Estelle, 7, 87, 88, 89, 208, 265, 316, 321, 331, 359, 388, 397
Adell, Teri, 87, 88, 266, 294, 359
Akin, Ted M., 161
Allen, R.E., 26, 149, 151, 163
Allen, Samuel, 185
Alston, George, 32, 43, 98, 109, 112, 117, 118, 141, 162, 163, 164, 165, 178, 277, 293, 360, 361, 389
Alston, Jane, 41, 293, 295
Alston, Mary Ann, 98, 321, 366, 371, 385
Alston, Patty (*nee* Matson), 16, 29, 41, 45, 73, 88, 103, 109, 110, 111, 112, 113, 114, 115, 131, 155, 189, 239, 258, 264, 274, 293, 318, 319, 345
Alston, Tommy, 293
Amand, Wilbur, 151
Amato, Michael, 230, 259
Anderson, John, 14
Andrews, Forest, 160, 162, 355
Angelovic, Joseph W., 185
Arkwright, William, 15
Armour, Mrs. Philip D. Jr. (Julia), 198, 199
Armstrong, 15
Atkins, Variell, 161
Ayers, Roy, 320

B

Bahr, Bob, 303
Bahr, Bonnie, 300, 303
Bahr, Ed, 239, 300, 303
Bahr, Sandra, 303
Bailey, Jon, 163
Baker, Harold, 25
Bamford, 163
Barber, L.E., 24
Barlow, Bobby B., 159
Barnes, James, 24
Barthold, Mrs. J.P., 151
Barton, Gordon, 56
Baruch, Dr. & Mrs. Herman B., 25
Batchelder, Roger, 155
Bates, Betty, 80, 81, 295
Bates, Lois, 80, 81
Bates, Mary Ellen, 159, 252
Beales, Raymond (Ray), 25, 52, 64, 150, 154, 165
Beaman, Art, 153

Beckwith, Ludell, 267
Belleville, W.E., 150
Benson, Lynn, 364
Berbit, Lisa, 87, 255, 294, 396
Berbit, Marshall & Thea, 87, 89
Berci, Carmen, 108
Berd, Alice, 161, 167, 172
Berd, Mr. & Mrs. Walter, 99, 100, 101
Bergland, Clayton & Patricia, 296, 309
Berners, Dame Juliana, 11
Beyrer, Eileen, 282
Beyrer, L., 89
Beyrer, Ray & Linda, 163
Beyrer, Raymond, 161
Billey, Louise, 79, 80, 131
Billings, Michele, 86, 140, 320
Blaine, 12
Bonneford, Mathew & Marian, 163
Boothroyd, M.J., 167
Booxbaun, Donald (Don), 130, 136
Borie, Mrs. W.J.S. (Martha), 71, 154, 157, 158, 159, 163, 189
Bosley, Bonita, 98, 371
Boughey, Sir Thomas, 13, 14
Bracy, Ed, 324
Brady, Maureen, 16, 35, 38, 45, 73, 74, 103, 109, 113, 114, 115, 239, 256, 264, 274, 318, 345
Brainard, William, 160
Breslin, John, 120
Briggs, Dorothy, 160
Brown, Ben, 147, 154
Brown, Mrs. Frederick (*former* Mrs. R. Gilman Smith), 94, 95, 153, 161, 185
Brown, Sherwood & Sandra, 163
Buchanan, Betty, 23
Buesing, Barbara, 157
Buoy, John, 185, 202
Buoy, John & Phyllis, 397
Burns, W.C., 146
Butler, Archie, 15
Butt, Mr. & Mrs. James, 216, 356
Buttram, Georgia, 54

C

Cabot, Patricia A., 320
Cacchio, Alex, 203
Cacchio, Ray, 66, 190, 203, 204, 209
Caius, Dr. Johannes, 11
Callahan, Dennis, 160
Callahan, Donald (Don) & Carol, 64, 65, 66, 214, 342
Callahan, Dorothy, 30, 31, 34, 76, 77, 156, 159, 160, 161, 162, 252, 272, 374
Cameron, Henry, 22
Cande, Don, 204

Cande, Mrs. Don (Kathleen), 190, 204, 209
Carey, Andrew, 130
Carey, Mr. & Mrs. Andrew M. (Andy & Mary), 54, 55, 56, 57, 58, 59, 102
Carey, Mary, 155
Carswell, Lawrence D. (Laddie), 32, 71, 72, 76, 92, 109, 110, 127, 148, 153, 155, 159, 163, 178, 189, 313
Cavalier, Carlos, 147
Chassels, A. McNab, 15
Chevrier, Eudore, 17, 18, 145, 147, 191
Chick, Elmore, 198
Christensen, Dr. C.A., 199, 201
Christensen, Dr. & Mrs. C.A., 196, 197, 203, 208
Chute, Tom, 302
Clancy, Mary, 87
Clark, Anne Rogers, 106, 113, 133, 284
Clark, Elizabeth D., 159
Clark, Houston, 44, 96
Clark, James Edward, 286
Clement, Charlie, 72
Coleman, William C., 24
Comerer, Marshall Jr., 162
Commiso, Lawrence, 155
Constable, Col. R.R., 201
Cooper, Dick, 28, 32, 106, 107, 126, 134, 149, 150, 160, 161, 163, 171, 188, 268, 318
Cooper, Ruth, 162
Cornthwaite, Robert, 22, 147
Costello, Mary V., 116, 158
Cowley, Nancy S., 69, 70, 143, 234, 240
Craig, Lew, 201, 205
Crane, Mrs. Francis V., 39
Crisanti, Karen (Karen Prickett), 304
Crook, Harry, 18

D

Dagliesh, J.C., 14
Daru, J., 163
Dash, Susan, 75, 176
Davis, Barry, 16
Davis, Betty Bates, 80, 81, 295
Davis, Frank Foster, 358
Davis, George, M.D., 159
Davis, Henry, 192
Dayton, Jeanne C., 156
DeBoth, Joanne, 268, 317
Del Deo, Ralph, 93
de Groen, Leonard, 158
DiDonato, Bud, 255, 317, 334, 340
DiDonato, Bud & Judy, 340
DiDonato, Judy, 340
Diffendaffer, Vivian, 155, 163

Dixon, Ed, 172
Donavan, Catherine, 187
Douglas, Leah L., 155
Downing, Melbourne, 85
Dreiseszun, Steve, 210, 211, 297, 301, 311
Drew, Margaret, 24
Dunham, Tad, 16
Dunn, Janice M., 257, 276

E

Eadie, James & Irene, 51, 265
Eadie, Jim, 51, 52
Earl, Maud, 10
Earle, David P., 22, 146, 185
Ebert, Ray T. & Helen, 283
Edgarton, J., 14
Edwards, Paul, 161
Elder, Dr., 154
Elder, Mrs. W.W., 151
Eldredge, I., 70
Eldredge, Ted, 59
Engle, Gary E., 159, 163
Engle, Gary & Mary, 162
Engle, Mary Jane, 162, 163
Epstein, Marilyn, 25
Evan, Billy D., 162
Eversfield, C.C., 13

F

Fagan, Harrison, 172
Ferguson, Henry, 21, 148, 185
Ferguson, John, 24
Ferguson, Walton Jr., 185
Ferguson, Mrs. Walton, 62, 146
Ferguson, Mr. & Mrs. Walton Jr., 21
Ferris, G.W.G., 146
Fitch, Ezra, 185
Fleishman, Mrs. Al, 240
Fleishman, Mr. & Mrs. Al, 301, 302
Fletcher, Mrs. John G. (Ruth), 62, 249
Foote, Robert D., 21
Forbes, Jackie Matson, 109
Forbes, James, 154
Ford-Lowe, Mrs. T., 12
Fordyce, Donald, 25, 146, 147
Forsyth, Jane Kamp, 324
Forsyth, Robert S., 39
Fortuna, Dorothy, 89, 126, 156
Fortuna, Mr. & Mrs. James O., 76, 77, 161, 324
Fortuna, Jim, 156
Fox, Robert, 19
Foy, Marcia, 69
Franco, Eli & Frances, 161, 163
Franklin, W.B., 158
Freese, Kathryn & Lynn, 83, 84, 137, 347
Funk, Jack, 161

G

Gallagher, Ben, 23
Gamache, Barbara, 161
Garcia y Garcia, German, 216
Gardner, J.P., 13
Gardner, W.H., 17
Garetano, Karen Adell, 7, 87, 89, 138, 166, 221, 264, 285, 288, 289, 290, 291, 293, 295, 327, 332, 350, 376, 388
Garvan, Mrs. Francis P., 66
Garvan, Peter, 66
Garvan, Mrs. Peter (Wilhelmina), 66
Gasow, Julie, 19, 22, 26, 28, 32, 33, 42, 43, 62, 74, 84, 85, 103, 104, 105, 106, 107, 112, 115, 125, 134, 145, 147, 149, 150, 151, 154, 158, 159, 160, 162, 163, 164, 171, 184, 188, 229, 231, 234, 252, 253, 272, 273, 288, 323, 326, 338, 346, 355, 372, 382, 383
Gates, Barbara Jane, 62, 162
Gates, Harvey, 362
Geiger, Robert C. (Bob), 194, 205
Geiger, Tillie, 187, 208, 362
Geiger, Robert & Tillie, 170, 362
Gibbs, Dr. Mary B., 84, 109, 167, 179, 247, 268, 293, 371, 384
Gies, E.C., 155
Gifford, Dr. A.C., 23, 121, 145
Gilmour, H.D., 19
Glassford, Andrea, 82, 83, 130, 216, 275, 356, 378
Glassford, Tom, 57, 82, 356
Gough, Lillian, 161, 163, 284
Gough, Robert, 43, 126, 164, 269
Gough, Robert & Lillian, 31, 39, 107, 158, 178, 243, 321, 373, 389
Gould, Mrs., 148
Graham, Janie, 166
Grant, Patricia, 160
Greening, Mrs. Charles (Ruth), 202
Greenwald, Leonard, 154, 155, 158
Grierson, H., 15
Groombridge, Lew, 149
Guggenheim, Col. & Mrs., 25
Guinta, Peter, 391
Gunderson, Ted, 157

H

Hadley, Fred, 147, 149, 150
Hagley, J.P., 14
Hale, Thomas, 163
Hall, Jim, 65
Halliday, Reginald, 185
Hamann, Mary L., 379, 395
Hamilton, Duke of, 14
Hamilton & Brandon, Duke of, 14
Hampton, Mrs. Virginia, 163
Hankwitz, Reed, 87, 155

Hansen, Liz, 67, 222
Harding, John, 64
Harkins, Bruce & Jeane, 48, 86, 87
Harris, Clint, 59, 60, 61, 159, 162, 269, 317, 330, 398
Harris, Louise, 158
Harris, Parker, 79
Head, Graham, 187
Heavisides, Douglas, 160
Heck, Clyde, 151, 154, 155
Heckman, Winifred, 63, 178
Hendee, Mr. & Mrs. Charles F., 52, 53, 54, 67, 269, 317
Hendee, Gwen, 320
Hendee, Mary Lee, 59, 330
Henneberry, Janet, 27, 148, 151
Herbert, Sir Hugo Fitz, 14
Herriman, Lloyd, 194
Hertwig, Hap & Alice, 111
Hertz, Michael & Barbara, 132
Herweg, Alice, 154
Higgs, A., 15
Higgs, George, 24, 146
Hill, Eva, 27
Hill, Howard E., 301
Hilt, John, 52
Hilts, Mrs. Erwin R., 147
Hines, Beryl D., 84, 111
Hobbs, Georgia, 159
Hoffman, H. William, 162, 163
Hogan, Julie, 8, 102, 103
Hooper, Dorothy Moreland, 14
Hopkins, Dana, 36, 61, 62, 63, 72, 74, 135, 139, 249, 250, 251, 262, 281, 283, 322, 325, 396, 406
Hopkins, Mr. & Mrs. Lathrop, 148
Hopper, Richard, 154
Hosteny, Mary Jo, 43, 88, 115, 271
Howard, Juanita Waite, 51, 118, 119, 120, 121, 122, 128, 162, 172, 242, 257, 276, 326, 327
Howard, Peggy, 286
Howard, Susanne B., 117, 118, 360
Hric, Al, 201
Humphrey, William, 14
Hunt, Fred, 150, 155, 158
Hunt, Mary Agnes, 147
Hunt, Mr. & Mrs. Fred (Fred & Mary Agnes), 23, 24
Hutchinson, W.J., 185
Hyslop, Jim, 93

I

Imrie, Mildred, 150, 260
Ingalls, David S. Jr., 50, 201

J

Jackson, Mrs. C. K., 147
Jackson, Fred, 148, 151, 163, 187

Jenkins, Karen A., 320
Johnson, Arlene, 224
Johnson, Candace, 215
Johnson, Stuart, 29, 61, 71, 72, 154, 157, 158, 251, 406
Johnson, Vern & Peggy, 160, 305, 307
Johnson, Virgil, 60, 155, 158, 159
Johnston, Harry, 17
Jones, C. S., 15
Jones, Ken, 194

K
Kelly, Kathleen, 43
Kemp, Cecil & Nancy, 115, 116, 346
Kendrick, William L., 83, 84
Kent, John & Godfrey, 13
Kineon, Forsyth, 49, 50
Kineon, Mrs. James C., 49
Kirby, Albert, 159
Kirby, Bill & Ruth, 319
Kirk, Debbie, 84, 161, 293, 371
Kirk, Kathy, 85, 293
Kirtland, Mr. & Mrs., 150
Klembara, Dr. Andrew, 151, 154
Klocke, Mrs. E. A., 27
Knapp, Lester, 24
Knight, Edward Dana (Ed), 25, 118, 146, 147, 148, 149, 150, 151
Kniola, Dennis, 108
Knoop, A. Peter, 188, 271
Koval, Lawrence, 162, 163
Kunhardt, Kingsley, 195

L
Lambe, Lady, 15
Lang, Billy, 20, 148
Langhans, Daniel, 365
Langhans, Daniel K. & Marie, 64
Larsen, Jo Ann, 163
Larsen, Wallace, 18
Lee, M. N., 15
LeFavour, Walter S., 146
Leffingwell, Ernest de K., 25, 146
Leighton, Robert, 11, 12
Leonard, John, 311
Leonard, Martha, 300, 301, 309, 310, 311
Leonard, Ralph G. (Bud), 299, 302
Lewis, Reginald, 148
Libeu, Mr. & Mrs. Lawrence, 306, 307
Linfesty, Tom, 186
Lloyd, Freeman, 17, 21, 191
Lopeman, E. K., 149
Lorentzen, Kathleen Reiss, 96, 97, 219
Lorenz, Candy, 198
Lorenz, Dave, 198, 200
Lorna, Countess Howe, 11
Luchsinger, Rodney C., 102

Ludwig, Joan, 281
Luley, Theresa A. (Terry), D.V.M., 304, 305

M
Mabrey, Sharon, 108, 109, 163
McClandish, William L., 147
McCune, Mary, 154
McDonald, David, 15
McDonald, Kyle M., 27, 119, 187
McGinnis, Ray, 6, 119
McKelvy, Mrs. William, 149, 150, 151
McKinney, W. E., 151
McLean, Robert, 191, 194
McQueen, Larry, 197
McQueen, Stanley, 201
Magill, Wayne D., 158, 163, 267
Magill, Wayne & Phyllis, 101, 102, 158
Maginnes, Helen M., 90, 278, 279, 339
Maker, Peter, 154
Marlin, Elmer & Billie, 311
Martin, Bryan K., 163
Marvin, John, 101
Marx, Susan (Mrs. Sid Marx), 162
Mason, Bethany Hall, 155
Mathis, Elaine, 355
Matson, Mr. & Mrs. A.W. (Al & Elsie), 29, 87, 109, 154, 189
Matson, Billy, 110
Matson, Elsie, 111, 112, 153
Matson, Susan, 162
Mau, Mr. & Mrs. Richard, 161
Mellenthin, Herman, 203
Menhall, James, 147
Menhall, Mr. & Mrs. James E., 25
Merriman, Mrs. Alexander B., 240, 245
Merriman, Mr. & Mrs. Alexander B., 123, 124, 125, 245, 313, 352
Merriman, Anne & Carrie, 240
Merriman, John, 97
Metzger, Everett, 214
Milbank, Dr. Samuel, 149, 192, 193
Milbank, Dr. & Mrs. Samuel, 25
Mildon, J. H., 13
Miller, Christine, 115
Miller, Dr. R. B., 24, 147
Millet, Jeanne, 159
Mitchon, Connie, 125, 212
Moffit, Mrs. A. R., 148
More, Elliot, 70, 99, 167, 181
More, Linda, 70, 143, 182
Morin, Mrs. W.A.M., 147
Morrow, Norman, 148, 151, 153
Morrow, Robert, 24, 99, 148, 150
Muchtin, J., 89
Mueller, Kurt, 328

Munn, Dr. Aristine Pixley, 25
Murphy, John P., 155
Murr, Louis, 117, 120
Murray, Ken, 96
Murray, Ken & Virginia, 97
Murray, Lee, 158, 160

N
Neilson, C. F., 146
Neilson, Howard Short, 21
Nelson, Frances, 67, 277, 309
Nelson, Francie, 47, 66, 67, 68, 133, 218, 222, 280, 337, 344, 386
Nelson, Russ & Frances, 67
Newton, Mrs. Benjamin, 24
Nicholas, Anna Katherine, 10
Nichter, A. M., 24
Northey, Howard, 51
Novick, Alan & Sonnie, 44

P
Parham, Gordon, 158
Parkening, Lucille M., 26, 27, 28
Parker, Barbara, 123
Patterson, Mrs., 51
Paton, Gordon, 151, 154
Paul, Mr. & Mrs. Vincent J., 154
Pease, Noel & Ardella, 113, 163, 261
Pemberton, Ronald, 161
Peppers, Doris, 308
Peppers, Larry, 308
Phillips, C. A., 14
Phillips, Henry & Tekla, 77
Pirie, John T. Jr., 199, 200
Placey, Hollis J., 18
Pokorney, Nancy, 83
Pope, Anne, 32, 34, 35, 37, 39, 61, 70, 71, 72, 73, 74, 75, 111, 115, 127, 129, 135, 136, 144, 156, 158, 160, 161, 163, 173, 174, 175, 176, 178, 179, 180, 181, 182, 183, 189, 233, 243, 256, 260, 261, 269, 270, 271, 284, 298, 314, 343, 349, 369, 372, 373, 385, 389, 395, 397, 406
Porges, E. D., 200
Porta, Albert Della, 161
Price, W.A., 149
Prickett, Karen, 51, 52, 101, 113, 172, 339
Prickett, Dr. Milton, 51, 52, 60, 159, 162
Pryor, Robert, 161
Pugh, George, 57
Putnam, Dr. Edwin D., 24
Pym, William, 27, 147

Q
Quay, Paul, 20, 154
Quirk, Joseph C. (Joe), 120, 148, 149, 185, 197

Quirk, Mr. & Mrs. Joseph C. (Joe & Phyllis), 148, 149

R

Radcliffe, Talbot, 66
Randall, Emmett, 24, 145
Randall, William L. & Elaine P., 105, 154
Randolph, Edna, 97, 163
Rayne, Derek, 340
Redden, Dr. Joseph E., 154
Reeves, Lloyd, 155
Reeves, Mrs. Lloyd, 155
Reikhoff, Connie J., 162
Rich, Anne, 109
Rich, William W., 109, 163
Riddle, Maxwell, 80, 111, 120
Ritchey, John, 19
Ritter, Courtney, 98
Ritter, Debbie, 103, 385
Ritter, Ron & Debbi, 98
Ritter, Susan, 98, 366
Robb, Donald, 161
Roberts, Ann, 59, 60, 159, 162, 287, 330, 398
Roberts, Lloyd, 60
Roberts, Mary, 97
Roberts, Percy, 105
Roberts, Seymour, 151, 155
Rockefeller, Don, 264
Roe, Bernice, 52, 127, 158, 159, 160, 272
Rollins, Marge, 82
Romig, Helen, 155, 158
Rosenberg, Alva, 105, 120, 166, 186
Ross, Joan M., 185, 270
Rottenberg, F.A., 15
Routley, Herbert S., 18, 146
Routley, Mrs. Herbert, 18

S

Sangster, George, 26
Sangster, Harry, 27, 149
Sayres, Joseph P., 379
Schenker, Henry, 25
Schmidt, Henriette, 77, 78, 79, 83, 226, 232, 236, 333
Schmitz, Bob, 100
Schulte, Raphael, 63
Schuman, James H. & Constance C., 161
Schwartz, Dave, 88, 265, 350
Schwerdle, Herbert, 153
Schwerdle, Elizabeth B., 159
Scott, Mary, 374
Scudder, Townsend, 147
Semke, Alice, 248
Shambaugh, Helen, 156
Sharpe, Isaac, 15
Shaw, Henry B., 15

Shellenbarger, Walt, 161
Sievers, Charles, 120
Skarda, Langdon, 144
Slagle, David, 113
Smith, Clifford, 163
Smith, Gilman, 153, 158
Smith, Mrs. R. Gilman (Mrs. Frederick Brown), 27, 78, 149, 151, 154, 155, 186, 187, 315
Smith, J. Winton, 13
Snelling, Anne E., 19, 43, 108, 159
Snyder, Donald, 160, 163
Sokup, George, 185
Spencer, J.W., 15
Staber, G.C., 149
Stapp, Edward & Lillian, 162, 163
Sternberg, Mr. & Mrs. R.G., 24
Stewart, Arthur & Sharon, 306, 307, 308
Stewart, James, 204
Stoddard, Walter, 146
Streng, Delores, 51, 52, 125
Sturdee, Mrs. E.A., 147
Suder, Carol, 155
Sullivan, Raymond, 158

T

Tacker, Joe, 159
Taisey, Earl, 162, 163, 165
Taylor, George, 14
Thomas, Richard N., 51
Thompson, Arlene M. (Mrs. Clark Thompson), 132, 162, 288, 396
Thompson, Bernie, 102
Thompson, Clark, 313
Thompson, Donna, 8, 102, 103
Thomson, Erica Huggina, 32
Thorsby, George, 147
Threlfall, Mark, 162
Tiedemann, Henry, 119
Tiedemann, Mrs., 368
Tomkinson, G., 15
Tourtelot, David M., 24
Tousley, Jacqueline, 106, 107
Toy, Charles, 22, 146, 147, 185
Trainor, William (Bill), 159, 272
Trimble, E., 15
Trotter, A.L., 15
Tucker, Bernardine, 154
Tyler, Howard, 65

V

Vale, Mr., 146
Valvo, Debra (Debby), 47, 116, 117, 207, 220, 231, 237, 275, 298, 299
Valvo, Paul, 238
Van Horn, Evelyn Monte, 192, 193, 206, 367
Vroom, Corky, 160

W

Wagner, Mayor Robert, 145
Wagstaff, David, 148, 185
Wagstaff, Mrs. David, 22
Walberg, Robert, 151
Walgate, Robert (Bob), 31, 79, 150
Walker, Lyman S. & Shirley, 162
Walsh, Helen, 26
Warwick, Mrs. James, 161
Waters, Bob, 342
Watson, George E. Jr. & Elizabeth, 49
Wear, Doris, 124
Weingarten, Barbara, 42, 88, 89, 221, 225, 230, 259, 285, 327, 359, 390, 391
Weingarten, Debbie, 285
Weingarten, Matthew, 213
Weingarten, Sharon, 132, 217, 218, 289, 390
Weingartens, the, 223, 392
Well, Ernest, 22
Wenger, J.A., 15
Westlake, W., 161
Westlake, G., 325
Westlund, Arthur, 155
Whitaker, Atha, 29, 30, 110, 148
Whitaker, E.H., 185, 189
Whitaker, Mr. & Mrs., 30
White, Mrs. Ralph, 121
Wigan, Mr. & Mrs. Lewis, 13
Wilbur, E.R., 185
Wilkerson, Mary Jane, 319
Wilkes, Herbert & Maxine, 158
Williams, Col. A.T., 13, 17
Williams, Ruth, 161
Willmotts, Mrs. C., 148
Wills, Robert, 80
Wilschke, Mrs. James S., 159
Wilson, Doris, 356
Wood, Gladys, 23
Wray, Catherine, 305, 306
Wunderlich, E.W., 199

Y

Yost, Howard, 215

Z

Ziessow, Madge, 36